ARCHITECTURE
AT THE END OF THE EARTH

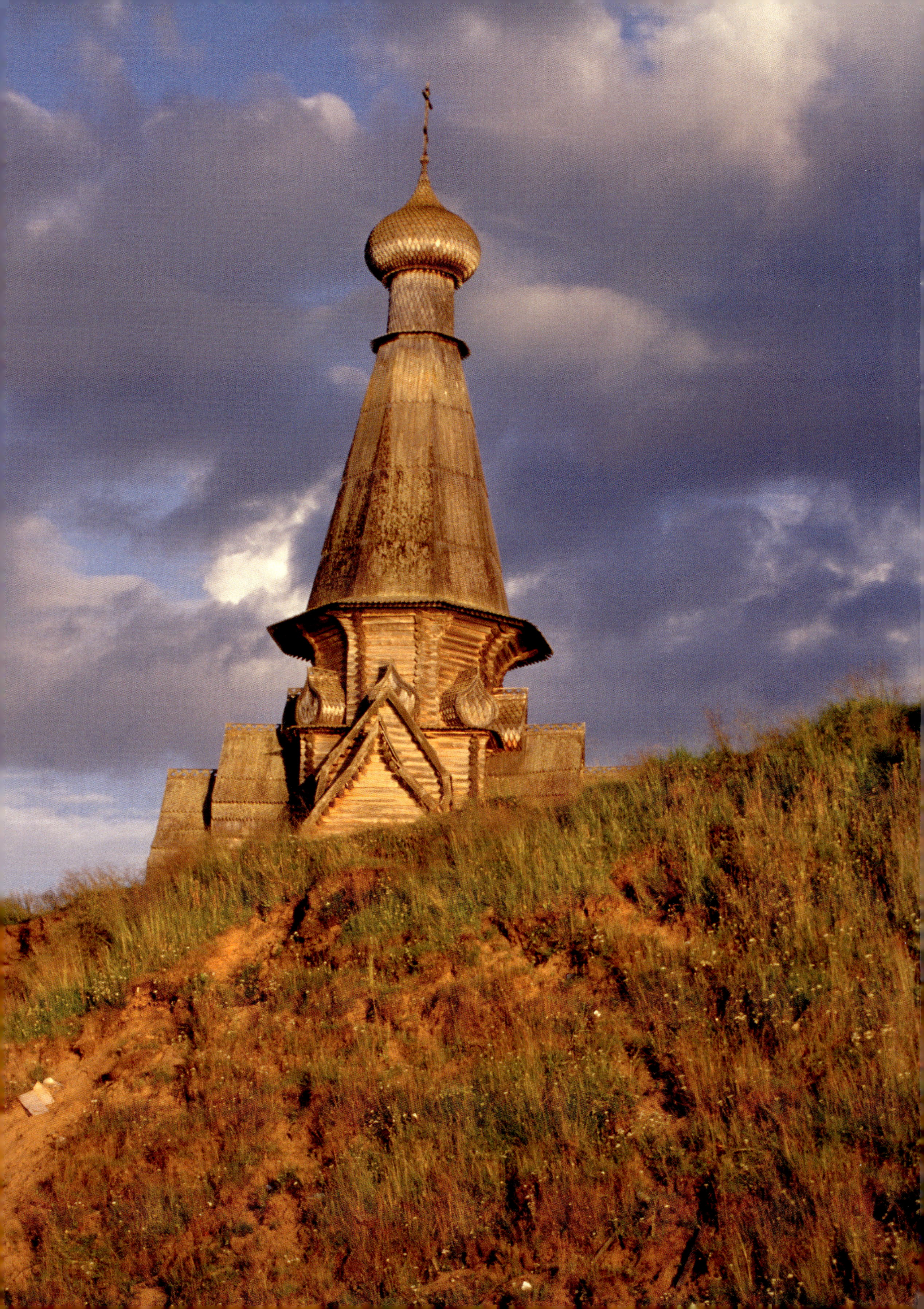

ARCHITECTURE
AT THE END OF THE EARTH

Photographing the Russian North

TEXT AND PHOTOGRAPHS BY

William Craft Brumfield

DUKE UNIVERSITY PRESS | DURHAM AND LONDON | 2015

Printed in the United States of America on acid-free paper ∞
Designed by Heather Hensley
Typeset in Garamond Premier Pro by Tseng Information Systems, Inc.

Library of Congress Cataloging-in-Publication Data
Brumfield, William Craft, 1944–
Architecture at the end of the earth : photographing the Russian North /
text and photographs by William Craft Brumfield.
pages cm
ISBN 978-0-8223-5906-7 (hardcover : alk. paper)
ISBN 978-0-8223-7543-2 (e-book)
1. Architecture—Russia, Northern. 2. Architecture—Russia, Northern—
Pictorial works. 3. Russia, Northern—Description and travel. 4. Russia,
Northern—Pictorial works. I. Title.
NA1195.N57B78 2015
720.947′1—dc23 2014046255

Frontispiece: Varzuga. Church of the Dormition of the Virgin (1674), northwest view above right bank of Varzuga River. Photograph: July 21, 2001.

Cover: Kimzha. Church of the Hodegetria Icon of the Virgin, southwest view.

Duke University Press gratefully acknowledges the generous support of Richard Hedreen, who provided funds toward the publication of this book.

IN MEMORY OF

Tamara Kholkina
(September 30, 1955–August 1, 2009)

Blessed are the pure in heart . . .

CONTENTS

ix ACKNOWLEDGMENTS

1 INTRODUCTION
Exploring the Russian North

21 INTO THE FOREST
A Note on the Architectural Heritage of the Russian North

29 ONE The Western Shore of the White Sea

73 TWO From the Vytegra Region to the Mologa River

115 THREE Kargopol and Its Surrounding Villages

151 FOUR From Vologda to Veliky Ustiug

207 FIVE Along the Northern Dvina and Beyond to the Arctic Circle

243 POSTSCRIPT
What Will Remain of the Heritage of the Russian North?

ACKNOWLEDGMENTS

The journey through the Russian North that I present in this book has unfolded over many years. During that period I have experienced the generosity of many individuals and organizations, both in the United States and in Russia. I will not attempt to place order on my memory; rather, the names are listed as they come to me: Dr. James H. Billington, Librarian of Congress, for many years of interest in my work and for providing the support that sent me to so many remote corners of Russia; Dr. Dan E. Davidson, president of American Councils for International Education, who has done so much to keep me in the field; Dr. Blair A. Ruble, formerly director of the Kennan Institute for Advanced Russian Studies in Washington, who supported many publications of my fieldwork. Tulane University has over the years provided the essential base for my work. Specific projects and periods in the Russian North have been supported by the John Simon Guggenheim Memorial Foundation, the National Humanities Center, the National Endowment for the Humanities (with their excellent magazine *Humanities*), the National Council for East European and Eurasian Research, and the American Councils for International Education. Special thanks are due to the Photographic Archives (now Image Collections) at the National Gallery of Art, which has housed the basic collection of my photographic work since 1985 with the steady guidance of curator Andrea Gibbs.

In Russia I am daunted by the challenge of acknowledging the generosity of so many people, a number of whom are no longer with us: Dr. Aleksei I. Komech, director of the State Institute of Art History during critical years of my work in the 1990s until 2007; colleagues at Pomor State University (now renamed Northern Arctic Federal University) in Arkhangelsk; Nelli Belova, for many years director of the Vologda Regional Library; Oleg Samusenko and Olga Bakhareva, friends in Cherepovets; Father Andrei Kozlov and his family (St. Petersburg). And to Moscow colleagues at the website Russia Beyond the Headlines for their supportive interest in my work over the past half decade.

The book itself would not have been possible without the extraordinary generosity and friendship of Richard and Betty Hedreen. In 2004 their support made possible a new edition of my fundamental work, *A History of Russian Architecture*. And now the Hedreens have enabled this present work with the dedicated professionals at Duke University Press, with whom I have had a productive relationship going back to the 1990s, when Duke published my *Lost Russia: Photographing the Ruins of Russian Architecture*. At the press I owe a special debt to the editor of this book, Miriam Angress.

The journey continues.

Introduction

Exploring the Russian North

In the popular imagination, virtually all Russia is "north," cold and imponderable. Yet within this immense Eurasian landmass, there is a region traditionally known as the "Russian North" that includes territories located within or near the basin of the White Sea. This space is crossed by water networks extending from the White Lake (Beloe Ozero) to the White Sea (Beloe Morye). (The names themselves speak volumes.) Of special interest are the contemporary regions of Vologda and Arkhangelsk. Despite the cataclysms of the twentieth century, this area of the Russian North still lays claim to a deeply rooted cultural coherence created by those who settled in its forests and moved along its rivers and lakes.

Today, the rivers have silted, and travel in the north occurs by road—or what passes for a road. The vehicle is all. The new Russians have their Mercedes and Cherokees, but for the true connoisseur of the Russian road, the ultimate machine is the UAZIK, Russia's closest equivalent to the classic Jeep. Four-wheeled drive, two gear sticks, two gas tanks (left and right), taut suspension, high clearance. Seat belts? Don't ask. The top speed is one hundred kilometers per hour, but you rarely reach that if you drive it over the rutted tracks and potholed back roads for which it was designed.

No place in Russia has more of such roads than Arkhangelsk Province, a vast territory that extends from the White and Barents Seas in the north to its boundary with Vologda Province to the south. A combination of poverty, government default on both a local and national level, and distances that exceed those of most

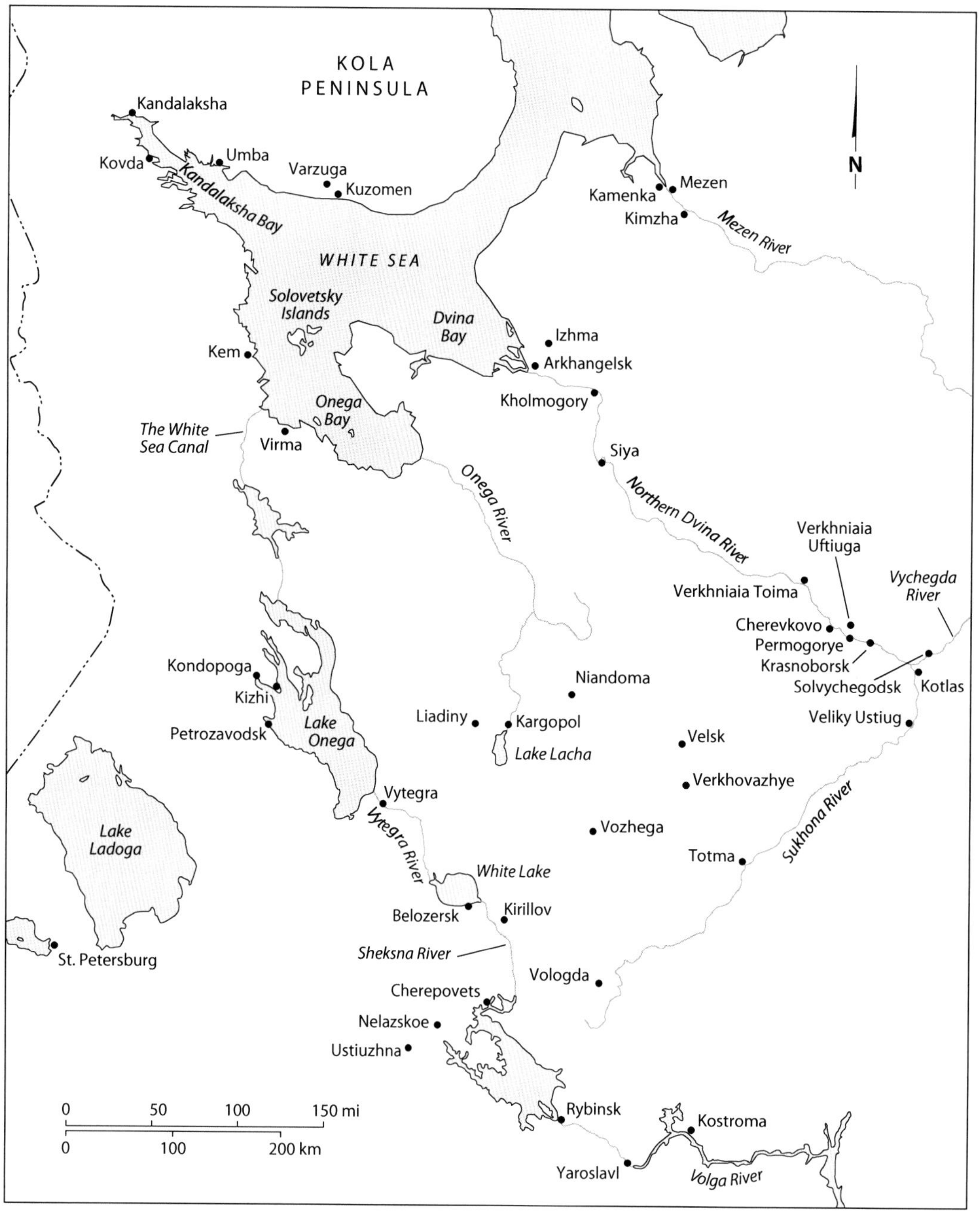

Area of the Russian North covered by the photography in this book.

western European countries have created some of the worst roads in European Russia.

Hence the UAZIK, whose name derives from the acronym for Ulyanovsk Auto Factory, located in the city of Ulyanovsk on the Volga River. Comfortable it is not, but an experienced driver can take this machine over rutted ice tracks in the middle of a snowstorm and not miss a beat. I should say at the outset that I am not such a driver, and I have only a vague idea as to how the machine works. I am, however, fluent in the Russian language, and that ability rescued many a challenging situation.

Although my first photographs of Russia were taken during the summer of

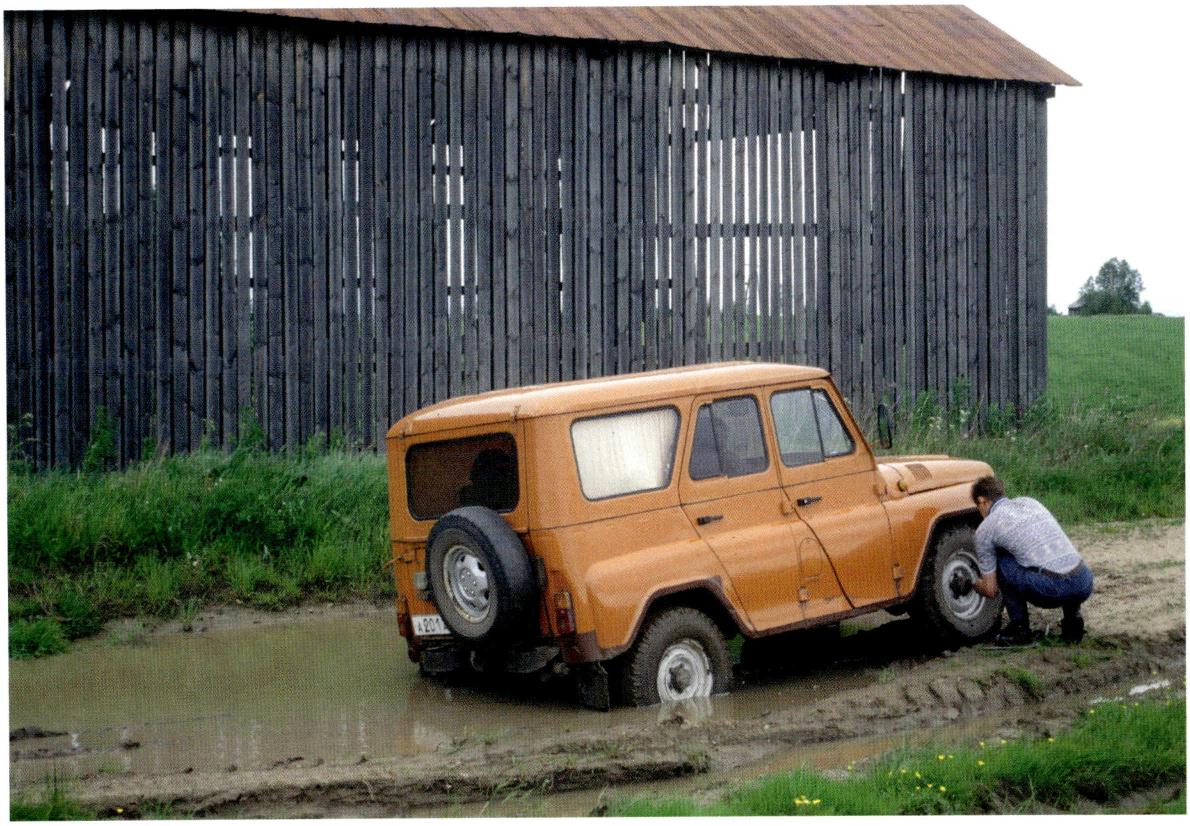

Driver engaging front-wheel drive on partially submerged UAZIK at village of Fedkovo, near Velsk. Photograph: June 14, 2000.

1970, my first limited foray to the North did not occur until 1988 (Kizhi Island), with return trips to the same area in 1991 and 1993. My deeper exploration of the area began only in 1995, but over the preceding two and a half decades I had created a substantial photographic archive and published fundamental books on Russian architectural history—including *A History of Russian Architecture* (1993, with a second edition in 2004). By the time physical and bureaucratic obstacles to travel in the North were overcome, I was prepared to see this area as an expression of time-honored traditions that I had long studied. After research came the road trips, and the drivers got me where I needed to go. My job was to keep the cameras ready and scan the horizon for onion domes. And in my travels throughout the North, the UAZIK performed superbly with or without roads.

The fact is, roads were an afterthought in the Arkhangelsk territory. Settlers, hunters, and traders moved primarily over a network of rivers, lakes, and portages that defined the area as a geographically distinct cultural entity. Indeed, the settlement of this part of northern Russia, its gradual development, and its eventual assimilation by Muscovy were based on a paradoxical set of circumstances. The wealth of its forests, rivers, lakes, and the White Sea itself promised considerable rewards to those capable of mastering the area; and yet the remoteness of the area, the relative paucity of arable land (usually limited to certain river plains), and the length of the harsh winters discouraged extensive population growth. Those who

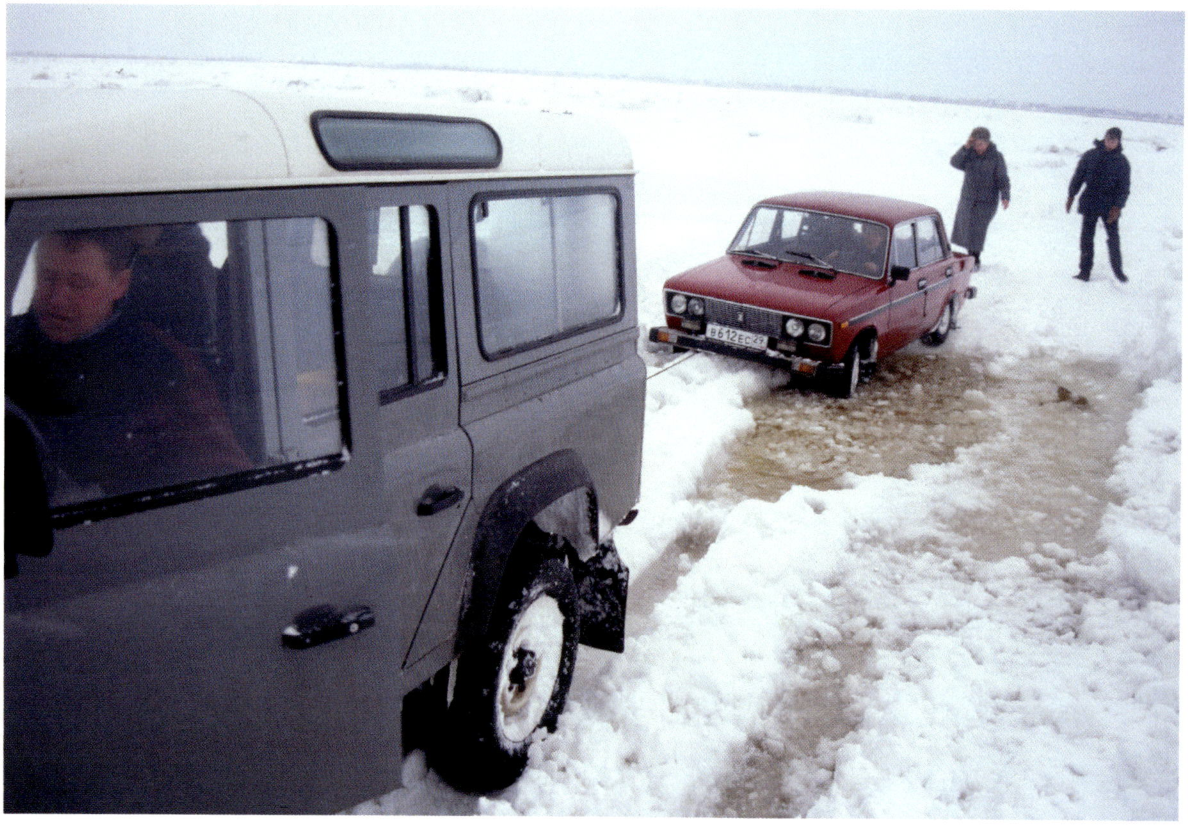

Car being pulled from icy slush on "frozen" surface of Mezen River between Mezen and Kamenka. Photograph: March 8, 2000.

succeeded in settling the area during the tenth through the thirteenth centuries proved to be sturdy, self-reliant farmers and craftsmen, a mixture of Slavs and Finnic tribes.

Moscow succeeded in colonizing the area during the next two centuries, and by the reign of Ivan the Terrible in the sixteenth century, the Dvina river system had become Russia's major route east to the Urals and west to England. Although the significance of this network declined after the founding of St. Petersburg, in 1703, the North continued to function as a critical artery, such as during the Second World War and the submarine race during the Cold War.

Nowhere is the former wealth of this area more evident than at Solvychegodsk ("Salt on the Vychegda"), which was once the capital of a Stroganov trading empire. Until recently, getting to Solvychegodsk was no simple matter. Coming from the richly historic town of Veliky Ustiug, some eighty kilometers to the south, one crossed to the east bank of the Northern Dvina over a ramshackle pontoon bridge across the Dvina just south of the grimy city of Kotlas, located at the confluence of the Dvina and Vychegda Rivers. In the winter cars also used a track plowed across the thick ice of the Dvina. Either route winds through the industrial detritus of Kotlas before reaching a ferry across the Vychegda River.

A ferry in this area typically consists of a small barge capable of carrying one or two vehicles. Along the deck are benches for hikers and bikers. Power is provided by a motor launch lashed to the side of the barge. That first trip, in July 1996, presented an empty landing on a chilly Sunday morning, and no one seemed certain that there would be a ferry at all. But after an anxious half hour, a few people with packs appeared, and shortly thereafter the ferry made its deliberate way toward our bank. When offered pay, the ferrymen refused with gruff good humor: "Today is the National Day of the River Fleet." And to prove the point, they turned up the radio with rousing music of Russian riverboat chanteys. The ride was choppy, but it was an ideal way to see this northern river, cold and windswept like the landscape. On the opposite side the barge ramp clanked down, and vehicles plunged into the sandy bank, as if from an amphibious carrier. A rutted track led through flat, marshy fields with small villages, and finally connected with a graveled road to Solvychegodsk.

Entering Solvychegodsk, which has some four thousand souls, is another of those Russian experiences that transport you back to the nineteenth century. One-story dwellings, usually of wood, mingle with low brick structures of the town's few Soviet-era enterprises and workshops. The first Russian settlements in the area probably arose in the fourteenth century with the support of medieval Russia's mercantile power Novgorod, whose explorers and traders would have recognized the value of a site near the crossing of two major river routes: north to the White Sea and east to the Urals. The merchant dynasty of the Stroganovs did not arrive until the middle of the sixteenth century, and soon thereafter the town was founded. As new trading routes led to a decline in its significance in the eighteenth and nineteenth centuries, the town became a small resort, known for its mineral waters and springs.

At the beginning of this century there were at least twelve brick churches here, of which eight were destroyed in the Soviet period, and two others left in various states of damage. But the jewels in the crown, the two Stroganov "cathedrals," still stand relatively unscathed. The earlier is a sixteenth-century cathedral dedicated to the Annunciation, and the other is an elaborately decorated seventeenth-century church dedicated to the Presentation of the Virgin.

Why were such grand structures built in so remote a location? One answer lies not far from the Presentation Church, in a salt spring now covered with a small log tower, a replica of the earlier Stroganov stockade. The area is replete with such springs, as well as a small brackish river, the Usol, and a salt lake, the Solonikha. The production of salt is now taken for granted, but in the medieval era, it was one of the most valuable of commodities. In this part of the Russian North, an enormously profitable salt monopoly, derived from ample sources of brine, allowed the Stroganovs to create a private empire at Solvychegodsk. Although miserly in most respects, the Stroganovs spent immense sums on the arts and crafts in the North of Russia during the sixteenth and seventeenth centuries. The term "Stroganov style" defines elaborately ornamented forms in music, icon painting, and architecture, as well as in the applied arts—a style that appeared wherever the Stroganovs had major operations, from Solvychegodsk to Nizhny Novgorod, on the Volga River, to Perm in the Ural Mountains.

The most lavish example of Stroganov architecture is the main church of the former Monastery of the Presentation of the Virgin. During the winter, services in the Presentation Church are held only in the warmer, south gallery. In March 1998, however, Father Vladimir, the young priest of the parish, allowed me into the main sanctuary after noon services on a bright Sunday. The interior was intensely cold, but the sunlight streaming through the high south windows dramatically illuminated the iconostasis. I hurriedly fumbled with my cameras to take as many shots as possible (the priest himself wanted photographs of the interior), and within minutes I was perspiring, despite the cold. Rarely has a small parish received such lavish premises.

Of course in the winter, the Vychegda ferry does not operate, and we skidded in our UAZIK upriver toward a frozen pontoon bridge at Koriazhma, a former monastic settlement now notorious as the site of one of Russia's largest paper mills. The town itself is pleasant enough; but in warmer weather the smell spreads for dozens of kilometers, and pollution is an ever-present factor. It is impossible to compute the ecological cost of such economic mainstays, but on the road we stopped at an abandoned church near the tiny village of Niuba.

A young boy, perhaps eight or nine, clad in a tattered padded coat, approached us. Despite the appearance of poverty, his face was bright and clean, and his voice clear as he answered my questions about the village. Then I noticed that one sleeve was empty. With a whisper I drew this to the attention of Sasha, the driver, and he bluntly asked: "What happened to your arm?" The child's calm reply, starkly brief: "Netu" (Not there). This clearly was a kid wise beyond his years, but what could anyone say to explain the defect that left him without an arm—and the state of poverty that left him without hope of a prosthetic? As we drove away, he slowly walked along the snow pack of the road, followed by his small dog and content as only a child can be on a bright and idle Sunday afternoon.

From this far southeastern corner of Arkhangelsk Province, it is possible to shuttle by train 250 kilometers due west to the other side of the province. At Konosha junction, the track merges with the main line north to Arkhangelsk. But there is no reason to rush, for this region around the town of Kargopol contains some of Russia's best preserved ancient villages. Kargopol, too, is a formerly wealthy trading center that time and fortune have passed by. And like Solvychegodsk, it is not easy to reach. The trains stop at Niandoma, a singularly graceless settlement whose main occupation — apart from the railroad — is the local forest products industry. From Niandoma Station, regular bus service runs to Kargopol, one hundred kilometers to the west.

The other, and faster, possibility is to hire a car for a fare that can be split three ways if there are additional passengers. For my first trip, at the end of February 1998, I chose the car. My train arrived at two in the morning, and in blustery winter weather I did not care to wait another forty minutes for a bus whose existence seemed very doubtful. (I later heard that the bus was right on time.) The car proved a mixed blessing: five passengers jammed into a small Zhiguli, whose driver played an endless, mediocre rock tape at ear-splitting level as he careened over a snowy road at eighty to one hundred kilometers an hour.

After an hour and a half, I finally stumbled out of the car into a snow drift while the driver vaguely pointed in the direction of the "hotel," and drove off. A brisk wind, a meter of snow, a barking dog, a couple of dimly lit windows, and one street light. I felt a sense of isolation intensified by the dull roar that remained in my head after the rock tape from hell. Although the refuge turned out to be only a block from where I uncertainly stood, my disorientation was so great that it took another half hour of stumbling and disturbing law-abiding local citizens before I desperately rang the bell at the small and very discreet two-storied hotel. Miraculously, a concierge appeared with an electric kettle and a space heater, and I — the only guest in the entire hotel — was escorted to a room on the second floor.

Kargopol still preserves the feel of a northern provincial town of the nineteenth (or eighteenth) century. By the turn of this century it had approximately three thousand residents and twenty-two churches (including those of wood), as well as two monasteries. Like other ancient Russian towns that were bypassed by railroad construction, such as Suzdal, Kargopol became a backwater. Unfortunately, this did not save its monuments of art and architecture after the revolution. During the Soviet period, half of the town's churches vanished through neglect or demolition.

Yet however difficult the struggle to preserve the legacy of historic architecture in Kargopol itself, the crisis is more acute still in the villages of the surrounding region, renowned for containing some of the best examples of log architecture and folk art in Russia. On a gray day in late February, I had my first view of this abandoned rural treasure as Viktor Sheludko and his wife took me over snow-covered lanes in a Niva vehicle of respectable age. When we got to the village of Oshevensk, sixty kilometers to the northwest of Kargopol, there was momentary uncertainty as to whether we could enter: the pine logs of the wooden bridge were being replaced. Enough remained to allow one lane of traffic, and as we passed over this beautifully designed structure, the fragrance of freshly cut pine planks came through the damp air.

Oshevensk was a wealthy and large village, and it is now one of the best preserved, with local inhabitants renting some of its log houses to summer visitors. Thus the mobility of new Russia gives hope to some otherwise neglected rural settlements. Oshevensk contains not only the exquisite miniature Chapel of St. George (now under restoration), but also the log Church of the Epiphany (1787), with its tent tower over the sanctuary and a detached bell tower. The interior has one of the largest spaces among wooden churches in the Kargopol area, and its icon screen and braced, painted wooden ceiling (known as a *nebo*, or "heaven") are staggering in their extent and color. I was informed by Olga Stepanovna, who kept the keys, that regular worship services are not held here, but women from the community frequently gather on Sundays to sing hymns in this church. Thus devotion returns in its most basic and sincere form.

One of the most remarkable examples of art and architecture in the Russian North is located at the small village of Liadiny, thirty kilometers north of Kargopol. This extraordinary and now all-too-rare ensemble consists of three parts: a summer Church of the Intercession (1761), with tall tent tower; a winter Church of the Epiphany (1793), with its panoply of cupolas; and a large bell tower. Both churches have distinctive designs, and the combination of icon screen and "heaven" inside the Intercession Church is the most striking that I have seen. This three-part ensemble of churches was once common in wealthy northern farming communities, but most have disappeared.

Liadiny, and its state dairy farm, have lost even the modicum of prosperity of the Soviet era. The elderly woman who opened the church for us was spirited, but how much longer can she continue her duties? And will anyone take her place? As I photographed the Liadiny churches, the brief, angry comments of local farm workers who walked by made it clear that preserving these priceless monuments was not one of their priorities. Their life is hard, and I would be the last to criticize them; but indifference and vandalism have degraded the condition of village churches. In 1998 Lidiia Sevastianova, director of the Kargopol Museum of History and Art, said that the Epiphany Church at Liadiny was in desperate need of restoration, and she gave me a detailed estimate of the sum needed to do preservation work for the entire ensemble. Funds were eventually found to complete the restoration of the structure of the Epiphany Church. (The art on its interior had long since disappeared.)

But just as there were signs of improvement, tragedy struck in a most literal sense. On Easter morning, May 6, 2013, the tower of the Intercession Church was struck by lightning. Although a lightning rod seems to have been in place, that is apparently not a guarantee of protection again certain strikes. The fire quickly consumed the tower and the main structure. With the intense heat, the nearby bell tower also caught fire. Fortunately, quick response enabled the Epiphany Church to survive. But the jewel in the crown, the Intercession Church, was destroyed. Even should funds be found to construct a reasonable copy of the church (unlikely), the unique interior, beautifully painted and adorned, can never be regained. My copious documentation of the interior will provide a record, but that is slight consolation.

The Onega River flows north and empties into the Onega Bay, in the southern part of the White Sea. Nearby are the Solovetsky Islands, the culminating point of a journey through Arkhangelsk Province. Geographically, the islands form one of the most curious natural environments in Russia. Historically, the very name "Solovetsky archipelago" resonates with both tragedy and heroic endurance, for it was here, in 1923, that the first specially designated concentration camp was established by the Soviet regime. Aleksandr Solzhenitsyn has already given us an incomparable account of that monstrosity, which metastasized throughout the Soviet Union in the 1930s and gave rise to the phrase "Gulag archipelago."

The most impressive way to approach the islands is by boat from the Karelian town of Kem. The monastery rises from the water, a floating citadel of towers and domes. For the strong of stomach, there is also an air option, from Arkhangelsk, on a twin-engine plane. Although less haunting than the approach by boat, the small plane provides an unforgettable view of the northern forests—pine, fir, larch, aspen, birch—merging into the taiga along the White Sea.

There is evidence that the Solovetsky archipelago was settled—or visited—by humans as early as four millennia ago. Not until the beginning of the fifteenth century did the island chain attract the attention of a few hardy monks, part of a wave of monastic expansion throughout the Russian North in the late fourteenth and fifteenth centuries. The first, tentative settlement occurred in 1429 when the monk Savvaty joined forces with one Herman, an illiterate hermit who had explored the archipelago. Despite the severe winters, sea currents moderated the climate, and the surroundings provided sufficient food for survival.

The elderly Savvaty's death, in 1435, brought an end to this first attempt, but the following year, another monk, Zosima, returned to the island and founded the Transfiguration Monastery. All three men were canonized by the Russian Orthodox Church. The great flourishing of the monastery occurred in the sixteenth century, under the direction of Philip Kolychev, a Moscow nobleman who spent twenty-five years at the monastery, before being called back to Moscow by a suspicious Ivan the Terrible—who had Kolychev tortured and executed. He, too, was canonized.

The monastery's dramatic fate took another tragic turn in the middle of the seventeenth century, when dissenters known generally as Old Believers refused to accept certain liturgical reforms. The monastery was a leading point of resistance, and after a seven-year siege by tsarist troops, it fell only when one of the monks betrayed the fortress through a secret entrance. The subsequent execution of the monks cast a pall over the monastery, but it gradually rebuilt over the following centuries—until the modern cataclysm of war and revolution.

In 1921 the Bolsheviks expropriated the monastery. Two years later, in 1923, a mysterious fire spread throughout the great stone churches and reduced their interiors to ashes. There are legends among the people as to who was to blame (the Bolsheviks, the monks themselves), but a once flourishing island was reduced to devastation.

Soon thereafter the archipelago became the site of a prototypical concentration camp that malignantly expanded. Aleksandr Solzhenitsyn and Dmitry Likhachev have provided definitive accounts of the Solovetsky camp, which was conveniently proximate to the White Sea–Baltic Canal (1931–33), the first major Soviet infrastructure project built by slave labor. In the 1930s the system spread throughout the Soviet Union as the "Gulag archipelago." Superseded by far larger complexes, the Solovetsky camp closed in 1939, and the territory was for many years a military base.

Attempts to restore the monumental Transfiguration Monastery began only in the 1970s, but work accelerated during perestroika, as students and other volunteers from Moscow streamed northward in the summers to help in the laborious task of renovation. With solemn ceremony in August 1992, Patriarch Aleksy consecrated the return of the relics of the monastery's founders, and the restored bells again rang out. Although only a few monks live in the monastery, its renaissance is visually stunning.

The Solovetsky Islands convey a strange sense of enchantment, whatever the season. But on those long summer days when the sun is not blocked by rain clouds, the monastery is suffused with a fantastic range of solar light that gradually illuminates all sides of the citadel and its churches. On a late summer evening, this light gives added meaning to the monastery's dedication, the Transfiguration—which is, after all, devoted to the miracle of light.

TOWARD THE ARCTIC CIRCLE: THE ENCHANTMENT OF KIMZHA

And then there is Kimzha. On the upper reaches of the Mezen River, in northeast Arkhangelsk Province, there are pockets of population that seem to exist in another time. Among them is Kimzha, located near the Arctic Circle and perhaps the most distinctive village I have seen in decades of travel throughout Russia. Most maps do not show this rural hamlet, though it stands near the intersection of two rivers, the Mezen and the much smaller Kimzha. Its population varies between winter and summer: a couple of hundred in the winter, and a hundred or so more during the summer, when relatives visit.

Because Kimzha lies buried under severe winter conditions for much of the year, it was appropriate that my first experience of the place occurred in early March 2000. The summer prior, in 1999, I had seen a photograph of the Kimzha church, consecrated in the 1760s and dedicated to the Odigitria Icon of Mary. It showed five soaring towers and cupolas over a structure of massive larch logs. It was enough to convince me that I had to reach this place. Friends in Arkhangelsk warned me of the difficulties: Kimzha would be impossible to reach by land in the summer because of the lack of roads.

Formerly, there was limited scheduled transportation by water from Arkhangelsk, but that had ceased with the collapse of state subsidies. Another possibility was to travel by small plane from Arkhangelsk to Mezen. But I wanted to experience the terrain between Arkhangelsk and the Mezen River, and for that I was told of another mode of travel: over a temporary winter road or *zimnik*.

Fortunately, I had *blat*, an essential Russian concept that combines "pull" and "connections." Since 1998 I had maintained close contacts with Pomor State University in Arkhangelsk, at that time the leading university in the White Sea territory (Pomorye). The first vice-rector of the university, Yury Kudriashov, was a native of Mezen; and while he had long since left the area, he had maintained contact with childhood friends such as Peter Kondratyev, the director of a lumber factory in Kamenka. Kondratyev provided me with a driver from his company motor pool and a Land Rover, one of several that made weekly runs between Arkhangelsk—the power center—and the twin towns of Mezen and Kamenka. For the driver, this was a regular, if demanding, shuttle trip. For me it was something else entirely.

When we left Arkhangelsk in the early afternoon of March 7, the sun was bright and the frost hard. The Land Rover sped over a paved road along the right bank of the Northern Dvina River until we approached the mouth of the Pinega

River, some one hundred kilometers to the southeast of Arkhangelsk. At that point we turned east and moved along a reasonably smooth gravel road near the right bank of the Pinega until we reached the town of the same name. The gently rolling terrain had presented few challenges to the Rover. A tractor grader kept the surface even, and high snow banks provided insurance for the occasional skid.

Beyond Pinega, the way to Mezen forked sharply to the north from the main road, and we soon approached the deep taiga forest. The grades became much more primitive, and the track narrowed. This was the beginning of the zimnik. Despite the apparent remoteness of the area, the track to Mezen carries a small but steady stream of traffic—including, to my amazement, twice-weekly service in small buses. And where there are drivers, there will be road stops. In the tiny village of Chizgora, we stopped at a log hut with the usual assortment of engine oil, beef jerky, soap, and ramen noodles. A stocky militia captain ate microwave-warmed *pelmeni*, and in the corner a small television projected a flickering black-and-white image of Jamie Lee Curtis in *A Fish Called Wanda*. It would have been funny to watch the scene where John Cleese seduces Curtis with a recitation of some of the most elegant nineteenth-century Russian poetry, but we had a ways to go.

As we drove, the forest suddenly thinned, and the road improved into a straight causeway through what appeared to be a marsh. Although the hour was close to eleven, floodlights loomed in the distance. Excavators tore at rock-hard earth, and the roar of heavy dump trucks shattered what had been the unbroken silence of the forest. The driver explained that "they" had decided to build an all-year road through forest and marsh directly to Mezen, via Kimzha. In the meantime we plunged back into the forest, with nothing in front of the headlights but a snow track and endless rows of fir and pine trunks. Around midnight, the driver, nodding and exhausted, mumbled that we were finally there.

To arrive at Kimzha in the middle of a winter night produces an unsettling impression, all the more because the first thing one sees is not the village—which is located to the side of the road—but a group of large crosses, stark and ghostly in the sharp contrast of the headlights' glare. This was a startling apparition, and eerily beautiful. But, I wanted to know, where was the village and my promised shelter? Despite the late hour a workshop on the edge of Kimzha was brightly lit, part of a service area for the road builders. The directions we received there took us into the village, where we again lost ourselves in a maze of log walls. Stumbling through snowdrifts, I found the small log house where I was to spend the night. Before going inside, I looked upward and saw the aquamarine shimmer of the aurora borealis. This was the last clear sky I would see in the Mezen region on this

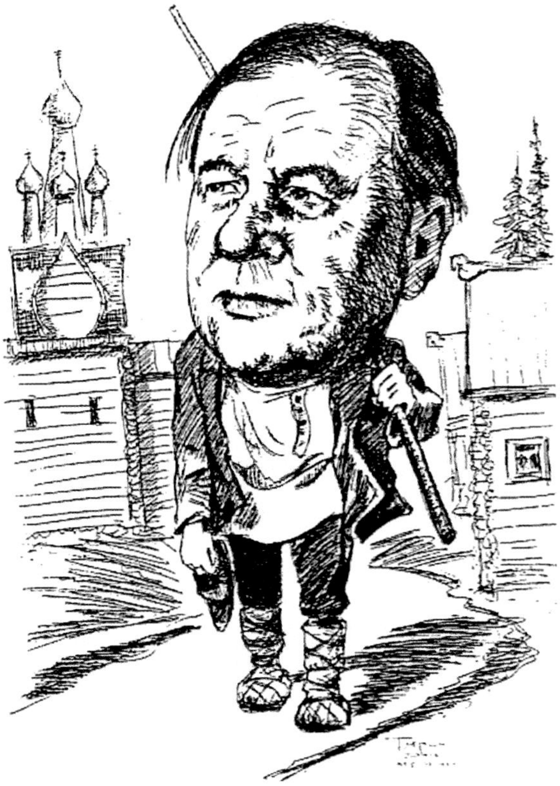

trip. The next hour brought a new weather front of constant snow and wind for the next three days. But in that brief moment I could clearly see the looming specter of the Kimzha church.

As for my accommodations, I had been told that the house was new—unfinished, as it turned out. But the small abode was warm and dry, and I had no trouble with the spartan room, with its window that looked out upon the village. The next morning my host, Georgy Fedorkov, and his brother (both retired on a pension from the lumber plant) provided a hearty breakfast of kasha, fresh milk, and simmering beef stew. The wind and snow continued unabated, and my attempts to call Mezen from a neighbor's house failed; the telephones were out. Kondratyev had planned to bring me from Kimzha to Mezen, but I was stranded in the middle of a snowstorm.

Drawing of author with Kimzha village and Church of the Hodegetria Icon of the Virgin in the background. Artist: Aleksandr Tiarin. Originally published March 22, 2001, in the Arkhangelsk daily *Pravda Severa* to accompany the article "William Brumfield, Enchanted Wanderer," by Sergei Domoroshchenov. Republished in Domoroshchenov's book *Svoi korabl* [My ship] (Arkhangelsk: Pravda Severa, 2002).

Despite the stiff wind and treacherous snow drifts, I decided to photograph as much as I could, partly as a way to relieve the tension. The church, of course, was my primary objective. This was the sole surviving example of its type, apparently created by a group of carpenters active only in this part of the North. The brilliance of their design, perfectly proportioned, is still a source of amazement to me.

But for all of the monumental power of the church, what surprised me still more was the extent to which the village's massive log houses, built during the late nineteenth and early twentieth centuries, had been preserved. This was not an open-air museum, with a few reconstructed log buildings. Yes, some of the houses had been abandoned or at least shuttered for the winter, while a few others had been modified with plank siding. Yet the main thing was that Kimzha remained a functioning, living environment.

How to explain this degree of preservation—of the buildings and of the community? Perhaps the very absence of roads, the "isolation factor," protected the integrity of the environment. Yet that alone was not sufficient to explain the survival of Kimzha, when hundreds of other villages throughout the North had vanished. It occurred to me that the existence of the church, although closed until 1999, might have contributed to the village's endurance. I decided to revisit Kimzha under more favorable conditions, during the summer, in order to explore further the sources of its strength.

The morning's photography produced two rolls of film before driving snow threatened the workings of camera and lenses. By eleven my primary concern centered on finding transportation to Mezen before the roads became completely snowed in. Fedorkov suggested that I turn to the road builders, whose shop I had seen the night before. Now I got a closer look. Even under clement conditions, it is extremely difficult to build a road straight through a northern swamp. I was told that the crews work throughout the year, day and night, on a week's rotation. At this rate the road should be completed within another two years. In view of the budget difficulties in the Arkhangelsk region, it is unlikely that the project would have gotten this far without some form of subsidy or promise of a payback in natural resources.

I looked into the equipment garage, saw a bulldozer under repair, and wondered what could ever bring this inert lump of metal back to motion. The blade was encrusted with a type of local clay that hardens to the consistency of rock, especially in the winter. While we discussed the possibility of my hitching a ride to Mezen with one of the road crews, I managed to see the bunkhouse and workroom, thick with cigarette smoke, as well as the canteen, where a fresh load of bread baked in a nearby village had just arrived. The hash hound, who appeared to be just out of the army, cooked up a crude but edible, calorie-laden fare of several dishes. I could only eat my way through two.

At noon we heard of a group of surveyors who were heading to Mezen in their UAZIK and were willing to take me along. As they packed their gear, a small car drove up with three passengers—Russian Baptist missionaries from St. Petersburg who had come to the Mezen region to spread the Good News and distribute copies of the New Testament. A bit later I noticed one of the crew idly thumbing through a copy in the bunkhouse, where only a little before a quick card game was in full swing with the usual incessant profanity. As for the villagers, one noted laconically: "They won't get very far here." While I pondered that judgment, a woman in a quilted jacket opened the long village stable, and out came several horses, some of whom rolled in the snow, while others ambled through the drifts. I remember very clearly the rime of snow on their dark coats.

In Aleksandr Solzhenitsyn's novel *First Circle*, the ruins of a church tower cause a member of the Soviet elite to ponder his previously unexamined fate. Certain cultures seem drawn to their ruins, their relics, their ghosts, and their shadows. Russia is one such culture. The American South is another.

During my work in the North, Russian colleagues often commented on similarities between their attitudes and what they interpreted as my southern spirit of respect for tradition and cultural legacy. Indeed, it has been easier for certain Russians to accept me as the representative of a region (even one they know primarily through the translation of *Gone with the Wind*) than as a citizen of the United States.

But the affinity between Russia and the American South first struck me during a stay in Leningrad in 1971. The beauty of the city, even in its decrepitude, haunted me—and reminded me of New Orleans, founded fifteen years after Petersburg. The original designs of both owe much to French military engineering. That year I also gained a deeper appreciation of the appeal of southern literature in Russia. Translations of Faulkner's novels and productions of Tennessee Williams plays were the most obvious examples, and my still imperfect Russian described mysterious New Orleans to Russian listeners.

The Russian North has in common with the American South the feeling that, as Faulkner himself put it, "the past is not dead. In fact, it's not even past." In the Russian North I visited dozens of villages whose surviving architecture bears witness to creative and resilient cultural traditions. Unfortunately, many villages have disappeared or been depopulated as the result of demographic shifts and the aftermath of the Soviet regime's economic and social policies (including ruthless collectivization).

Russia and the South also both have ghosts in a more traditional sense: those who have fallen in battle on blood-stained ground. In the course of travels throughout Russia, I have noted—and in many cases photographed—war memorials that exist in almost all Russian settlements, even small villages such as Kimzha. One can endlessly debate the reasons and responsibilities for this huge loss of life, but the scale of the sacrifice is beyond debate. Growing up in the American South, I gained an interest in military history that has continued to play a role in my understanding of Russia. I have taken this interest—in a very personal sense—as a lesson in defiance: to take from every setback a determination to recoup. By going north I return to the South.

After the winter visit, I could think only of returning to Kimzha with summer light. In late July 2000, again in Arkhangelsk, I purchased a plane ticket to Mezen and left from the small regional Vaskovo airport. The view from the air was spectacular during the hour-long trip. The taiga forests, bogs, and meandering rivers took on an otherworldly look. I could scarcely imagine the terrain that I had covered with such difficulty a few months earlier.

Upon arrival in Mezen I was escorted by the major who headed the local militia and, after due formalities, was driven in a brand-new UAZIK to the village of

Dorogorskoe, across the Mezen River from Kimzha. There I met the head of the local village council, Aleksei Zhitov, who made it clear that he pretty much controlled what happened in Kimzha. Not an easy job, as it happens, and the silting of the Mezen River has made it much harder. As I later saw, simply getting a small barge of fuel oil over to the other side was a very difficult, even dangerous, operation — and without oil the village of Kimzha has no electricity. It came as no surprise to learn that Zhitov was suffering from a serious ulcer.

A local fisherman got me up and over the river to Kimzha in an aluminum boat with a sputtering outboard. Now I was here, but where was the sun? After leaving my gear in Fedorkov's house, I moved through the village with two cameras. What a relief to walk without the constant impediment of snow drifts, however picturesque. Now the land was swathed in green, and I staunched my disappointment over the sun. A stiff wind was pushing the cloud layers around. A group of children followed me, the visitor from another planet, with a patter of questions. Then the sun appeared. As I ran toward the center, with the village kids cheering in my wake, the church acquired that rich glow that only late northern light can impart.

The next days brought the same alternation of cloud and sun, and I had time to contemplate the ever-changing image of the church. I also met some of the people from the local parish. This dedicated group — predominantly women — had succeeded in 1999 in having the padlock removed from the church, which was then reconsecrated by an Orthodox priest.

Although there is no resident priest and no regular service, the church is now opened by the women of the church committee at ten in the morning. They have also created a small prayer table (the altar has not been re-created) with an icon of the savior. The door over the vestibule has a reproduction of one of the "tenderness" icons, with Mary and the Christ child. The church ladies are very concerned about the state of the building, and worried that Zhitov is unwilling to make basic repairs, particularly to the windows. Their appeals to various foundations have so far gone unheeded, although the church is a registered national landmark. A rather slipshod attempt at restoration in the 1980s has long been abandoned, and this, too, has disfigured the appearance.

As I asked about the parish, I also learned more about the community. Although the former dairy kolkhoz, surrounded by rusting machinery for which there is no fuel, is a shadow of its Soviet size, a large part of the dairy herd has reappeared through individual ownership. I had ample opportunity to partake of the fresh milk, cottage cheese, and *ryazhenka* (similar to buttermilk) produced throughout the week by individuals who own one cow or a few. The villagers are also sustained by the forest and by the rhythm of its seasons — a time for berries, a time for mushrooms, a time for hunting and fishing. Late one afternoon Elena Repitskaya and Antonina Mamontova arranged a tasting session at which I sampled over a dozen types of jams and other concoctions from the various types of local berries. No Moscow restaurant could offer better.

It also came as a surprise to find that Kimzha has retained a number of residents in their thirties, with young children. These families tend to be large and are of modest means. Much of their income will eventually go to educating their children in a large town. But in the meantime these families — and others who come for the summer — are quietly proud of being a part of the village.

Like all complex environments, Kimzha does not submit to easy definition. I came to realize that it was not some isolated pocket of the past. The villagers no longer sit around singing authentic folk songs. Many of the residents are retirees from the lumber plant, and their children have moved to larger places. When they return for the summer, more urban elements appear in the culture of the village. Television is widespread. In other words, life here shares much with life anywhere in Russia. And yet, these surviving ancient villages are essential microcosms of Russian traditions, many of them now forgotten.

Fortunately, I had succeeded in photographing the Odigitria Church before a decision was made to restore it a few years later. As is often the case in such remote locations, the project was clumsily managed from Arkhangelsk, and as late as 2010, there were concerns that the components would rot before the task was completed. More recent information suggests that at least the roof is back in place. One can only hope that this unique, soaring wooden church will remain, when so many others have been lost.

VARZUGA: BACK TO THE KOLA PENINSULA

Few places in the Russian North give a greater sense of the elemental force and beauty of nature than the village of Varzuga, situated on the high banks of a river of the same name in the southern part of the Kola Peninsula. The Solovetsky Islands rival Varzuga in their strange beauty, and indeed Varzuga was long associated with the Transfiguration Solovetsky Monastery located on the other side of the White Sea to the south (of which more later). But Varzuga, located near the Arctic Circle and set within a background of high sandy hills covered in juniper, pine, and small birch, projects its own unique aura. I can think of no more appropriate setting for one of the most impressive tower wooden churches of northern Russia — the Church of the Dormition of the Mother of God, standing since 1674.

I had long thought of the possibility of traveling to Varzuga to see the Dormition Church, but the specific means of getting there had eluded me. However, in the spring of 2001 I found an ally in Nikolai Utkin, a specialist in traditional wooden architecture of the Arkhangelsk region. We departed from the Arkhangelsk station on the evening of July 18 and proceeded by rail to Kandalaksha, a major rail station on the Murmansk Railway. Passing through Petrozavodsk, the capital of Karelia, we arrived at Kandalaksha at ten thirty the following evening. We made few specific arrangements, but had high hopes.

On the morning of July 20, we took an early bus eastward from Kandalaksha along the Tersky Coast to the regional center of Umba. There we descended upon the startled local administration to ask for the best way to Varzuga. The answer was difficult: once-weekly scheduled transportation would not be for several days. Private cars were available for hire, but at a steep price inflated by the fact that Varzuga had become an attractive destination for sport fishermen with ample money. The alternative was to stand at the turnoff to the road to Varzuga. The local police stopped cars headed in that direction and vouched for us, but no driver was going all the way to Varzuga.

After lunch we explored the other side of Umba, where the parish priest was working with carpenters on restoring a nineteenth-century wooden church located on the left bank of the fast-flowing Umba River. Restoration of the church, which was surrounded by a few wooden houses as well as docks and boat sheds, seemed to me an excellent idea, yet I later found out that part of the parish objected to its relatively distant location and wanted to remain in the temporary place of worship closer to the center.

Later in the afternoon we walked back across a low wooden bridge to the center of Umba and continued our wait for a passing car to Varzuga. As the hour approached eight in the evening I began to wonder about the possibilities for reaching Varzuga, even though the summer sun was still very high and rich this far north. In this mood of languid resignation I hardly noticed a passing car with an attached trailer filled with boxes of vegetables. But Nikolai did, and after a brief conversation, he motioned to me with a quick gesture. Just like that, we were on our way.

The memory of this trip still seems miraculous to me, and not just because of the unexpected serendipity of our meeting. (The driver and his wife were on their way back from a large market with garden vegetables to sell in Varzuga.) As the sun dipped lower behind us, the light became richer, bathing the coastal landscape with its small pines in a warm orange glow. And the road itself, a mixture of red clay and sand, shared in that glow. With the solid clay base and packed sand as a leveling agent, this coast road was virtually without ruts or bumps, and in most places smoother than asphalt. The car flew along, and I began to have hope that we would get to Varzuga to share the last, best part of this rich light.

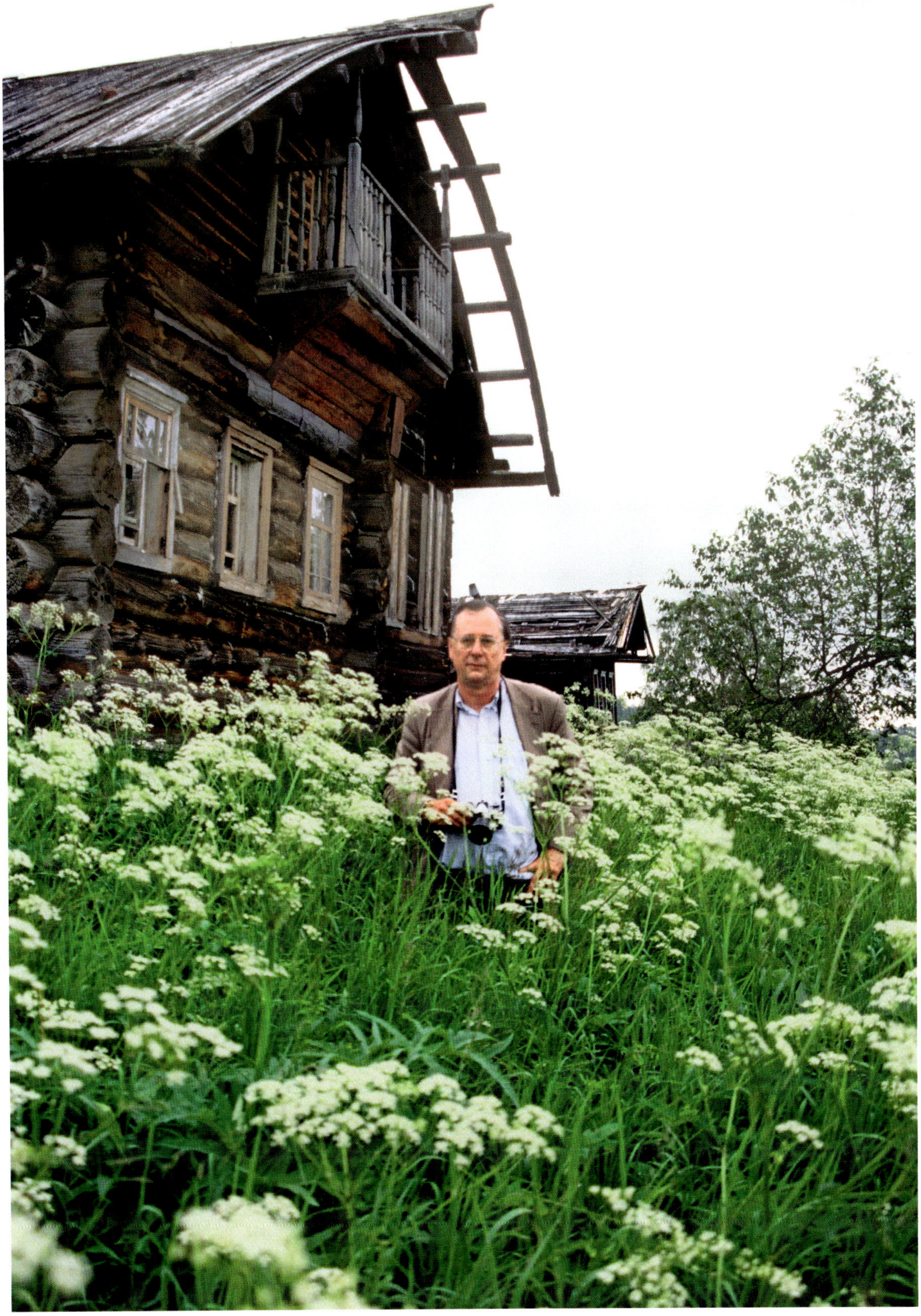

Author with abandoned log house in the background, Shelomya village, Arkhangelsk Province. Photograph: June 22, 2000.

We did, despite a tense interval of several kilometers when we turned north from the shore onto a deeply rutted sandy track through a pine forest leading to Varzuga. I saw the towering form of the Dormition Church just as we cleared the forest on a short descent into the village. The car had not come to a complete stop before I was out the door with my cameras. For the next hour (already after ten in the evening), I photographed the Dormition Church and its neighbor, the nineteenth-century "winter" Church of St. Afanasy, until the bemused driver insisted that he had to get us across the river to the house of Peter Zaborshchikov, our host for the next few days. As we crossed the Varzuga in a low, wooden skiff, I saw the Dormition Church not so much receding as taking more clearly its place in the surrounding landscape.

Although there may have been a settlement on the site as early as the twelfth century, initial references to the village of Varzuga date from the fifteenth century, when it served as an outpost of Novgorod and flourished through its advantageous location on the Varzuga River, near the abundant fishing grounds of the White Sea. In 1450 the prominent Novgorodian Marfa Boretskaia (Marfa posadnitsa, renowned in Russian history for her attempt to defend Novgorod's ancient independence against the encroaching power of Muscovy) donated her holdings along the White Sea to the recently established Solovetsky Monastery.

As the village developed along both sides of the river, churches were also built on both sides. But nothing in Varzuga would rival the elevated form of the Dormition Church, created by a master builder known as Kliment in 1674. An early twentieth-century photograph reproduced in the first edition of Igor Grabar's *Istoriia russkogo iskusstva* shows a soaring tower clad in planks and painted white—a modification that dated to the middle of the nineteenth century. Fortunately, other changes in 1867 did not substantially affect the original form, which was largely restored (at least on the exterior) in 1973. The remarkable stability of this, as well as other large tower churches of the Russian North, is grounded in a thorough understanding of the properties and strength of the pine logs composing the main structure.

Both Kimzha and Varzuga are living environments that exist in a rapidly changing world with new hopes and expectations. They are not museum displays. At the same time, there are legitimate concerns about preserving their traditional wooden architecture. Each village will survive in some form, but Russia can ill afford to lose the aesthetic and cultural traditions so richly embodied in these two outposts of the North.

Into the Forest

A Note on the Architectural Heritage of the Russian North

The Russian North is part of a vast boreal forest, or taiga, and its traditional architecture reflects that elemental fact. We can assume that indigenous Finno-Ugric peoples, as well as Russian explorers and settlers from the medieval commercial center of Novgorod, possessed the skills for constructing durable log structures. The northern climate and terrain made such skills essential.

The Russian presence in the North also brought the spiritual culture of the Orthodox Church, which had rich traditions of building in both wood and stone. Although log churches and chapels might have been built in the area as early as the eleventh century, the earliest surviving masonry structures appeared only at the end of the fifteenth century, as control of the region shifted from Novgorod to Moscow. The most notable example is the small Cathedral of the Nativity of the Mother of God at Ferapontov Monastery (discussed in chapter 2). Apart from its historical significance, the temple contains stunning frescoes by the Moscow painter Dionisy, among the great achievements of medieval Russian art.

Despite difficult conditions and the paucity of skilled masons, the sixteenth century witnessed the creation of a number of impressive brick churches in the North. Of special interest are cathedrals in Vologda and Solvychegodsk, as well as the ensemble of the Solovetsky Transfiguration Monastery. These structures derive from the church architecture of medieval Novgorod and Moscow, but with distinctive local modifications noted in the following chapters. (The characteristics of medieval Russian church architecture are given a detailed examination in my book *A History of Russian Architecture*.)

The seventeenth century witnessed an acceleration of masonry church construction in the North. The structures were less daring in scale and execution than during the preceding century, but more highly decorated. Both Vologda and Veliky Ustiug have numerous examples from this period. At the beginning of the eighteenth century, the reign of Peter the Great brought fundamental stylistic changes inspired by European architecture. Baroque and neoclassical styles soon found their way to church as well as secular construction in northern towns, with their commercial links to St. Petersburg. Once again, local variations led to highly idiosyncratic decorative styles exemplified in northern merchant towns such as Totma and Veliky Ustiug.

Yet overwhelmingly the architecture of the Russian North was based on wood. By virtue of their settlement within a forested zone, Russian knowledge of the properties of wood was ingeniously applied to churches, dwellings, and fortifications. Fire and the inevitable process of decay have long since destroyed the work of early medieval Russian carpenters. Little has been preserved from before the eighteenth century, and attributions of log churches to the fifteenth and sixteenth centuries are rare. Nonetheless, much commentary on the characteristics of early Russian wooden architecture has proceeded on the assumption that such traditional forms were inherently conservative and can be inferred from surviving log buildings of a later period.

The oldest examples of Russian wooden architecture are churches, which could last as long as three to four centuries, assuming that decayed logs were promptly replaced (a common procedure) and the roof maintained. The simplest type of wooden church resembles the basic unit of the peasant house, with its pitched roof and rectangular "cell." The plan is linear, along an east–west axis, with one unit for the service and another, the *trapeza*, as a form of vestibule. Such churches often have two additional units: an apse containing the altar on the east and a bell tower attached to the vestibule on the west. The more elaborate churches of this type, like the larger peasant houses, were decorated with carved end boards (*prichelina*) protecting the roof beams, and with carved galleries on raised porches. The variations on this form are many. Some examples display multiple gables with extensive carving and high pitched roofs.

The vertical line is much more emphatic in a type of wooden church known as the "tent" (from the Russian word *shatior*), so named for the shape of its central tower. This type has a centralized plan consisting of a cuboid core that supports an ascending eight-sided tower. More complex variants display a cruciform plan with flanking domes. Often the core projected a gallery on three sides, raised above the highest snow drifts on a system of extended logs (*pomochi*). Details such as the gallery remind us how closely aesthetics and function were combined in log churches.

The disfavor directed toward the "tent" tower by the church hierarchy in the late seventeenth century resulted in a waning of that design. Yet the Russian love of verticality in church design found expression in a third type of log church, the tiered (*yarusnyi*) structure, in which a pyramidal silhouette ascends in a series of diminishing octahedrons over the main part of the building. The vertical design of this church is accented by decorative barrel-shaped gables over the arms of the cruciform plan and repeated in smaller forms above the octahedrons. In the tiered form, as in most of the other types surveyed above, there were two basic methods of joining the pine logs: the notch (*oblo s ostatkom*) for round logs, and the mortised dovetail (*v lapu*) for both round and squared logs. The dovetail was used when greater precision of detail and stability were required.

Whatever the form, the methods of construction demanded a careful series of steps. The logs were cut in late fall after the final ring of the tree—usually pine, with some fir—had hardened, and they were left on the ground until the beginning of building season, in late spring. Logs were then taken to the construction site, where master carpenters trimmed, notched, and if necessary, planed them. The most common tools were the ax (of which there were various types adapted to specific functions) and the adze, as well as wedged spikes for splitting logs and a primitive type of spokeshave, or drawing knife, for making concave incisions along a log. Russian log structures rarely used clay caulking but relied instead on the tight fit of one log above another, with materials such as moss or hemp for insulation in dwellings. There was little use for saws, which would have opened the grain of the wood to moisture, as opposed to the proper stroke of the ax, which closed the grain. Nails were also traditionally dispensed with, even in the roof, whose planks—usually double-layered—were designed with a groove fit and wedged at the top into a ridge beam.

Whether notched or dovetailed, the logs just beneath the roof were usually extended in length, so as to support an overhang for protection against moisture runoff. This flare (*poval*) is one of the most graceful, if unobtrusive, details of Russian wooden architecture, and is completely functional. The tips of the roof planks often displayed carved tips, which in sunlight cast a bold pattern of shadows against the texture of the log walls.

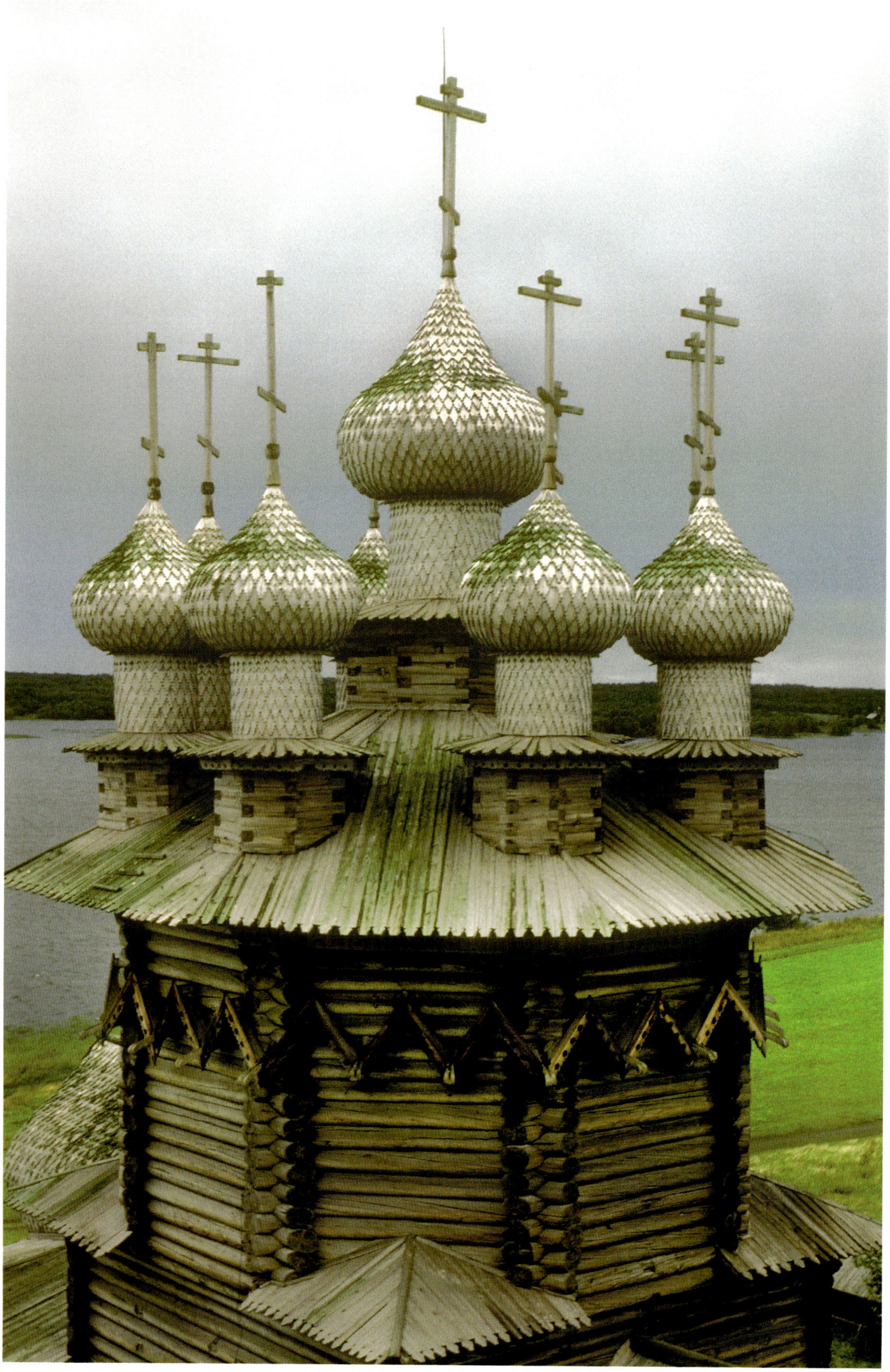

KIZHI POGOST. Church of the Intercession, cupolas, northwest view from bell tower. Photograph: August 18, 1988.

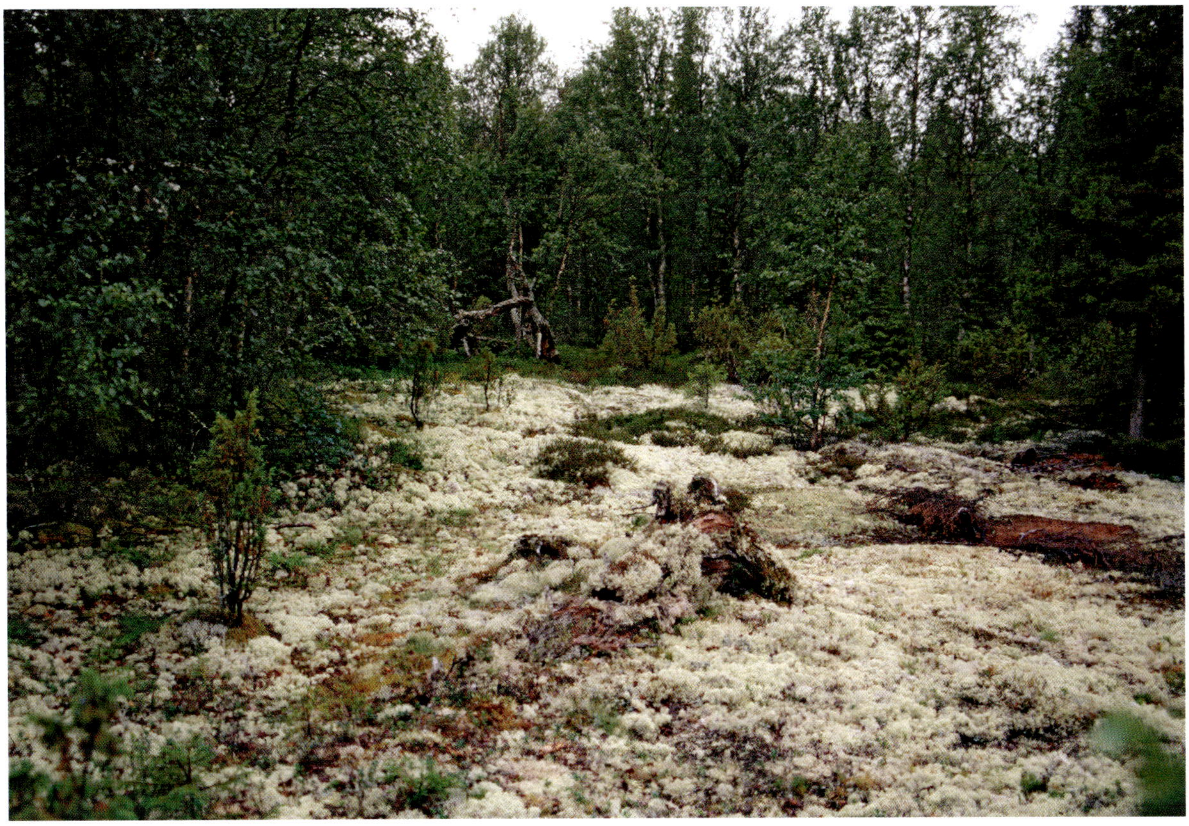

Moss-covered glade in forest beyond Varzuga. Photograph: July 22, 2001.

If the church culminated in a "tent" tower, the base of the tower would be surrounded by an overhang at a much lower angle (*politsa*). Such towers were usually planked, but in some instances they were covered with carved shingles, as were the cupolas. These shingles (*lemekhi* or *cheshui*—"fish scales"), among the most ingenious features of Russian wooden architecture, were curved and wedged to follow the contours of the wooden frame underneath. Typically the shingles were carved from moist aspen, which ages from a golden hue to silver and forms a brilliant contrast to the dark walls of aged pine logs.

The soaring vertical superstructure provided a system of ventilation to preserve the structure from rot. Yet the superstructure of tall wooden churches was not usually visible from the interior, which was capped at a low level by a painted ceiling, or "heaven" (nebo) that prevented heat loss over the central part of the church.

It was not uncommon in Russian settlements to have paired churches at a venerated site called a *pogost*. Usually connected to a cemetery, the pogost might have a large church for summer worship and a smaller one (more easily heated) for the winter. The churches were not built simultaneously; the ensemble evolved as parish means permitted. But the concept was always present. The final element of the pogost ensemble was a freestanding bell tower with a tent roof between and

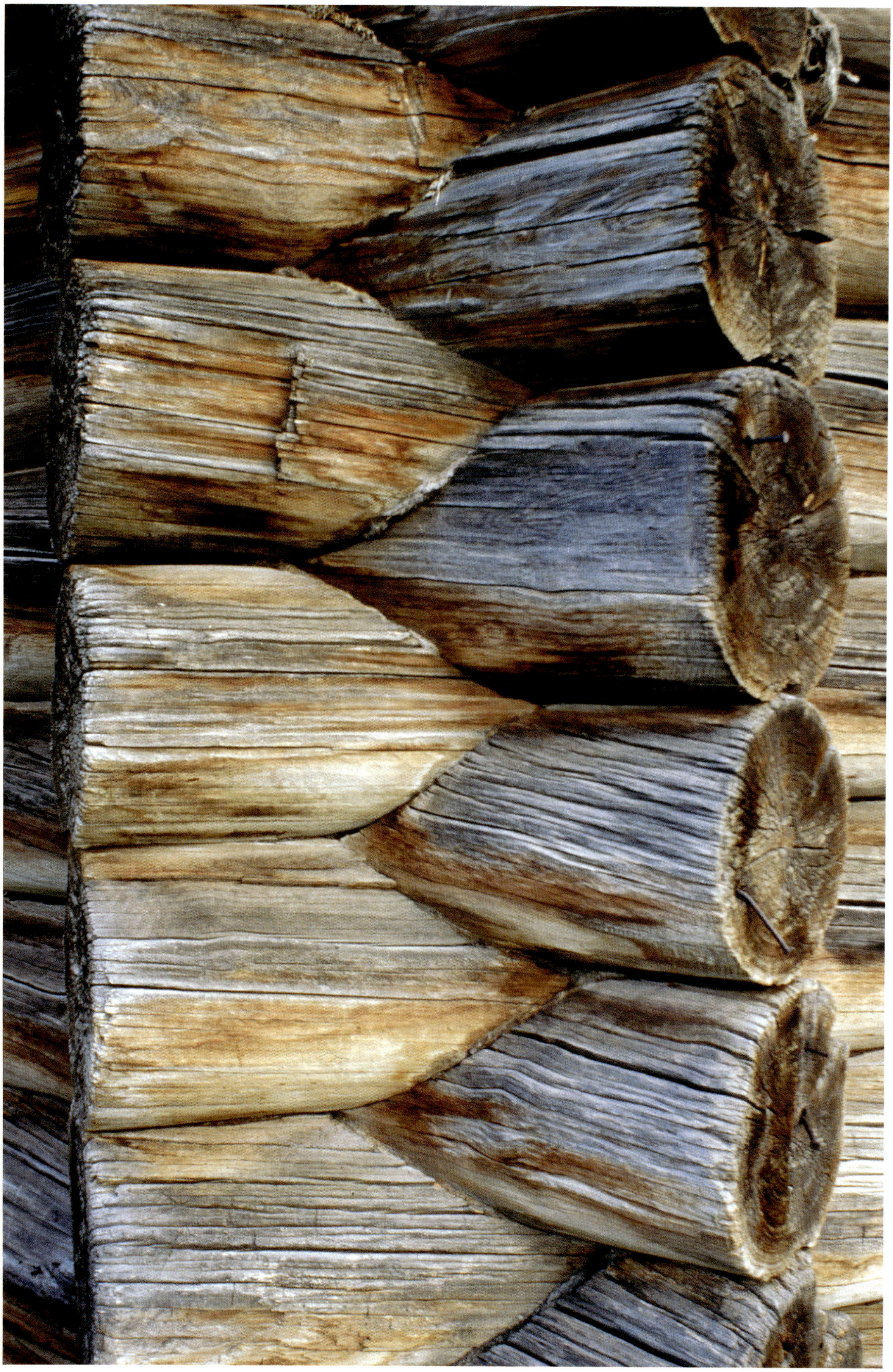

KIMZHA. Church of the Hodegetria Icon of the Virgin, log construction, apse wall. Photograph: August 1, 2000.

in front of the two churches. The pogost could be enclosed by a low wall of horizontal logs on a base of fieldstone, with square towers at the corners. The supreme example of the pogost—and of the genius of Russian wooden architecture—can be found on Kizhi Island in the northwest part of Lake Onega (see chapter 1).

The extraordinary variety and beauty of Russian log churches should not obscure the main purpose of wooden architecture, which was to provide housing. Although log houses were often humble affairs and even in the best cases would not have rivaled the distinctive form of the church, they, too, demonstrated artistry of design as well as economy of function.

The center of the peasant log house—whatever its size—was the large masonry stove used both for cooking and for heating the main living space during the long winters. The stove could be ventilated in two ways that define the basic types of peasant house: the "white" and the "black." In the former the smoke was released through a brick chimney, while in the latter the smoke drifted up toward the ceiling and along a wooden duct that collected the smoke and expelled it. This "black" variant was common even for large houses; and due to the ingenuity of the design, the smoke did not foul the entire living space, but only an area under the roof that could be scraped down.

The house typically formed the main component of an enclosed yard (*dvor*). In the more severe climate of the far north, these units were combined into a single, self-sufficient structure with three basic configurations: a long rectangular structure (known in Russian as *brus*) with the living quarters on one side and barn space for storage and livestock extended on the longer side; a rectangular structure with the barn attached to the side and extending back at a right angle (*glagol*); and, the most complex, a two-story structure with the living quarters in front and the barn in back under a greatly extended roof (*koshel*).

Whether large or small, log houses were traditionally decorated with window surrounds and end boards that were carved or sawn in intricate designs. In the eighteenth and nineteenth centuries, patterns derived from folk motifs became particularly elaborate. During the same period, carpenters began to adapt urban architectural motifs such as baroque window surrounds that they observed during seasonal work in the cities, or at the country dachas of city residents.

For large northern towns such as Vologda, wooden houses were the majority well into the nineteenth century. With the spread of sawmills, the log walls of these houses were frequently covered in plank siding, which provided opportunities for still more elaborate designs. Vernacular architecture thus served as a showcase for artisanal skills that reflected the owner's prosperity and link with Russian peasant traditions. Indeed, during the nineteenth century the northern log house became a symbol of national identity.

The achievements of Russian master carpenters can be seen both as a highly developed, specific response to a demanding physical environment, and as an expression of values that can also be traced in Russian masonry architecture: the striving for verticality in church architecture, with its symbolic relation to God; the fondness for elaborate ornamentation; and a plasticity of structural form. The rigors of the far northern climate produced a shelter environment that excluded or reduced light—even in the precious and limited time when the sun was visible. The windows were small, and interior lamps—where they existed—were dim. All the more necessary and comprehensible was the urge to create vivid, towering forms of churches that would catch and reflect the light, whether from the blinding sun of a short winter day or on a long summer evening. Such forms reaffirmed the survival of the community and sustained the spirit of those who sought refuge in the northern forests.

Let us now go into the forest.

ONE *The Western Shore of the White Sea*

VARZUGA ON THE KOLA PENINSULA

The historic Russian North—particularly the area around the White Sea—was for centuries dotted with settlements sustained by the northern forests and by the bounty of the sea. One of the most important is the large village of Varzuga in the southeastern part of the Kola Peninsula (Murmansk territory). The village—with its four wooden churches—is situated on both sides of the Varzuga River some twenty kilometers north of the point where it empties into the White Sea. Each side of the village is nestled in a backdrop of high sand dunes covered with juniper bushes. Farther inland from the dunes are small coniferous forests. The landscape is especially beautiful in the summer, when the long, dark winters are compensated by almost constant light.

Official sources state that the current population of Varzuga is approximately nine hundred, but this figure includes other villages in the area. The 2002 census gives Varzuga itself 351 residents. (By contrast the population in 1910 was approximately one thousand.) The village was first mentioned in written sources in 1466, when the area was still nominally under the control of the medieval trading city of Novgorod. By the end of the fifteenth century, the area had entered the domains of Muscovy.

Varzuga's prosperity was brutally interrupted in 1568, when the village was raided as part of a campaign by Ivan the Terrible to extort further revenues for his incessant military campaigns. From the sixteenth to the latter part of the eighteenth century, Varzuga was economically linked to various monastic institutions, in particular the powerful Transfiguration Monastery on the Solovetsky archipelago in the southwestern part of the White Sea.

At first glance Varzuga appears isolated, with primitive service to the regional center of Umba over a largely unpaved coastal road. Conditions have improved over the past decade, however, and there is now an upgraded dirt road from Varzuga to Umba. And from Umba there is a paved road to the major rail station at Kandalaksha. Varzuga has also recently been connected to the regional power grid, which ensures a dependable power supply.

For centuries, the basic asset of Varzuga has been its fishery, which continues to exist under skillful local management in the post-Soviet era. This enterprise provides jobs and a measure of economic stability for local residents, some of whom have lived in the area for generations. In recent years Varzuga has gained another source of income based on its reputation as a prime location for salmon fishing. Sportsmen from Russia and abroad arrive for deluxe fishing packages that include ready access to the town (helicopter flights are an option) and well-stocked cabins farther up the Varzuga River. Sports tourism has become a boon to many residents of Varzuga and is closely related to the fishery.

With this dependence on fishing, agriculture has occupied a limited role in the life of Varzuga. In the summer the residents cut hay for the livestock that most households possess. And there are the essential vegetable gardens. The climate and location work against more extensive crops. The emphasis on fishing also affects the design of the village's traditional log houses, which are smaller than those of northern agricultural villages such as Kimzha (see chapter 5). Ironically, with their relatively favorable economic position, village residents often seem less willing to maintain traditional log houses built several decades ago. New houses—some of log construction and some of masonry—are increasingly preferred to traditional dwellings.

For all of its resources, what endows Varzuga with a distinctive cultural presence is the wooden Church of the Dormition of the Virgin, which rises thirty-four meters above the high right bank of the river. Remarkable for its construction logic as well as its beauty, the core log structure, from 1674, has withstood time and the elements in its exposed location. A number of modifications were made in the nineteenth century, and both exterior and interior were clad in plank siding. A restoration completed in 1973 returned the upper part of the church to its original appearance. On the interior the icon screen was dismantled for restoration, and work slowly continues on the main surviving icons, which date from the seventeenth and eighteenth centuries.

The main place of worship for Varzuga is the adjacent nineteenth-century Church of St. Afanasy. It is called a "winter church," because its lower dimensions allowed it to be heated for year-round use. There are also two small churches on the left bank—the Church of St. Nicholas (probably the first church to be founded in the area) and the Church of Apostles Peter and Paul.

But within this bucolic setting, there are sharp controversies, such as the one that arose from the recent rebuilding of the bell tower near the Dormition Church. The original bell tower adhered to the octagonal form traditional in the North and exemplified at the village of Liadiny (see chapter 3). At Varzuga the new bell tower is in a very different, quadrilateral design, whose ungainly shape has outraged preservationists. The church's position is that the structure in its current form is needed to support a heavier weight of bells, but that is a questionable argument. Traditional design is not just a matter of aesthetics but also requires consideration of the historic environment within which these northern wooden churches have existed.

At the mouth of the Varzuga River on the White Sea is the small fishing village of Kuzomen. Although Kuzomen has no church, the sand dunes at its edge are marked by the startling apparition of weather-beaten wooden crosses at an abandoned cemetery. Eternal rest at the shifting line between land and sea.

KEM ON THE WHITE SEA

To the south of Kandalaksha, the White Sea coast is dotted with inlets, the occasional town, and picturesque, windswept villages such as Kovda and Virma. Among the most important settlements is Kem, a regional town known to most visitors as a major route to the Solovetsky archipelago and the great Monastery of the Transfiguration. Yet the town itself has a dramatic history, which, like that of the Solovetsky Islands, combines elements of ancient spiritual quest with modern tragedy.

The very setting of Kem is dramatic, with a rocky coastline bounded by a dense forest that reaches the west shore of the White Sea. The historic part of town is located primarily on an island known as Lepostrov (Läppäsaari in Karelian), flanked by the arms of the small Kem River near its confluence with the sea.

During the medieval period these northern lands were tenuously held by the commercial power of Novgorod, whose authority was already tested to the limit by Moscow's expansion. In 1450 Novgorod granted the settlement at the mouth of the Kem River to the Solovetsky Transfiguration Monastery, which had been formally established in 1436 on a group of islands in the southern White Sea.

Through this grant the Solovetsky Monastery, protected on its sacred archipelago, acquired a land base and port some sixty kilometers over water to the west.

Because of its strategic location, Kem gained the attention of hostile neighbors in the late sixteenth century. Ivan the Terrible was at that time mired in a protracted conflict known as the Livonian War (1558–83), which in its latter phase involved a struggle with Sweden for control of the eastern Baltic region. In 1589 Kem was raided by Finnic forces, and in 1590 the region was attacked by the Swedes. The following year Moscow reaffirmed Solovetsky Monastery's title to the Kem territory. The power of the monastery allowed it to function as a surrogate for an exhausted Muscovy, and during the next century Kem was defended and fortified under the monastery's direction.

Kem was briefly returned to state control from 1704 to 1711 during the early phase of Peter the Great's struggle with Sweden known as the Great Northern War (1700–1721). With Peter's victory over King Charles XII at Poltava (July 1709), pressure on Russia's White Sea territory diminished.

To symbolize Russian power in the area, the Cathedral of the Dormition was erected in Kem in 1711–14. That this extraordinary log structure should be designated a cathedral is indicative of the distinctive culture of northern Russia. Its three tent towers, which signify the presence of three altars, soar above an elevated location on Lepostrov. Although partially obscured by trees, the Dormition Cathedral is still the town's dominant landmark.

Despite wooden scaffolding from an ongoing restoration, the west (front) facade of the Dormition Cathedral is largely visible. A decorated porch leads to a wide one-story structure with low pitched roofs. The ascending levels of three roofs provide a harmonious pedestal for the central tower, which rises from a square base to an octagon that supports an eight-sided "tent" tower. Some thirty-six meters high, the tower is crowned with a wooden cupola and cross. It is flanked by two smaller towers over chapels attached to the north and south of the main structure.

The church interior begins with a spacious vestibule (or refectory), whose trimmed log walls are lined with benches. In the center are massive painted log columns that support key elements of the roof. A portal leads from the vestibule to the main worship space, whose icon screen on the east wall has been partly preserved and is being restored. Behind the screen is the primary altar, dedicated to the Dormition. The octagonal upper space culminates in a ceiling of planks arranged in a chevron pattern. The west wall supports a small wooden choir gallery.

To the right of the main space is a chapel dedicated to St. Nicholas. To the left is the north chapel, with an altar dedicated to Saints Zosima and Savvaty, founders of the Solovetsky Monastery. The north chapel has a separate entrance from the outside. More easily heated than the main space, this chapel is used for winter worship. The territory of the Dormition Cathedral also has a separate chapel built around 1710 and dedicated to the Trinity. Square in shape, the interior of this small structure contains a remarkable carved votive cross associated with Peter the Great.

Despite clumsy modifications in the nineteenth century, the preservation of the Dormition Cathedral after three centuries of turbulent history is a miracle, particularly in view of the destructive antireligion campaigns of the Soviet period. Yet the slow pace of its restoration gives cause for concern.

Kem remained under the control of the Solovetsky Monastery until 1764, when Catherine the Great initiated reforms that curtailed monastery holdings. At that point the town became a part of various administrative divisions in the White Sea area. During the nineteenth century, the town existed primarily on the basis of fishing. The rocky soil could only support subsistence farming for its some two thousand inhabitants. In 1903 Kem gained a large masonry church, the Cathedral of the Annunciation. Severely damaged during the Soviet era, the church is now being restored as part of the recently established Monastery of the New Russian Martyrs and Confessors.

Kem's growth was stimulated during the First World War with the construction in 1915–17 of a strategic railroad through the town to the new port of Murmansk. Following the Bolshevik revolution, Kem was occupied in 1918 and 1919 by White troops and briefly by an Anglo-American force. With the return of Soviet power, Kem rapidly became a part of the system of supply and administration for a penal camp established by the Cheka (the Soviet political police) in 1919 on the territory of the former Solovetsky Monastery. In 1921 this prison was named the Solovetsky Camp of Special Designation (abbreviation: SLON), described by Aleksandr Solzhenitsyn in his *Gulag Archipelago*. The camp was closed in 1939, yet the Gulag system continued to expand. A large wooden votive cross now stands on a rocky elevation near the harbor to commemorate the fate of those who embarked from Kem to this sinister destination.

During the Second World War, Kem served as an important station on the critical rail route for allied lend-lease deliveries through the port of Murmansk. Although much of southwestern Karelia (including Petrozavodsk) was occupied by Finnish forces until the summer of 1944, the railway continued to deliver vital supplies via a link around the south shore of the White Sea to the Arkhangelsk–Vologda main line.

After years of declining numbers, the population of Kem has stabilized at around twelve thousand. Easily accessible on the major rail line from Petrozavodsk, the town is sustained in part by the revived Solovetsky Transfiguration Monastery, which attracts an increasing number of visitors.

THE SOLOVETSKY TRANSFIGURATION MONASTERY

No site in the Russian North carries more historical weight than the Solovetsky Transfiguration Monastery, located on Great Solovetsky Island, part of an archipelago in the southern part of the White Sea. The islands form one of the most curious natural environments in Russia. Although buffeted by northern winds and sea currents, the same currents also moderate the northern climate and produce a rich ecological diversity.

The origins of the settlement on the Solovetsky archipelago can be dated to 1429. At that time the monk Savvaty, who had been tonsured at the St. Cyril-Belozersk Monastery, joined forces with Herman, an illiterate hermit who had periodically visited Solovetsky Island. The elderly Savvaty died in 1435, but the following year another monk, Zosima, returned to the island and founded a monastery dedicated to the Transfiguration of the Savior. Despite many hardships, the monastery took root under the direction of Zosima, who died in 1478. During this early period the monastery belonged to the domains of the Russian city-state of Novgorod, but after Novgorod's subjugation to Moscow in 1478 the Muscovite grand princes reaffirmed the strategic importance of this remote monastic outpost.

A new era began with the arrival of Philip Kolychev, a Moscovite monk of noble origins who left his privileged existence in 1537, joined the Solovetsky monastic community, and in 1547 became its spiritual leader (*hegumen*). During the next eighteen years Philip guided an ambitious program of construction that transformed the monastery and created monumental buildings of stone and brick such as the great Cathedral of the Transfiguration of the Savior (1558–66) and the Refectory Church of the Dormition (1552–57), among the most impressive manifestations of late medieval Russian architecture. He also initiated a series of projects, including canals that improved the position of the monastery as a self-sustaining community. In the summer of 1566 he was called back to Moscow by Ivan the Terrible, who supported Philip's appointment as metropolitan (head) of the Russian Church. Philip's resistance to Ivan's misrule led to his exile and execution in 1569.

Nonetheless, construction at the monastery continued after Philip's death.

Other late sixteenth-century churches in the monastery include the Church of St. Nicholas (1577; razed and rebuilt in 1830–34); and the Gate Church of the Annunciation, built in 1596–1601 over the west gate and still standing, although much modified in the nineteenth century. Between 1582 and 1594 monks and hired labor manhandled thousands of granite boulders into place as the great walls and round towers of the monastery arose from the marshy ground.

Despite the conflicts of the seventeenth century, the Solovetsky Monastery remained one of Muscovy's most prestigious monasteries and one of the privileged religious centers, closely connected to the court. It received many donations, the churches were repaired, and other buildings were added in the eighteenth century. During the nineteenth century, the monastery became a major pilgrimage site, with its own steamship and hotel.

After the end of the Russian civil war in 1921, the Bolsheviks expropriated the monastery. Two years later, a fire of mysterious origins spread throughout the central stone churches and reduced their interiors to ashes. It was here, in 1923, that the Soviet regime established the first concentration camp. Superseded by larger camps, the Solovetsky camp closed in 1939, and the territory became a military base. Modest attempts to restore the monumental Transfiguration Monastery began in the 1960s, and in 1992 Patriarch Aleksy reconsecrated the relics of the monastery's founders with solemn ceremony.

In the summer, this far northern monastery is suffused with an unending display of light that illuminates all sides of the citadel and its churches, and gives added meaning to the monastery's dedication to the Transfiguration, the miracle of divine revelation and light. Travel to the Solovetsky Islands has traditionally been by sea from the Karelian town of Kem. I prefer the aerial option on a small twin-engine airplane from Arkhangelsk's Vaskovo airport. The view from the air is stunning.

THE VILLAGES OF KOVDA AND VIRMA ON THE SOUTHWESTERN SHORE OF THE WHITE SEA

For centuries the natural bounty of the White Sea has supported hardy souls willing to endure the severe climate. The sea's rocky western shore was dotted with ancient fishing villages that still remained at the beginning of the twentieth century. The modern age has dealt harshly with them. Most of the churches have vanished, and the few that have survived remain at risk.

Perhaps the most picturesque of these villages is Kovda, located near Kandalaksha Bay, an arm of the White Sea in the southwestern part of Murmansk Province. The village is perched on rocky cliffs above the point where the small Kovda River flows into the Startsev Inlet. The population of Kovda is officially listed as twenty (in 2010), with the addition of a few visitors in the summer. The few log houses that remain have carefully tended gardens carved into the hillside. Strings of dried fish, cured by the sun, are suspended along the sides of log walls. A few sheds and log saunas complete the picture in this craggy yet stunningly beautiful landscape.

At the beginning of the twentieth century, Kovda was a bustling commercial center, with a customs station, biological research station, and a number of sawmills—including one English and another Swedish. Remnants of those enterprises survive in the neighboring settlement of Lesozavodsky ("Sawmill") and Zelenoborsky. The building of the Murmansk Railway inland from Kandalaksha Bay during the First World War diminished Kovda's activity in favor of the railroad town of Kandalaksha, some twenty-five kilometers to the north.

Although Kovda dwindled, it retained its primary historical monument, the small log Church of St. Nicholas with an adjacent bell tower. A church had existed on the site as early as the fifteenth century, but the present structure dates from the beginning of the eighteenth century when the bell tower was also built. At that time the church was surrounded by a cemetery that was enclosed in a low log wall.

The plan of the St. Nicholas Church is modest, with an apse containing the altar in the east. The main part is a square structure with a double-pitched roof. At the top is an unusual squat cupola with a small nob supporting a cross. The entrance is at the west end through a vestibule that is wider than the central component and built of thicker logs. In this primitive design the two components are not linked structurally.

Like most wooden churches in the nineteenth century, the St. Nicholas Church had plank siding, which was removed during the Soviet period. Closed in 1960, the church was finally slated for restoration as a cultural monument in the 1990s. The bell tower was rebuilt in a simplified form, and restoration of the church itself began in 2003, albeit with frequent halts and sharp disputes. The church now has rather artificial-looking plank siding, but at the beginning of this century it was still possible to see the original log structure.

Farther south along the White Sea coast, the steep rocky outcroppings give way to salt marshes. In this setting, just over four hundred kilometers south of Kovda, stands another coastal village with a miraculously preserved log church. The village of Virma is located near the mouth of the Virma River, some thirty-five kilometers to the southwest of the town of Belomorsk, the northern terminus of the White Sea Canal in the Republic of Karelia. The 2010 census gives Virma a population of twenty-two souls, which makes it 10 percent larger than Kovda. A few wooden houses seem to float in the grassy marsh.

Like many other villages in the western part of the White Sea, Virma had for centuries been within the orbit of the great Transfiguration Monastery on the Solovetsky archipelago. Although the relationship was frequently contentious, these villages provided goods and labor, while the monastery attended to their spiritual needs.

The dominant landmark is the village church, built perhaps as early as 1625 and rebuilt in 1759. Dedicated to Saints Peter and Paul, the archaic structure rises like a living, organic form among the firs and other conifers that crowd the narrow coastline.

Unlike the Kovda church, the Church of Saints Peter and Paul has no bell tower. In compensation, however, it has a remarkable crown of five cupolas covered with silvery aspen shingles and surmounted with wooden crosses. The dramatic thrust of the cupolas rests on a distinctive flared roof—also clad in wooden shingles.

The roof rests above the ledge of a projecting cornice that protects the log walls of the square main structure from excessive moisture. As in the best examples of northern wooden architecture, function and beauty coexist in graceful harmony.

On the east is an apse crowned with the barrel gable, while the west part of the church consists of the usual low vestibule that could be heated for worship during the long winters. A small covered porch completes the linear design. The interior is being slowly refurbished as the church returns to active use. Few parishes can claim a lovelier place of worship.

WOODEN CHURCHES IN KARELIA'S KONDOPOGA REGION

With its ample forests Karelia is especially rich in traditional wooden church architecture. One of the most distinctive examples is in the town of Kondopoga, located on the shores of Lake Onega, some fifty kilometers north of the capital of Petrozavodsk. The site of one of Russia's largest paper mills, Kondopoga is generally known as an industrial town. With a population of some thirty-two thousand, it is the second largest city in Karelia and is readily accessible on the main railroad and highway route from St. Petersburg to the port of Murmansk, nine hundred kilometers to the north.

The origins of a settlement on the site of Kondopoga have been dated to the turn of the sixteenth century. Its favorable location on a bay near the mouth of the Suna River in western Lake Onega made it a natural site for trade and fishing. During the medieval period Kondopoga was considered part of the territory of Kizhi. All structures, including churches or chapels, were built of pine or fir logs.

Kondopoga's economic significance increased in the eighteenth century with the discovery of iron deposits that supplied the large metalworking factory established by Peter the Great at Petrozavodsk in 1703. In the middle of the eighteenth century, extensive marble quarries were developed at the nearby village of Tivdiya, located on a river of the same name. By the 1760s the marble quarried here could be transported to St. Petersburg via a system of waterways linking Lake Onega with the Neva River.

The growing importance of Kondopoga during the reign of Catherine the Great no doubt contributed to the construction in 1774 of the Church of the Dormition, one of the most remarkable monuments of wooden architecture in the Russian North. Situated on a narrow cape extending into Chupa Bay (part of Lake Onega), the Dormition Church could be seen over water like a beacon from a great distance.

To emphasize this prominent location, the master builders created a tower forty-two meters (138 feet) in height. Toward the top of this soaring octagonal structure of notched pine logs is a horizontal band resembling a chevron pattern. These small attached gables not only decorate the structure but also protect it from excessive moisture in this damp region. The bottom of each "V" has a wooden rain spout that collects and expels precipitation away from the log walls.

The church culminates in a tall "tent" tower covered in wooden shingles and crowned with a cupola and cross. Attached to the west of the main structure is an elevated vestibule, or refectory, that is reached on the outside by a decorated staircase attached to the south facade.

The inside of the vestibule is a clean area formed by log walls adorned with icons and painted posts that support and divide the space. The entrance to the worship space is through a painted doorway that frames a view of the icon screen. Passing from the low vestibule to the tower space creates an unforgettable impression. The tall interior, illuminated by window light, is bounded by an icon screen that conceals the altar.

The interior is covered by a painted ceiling, or "heaven" (nebo), a distinctive feature of northern Russian log churches. These "heavens" are an ingenious combination of traditional art and architecture. They consist of a polygonal form segmented by flat beams extending from the top of the walls to an elevated ring in the center. The beams incline upward and create a frame that is self-supporting between the walls and the ring where they meet at the center. The painted panels are in the shape of narrow triangles and are laid upon the inclined frame without fasteners. The number of triangular panels can vary, but in the Dormition Church there are sixteen. They depict angels, including the primary archangels. The ring in the center contains an unusual image of Christ as a priest standing at the altar.

During the Second World War, Kondopoga was occupied from early November 1941 until the end of June 1944 by Finnish forces, at that time allied with Germany. Although the town's industry was ransacked, the Dormition Church—located on the outskirts—was untouched. A thorough study and conservation of the church was undertaken in the 1950s.

In the 1990s the interior of the Dormition Church was again the object of careful restoration, even as the church was returned for active parish use. The complex balance between parish use and the need to preserve this unique historic structure (remote from the main housing districts) led to the construction of the new, more spacious wooden church, completed in 2009 and dedicated to the Nativity of the Virgin. It should be noted that Kondopoga also has one of the largest Lutheran parishes in Karelia.

There are a number of other wooden architectural monuments in the Kondopoga area, including the Chapel of the Kazan Icon of the Virgin in the village of Manselga. With a bell tower over the entrance in the west, the Kazan Chapel follows a typical form for wooden chapels in Karelia during the eighteenth and nineteenth centuries.

A distinctive expression of this traditional form is the late eighteenth-century Chapel of the Three Prelates, originally at the village of Kavgora in the Kondopoga region but subsequently transferred to the museum on Kizhi Island. This intricately crafted structure, with decorative carved end boards, culminates on its west end with a tall octagonal bell tower. Like the Dormition Church, it has an elevated covered stairway to provide access over the high snows of the Karelian winter.

The most unusual variation of the traditional wooden chapel in the Kondopoga region is the diminutive Church of St. Peter at Martsialnye Vody (a word play on the Russian for "mineral waters" and the god Mars). Martsialnye Vody was founded by Peter the Great in 1719 at the site of mineral springs and is considered Russia's first spa. Peter visited Martsialnye Vody on four occasions between 1719 and 1724.

It is possible that the Church of St. Peter was built to the tsar's own design, which combines traditional elements with a baroque dome over the main space.

Although the spa fell into decline after Peter's death in 1725, it was revived in the late nineteenth century and again in 1964. The Martsialnye Vody spa functions to this day, with the Church of St. Peter preserved as a link to the time of Peter the Great.

THE KIZHI POGOST ENSEMBLE

The forests of northern Russia between Lake Ladoga and the White Sea were once dotted with great ensembles of log churches. Now only a few precious examples remain, of which the most remarkable is situated on the small island of Kizhi, one of almost fourteen hundred situated in Karelia's Lake Onega. Detached from the mainland, the island has long been known as a sacred space. Its unusually picturesque setting exists within a length of only six kilometers.

Yet this beauty alone would not have saved the site from the decay and vandalism that destroyed so many other masterpieces of wooden architecture. For over a century, the efforts of some of Russia's leading preservations have ensured the protection of this legacy. In 1966 Kizhi achieved the status of a national architecture and historic museum. In 1990 it was designated a UNESCO World Heritage Site. Kizhi Island now contains some of the oldest surviving examples of Russian log buildings, including one small church—the Resurrection of Lazarus—dated perhaps as early as the end of the fourteenth century.

The supreme example of Russian wooden architecture is Kizhi's Church of the Transfiguration of the Savior, built in 1714 ostensibly in honor of Peter the Great's victories over the Swedes—although a Transfiguration Church had existed at Kizhi since at least the early seventeenth century. Located on open space in the southwest part of the island, the church formed the center of a *pogost*, a term which by the eighteenth century had come to mean an enclosed cemetery with a parish or district church.

As with St. Basil's on Red Square in Moscow, the main Kizhi church, with its many domes, produces an impression of overwhelming profusion and complexity; yet the design derives from rigorous structural and aesthetic logic. Its soaring pyramidal silhouette (thirty-seven meters high) signifies consecrated ground from a great distance, and the design of the structure reinforces that symbolic purpose at every point.

The core of the Transfiguration Church is an octahedron, rising in three tiers and buttressed by extensions ("arms") at the four compass points. These extensions are also stepped, thus providing platforms for additional cupolas: twenty on the structure, plus one at the top and another on the east side above the apse. This intricate pattern of cupolas and log structure is emphasized by the natural properties of the different woods: the dark walls of aged pine logs and the brilliant silver of the cupolas, covered with over thirty thousand curved aspen shingles tightly fitted over the cupola frame.

The design of this elaborate superstructure provided an efficient system of ventilation to preserve the structure from decay. Yet as was typical of tall wooden churches in the Russian North, the tower was not visible from the interior, which was capped at a low level by a ceiling painted with saints and archangels — known as a "heaven" — over the central part of the church. This "heaven" provided a culmination to the religious imagery of the icon screen in front of the altar. Unfortunately this particular "heaven" at Kizhi was lost during the Second World War, and we know of its form only through black-and-white photographs.

The Church of the Transfiguration was intended for use only during major church holidays in the summer. It was not uncommon in Russia to have paired churches, for summer and winter. At the Kizhi pogost, the adjoining "winter" Church of the Intercession, built in 1764, provides an admirable visual complement to the ensemble. Whereas the Transfiguration Church soars, the Intercession accentuates the horizontal, with an extended "refectory." Its crown of eight cupolas surrounding the main cupolas at the top of its octagonal core is a dramatic and satisfying resolution that enhances, rather than competes with, the form of the Transfiguration Church.

The final element of the original pogost ensemble at Kizhi is a bell tower with a tent roof between and in front of the two churches. Originally built in the late eighteenth century, it was rebuilt in 1874 and renovated most recently in the early 1990s. The pogost, with cemetery, is enclosed by a low wall of horizontal logs on a base of fieldstone.

In departing Kizhi Island we again see the soaring forms of the Church of the Transfiguration. Although less known than the great Gothic cathedrals, it is their equal as a daring expression of the spiritual impulse in architecture. The Transfiguration Church is now undergoing a thorough, complex restoration that will enable it to survive as one of Russia's defining monuments.

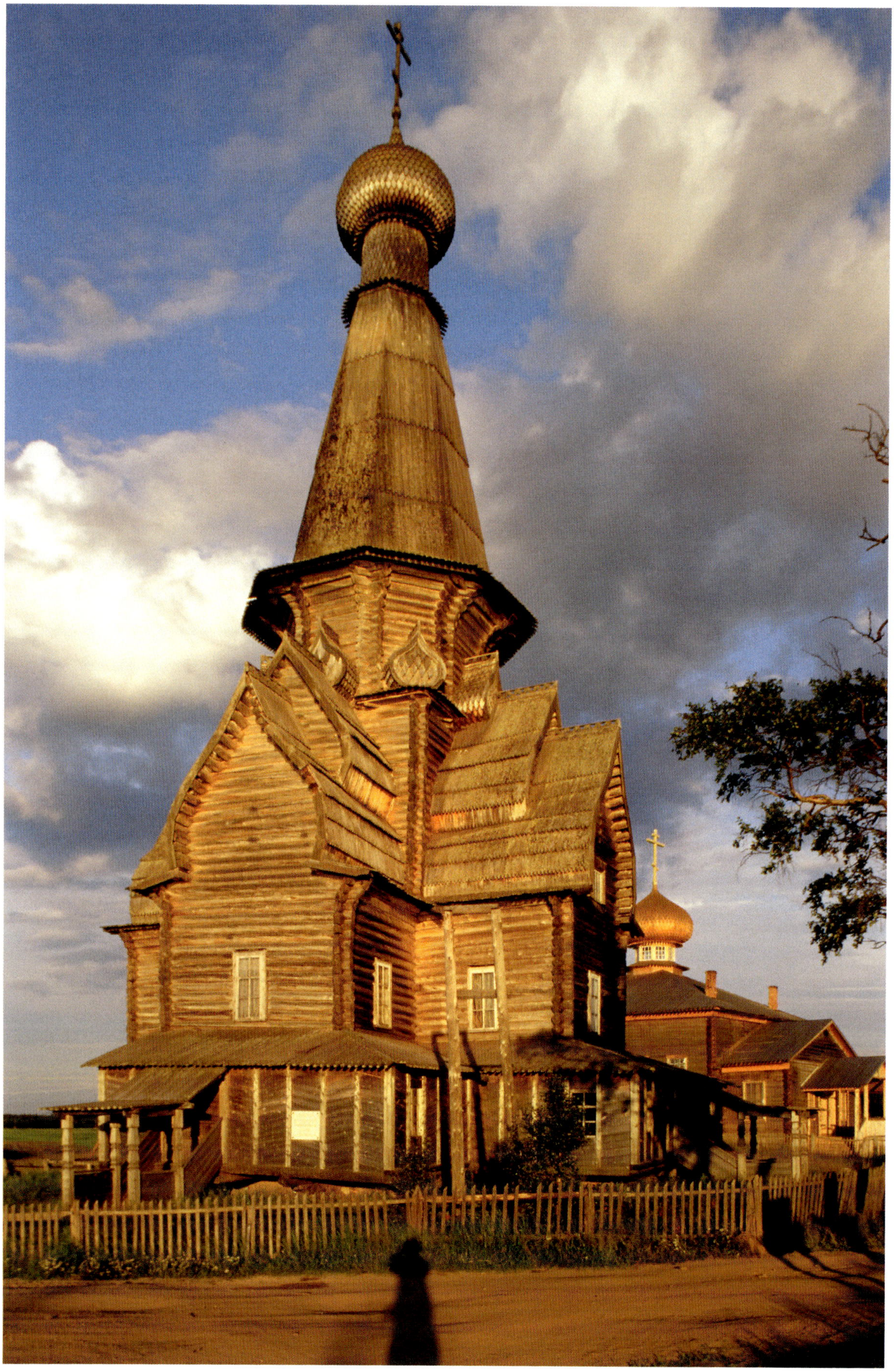

VARZUGA. Church of the Dormition of the Virgin, northwest view. Built in 1674. In 2011 the log walls were again covered with plank siding, as in the nineteenth century. Photograph: July 21, 2001.

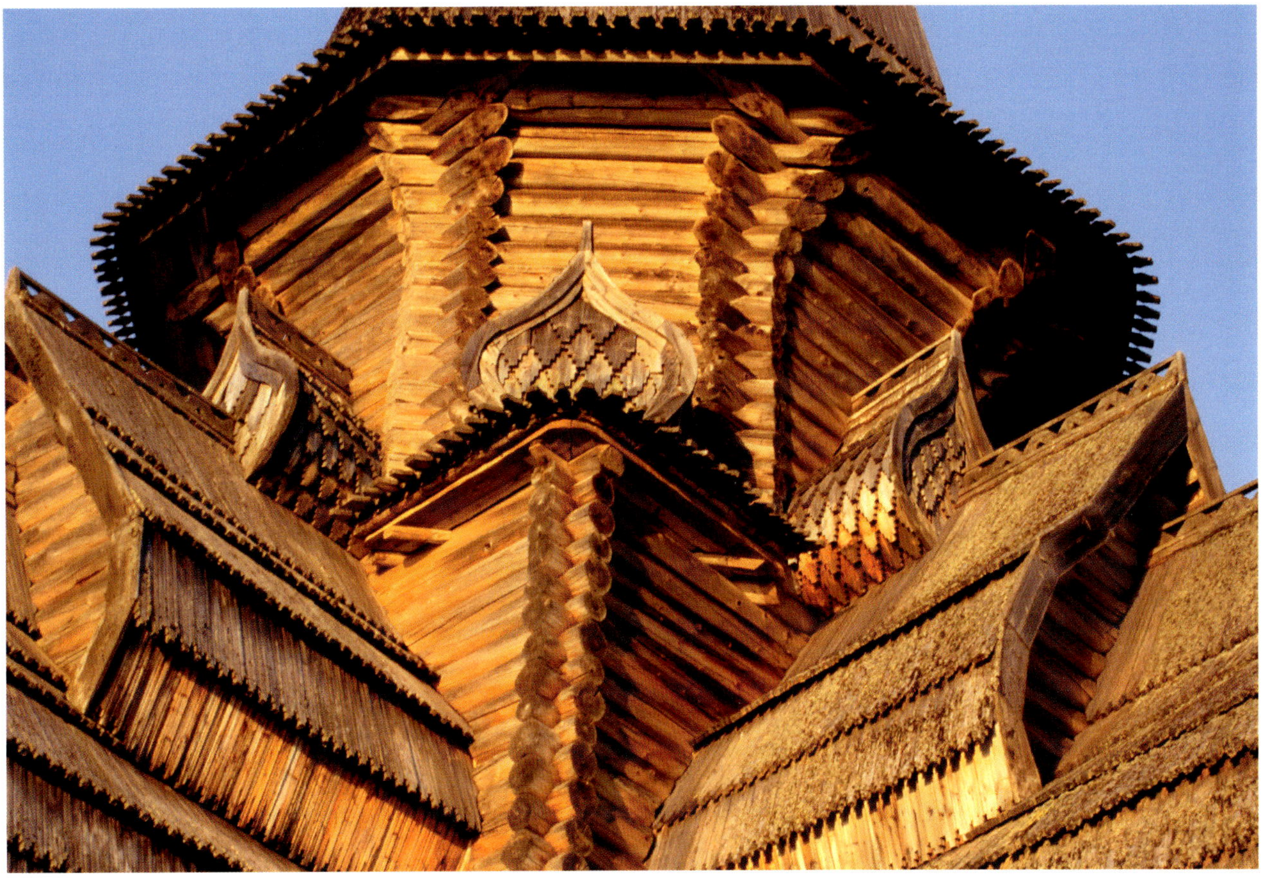

VARZUGA. Church of the Dormition, northwest view, upper structure. Construction details no longer visible because of new plank siding. Photograph: July 20, 2001.

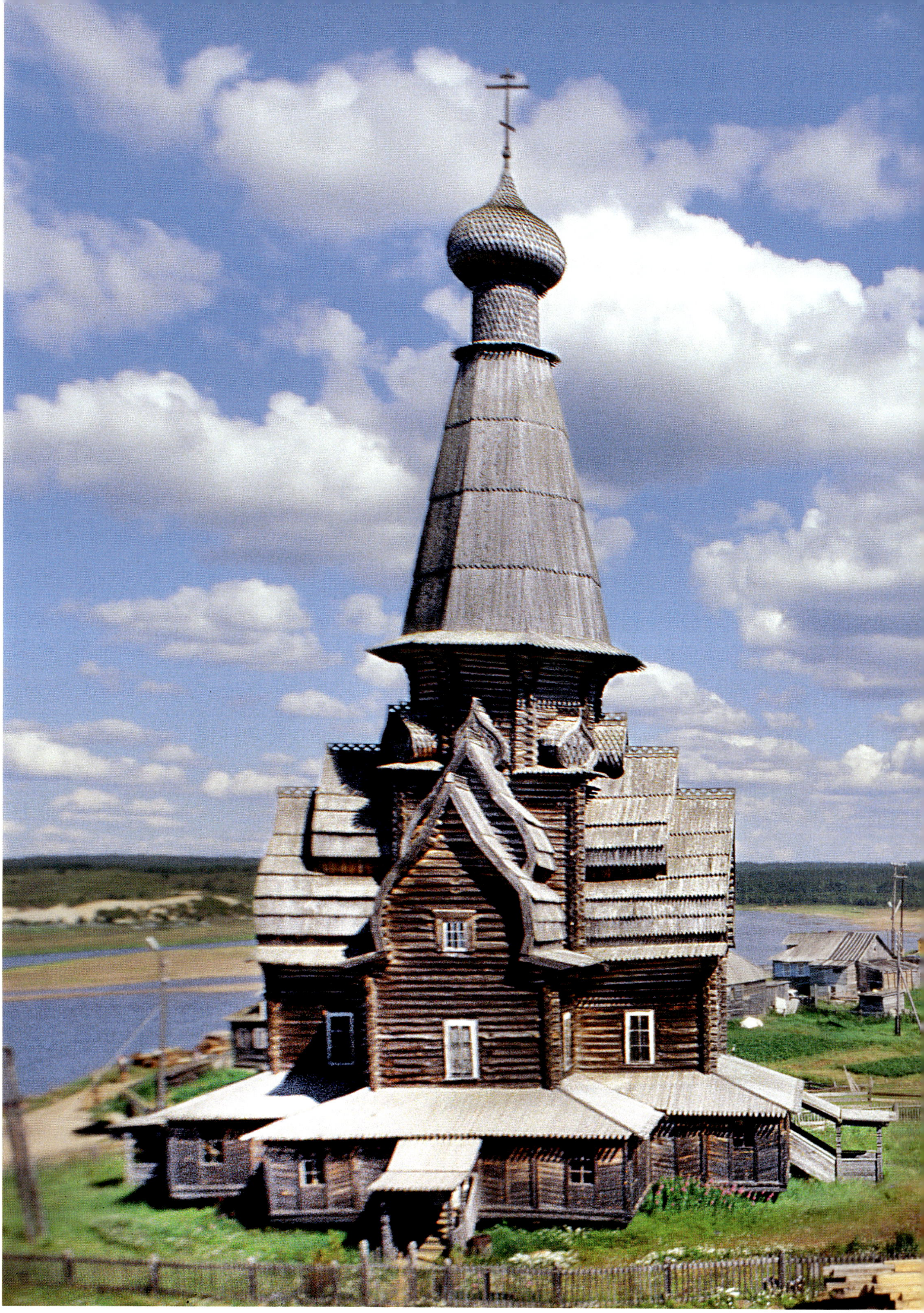

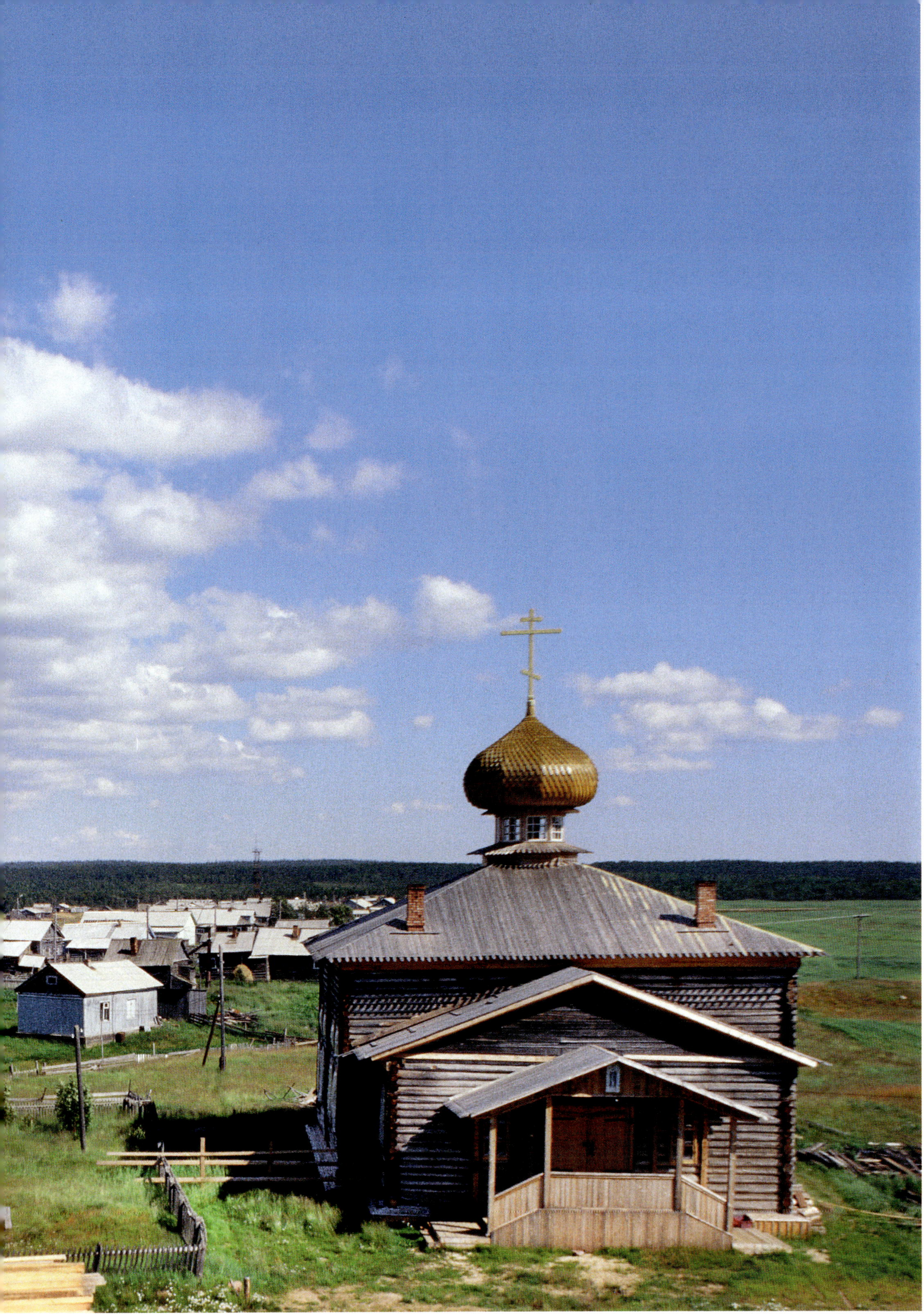

VARZUGA. Church of the Dormition on left. On right, Church of St. Athanasius the Great, built in 1854 for winter services. West view from bell tower. Background: Varzuga River. Photograph: July 21, 2001.

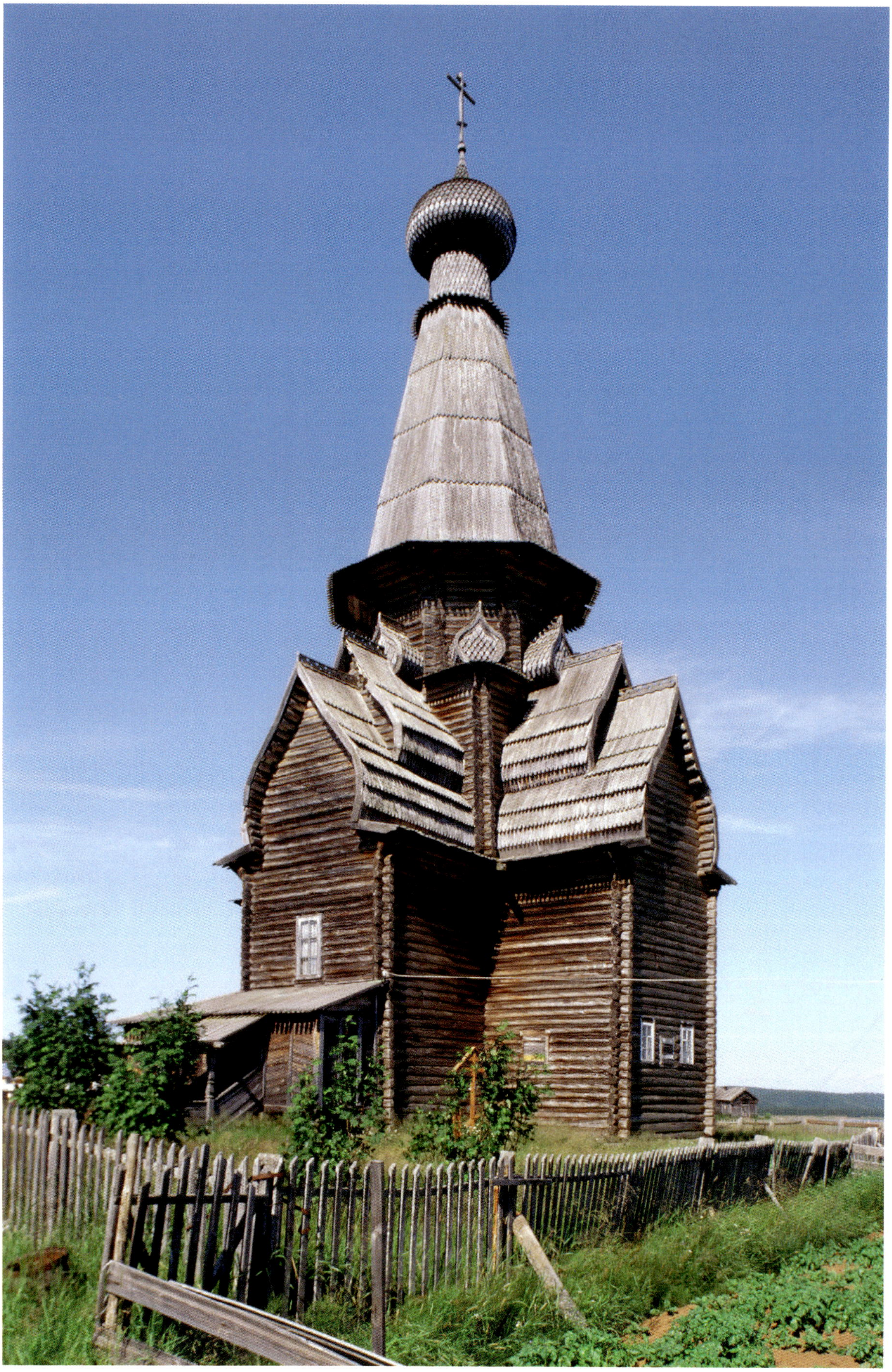

VARZUGA. Church of the Dormition, southeast view. Photograph: July 21, 2001.

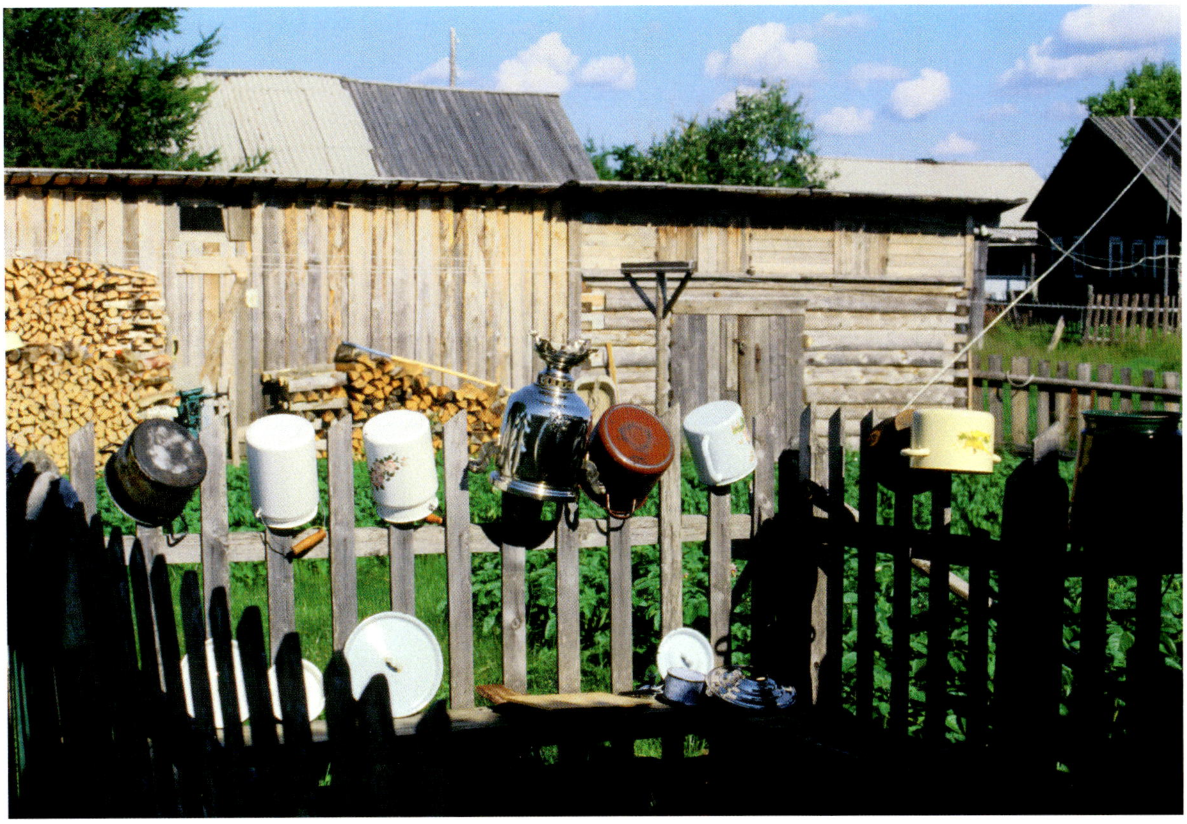

VARZUGA. Fence with washed pots and samovar, backyard of wooden house on left bank of the Varzuga River. Photograph: July 21, 2001.

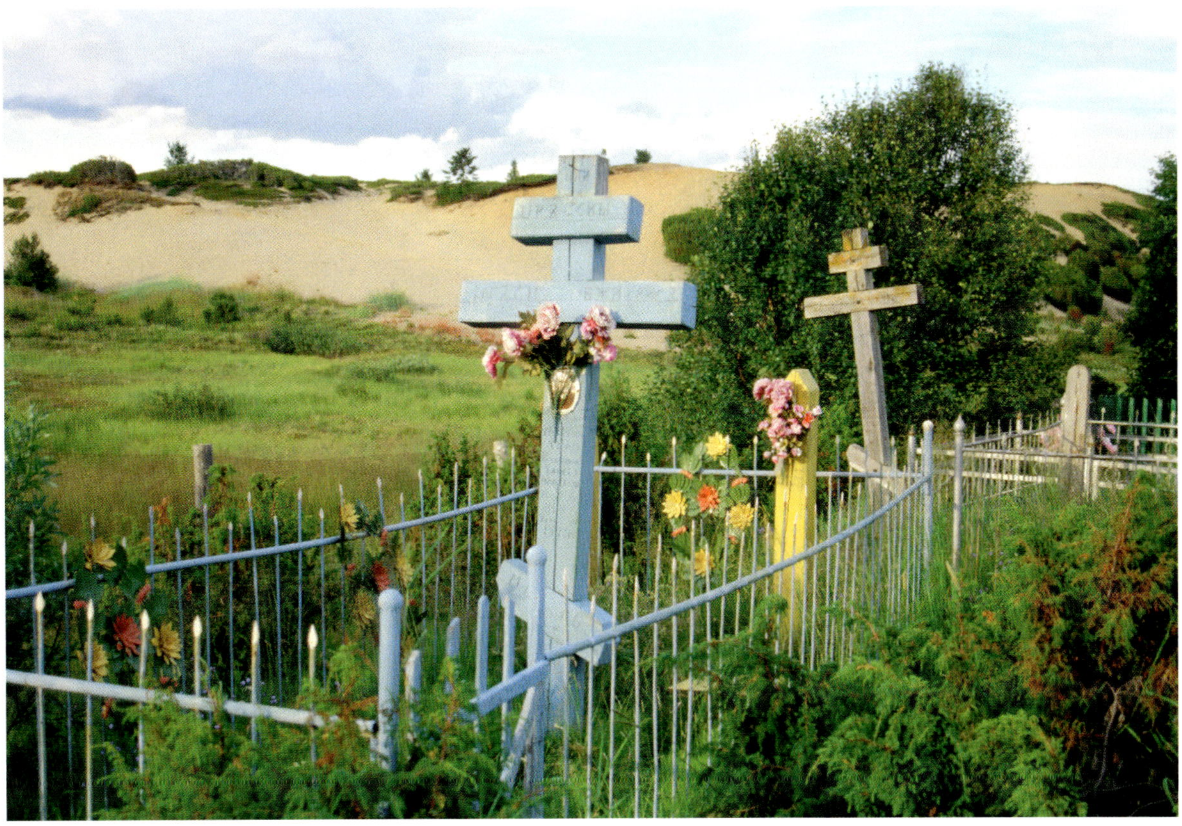

VARZUGA. Cemetery on left bank of the Varzuga River. In the distance, sandhills with juniper bushes. Photograph: July 21, 2001.

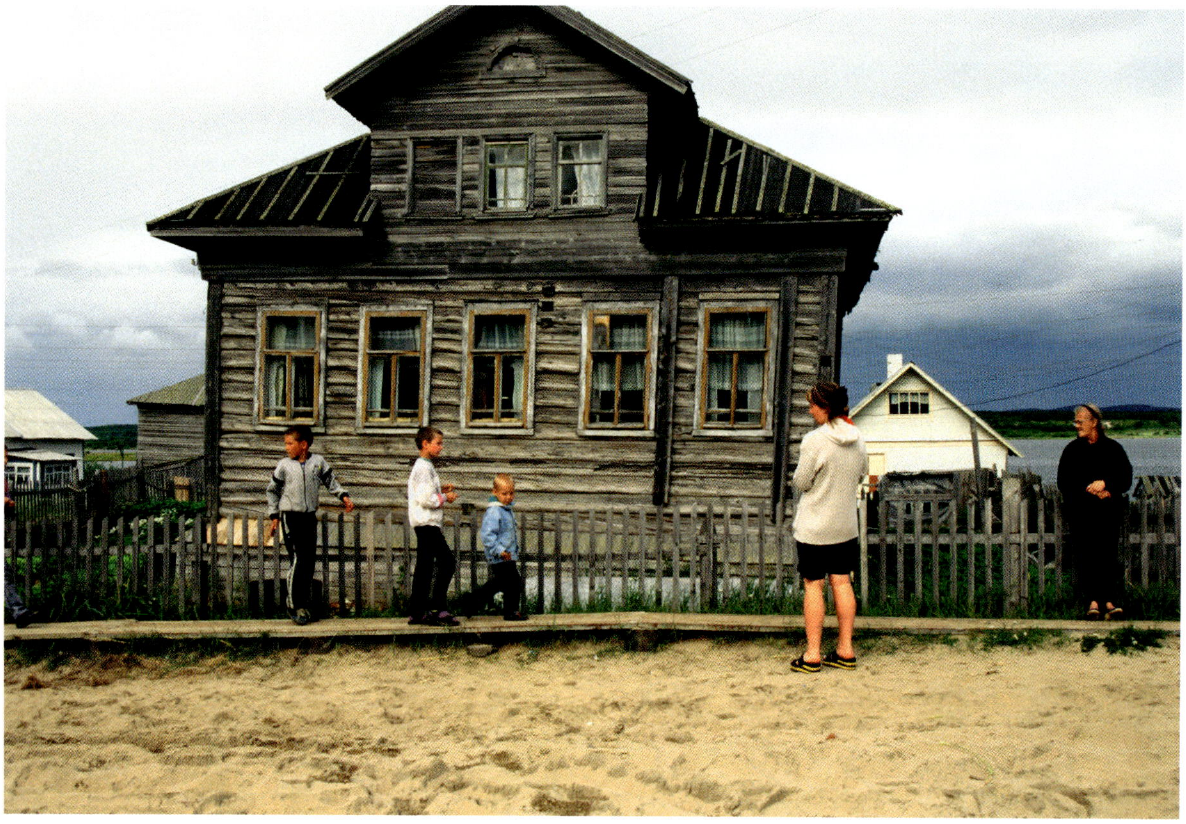

KUZOMEN. Nineteenth-century wooden house. Background: mouth of the Varzuga River. Photograph: July 23, 2001.

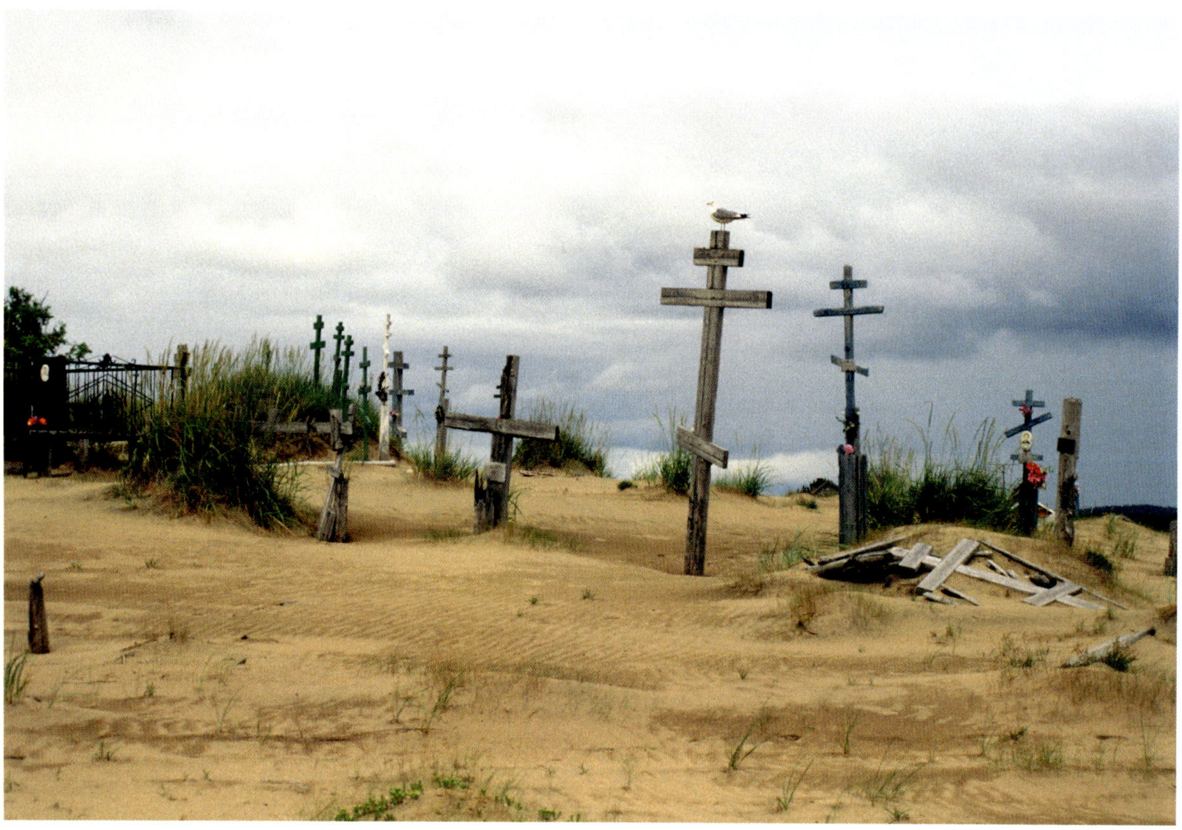

KUZOMEN. Cemetery in sand dunes near White Sea coast. Photograph: July 23, 2001.

KEM. Wooden Cathedral of the Dormition, west view. Built between 1711 and 1717. Photograph: July 25, 2001.

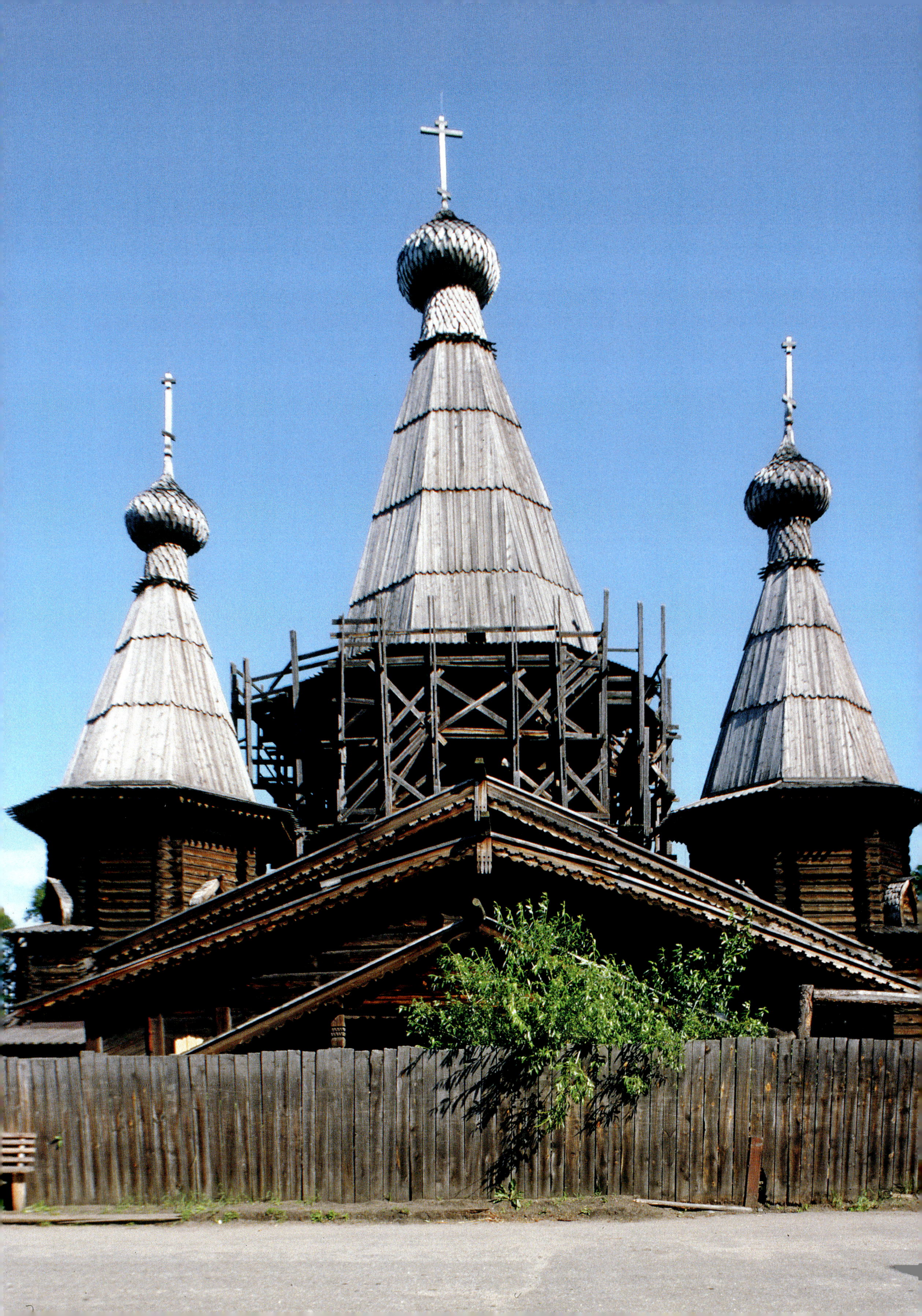

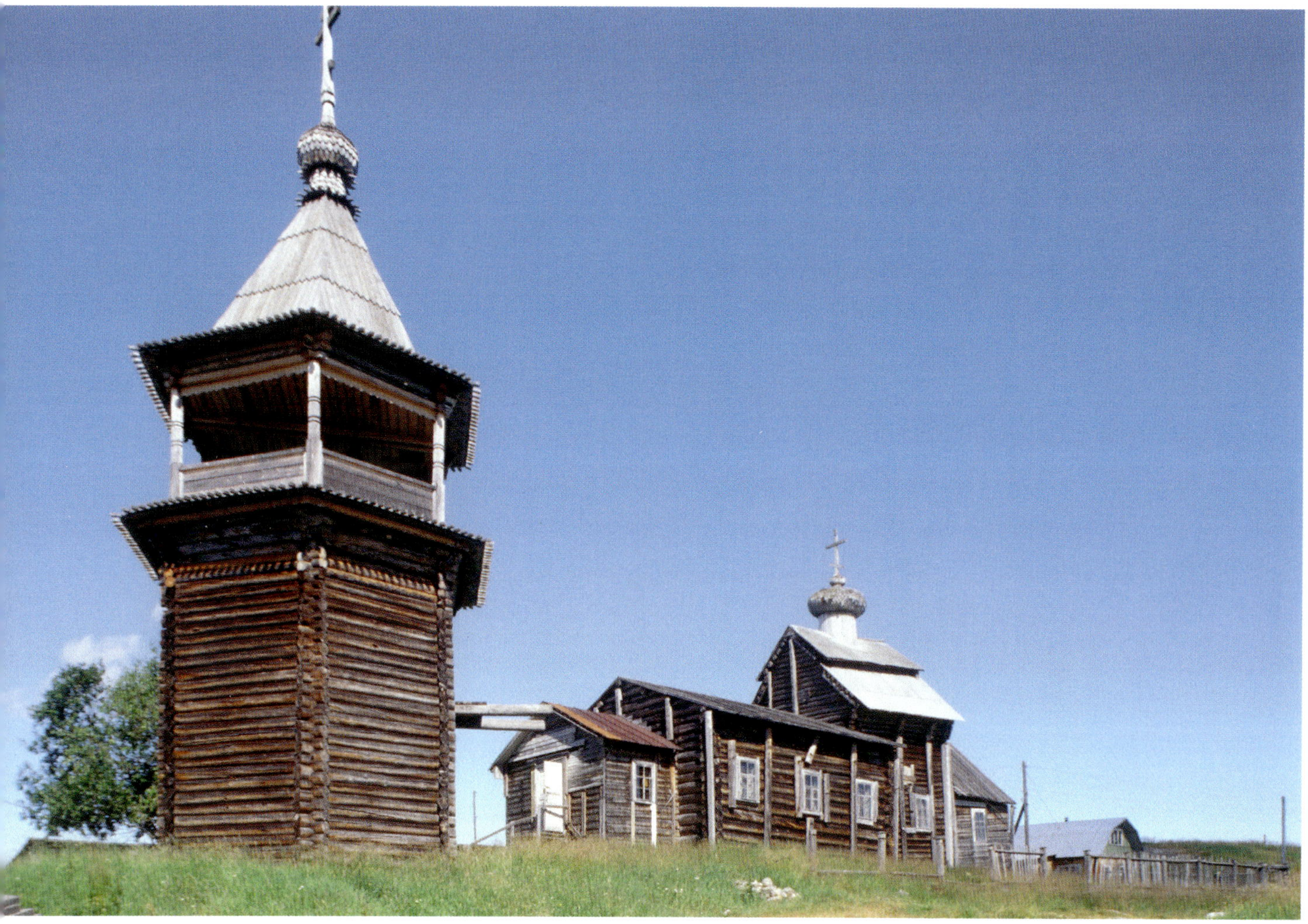

KOVDA. Bell tower and Church of St. Nicholas, southwest view. Built in 1705.
The log walls are now covered in plank siding. Photograph: July 24, 2001.

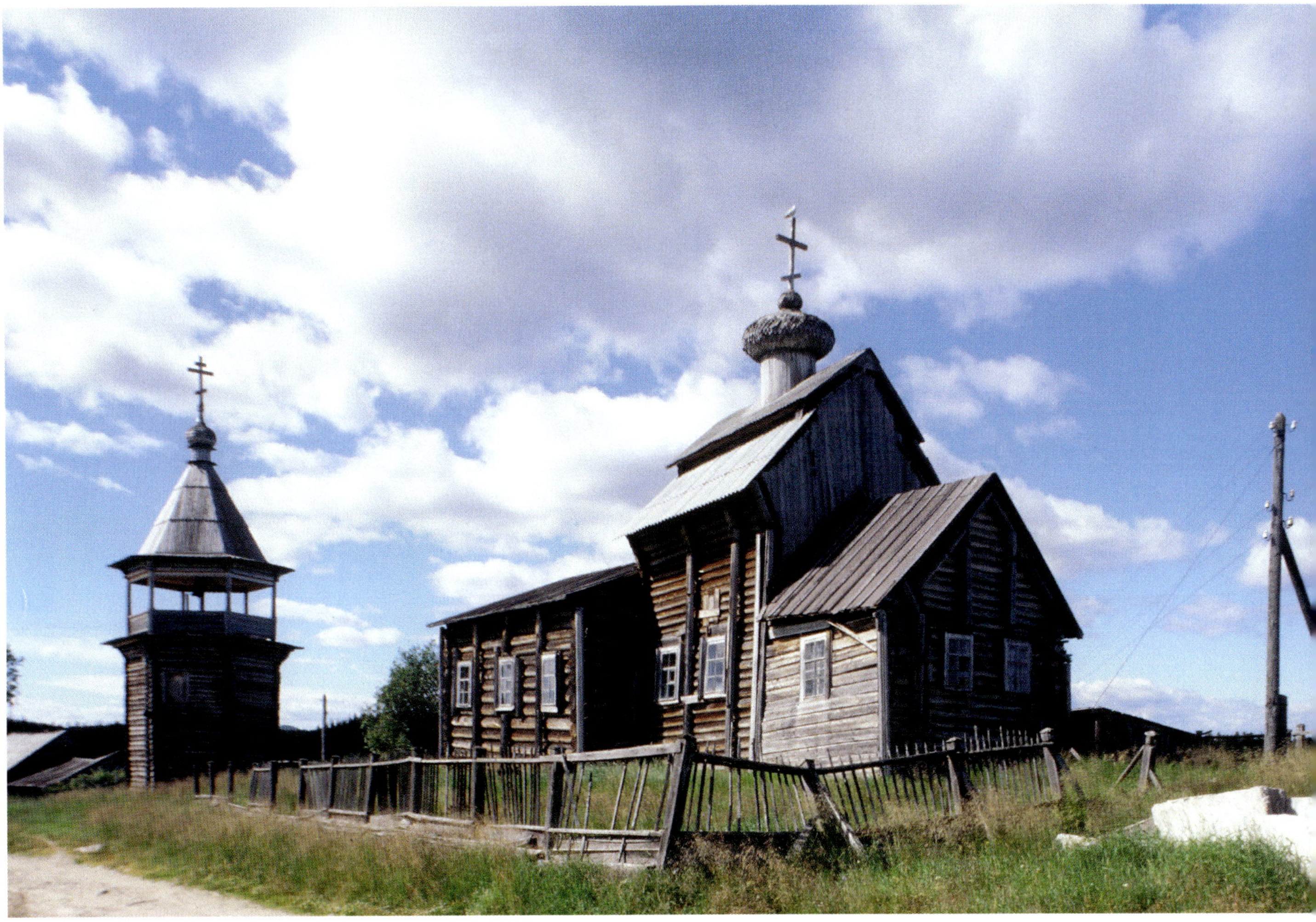

KOVDA. Church of St. Nicholas and bell tower, southeast view. Photograph: July 24, 2001.

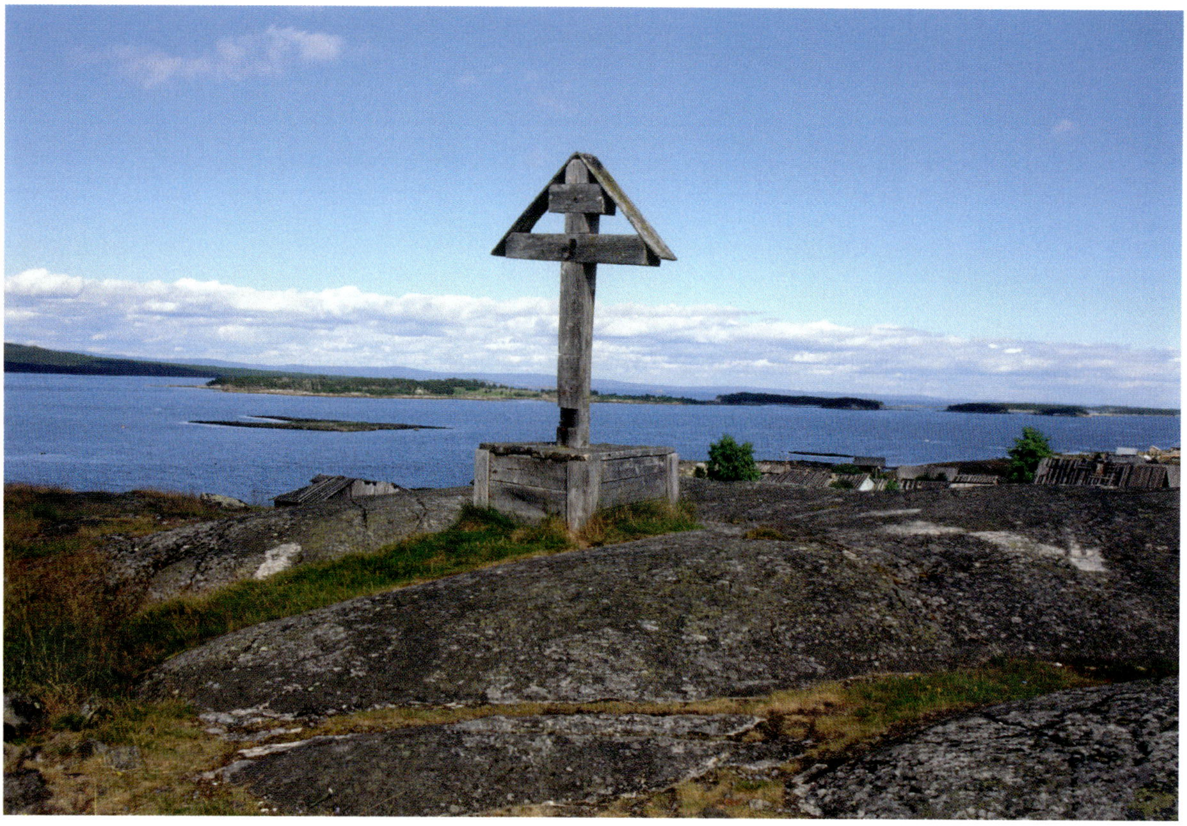

KOVDA. Votive cross overlooking Kovda Inlet of Kandalaksha Bay. Log houses are nestled beneath the rocky ridge. Photograph: July 24, 2001.

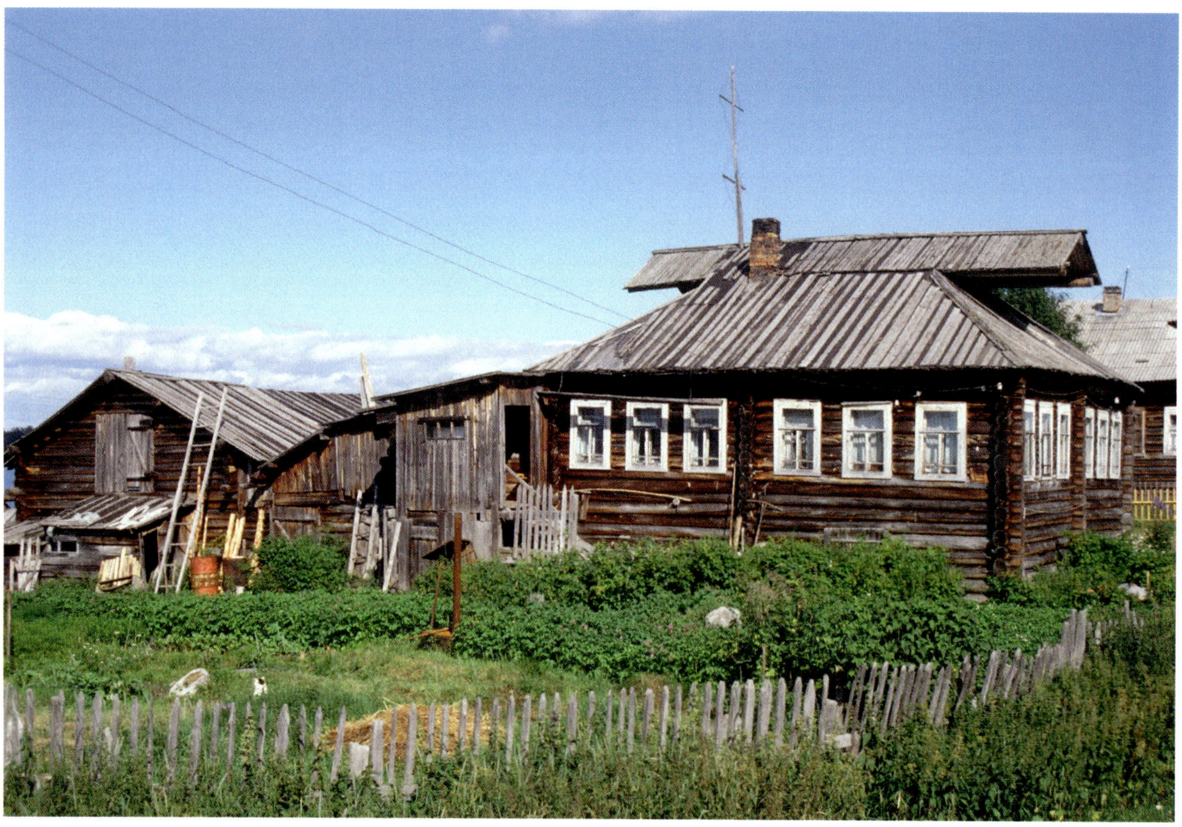

KOVDA. Log house with extended gable. On the left is a well-used log barn; in the foreground, a vegetable garden with potato plants. Photograph: July 24, 2001.

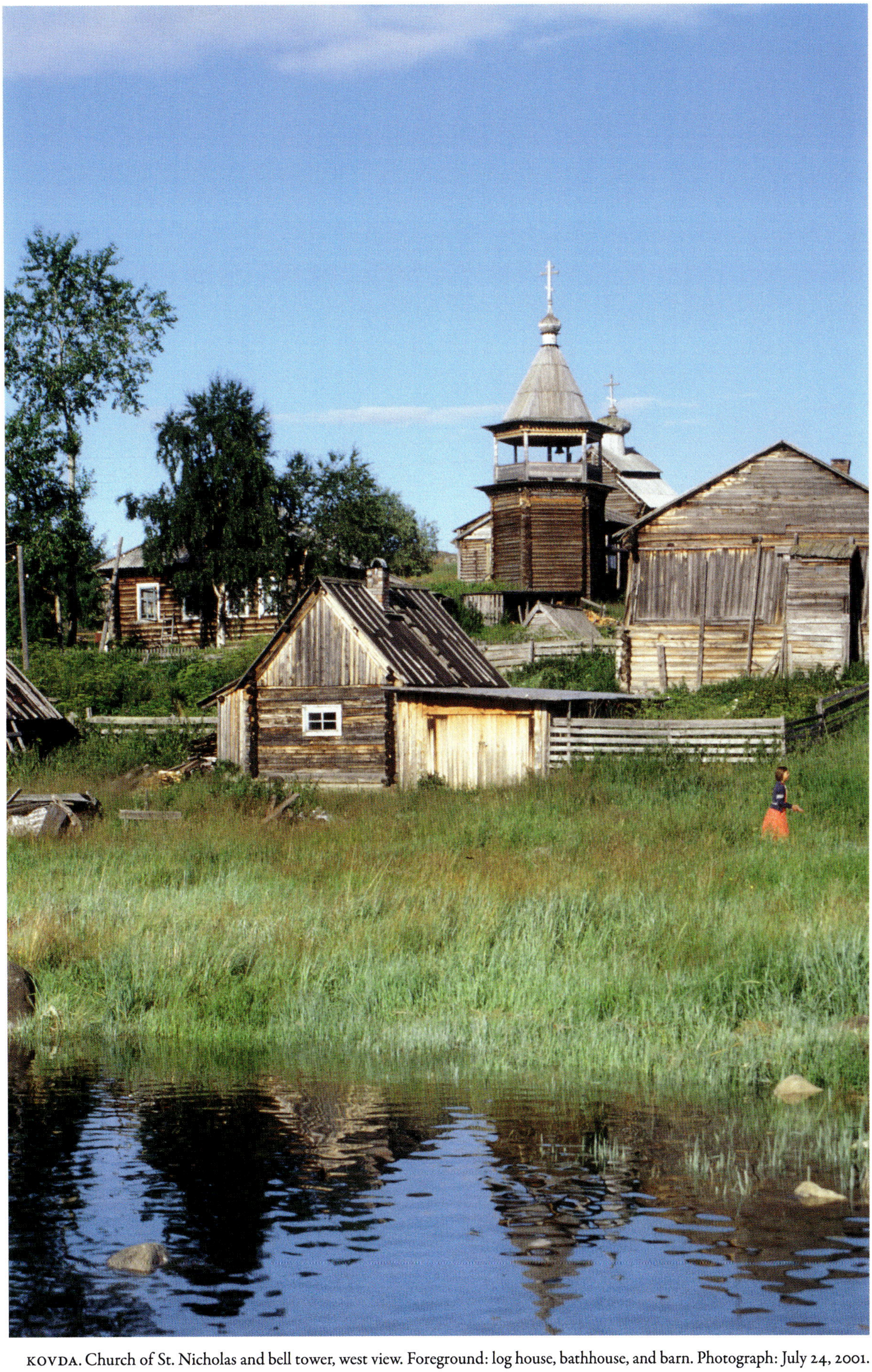

KOVDA. Church of St. Nicholas and bell tower, west view. Foreground: log house, bathhouse, and barn. Photograph: July 24, 2001.

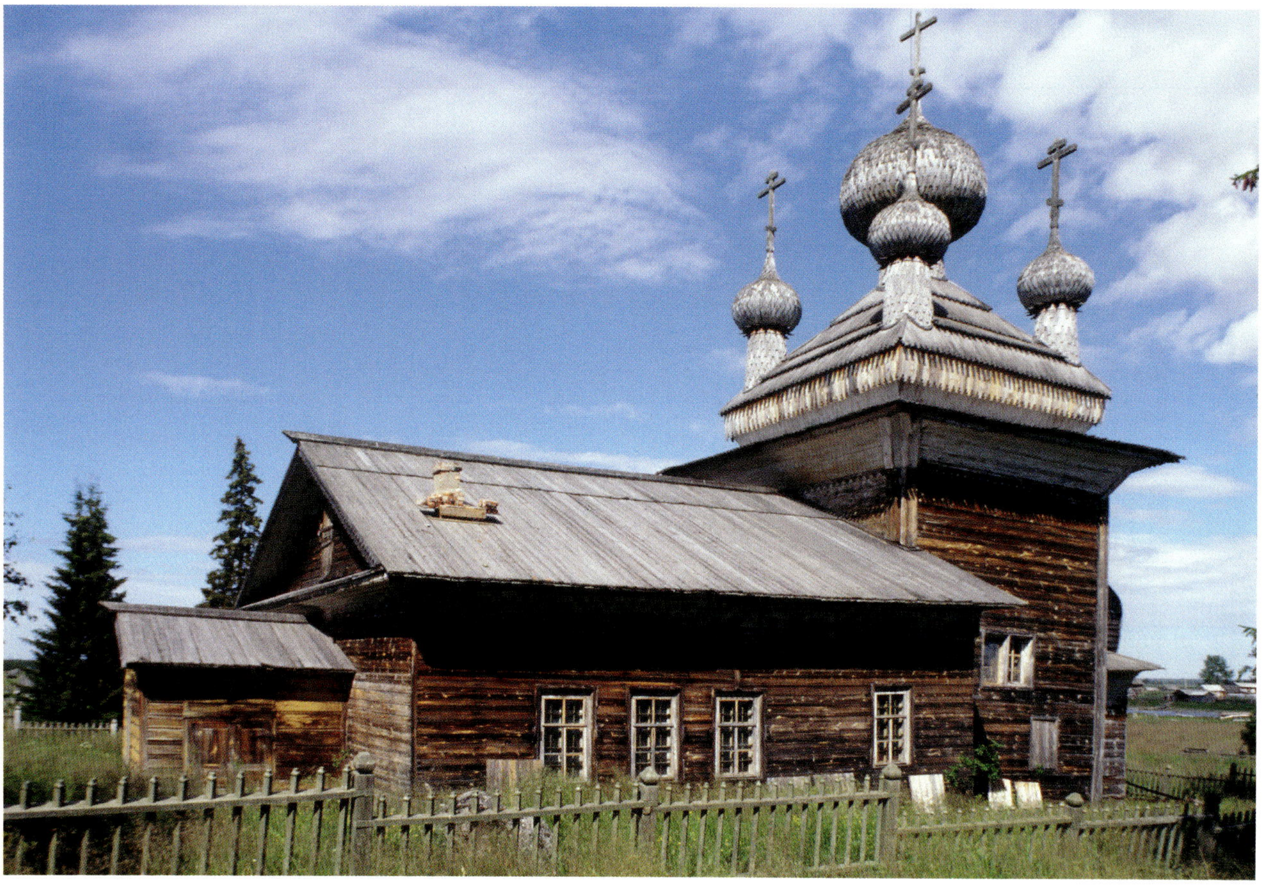

VIRMA. Wooden Church of Saints Peter and Paul, southwest view. Date of construction uncertain, after 1625. Photograph: July 7, 2000.

VIRMA. Wooden Church of Saints Peter and Paul, west view. Photograph: July 7, 2000.

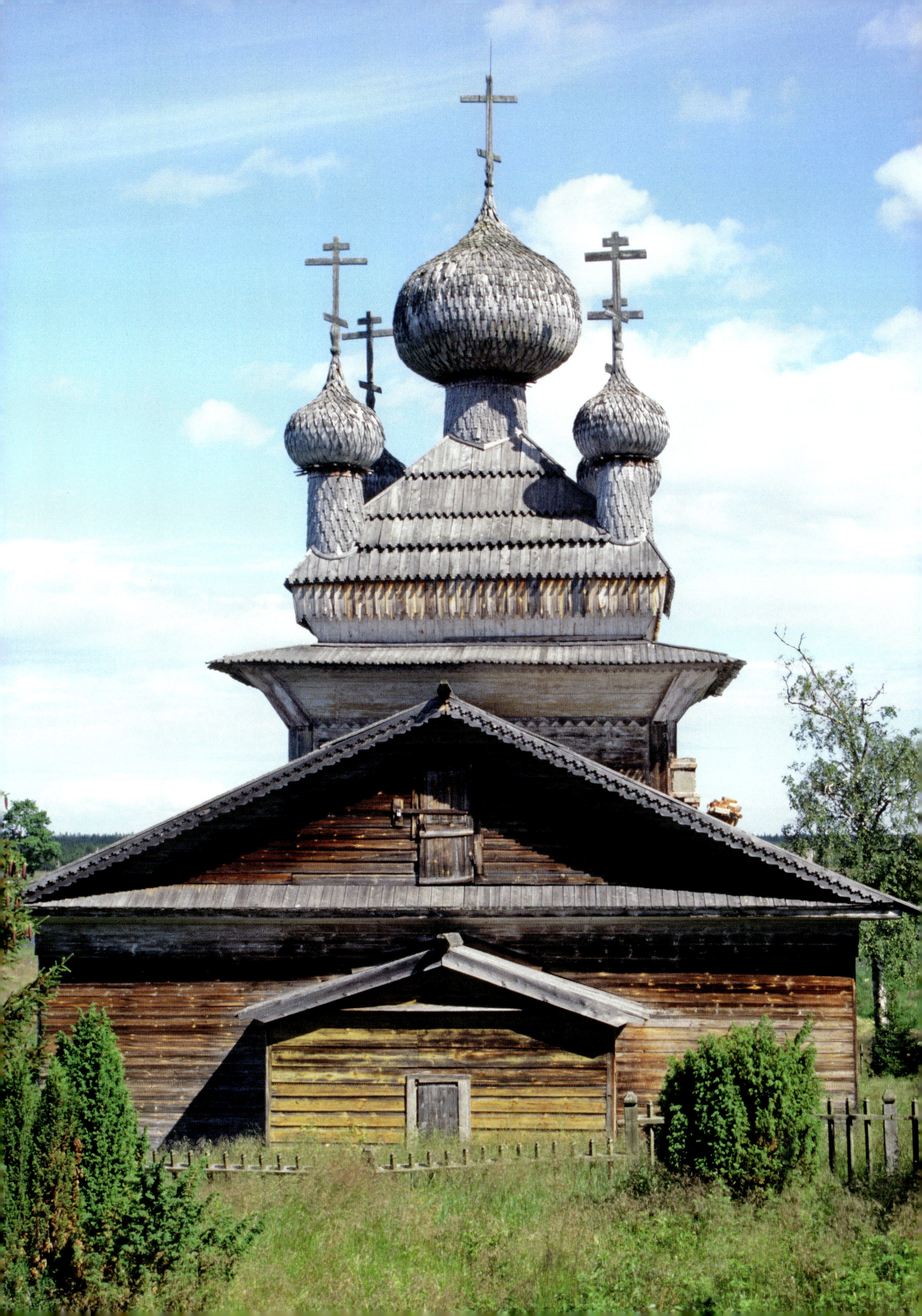

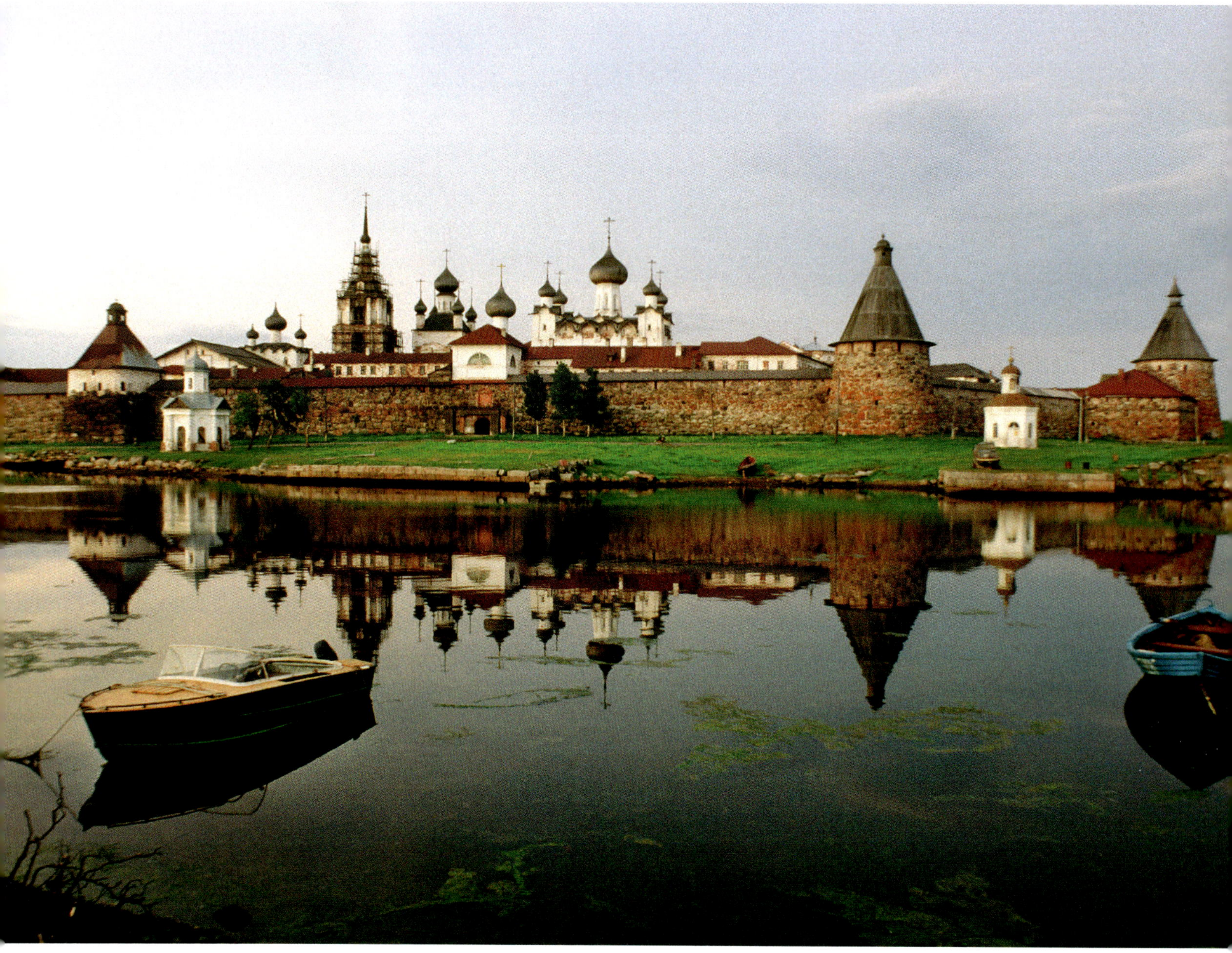

GREAT SOLOVETSKY ISLAND. Transfiguration Monastery, southwest view across Felicity Harbor. Calm at eleven in the evening after rainstorm. Photograph: June 29, 1999.

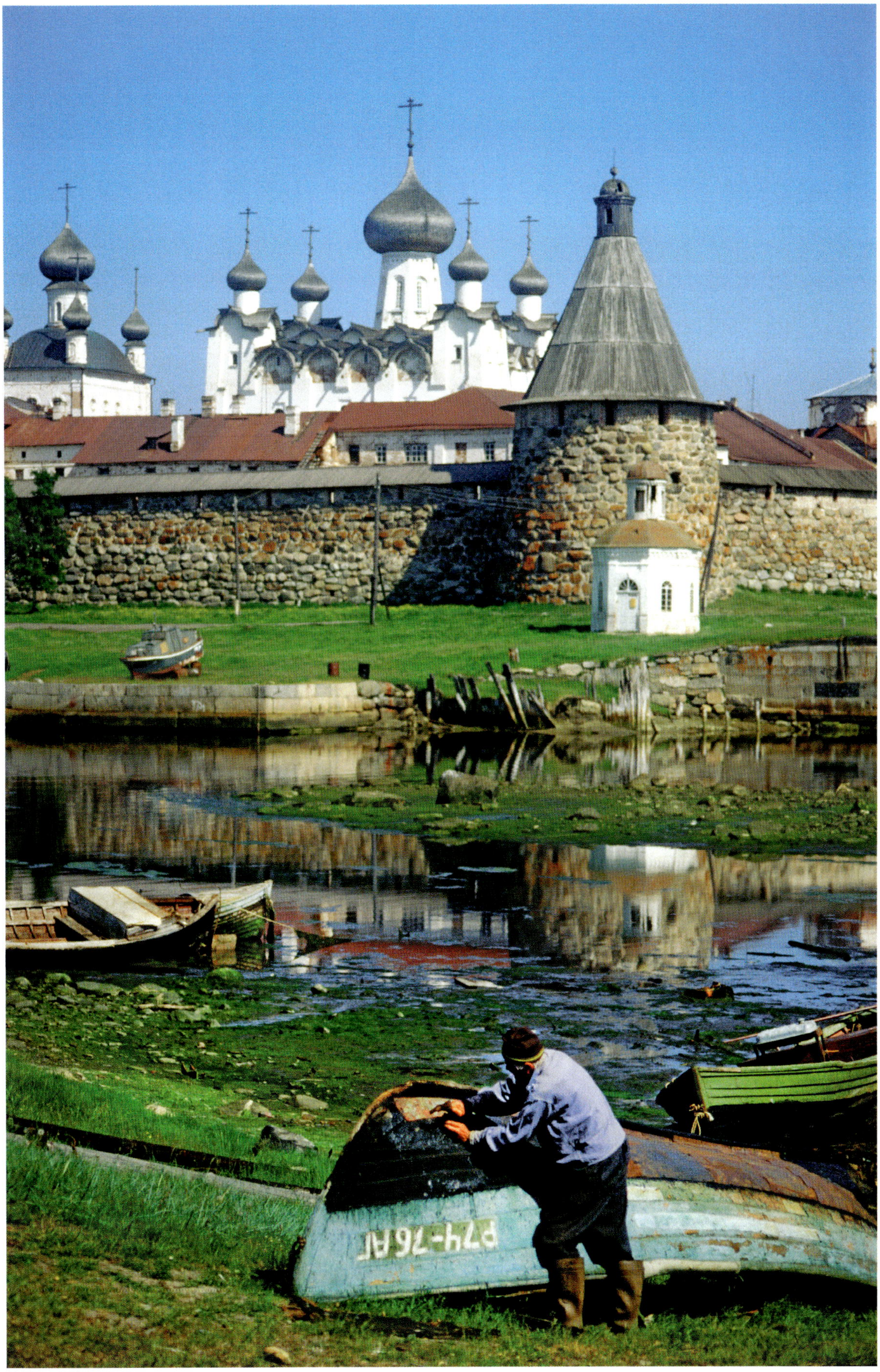

GREAT SOLOVETSKY ISLAND. Transfiguration Monastery, southwest view across harbor. Fisherman repairing copper sheathing. Photograph: June 30, 1999.

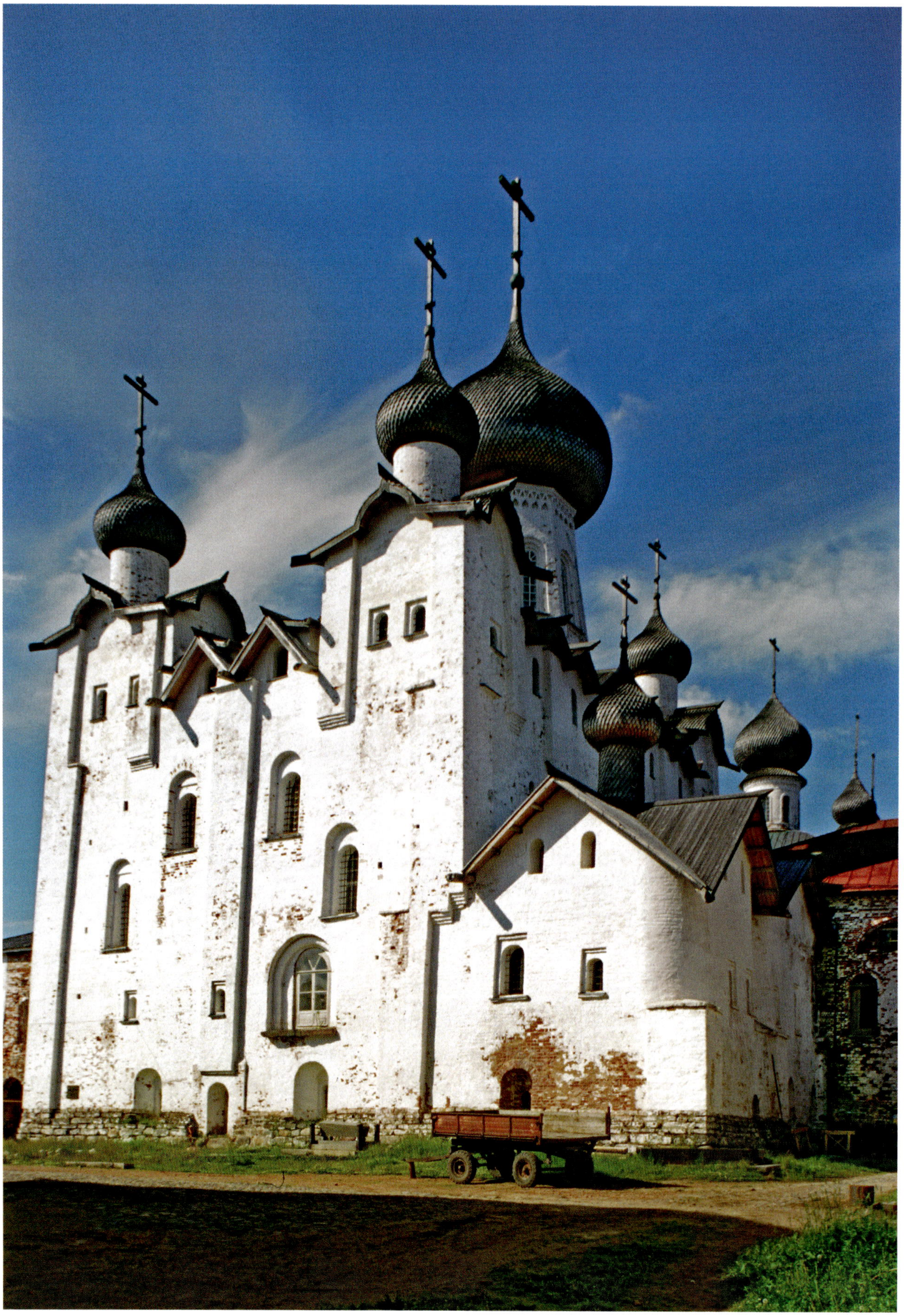

GREAT SOLOVETSKY ISLAND. Cathedral of the Transfiguration, Transfiguration Monastery, southeast view.
Cathedral built between 1556 and 1566. Photograph: July 25, 1998.

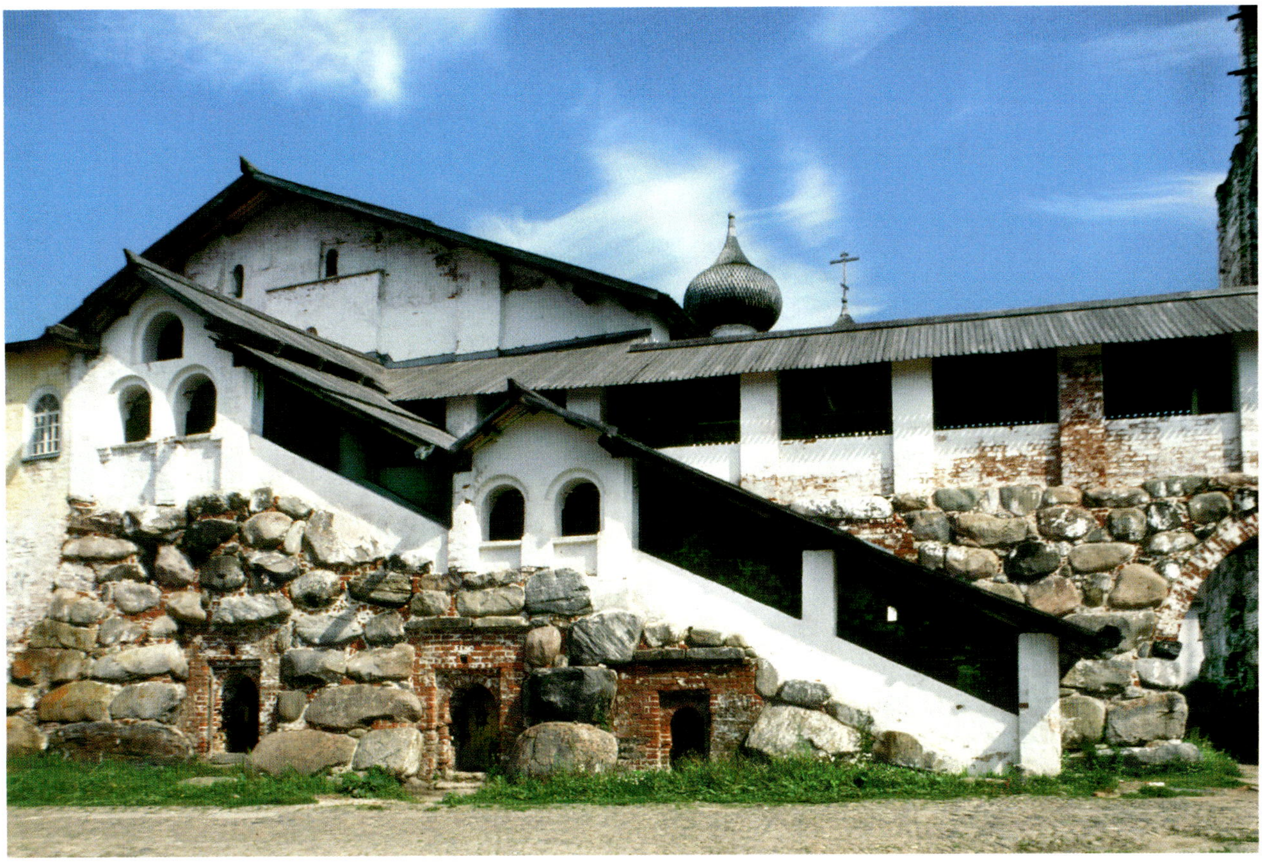

GREAT SOLOVETSKY ISLAND. Refectory Church of the Dormition and exterior gallery, Transfiguration Monastery, west view. Church built between 1552 and 1557. Photograph: July 25, 1998.

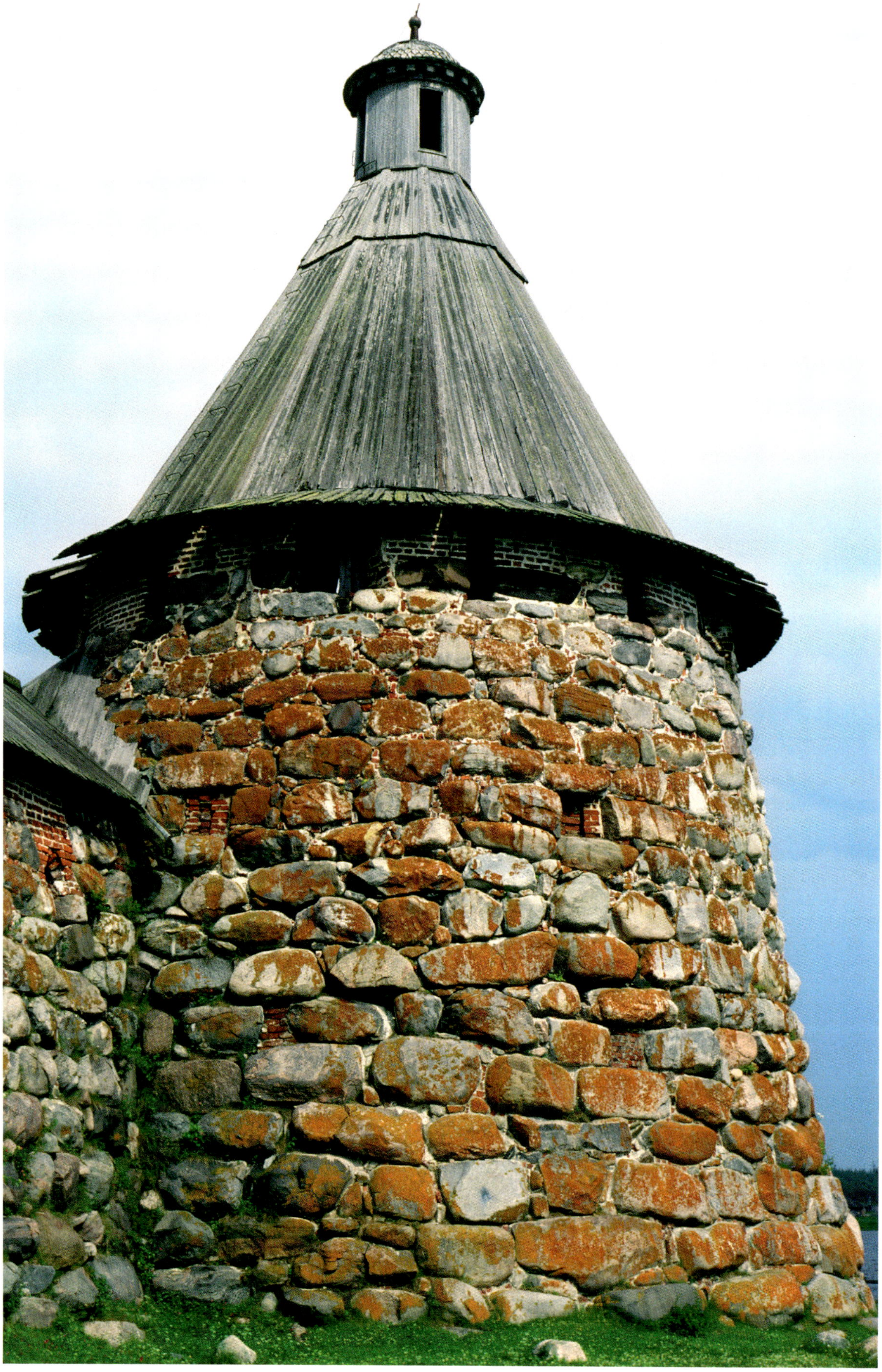

GREAT SOLOVETSKY ISLAND. Archangel Tower, southeast range of monastery walls, built in late sixteenth century from granite boulders. Photograph: July 26, 1998.

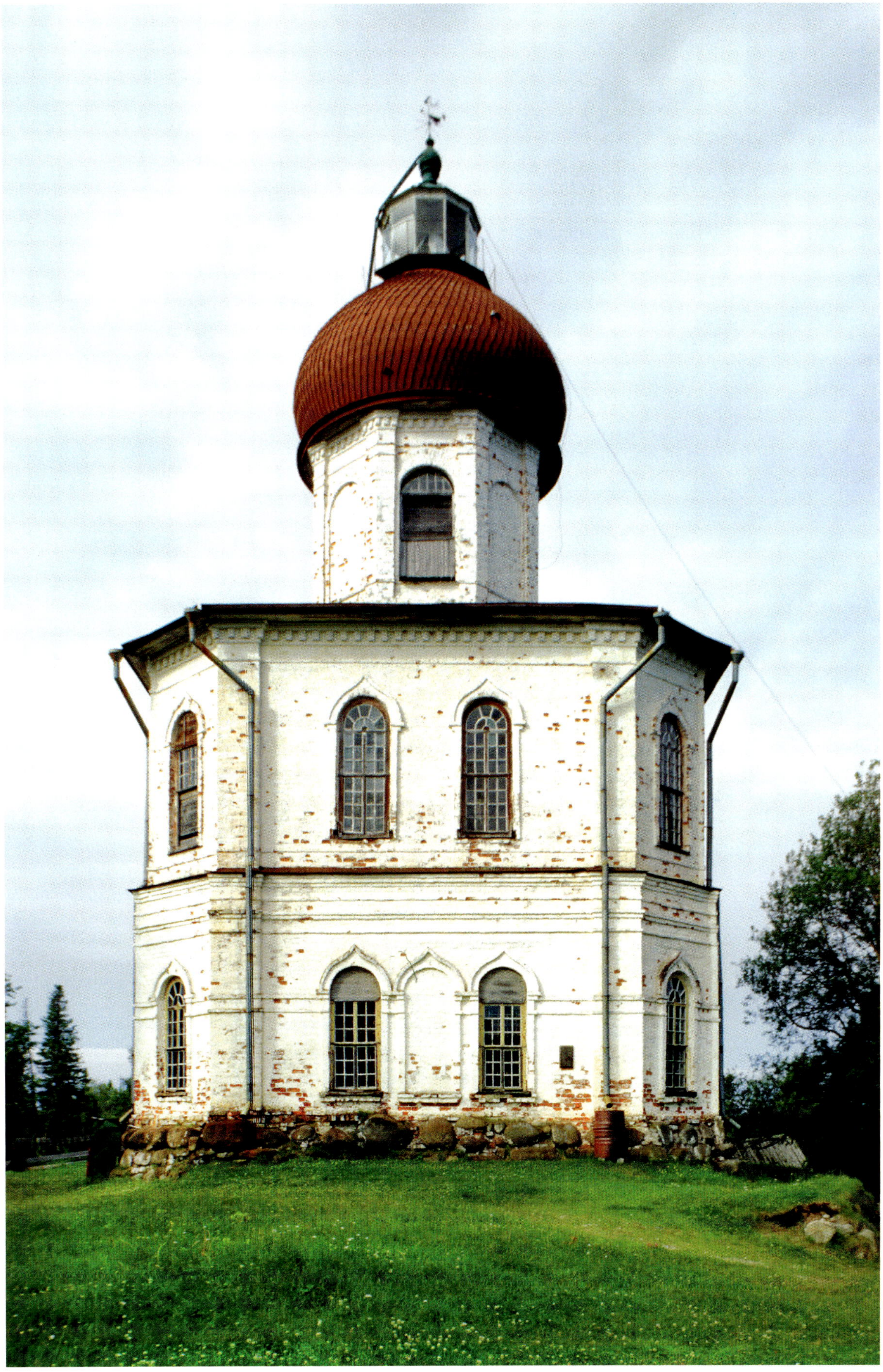

GREAT SOLOVETSKY ISLAND. Church of the Ascension, Sekirno-Ascension Skete, east view. Built in 1862 on the island's highest point. Lantern above cupola served as a beacon. In the 1920s and 1930s, the church was used as a punishment block, described in Aleksandr Solzhenitsyn's *Gulag Archipelago*. Photograph: July 26, 1998.

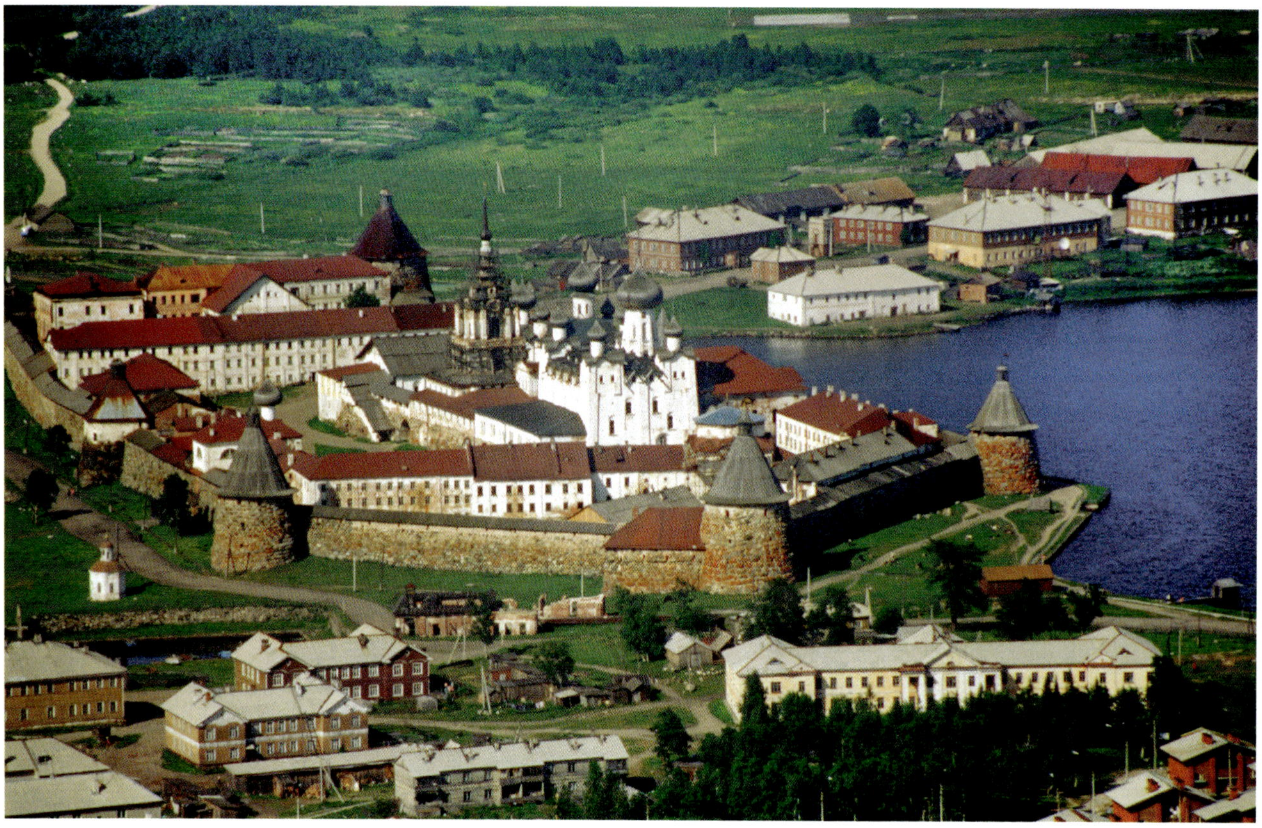

GREAT SOLOVETSKY ISLAND. Transfiguration Monastery, aerial view from southwest. Photograph: June 30, 1999.

GREAT ZAIATSKY ISLAND (part of archipelago). Wooden Church of St. Andrew, built in 1702. According to local lore, the church was built by Peter I as an expression of gratitude for rescue from a storm on the White Sea. Photograph: June 29, 1999.

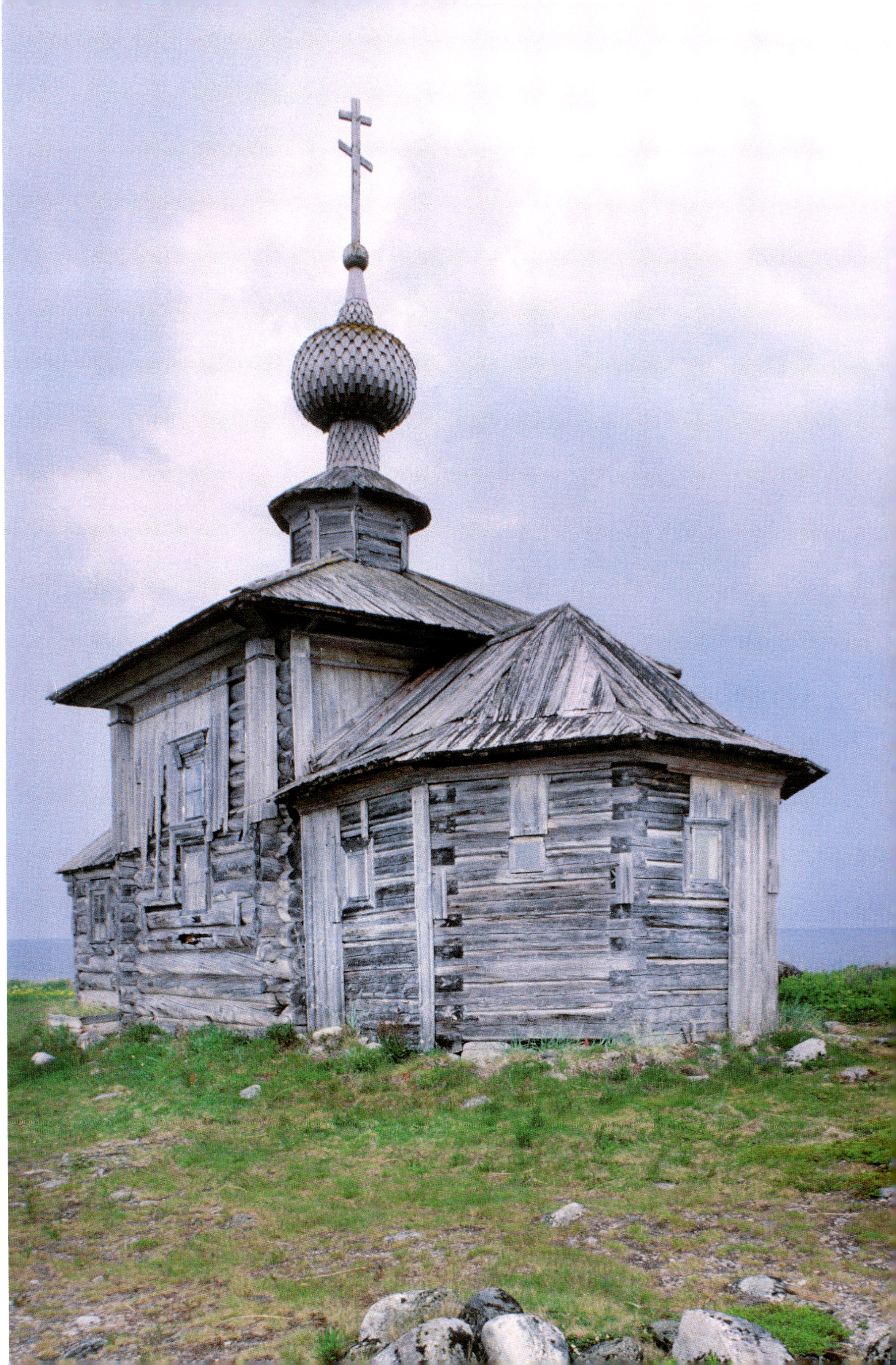

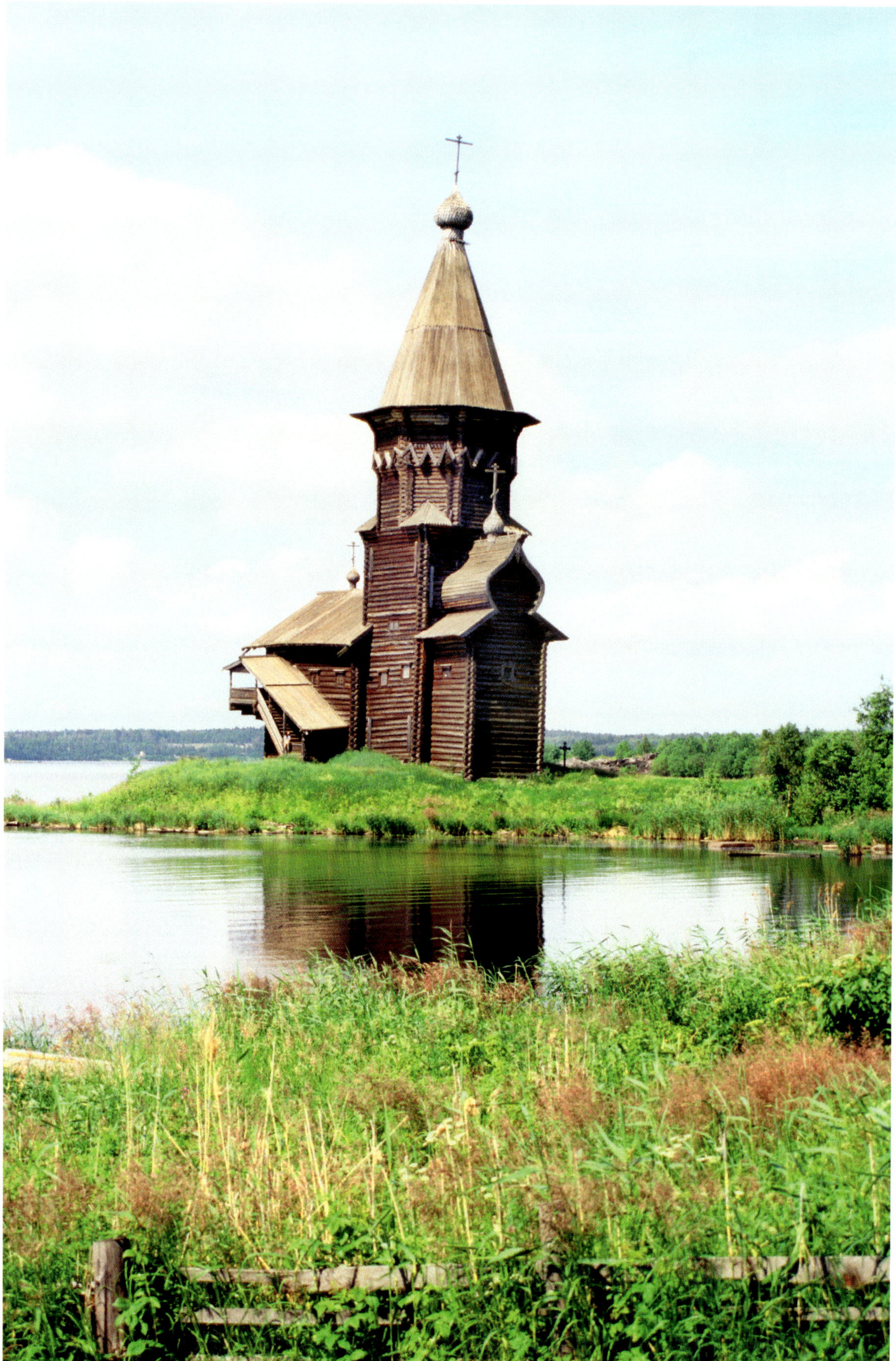

KONDOPOGA. Wooden Church of the Dormition, southeast view with Kondopoga Inlet of Lake Onega. Church built in 1774. Photograph: July 4, 2000.

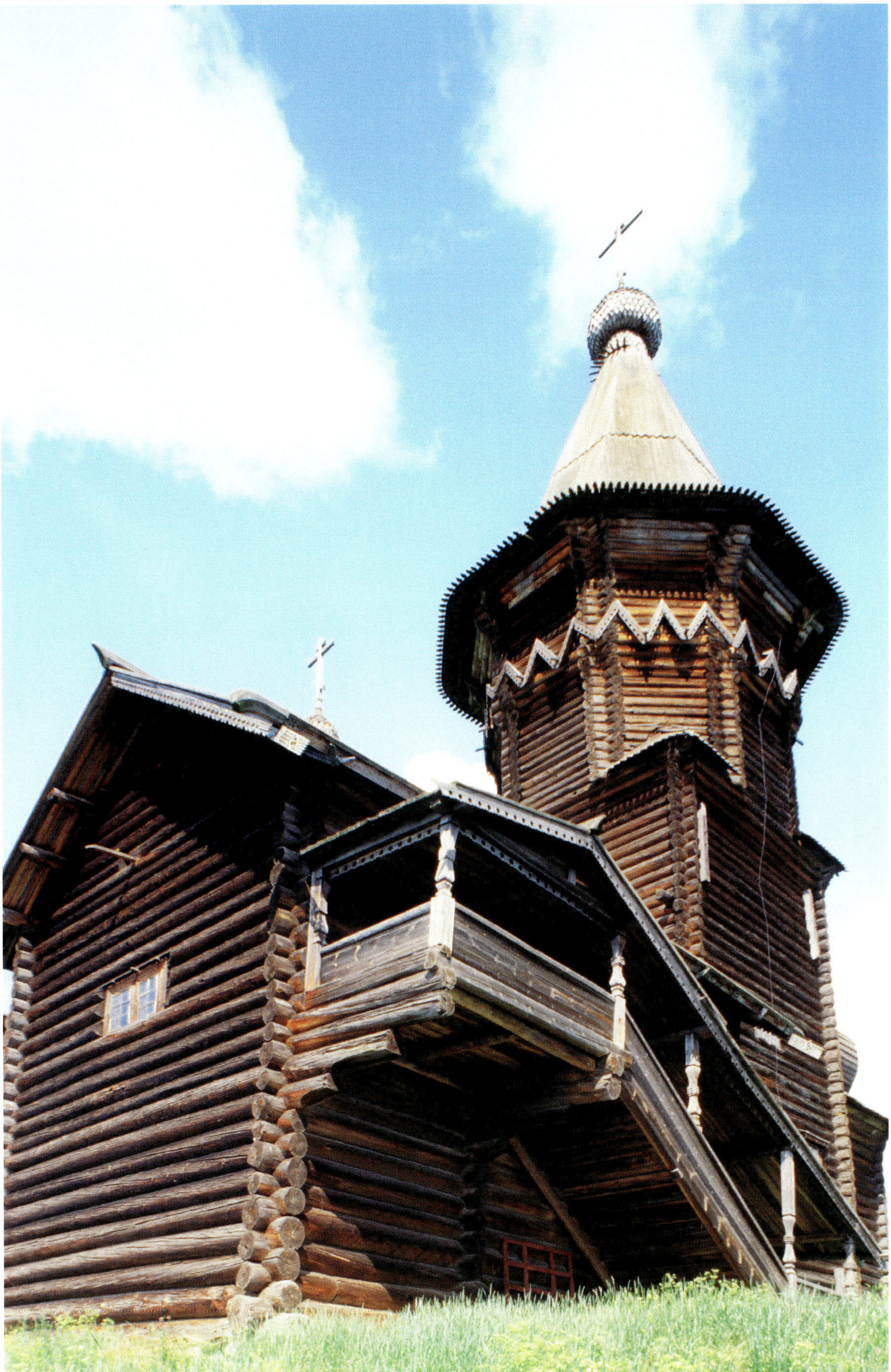

KONDOPOGA. Church of the Dormition, southwest view. Photograph: July 4, 2000.

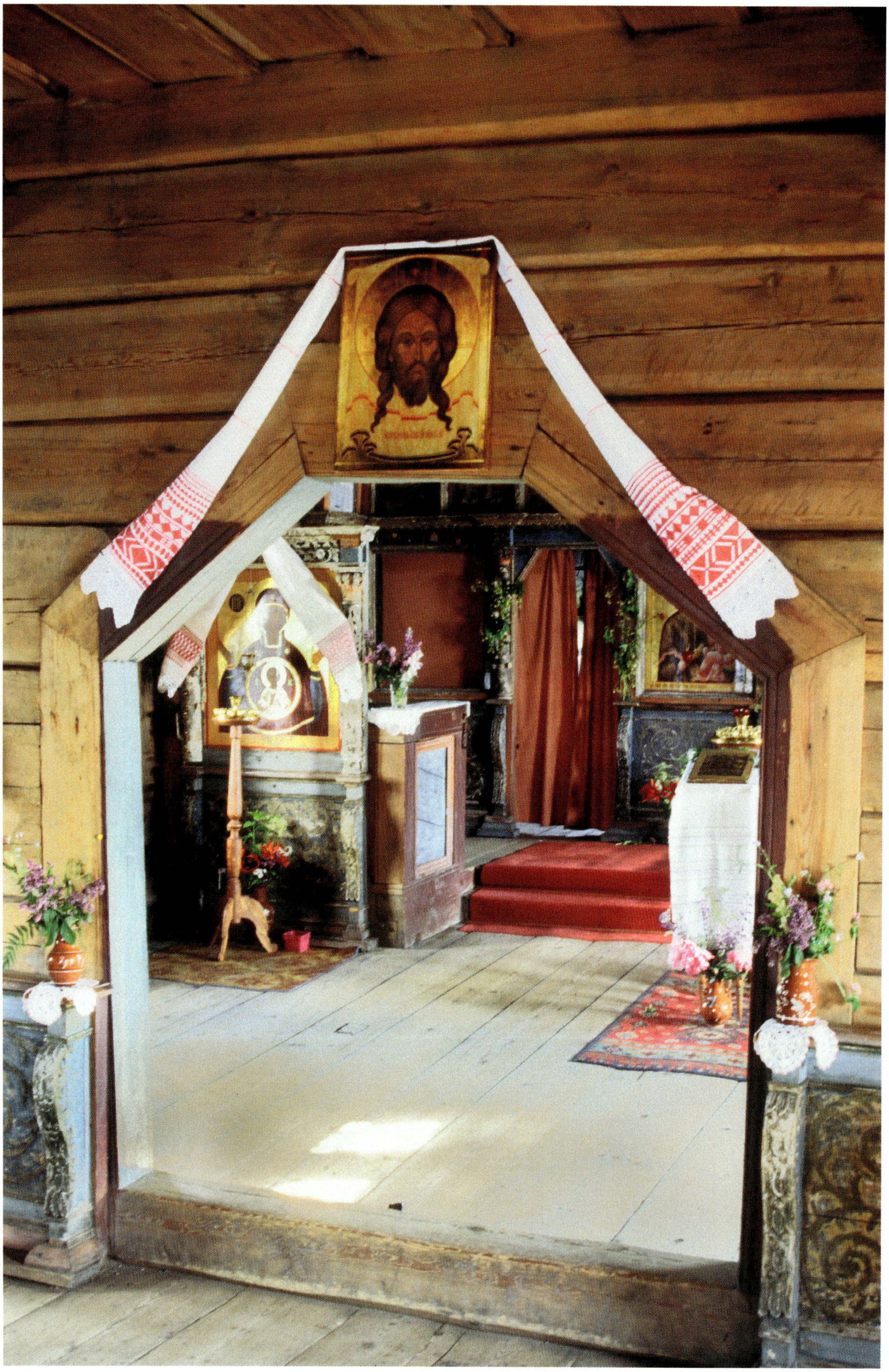

KONDOPOGA. Church of the Dormition, interior, view east from vestibule toward main space and icon screen. Photograph: July 4, 2000.

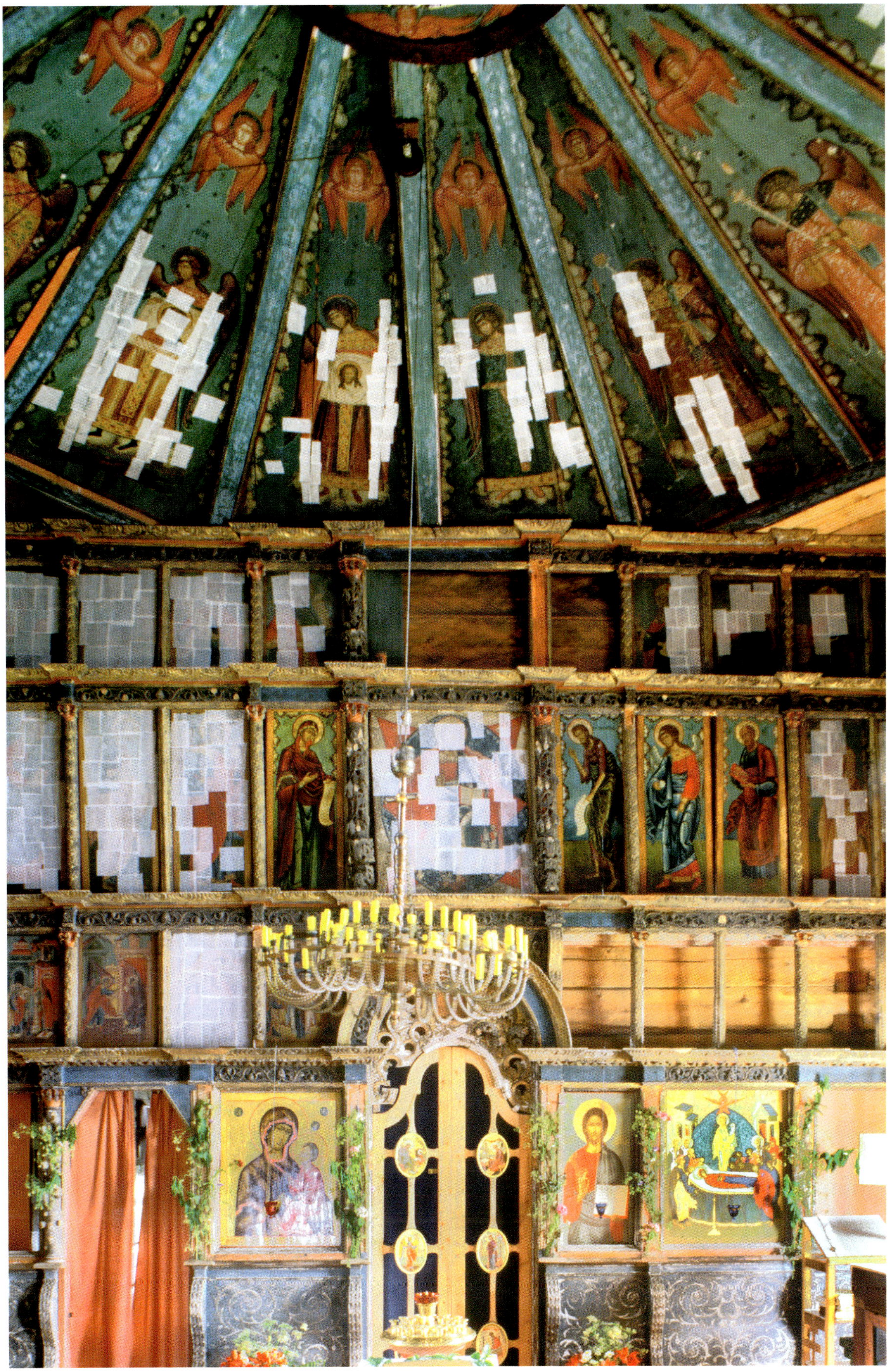

KONDOPOGA. Church of the Dormition, interior, icon screen. Photograph: July 4, 2000.

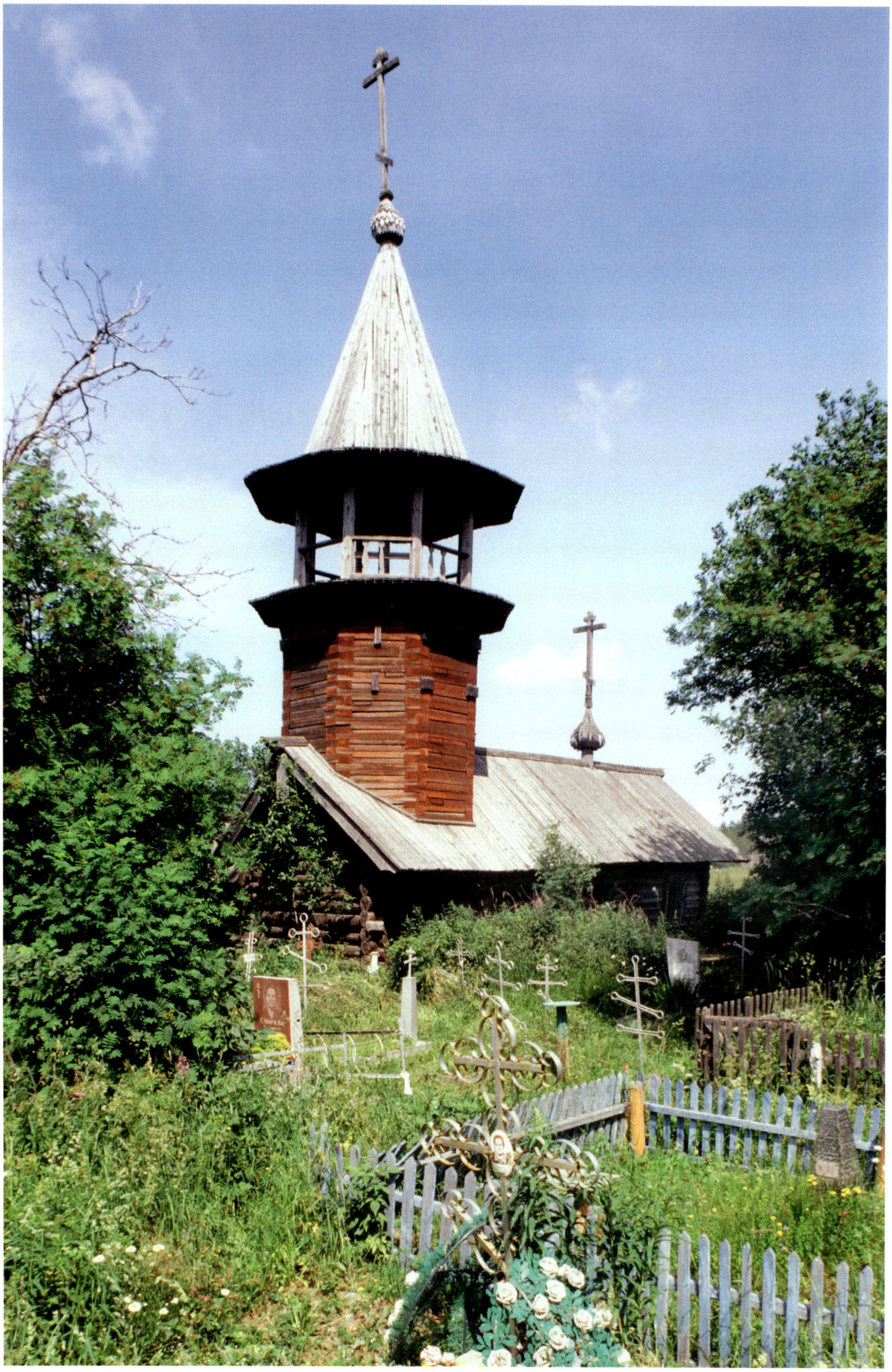

MANSELGA. Cemetery and Chapel of the Kazan Icon of the Virgin, southwest view. Date of construction unknown, presumably late eighteenth century. Photograph: July 4, 2000.

MARTSIALNYE VODY. Wooden Church of St. Peter, north view. Built in 1721. Photograph: July 4, 2000.

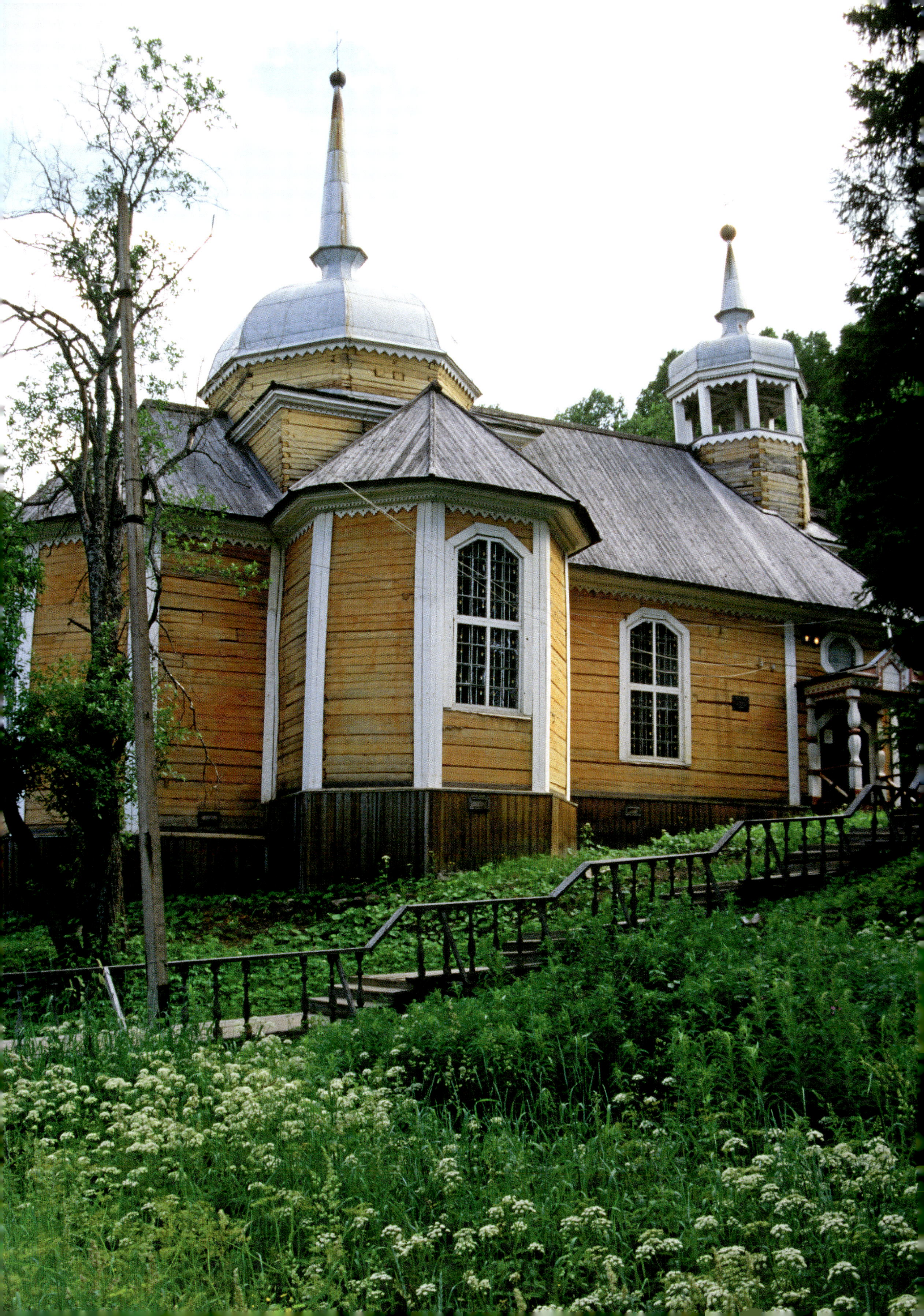

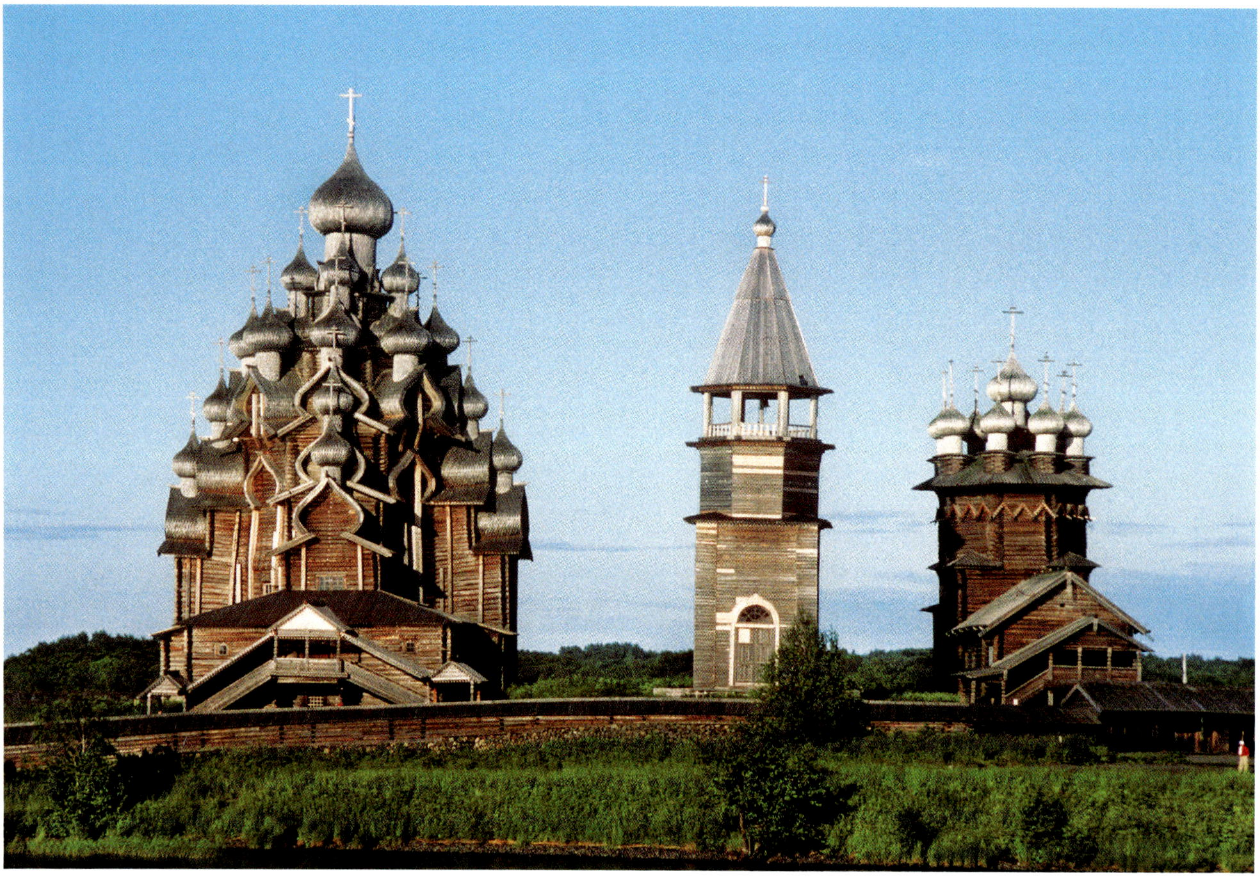

KIZHI POGOST. From left: Wooden Church of the Transfiguration (1714), bell tower, Church of the Intercession (1764), west view. Photograph: July 13, 1993.

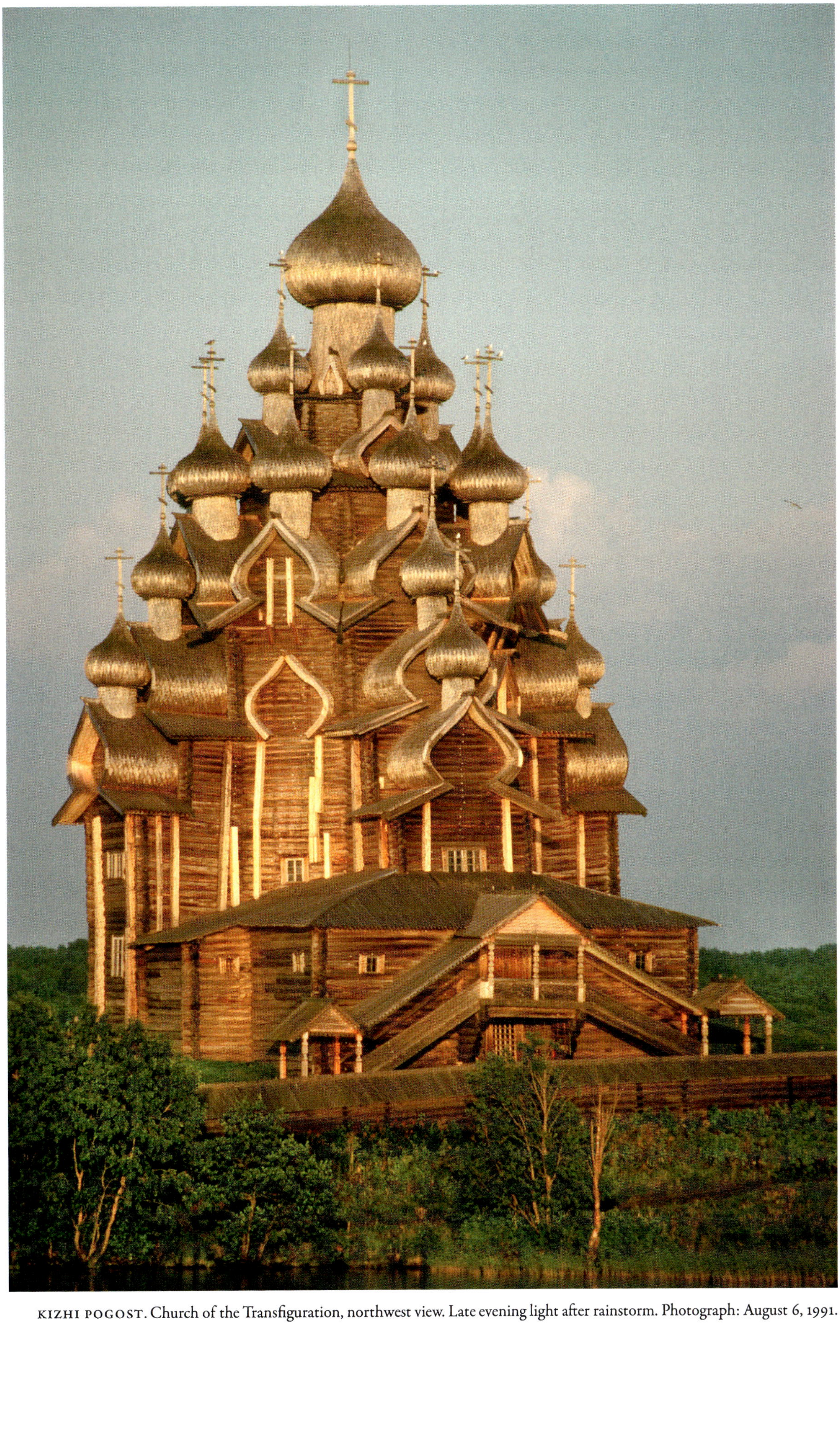

KIZHI POGOST. Church of the Transfiguration, northwest view. Late evening light after rainstorm. Photograph: August 6, 1991.

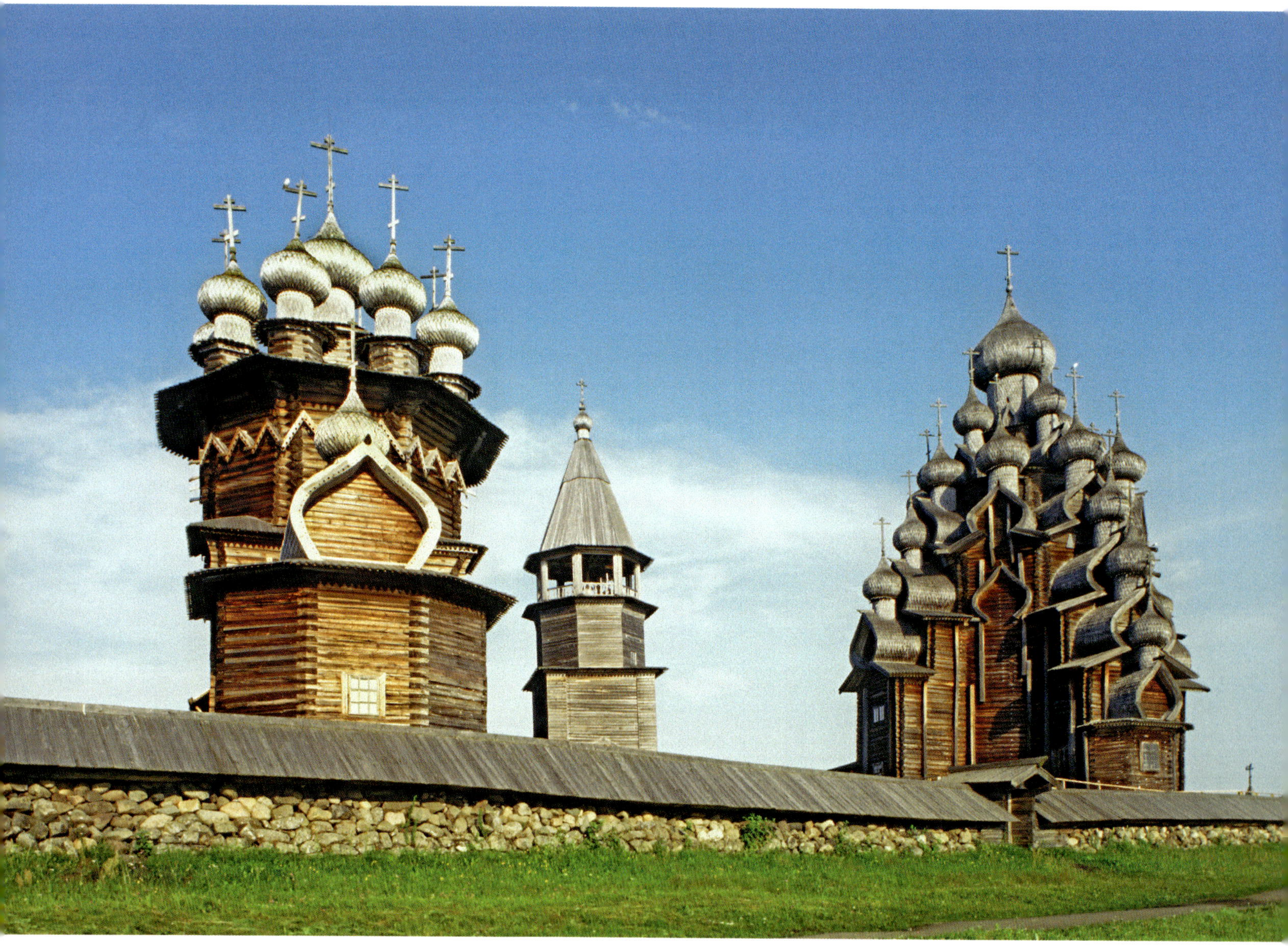

KIZHI POGOST. From left: Church of the Intercession, bell tower, Church of the Transfiguration, southeast view. Photograph: July 13, 2007.

TWO *From the Vytegra Region to the Mologa River*

THE VYTEGRA REGION: BETWEEN LAKE ONEGA AND WHITE LAKE

The small town of Vytegra (population around ten thousand) in the northwestern corner of Vologda Province might seem remote territory. Yet every summer, thousands of tourists who take popular riverboat cruises between Moscow and St. Petersburg pass directly by Vytegra, located on a small river of the same name.

Vytegra is first referred to in written documents at the end of the fifteenth century. By the early eighteenth century, the settlement had become a crossroads for trade between the northern port of Arkhangelsk and the city of St. Petersburg, founded in 1703 and designated the capital of Russia in 1712. The challenge of linking the new capital with the interior of the country led to the development of a canal system eventually known as the Mariinsky Waterway, connecting St. Petersburg with the Volga River Basin.

The first major component of the waterway was a canal that linked the Vytegra River, which flows into Lake Onega toward St. Petersburg, and the Kovzha River, which flows south into White Lake. In 1799 this segment was named the Mariinsky Canal, with Vytegra—officially designated a town in 1773—as its administrative center.

Although Vytegra was built primarily of wood, the town center had several substantial brick structures at the turn of the twentieth century, including administrative buildings, merchant houses, schools, and churches. Some of these buildings have been preserved, such as the Church of the Purification, rebuilt and consecrated in 1873 on the site of an earlier church. During the Soviet period, the building was given to the local history museum, but most of the space has now been returned to the church. Its cupolas are clearly visible from the cruise boats that pass through the Vytegra canal locks.

The region beyond Vytegra at one time had some of the most interesting wooden church architecture in Russia. The best surviving example is the Church of Elijah the Prophet at Saminsky Pogost, built apparently in the 1690s and covered with plank siding in the nineteenth century. Located on the right bank of the Samina River forty-five kilometers north of Vytegra, this superb structure with its soaring tent tower has recently been carefully restored. Although the nineteenth-century bell tower attached to the west facade was not rebuilt, the plank siding was retained as a means of protecting the log structure.

Next to this bold form, which has withstood the test of time, are the ruins of the Church of the Tikhvin Icon of the Virgin, erected in 1897 for use in the winter. Both churches were of logs, but the form of the Tikhvin Church followed a style of masonry architecture associated with Konstantin Thon, whose designs were a model for Russian churches in the nineteenth century. Imitating brick walls, the log structure of the Tikhvin Church lacked the coherence of the much earlier and more daring design of its neighbor, which still stands as a monument to the traditional virtues of northern log architecture.

No matter how well built, log structures will eventually collapse if not maintained. An instructive example is the pair of churches at the village of Paltoga, just to the west of Vytegra. The white brick Church of the Virgin of the Sign (Znamenie), built in 1810, still stands as a picturesque neoclassical ruin. Adjacent to it was the log Church of the Epiphany (1733), an unusual, beautiful form crowned with five cupolas. Already in a state of extreme disrepair in 2006, the church collapsed soon thereafter. Efforts have been made to conserve what is left of the lower structure, but the possibility of its complete reconstruction is dim.

BELOZERSK AND THE SOUTHERN SHORE OF WHITE LAKE

The river system descending from the Vytegra eventually leads to the White Lake, or "Beloe Ozero," the territory of one of Russia's most ancient settlements. The origins and early location of Belozersk, a town of some ten thousand in the Vologda region, are dim and uncertain. Nonetheless, "Beloozero" is considered among the oldest recorded settlements among the eastern Slavs, mentioned in the *Primary Chronical* under the year 862 as one of the five towns granted to the

Varangian (or Viking) brothers Riurik, Sineus, and Truvor, invited (according to the chronicle) to rule over the eastern Slavs in what was then called Rus.

Whatever the details of its history, it is clear from the name that the town was always closely connected with White Lake (Beloe Ozero), a large body of fresh water in northwestern Russia. Although smaller than Lakes Ladoga and Onega, White Lake is a pivotal link between those two lakes and the Russian heartland. On the southeast end White Lake drains into the Sheksna, a tributary of the Volga and the route of many summer cruise boats between Moscow and St. Petersburg.

The early Beloozero — as it was originally called — was at a different location on White Lake, and the town was again resettled until it occupied its current place in the late fourteenth century. As Moscow's power increased in the fifteenth century, Beloozero gained strategic importance as a bulwark on Muscovy's northwestern frontier and its water transportation routes. Ivan III (the Great) understood the significance of this location, and in 1487 he constructed a large fortress, or kremlin, whose earthen ramparts still stand.

The town prospered during the middle of the sixteenth century, particularly as a source of iron goods and fish. An impressive visible reminder of that wealth is the fortresslike Church of the Dormition, begun in 1553 on one of the town's highest points. Beloozero witnessed the disruptions of the latter part of the reign of Ivan the Terrible (r. 1547–84), when the town was included in his personal domain (*oprichnina*) and served as a place of exile.

The inclusion of Beloozero in Ivan's domains did not prevent it from experiencing the famine and disease inflicted on much of the rest of Russia in the late sixteenth century. And during the Time of Troubles (the dynastic crisis following the death of Tsar Boris Godunov in 1605), the year 1612 brought a full measure of devastation with the sack of Beloozero by a marauding force. With the revival of trade in the seventeenth century, Beloozero's location and natural resources again proved advantageous. During the reign of Aleksei Mikhailovich, the Cathedral of the Transfiguration was built within the kremlin in the 1670s.

With the founding of St. Petersburg in 1703, Beloozero found itself in a pivotal position between the Volga River Basin and the large northwestern lakes Onega and Ladoga, which led via the Neva River to the new imperial capital. In 1777 the town's name was formally changed to Belozersk, and the next year it gained a new plan as part of Catherine the Great's project to remake Russian provincial life by redesigning regional centers.

In the case of Belozersk the natural landscape and the design process were successfully united. A terrace effect created by the gentle slope of the town toward the lake to the north was utilized to create a leafy boulevard (now called Soviet Prospekt) parallel to the lakeshore. The boulevard was flanked by other east–west streets, which were in turn intersected with a system of north–south lanes leading to the lake. This design was dominated on the west by the high earthen walls of the kremlin, while small hills with churches anchored the south side. Despite the vandalism inflicted on these churches in the Soviet period, Belozersk's remoteness from economic development has preserved much of its center with nineteenth-century buildings.

The best general view of historic Belozersk is provided by the ramparts of the kremlin. This citadel is perhaps the best preserved example of a type of earthen fortress once widespread among the eastern Slavs. Roughly quadrilateral in shape, the fortress was protected on two sides by a moat. In the late seventeenth century, the ramparts were still surmounted with a log wall containing eight towers and two gates—all removed in the eighteenth century. Quite apart from the historical significance of the fortress, its high ramparts offer breathtaking views of the town and of White Lake.

KIRILLOV AND THE SHEKSNA RIVER

Throughout the North, waterways have long served as the main arteries of trade and commerce. Among the most important of these is the Sheksna River, a link in the waterway connecting the Volga River with Lake Onega in northwestern Russia. Each summer cruise boats operating between Moscow and St. Petersburg dock at the village of Goritsy on the Sheksna. From there, buses transport visitors some ten kilometers to the east to Kirillov, a small town that includes a few streets with nineteenth-century houses built by local merchants. Yet the stream of visitors is not there for the charming town, but for its extraordinary fortress-monastery, founded in 1397 by Kirill (Cyril), a Muscovite monk of noble origins.

In all of Russia there are few more impressive sights than the walls and massive towers of the St. Kirill Monastery. Its location, at Siverskoe Lake near the Sheksna River, was both remote and strategically important. With the revival of monasticism in Moscow during the fourteenth century, pioneer monks sought remote areas as a test of their ascetic faith and dedication. At the same time, Muscovite princes supported these efforts not only to spread and maintain the Orthodox faith, but also to consolidate Moscow's territorial expansion into the rich forests of the far North.

In the early fifteenth century, St. Kirill's monastery, formerly dedicated to the Dormition of the Mother of God, played a major role in supporting Moscow's dynastic stability. As a consequence, the monastery received major donations that by the sixteenth century made it one of the largest Russian monastic institutions, second in size to the Trinity–St. Sergius Monastery near Moscow. The first church to be built in brick and stone was the Dormition Cathedral, begun in 1496 and expanded with small picturesque attached churches over the next two centuries. The cathedral interior has a grand icon screen and seventeenth-century frescoes that are still under restoration.

One of the main patrons of the monastery was Basil III, grand prince of Moscow, who in 1528 made a pilgrimage to the monastery with his second wife, Elena Glinskaia, to pray for the birth of a son and heir. In the 1530s Basil sponsored two brick churches in the monastery, including the Church of John the Baptist, which became the nucleus of another monastery. Thus St. Kirill-Belozersky Monastery is actually composed of two monasteries (the Dormition and John the Baptist), as well as a settlement for lay workers protected by an ever-expanding system of walls. At the beginning of the seventeenth century, these walls would enable the St. Kirill Monastery to defend the area against marauders during a period of civil war and foreign invasion known as the "Time of Troubles."

A major surge in the monastery's fortunes occurred in the second half of the seventeenth century, when Tsar Aleksei Mikhailovich decided to rebuild the monastery as an impregnable monument to Moscow's dominance in the North. At that time, the most likely enemy was Sweden, which had already gained considerable territory held in medieval times by the Russian city-state of Novgorod. If Sweden attempted a deep invasion, the St. Kirill Monastery would stand as a firm obstacle. In 1653 Alexis decreed the expansion of the monastery's walls and towers, which rose over a period of several decades throughout the latter part of the seventeenth century.

Ironically, no hostile army ever came close to the citadel that had been rebuilt and expanded at such great effort. Its walls and towers only served as testimony to the Russian ability to erect masonry structures of enormous extent during the late medieval period. With his victories against the Swedes in the early eighteenth century and the founding of St. Petersburg (1703), Peter the Great fundamentally altered the geopolitical position of the Russian North.

The declining importance of the St. Kirill Monastery led to its neglect and decay during the eighteenth and nineteenth centuries. In the late nineteenth century, a revival of interest in Russia's medieval heritage led to restoration efforts that continued during the early Soviet period. In 1929 the first museum was established in the monastery. The onslaught of Stalinist industrialization and ideological repression undercut much of this work and led to great material losses, such as the melting down of the monastery's remarkable bell ensemble—one of the most important in Russia.

Only after the Second World War did the Kirill-Belozersk Museum revive its cultural potential. The territory of the monastery gradually became a major repository of Russian cultural treasures, with an excellent museum of sacred art. Part of the monastery has reverted to the use of the Orthodox Church.

FERAPONTOV-NATIVITY MONASTERY

Although the small village of Ferapontovo is not far from Kirillov and the Sheksna River, it is not included in cruise schedules between Moscow and St. Petersburg. Perhaps that is just as well, for its miniature monastery could easily be overwhelmed by large groups. Yet the frescoes within its main church are among the sublime creations of medieval religious art.

The monastery was established in 1398 on the shores of the small Lake Borodava. Its founder, Ferapont (1337–1426), was a monk of noble birth from Moscow's Simonov Monastery who had accompanied Kirill, another pioneering Muscovite monk, on his journey in search of solitude in the North. Within a year of Kirill's establishment of the Dormition Monastery on Siverskoe Lake near the Sheksna River, Ferapont left to form his own spiritual retreat a short distance to the east. He was canonized in the sixteenth century, and the northern monastery that he founded came to be known as Ferapontov, while retaining its original dedication to the Nativity of the Virgin.

The main entrance to the monastery is through a picturesque gate that supports two small churches dedicated to the Epiphany and St. Ferapont (1649). The center of the monastery is the Cathedral of the Nativity of the Virgin, rebuilt in brick in 1490, six years earlier than the Dormition Cathedral at Kirillov. The upper walls and cupola of the Nativity Cathedral were substantially modified, starting in the sixteenth century with work continuing through the eighteenth century.

The west entrance to the cathedral is flanked by frescoes devoted to the Nativity of the Virgin. They serve as an introduction to the work of one of medieval Russia's greatest artists, Dionisy, who painted the interior of the Nativity Cathedral in 1502 with the assistance of his two sons. The fact that such a renowned artist, accustomed to commissions for frescoes and icons from the court of Grand Prince Ivan III, should engage in work far to the north is further evidence of the close relations between these monasteries and Moscow.

The frescoes, in praise of the Virgin Mary and Christ, are extraordinary in the warmth of their colors and the delicacy of the figures. Due to the remote location and small size of Ferapontov Monastery, these frescoes did not undergo the repaintings typical of many medieval Russian churches and are well preserved, despite modifications to the structure itself. On a bright day, the compact space of the cathedral is suffused with vibrant color. The Ferapontov frescoes are now on the UNESCO World Heritage list.

In addition to the Nativity Cathedral, the main ensemble of the monastery includes the Refectory Church of the Annunciation (1530–31) and the Church of St. Martinian (1640), which features a tower roof. The ensemble is linked on the west by a raised gallery with a seventeenth-century bell tower. One of the great charms of Ferapontov Monastery is its natural setting, surrounded by lakes and forests that convey the haunting beauty of the Russian North. There is no clearer evidence that despite their asceticism, the pioneering monks who came to this region had a superb aesthetic sense.

USTIUZHNA ON THE MOLOGA RIVER

The Sheksna River eventually flows past the industrial city of Cherepovets, whose architecture is primarily a modern creation. To the west of Cherepovets, however, is another remarkable center of traditional Russian culture. Among the numerous historic towns of the Vologda territory, Ustiuzhna is perhaps the least known. Located on the Mologa River (a tributary of the Volga) in the southwest corner of Vologda province, the town is often confused with Veliky Ustiug, situated almost seven hundred kilometers distant in the northeast corner of the province. Ustiuzhna, whose current population is approximately ten thousand souls, is not particularly remote by Russian standards, yet it has no rail link and is several kilometers from the main road between St. Petersburg and Cherepovets.

Walking along the town's quiet streets (many of them unpaved) gives the impression of a provincial trading center that has changed little since the nineteenth century. The twentieth century, however, inflicted much damage here as in so many other provincial towns. Although every neighborhood seems to have its church, most of the churches were vandalized or destroyed during the Soviet period. Only one, dedicated to the Kazan Icon of the Virgin, is currently used for worship. Fortunately, this church and its frescoes form a masterpiece of Russian religious art.

Ustiuzhna's wealth in the medieval period was based on nearby deposits of bog iron suited to primitive smelting methods. The town was first noted for its iron in the mid-thirteenth century, when it became one of the earliest Russian centers of metalworking. Ustiuzhna reached the height of its iron production during the sixteenth century.

With the eighteenth-century development of the Urals as Russia's primary metal producer, Ustiuzhna settled into the status of a modest regional town. A major change in its appearance occurred during the reign of Catherine the Great, who in the 1770s brought order into the planning of Russia's towns. The Ustiuzhna plan, approved in 1778, skillfully connected the two main churches: the Cathedral of the Nativity of the Virgin and the Church of the Kazan Icon.

The Cathedral of the Nativity, built in 1685–90, is the oldest surviving church in Ustiuzhna. The exterior is relatively simple, but the interior has an extraordinary iconostasis whose style can be traced to work done in the Moscow Kremlin in the late 1680s. Its carved, gilded frame ascends in five rows in the canonical Orthodox pattern, from the Local Row at the bottom to the Patriarchs Row at the top. The cathedral currently serves as the town museum.

Ustiuzhna's other monument of religious art, the festively decorated Church of the Kazan Icon of the Virgin, was begun in 1694 by Grigory Stroganov (of the renowned Stroganov merchant dynasty), who had commercial dealings in Ustiuzhna. The Kazan Church contains a soaring iconostasis, but its glory is the full array of mid-eighteenth-century frescoes, painted in a robust style by masters from Yaroslavl. The frescoes begin in the small narthex, which includes the Seven Days of Creation, the Expulsion from Paradise, and the Last Judgment. The interior of the main structure creates an overwhelming impression, with depictions of the Passion of Christ, major church festivals, images of the Virgin Mary, and scenes from the vita of St. Catherine.

As for secular architecture, many of the town's houses and commercial buildings have survived. Despite losses during the twentieth century, the historic center of Ustiuzhna still evokes the cultural heritage of Russia's northern towns.

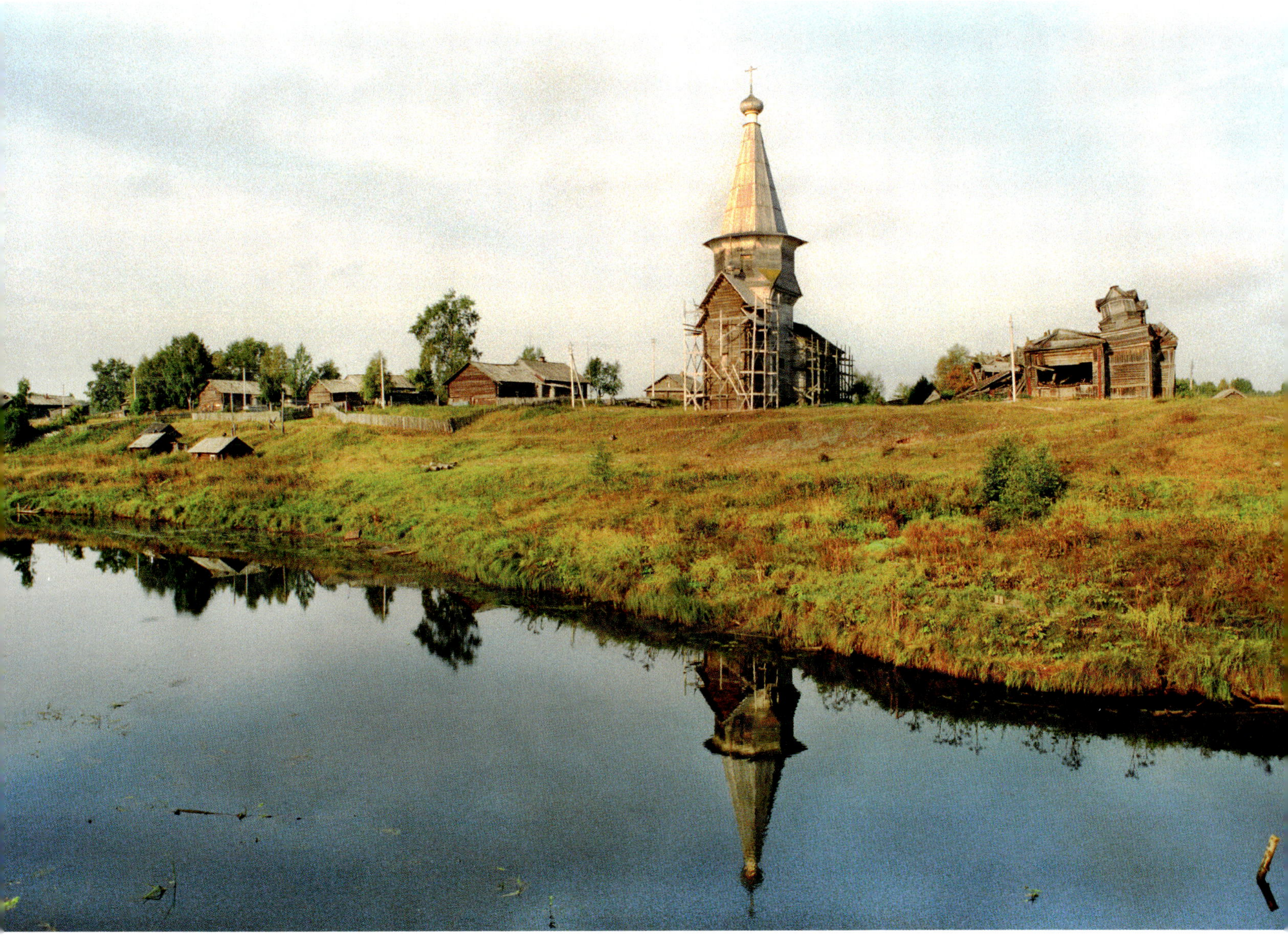

SAMINSKY POGOST. Wooden Church of Elijah the Prophet, with ruins of Church of the Tikhvin Icon of the Virgin, built in 1892. Northeast view across Samina River. Left: log houses and barns, with bathhouses nestled along river bank. Photograph: August 28, 2006.

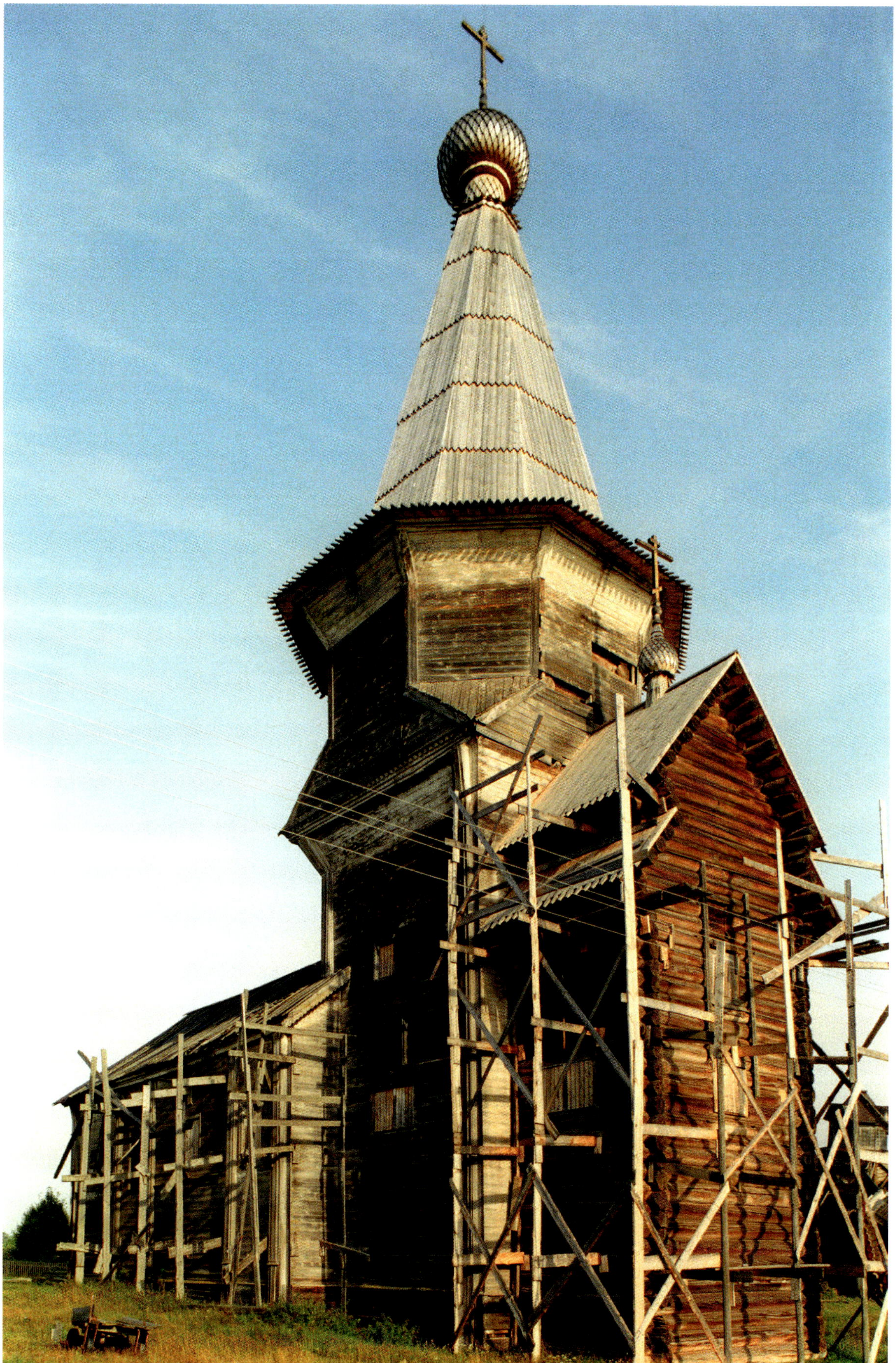

SAMINSKY POGOST. Church of Elijah the Prophet, southeast view. Built between 1692 and 1702. Photograph: August 28, 2006.

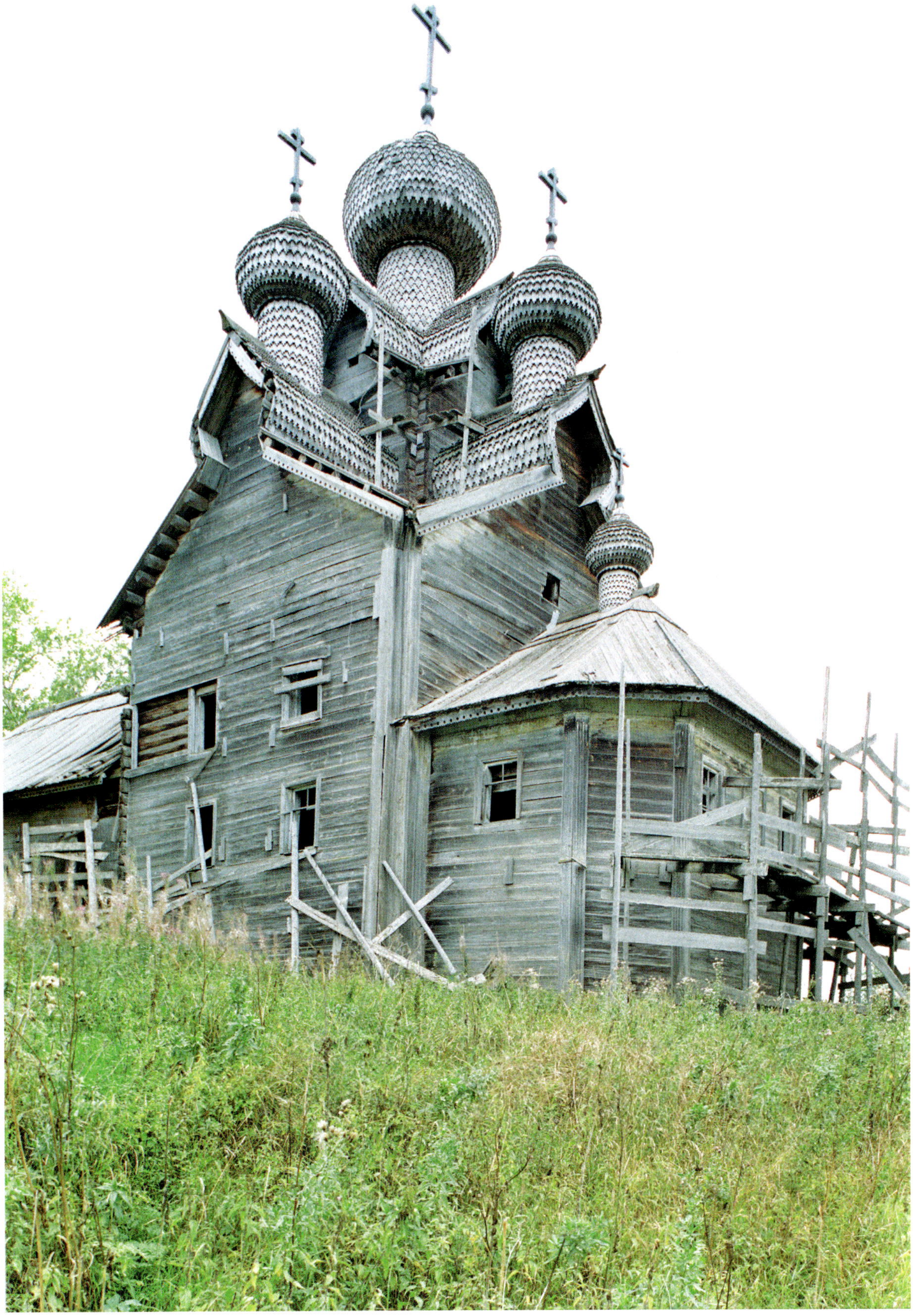

PALTOGA (Paltozhsky Pogost). Wooden Church of the Epiphany, southeast view. Built in 1733. Main structure collapsed in 2009. Photograph: August 28, 2006.

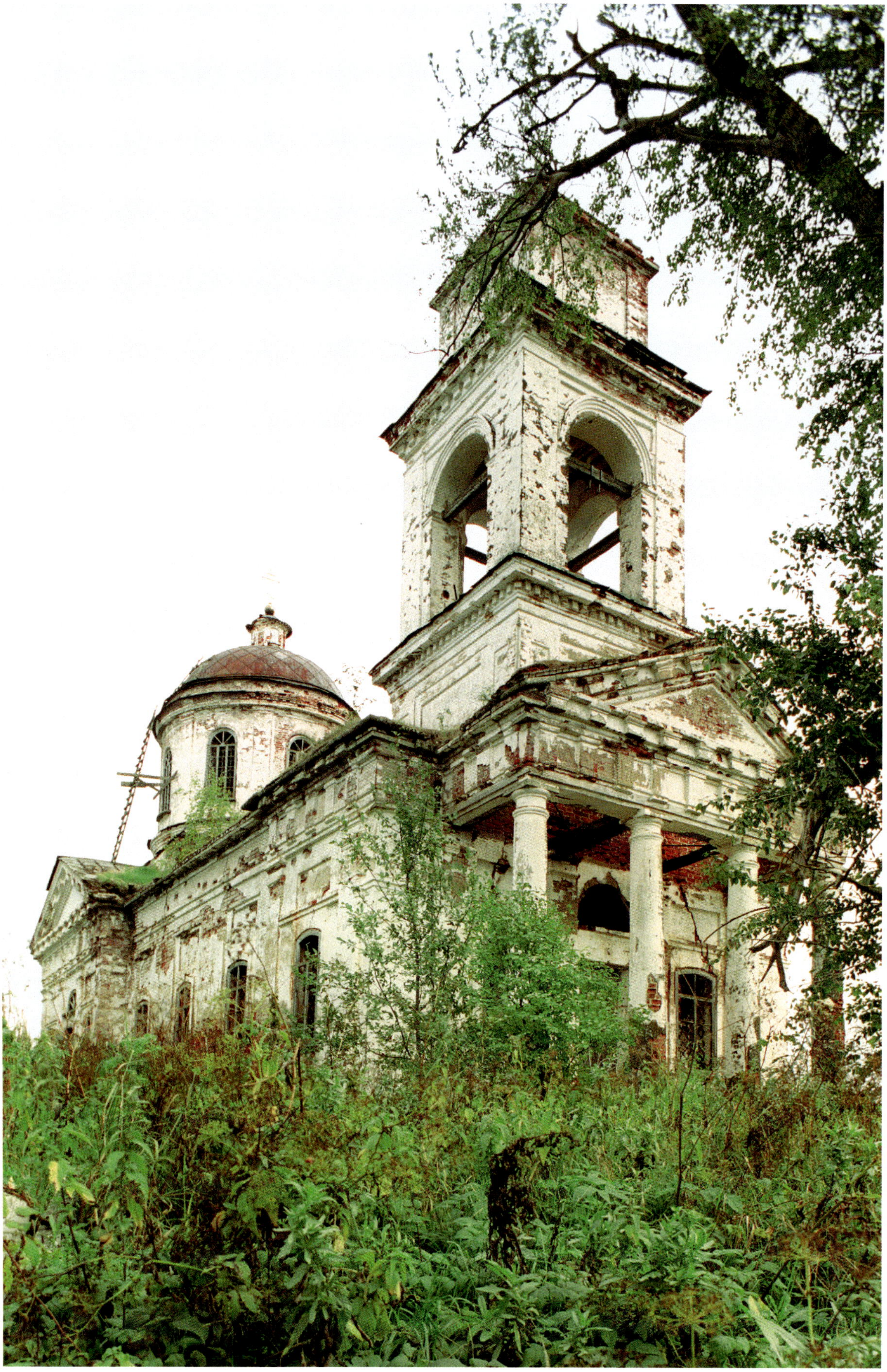

PALTOGA (Paltozhsky Pogost). Church of the Icon of the Sign, northwest view. Church built in 1810. Photograph: August 28, 2006.

VYTEGRA. Wooden Chapel of St. Isaac of Dalmatia, southwest view. Chapel built in 1881. Photograph: August 28, 2006.

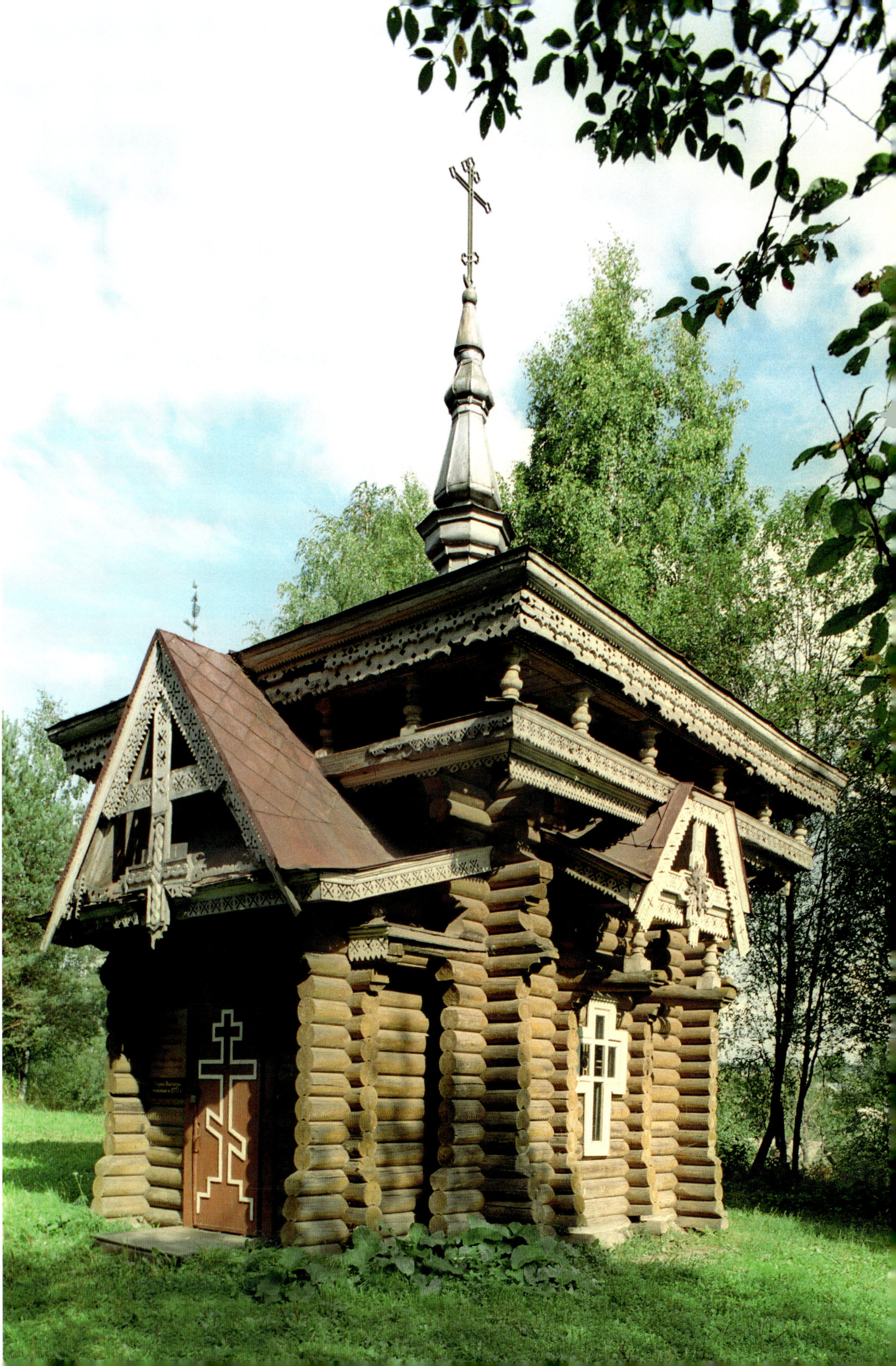

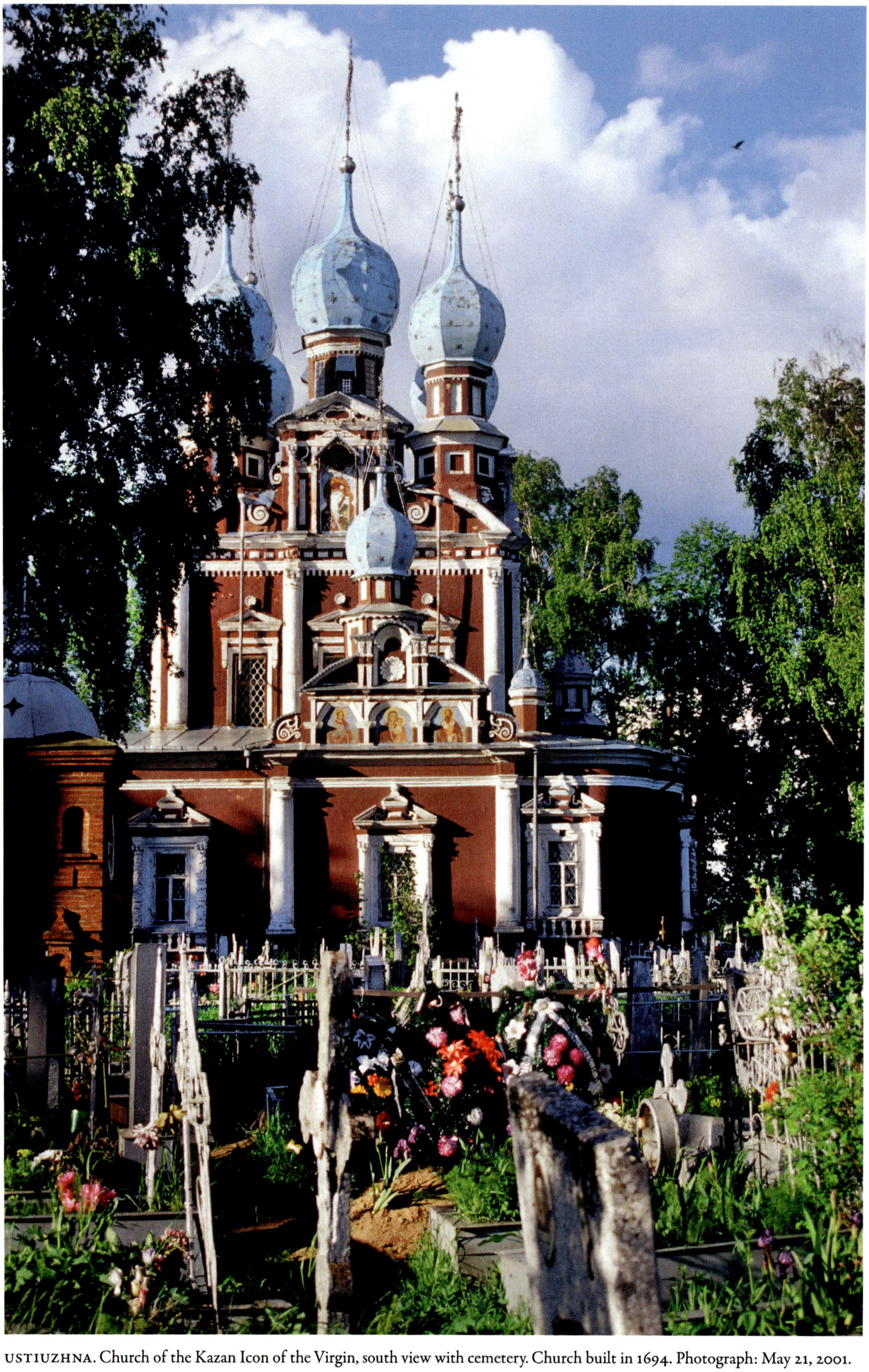

USTIUZHNA. Church of the Kazan Icon of the Virgin, south view with cemetery. Church built in 1694. Photograph: May 21, 2001.

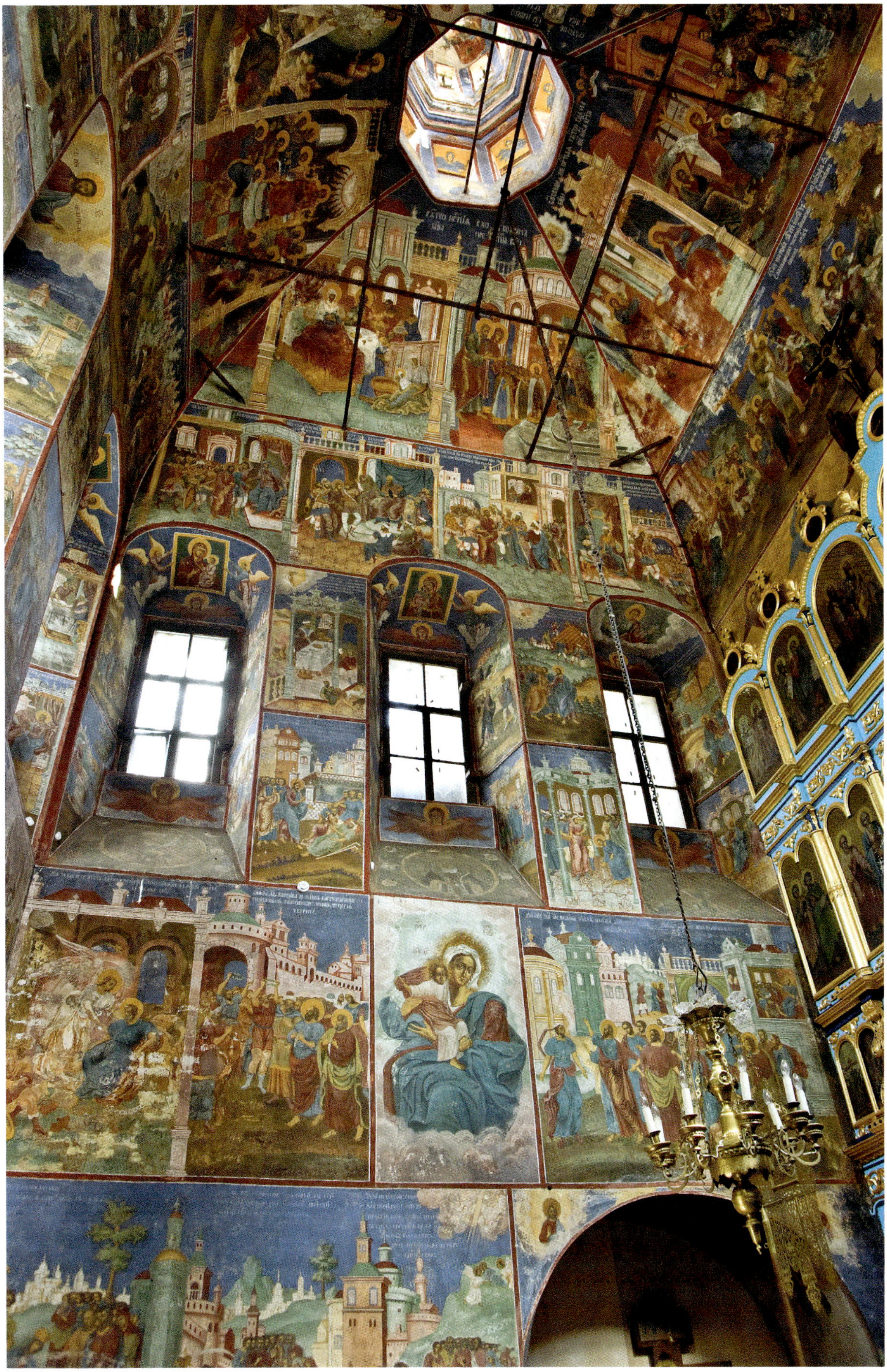

USTIUZHNA. Church of the Kazan Icon of the Virgin, interior, view north. Photograph: July 7, 2009.

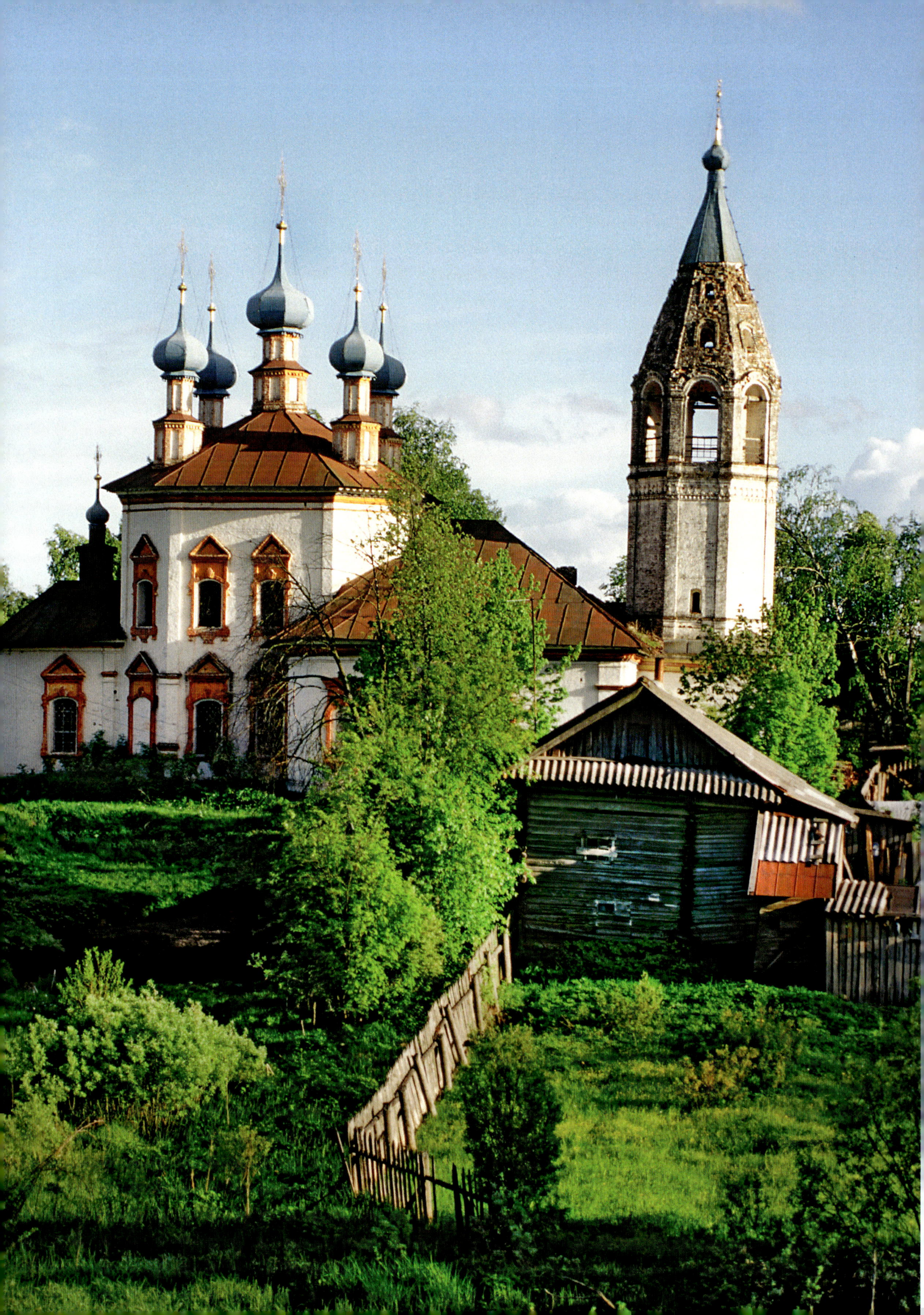

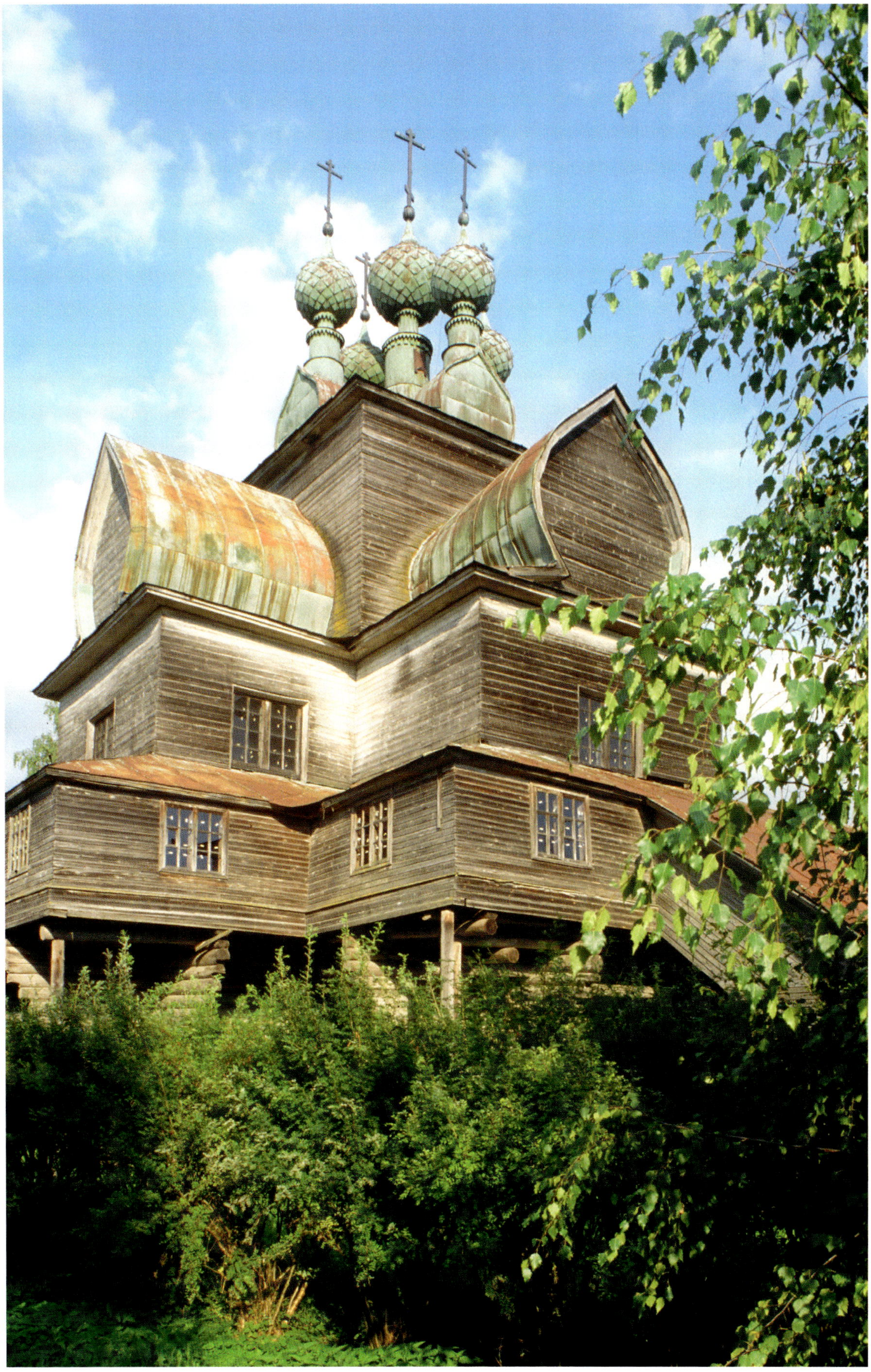

NELAZSKOE. Wooden Church of the Dormition, northwest view. Church built in 1694. Photograph: August 13, 2006.

USTIUZHNA. Church of the Annunciation, north view. Church built between 1690 and 1694. Photograph: May 21, 2001.

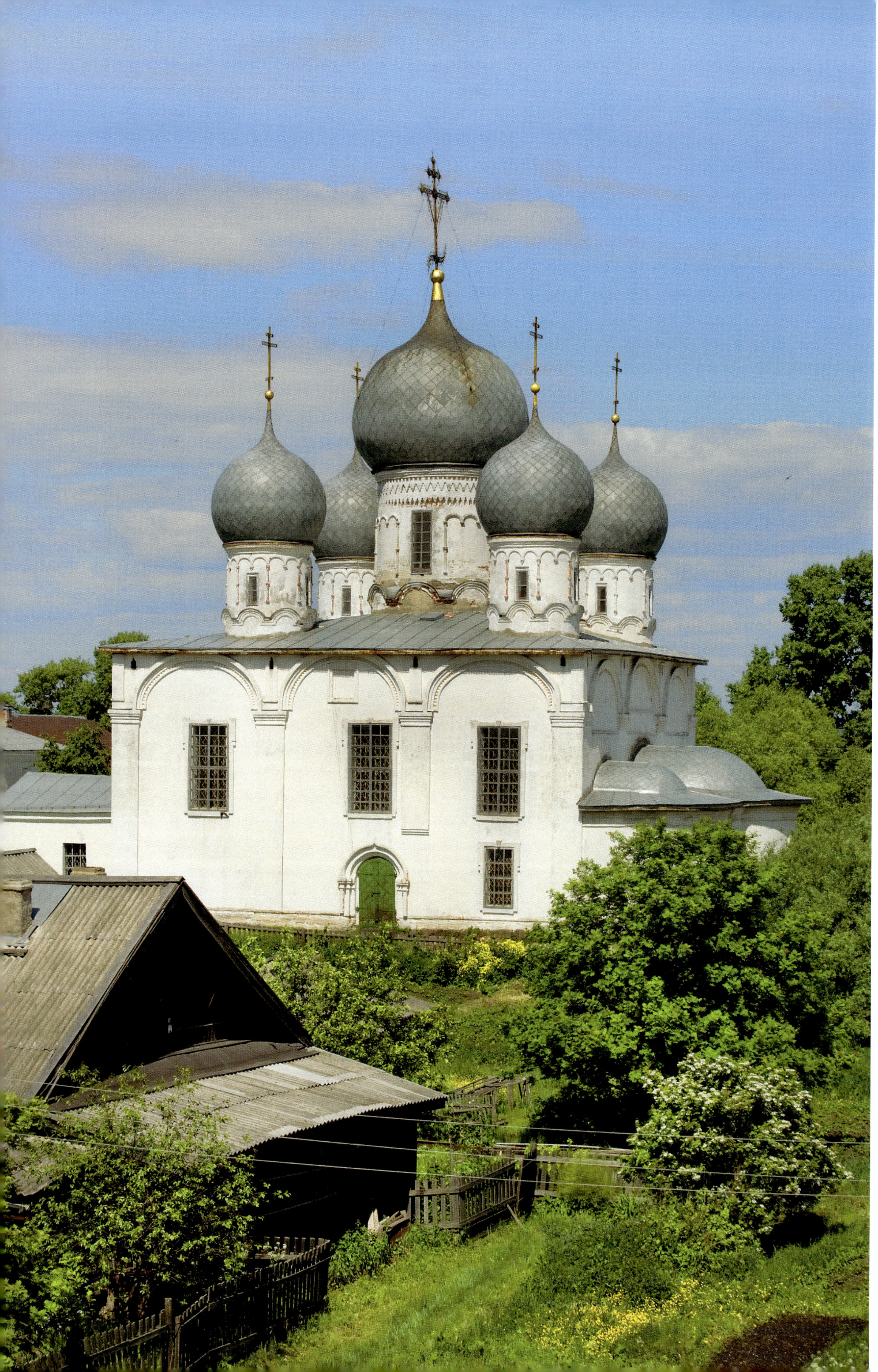

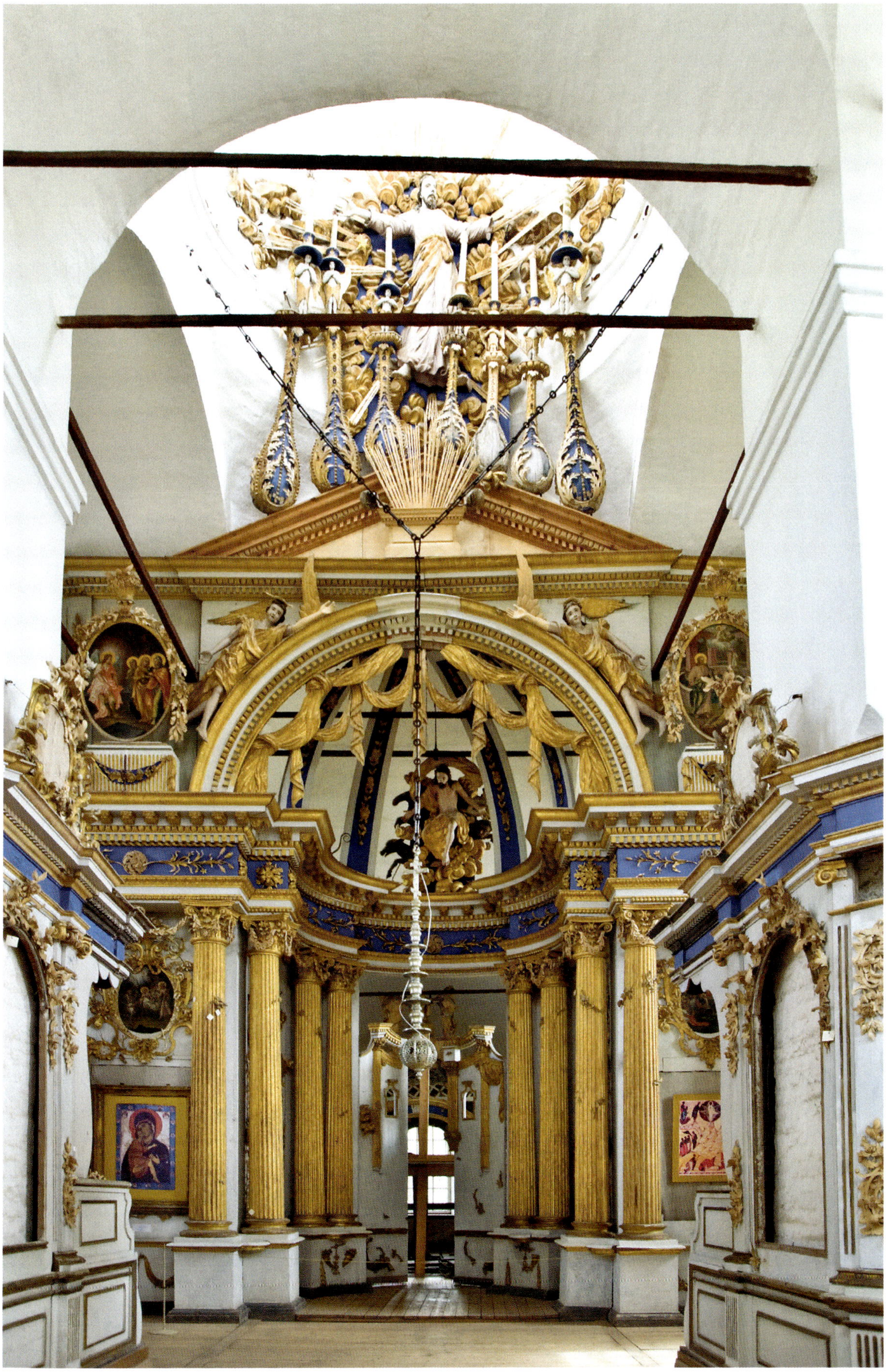

BELOZERSK KREMLIN. Cathedral of the Transfiguration, interior, view east toward icon screen. Photograph: August 8, 2009.

BELOZERSK KREMLIN. Cathedral of the Transfiguration, southeast view from kremlin rampart. Cathedral built 1668–70. Photograph: June 9, 2010.

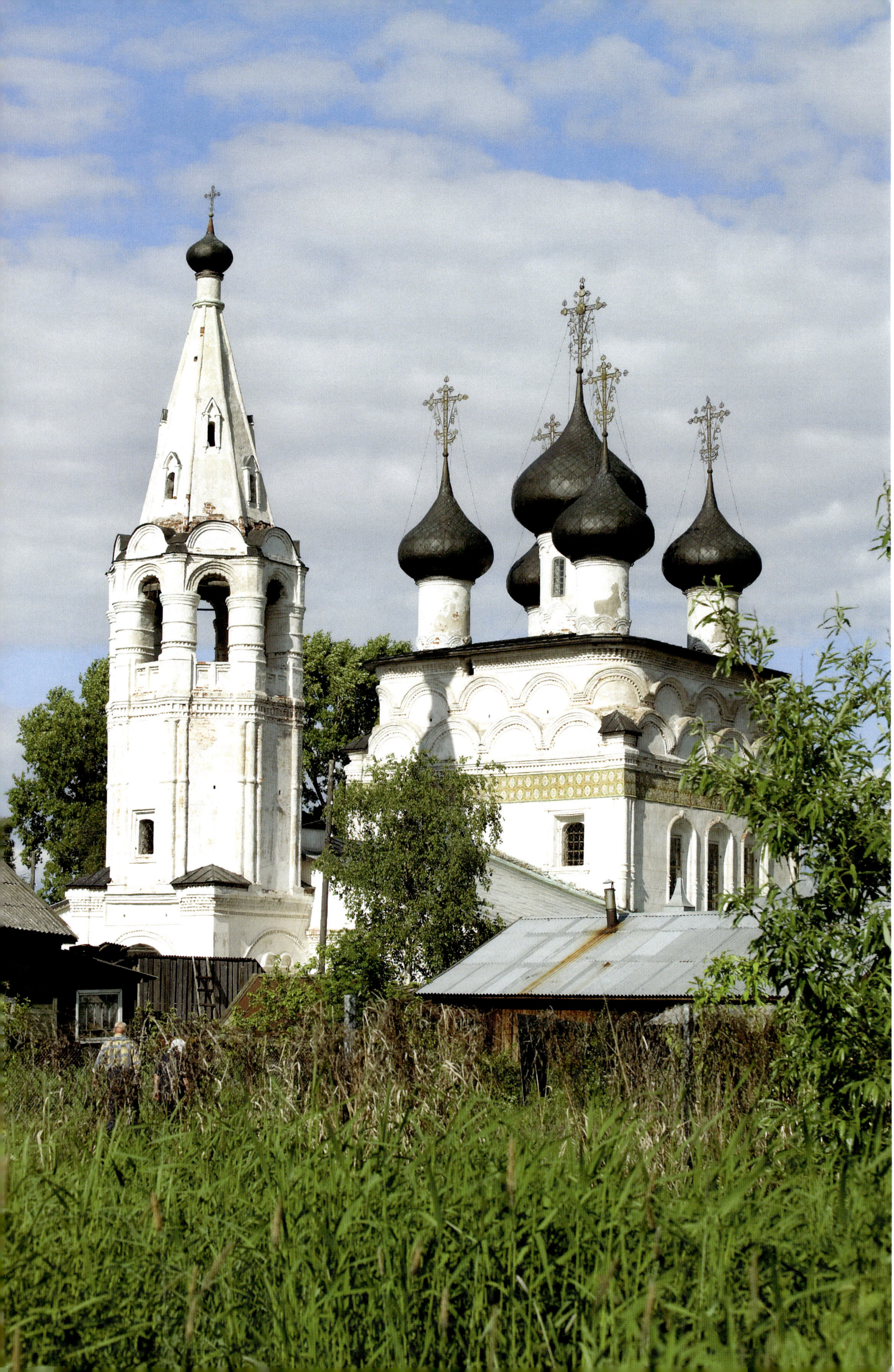

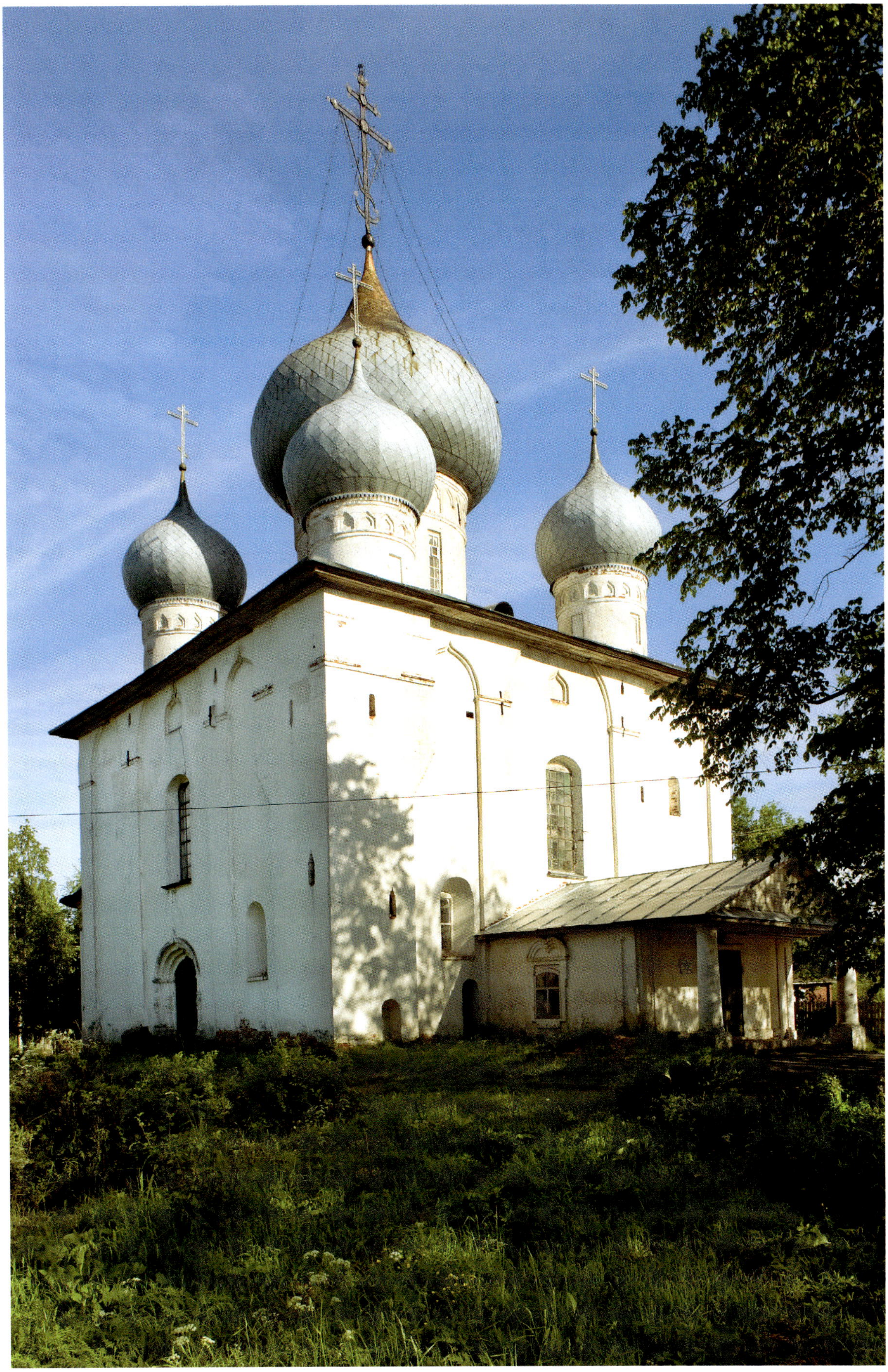

BELOZERSK. Church of the Dormition, northwest view. Also referred to as a cathedral, the structure was built between 1552 and 1563. Photograph: June 9, 2010.

BELOZERSK. Church of the Merciful Savior, southwest view. Church built in 1723. Photograph: June 9, 2010.

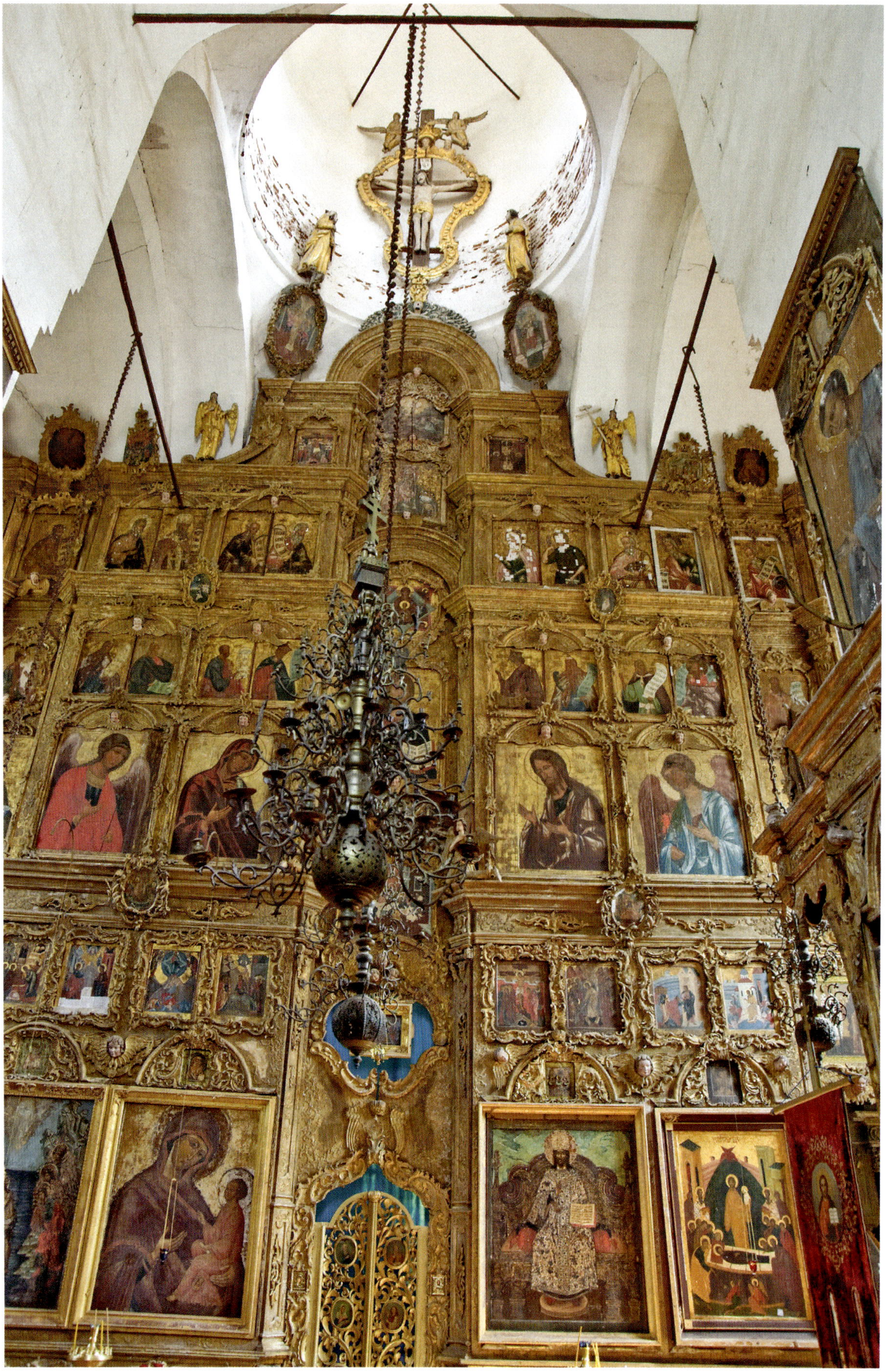

BELOZERSK. Church of the Dormition, interior, view east toward icon screen. Photograph: August 8, 2009.

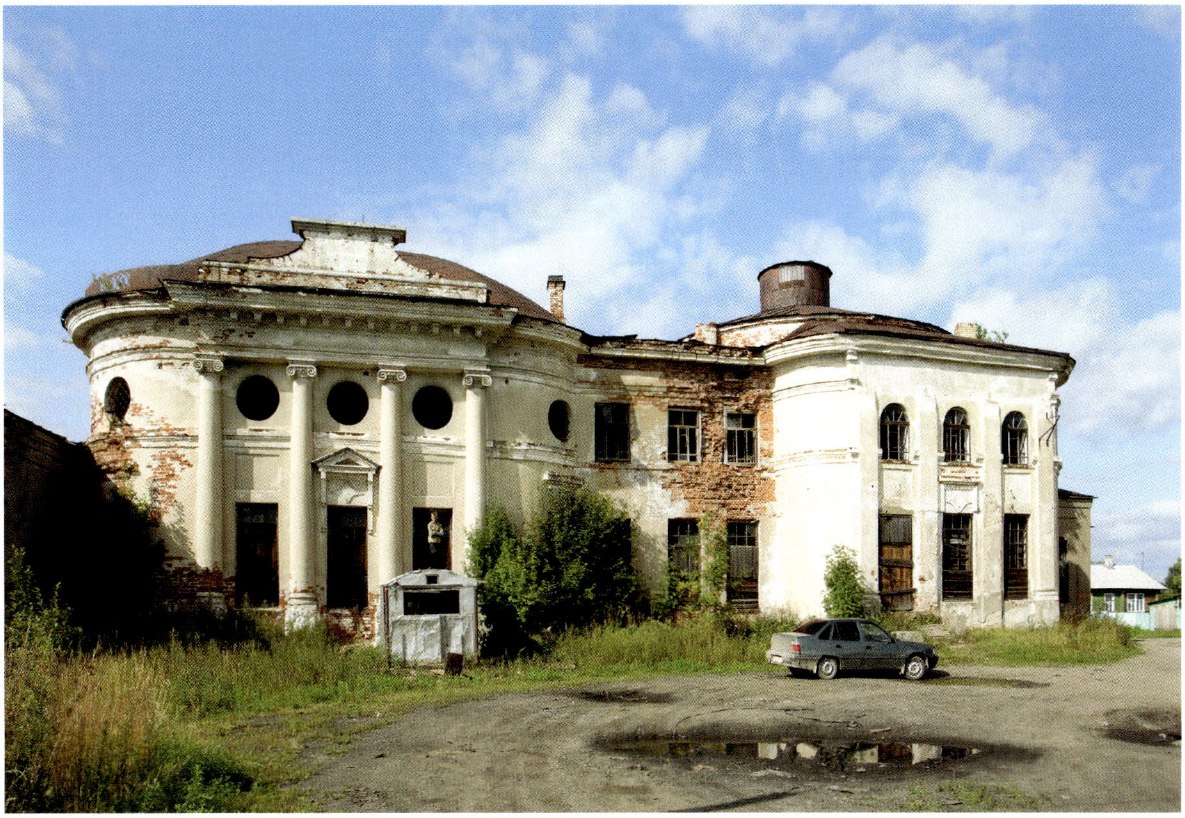

BELOZERSK. Church of the Trinity (Nativity of John the Baptist), south view. Monumental neoclassical temple, completed ca. 1800, stripped of domes and converted to factory workshop during Soviet period. Photograph: August 8, 2009.

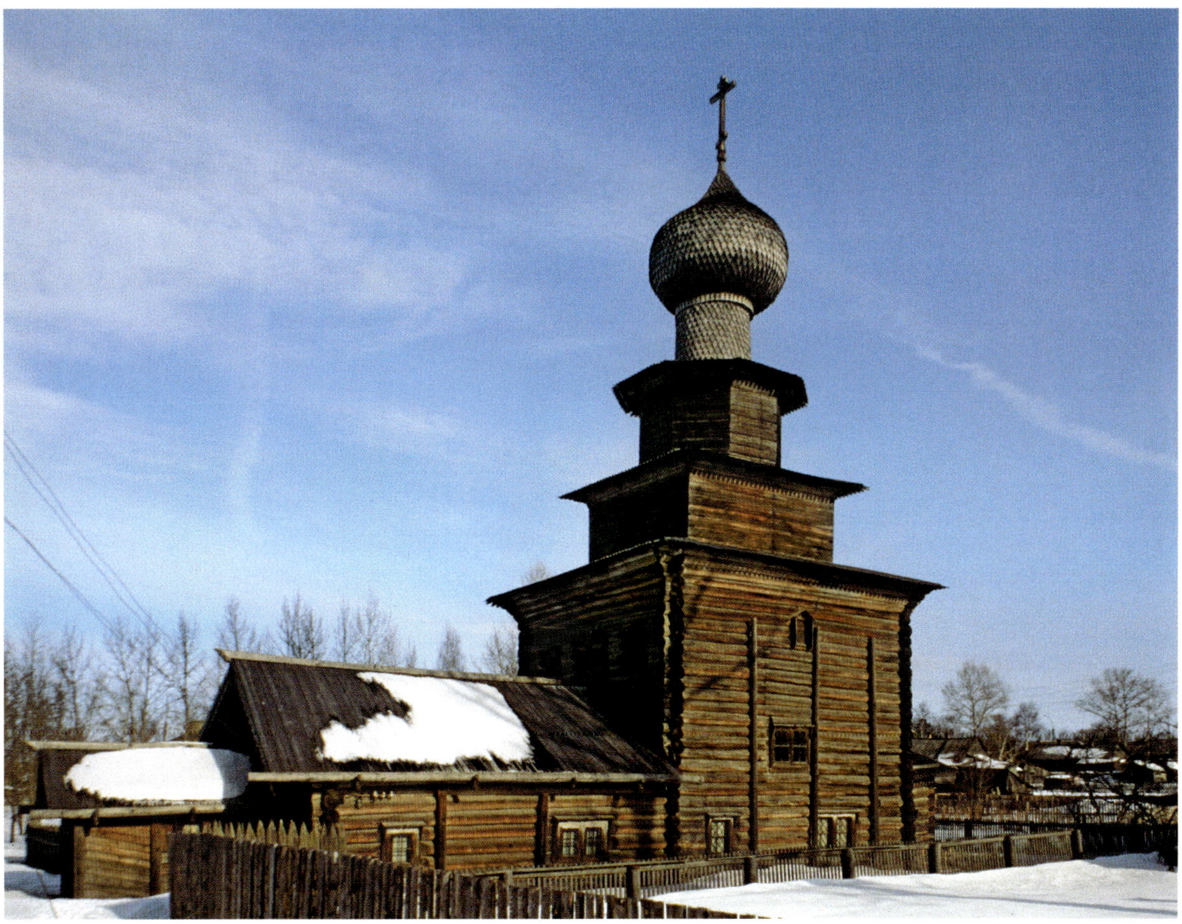

BELOZERSK. Wooden Church of Elijah the Prophet, southwest view. Built between 1690 and 1696, the church was disassembled for restoration in 2012. Funding complications have prolonged the restoration work. Photograph: March 3, 1998.

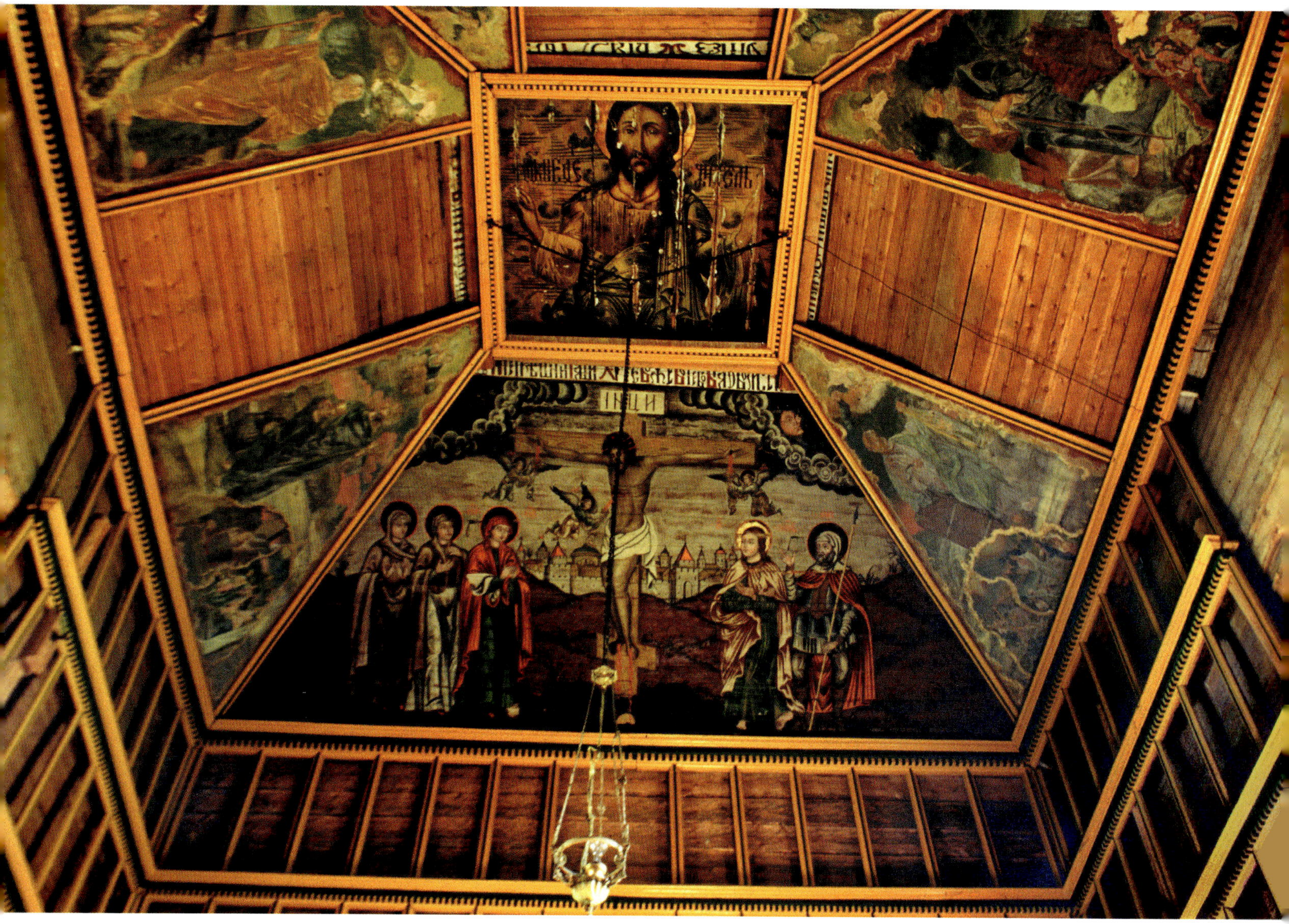

BELOZERSK. Church of Elijah the Prophet, interior with painted ceiling (nebo).
Photograph: July 23, 1999.

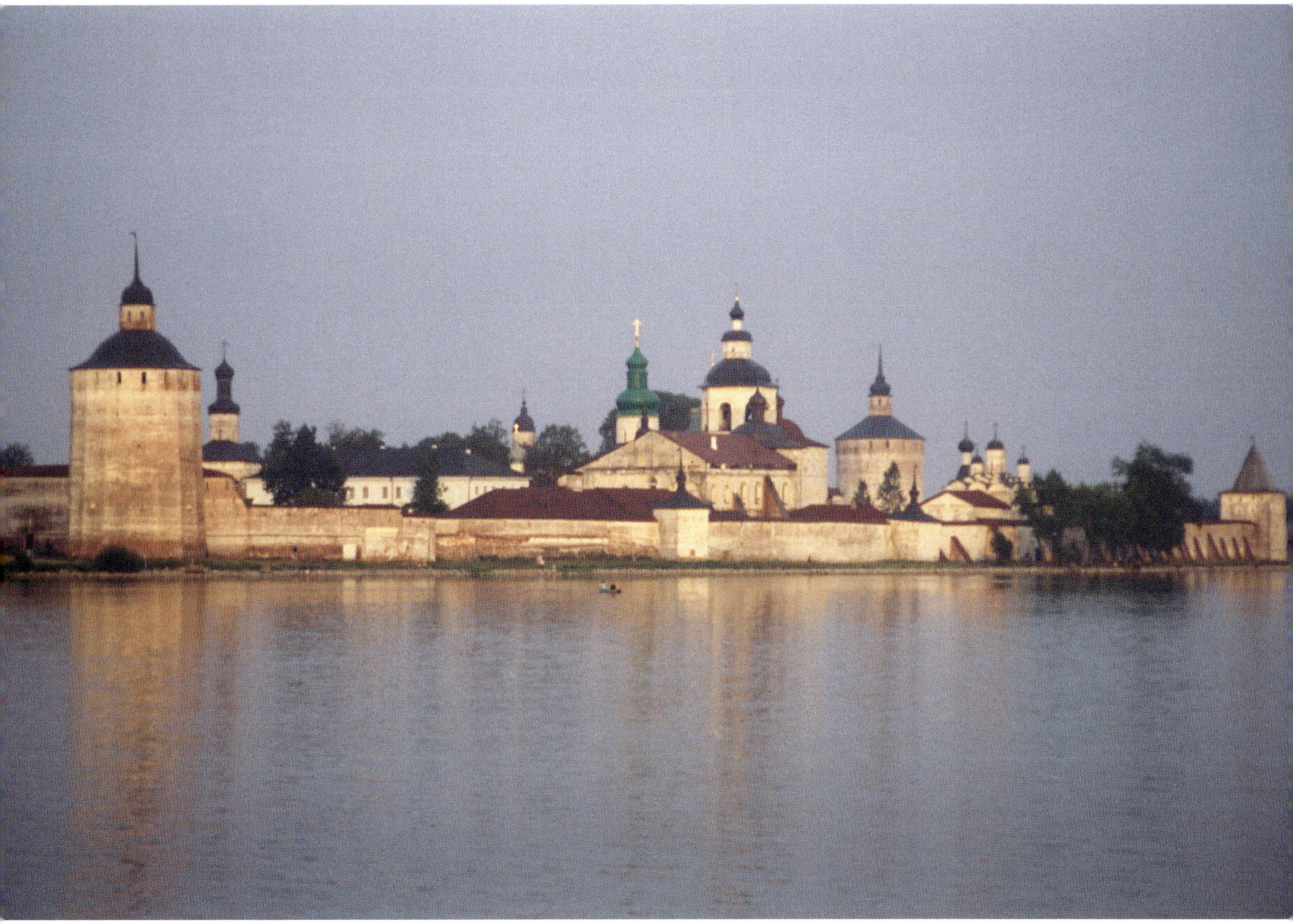

KIRILLOV. St. Kirill-Belozersky Monastery, view across Siverskoe Lake.
Left: Belozersk Tower. Photograph: July 14, 1999.

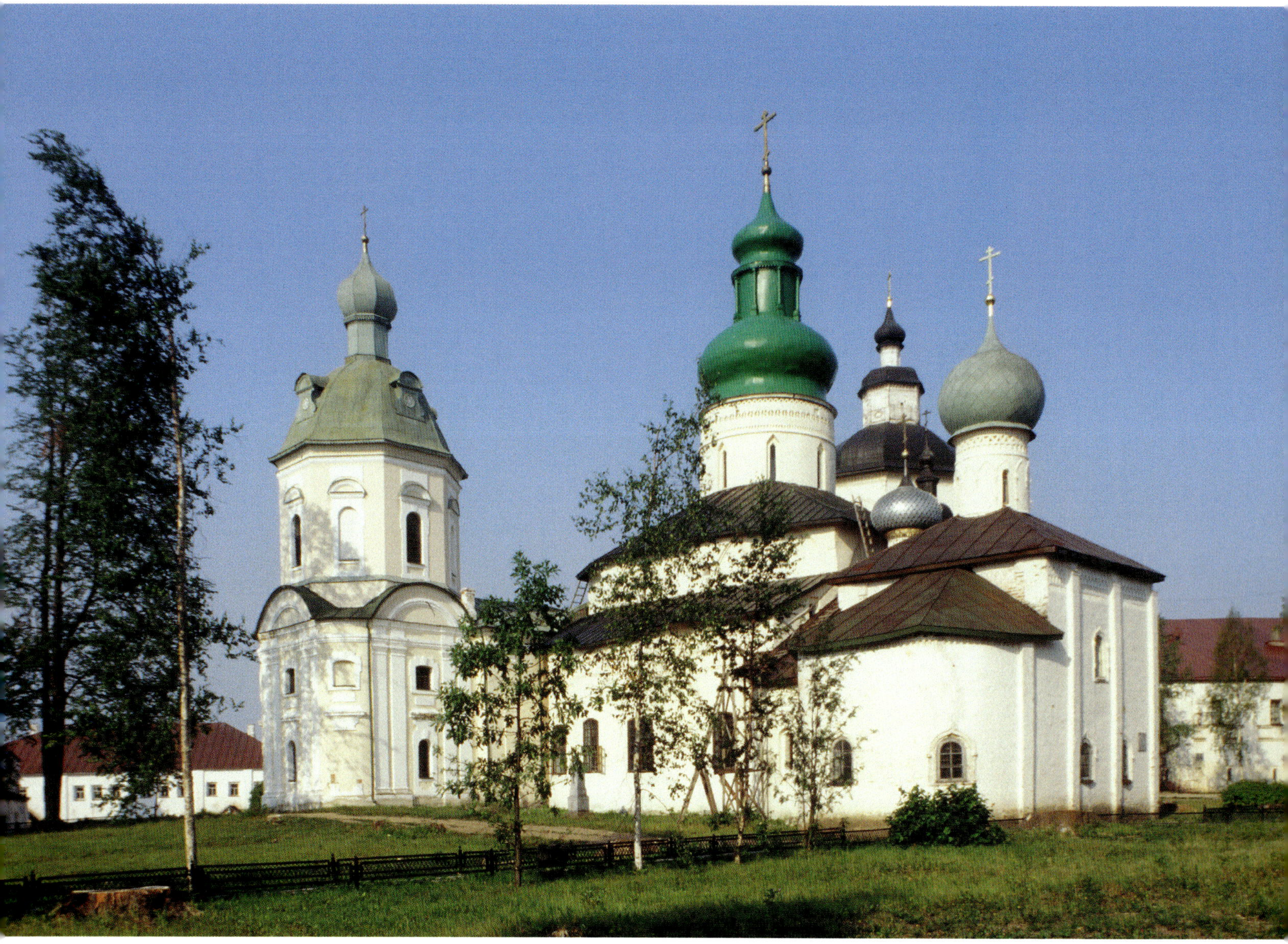

KIRILLOV. Cathedral ensemble, St. Kirill-Belozersky Monastery, northeast view. From left: Church of St. Kirill-Belozersky (1791), Dormition Cathedral (1497), Church of St. Epifany (1645). Photograph: July 15, 1999.

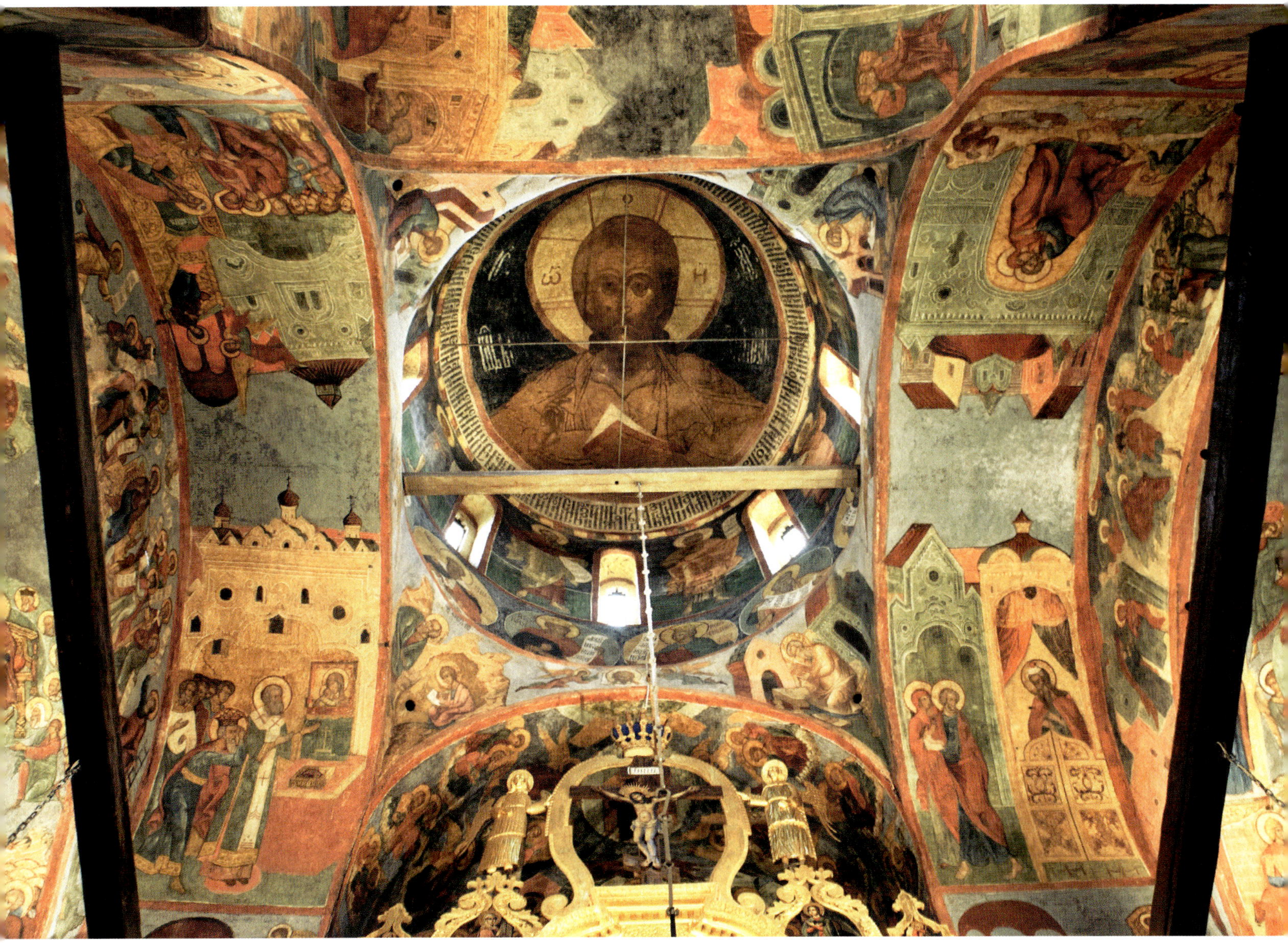

KIRILLOV. Cathedral of the Dormition, St. Kirill-Belozersky Monastery. Interior, view east, ceiling and dome frescoes with top of gilded icon screen. Photograph: June 2, 2014.

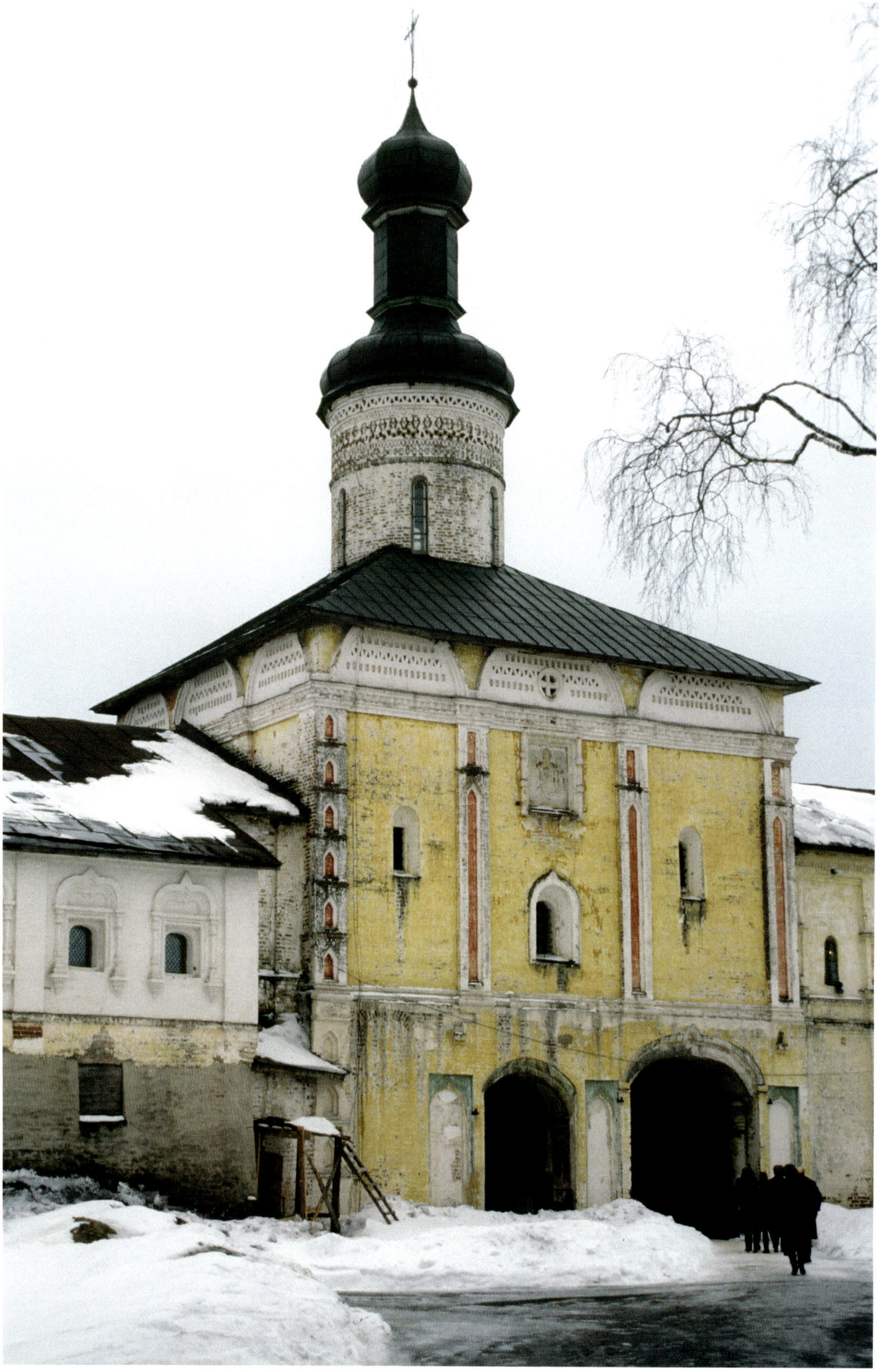

KIRILLOV. Church of St. John Climacus over Holy Gates, St. Kirill-Belozersky Monastery. Church built over main north entrance in 1572. Northeast view. Photograph: April 1, 2001.

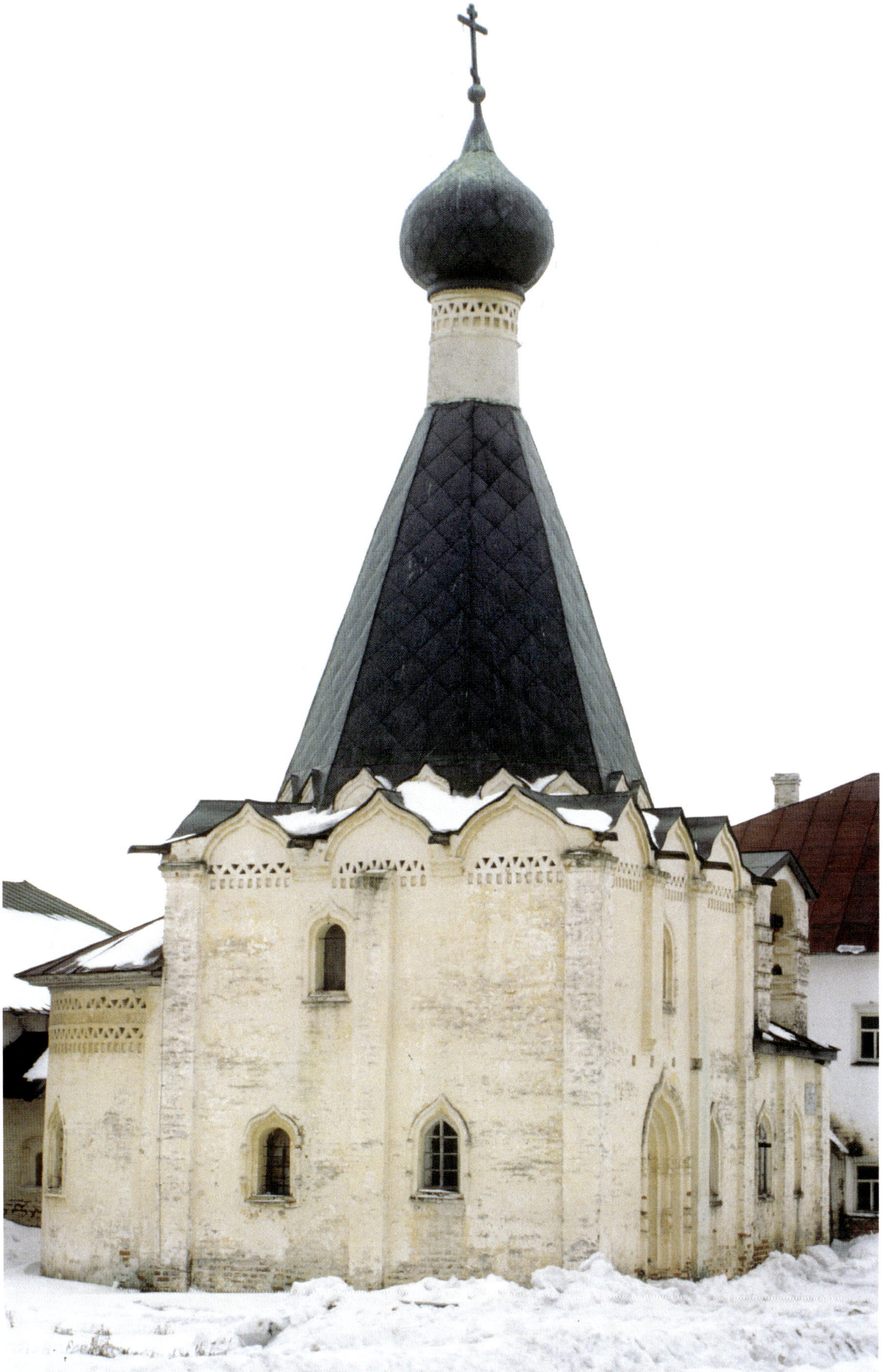

KIRILLOV. Infirmary Church of St. Evfimy, St. Kirill-Belozersky Monastery. Church built in 1653.
Northwest view. Photograph: April 1, 2001.

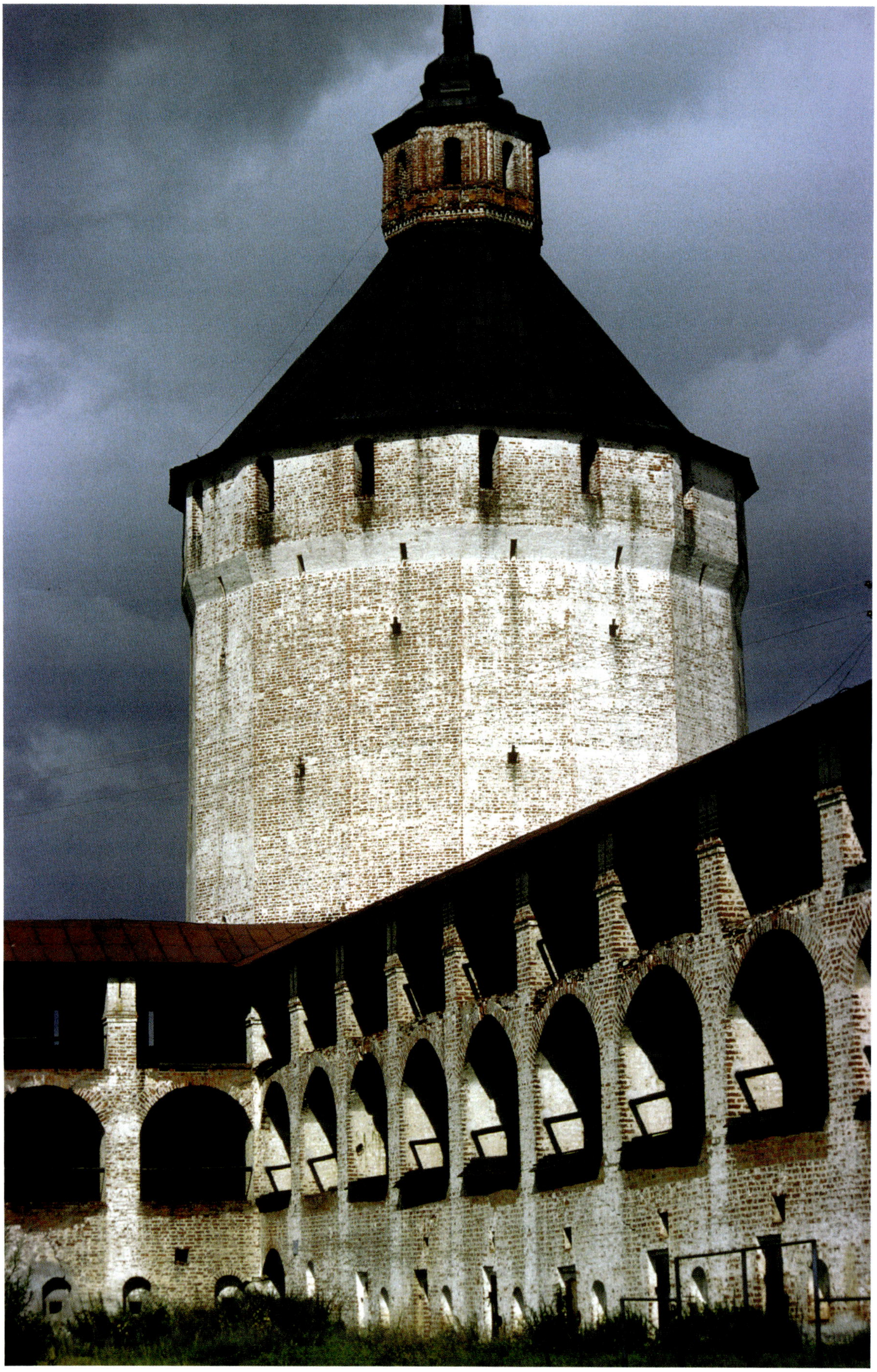

KIRILLOV. Ferapontov (Moscow) Tower, St. Kirill-Belozersky Monastery, northeast view. Tower built in 1660, walls during the following decade. Photograph: August 8, 1991.

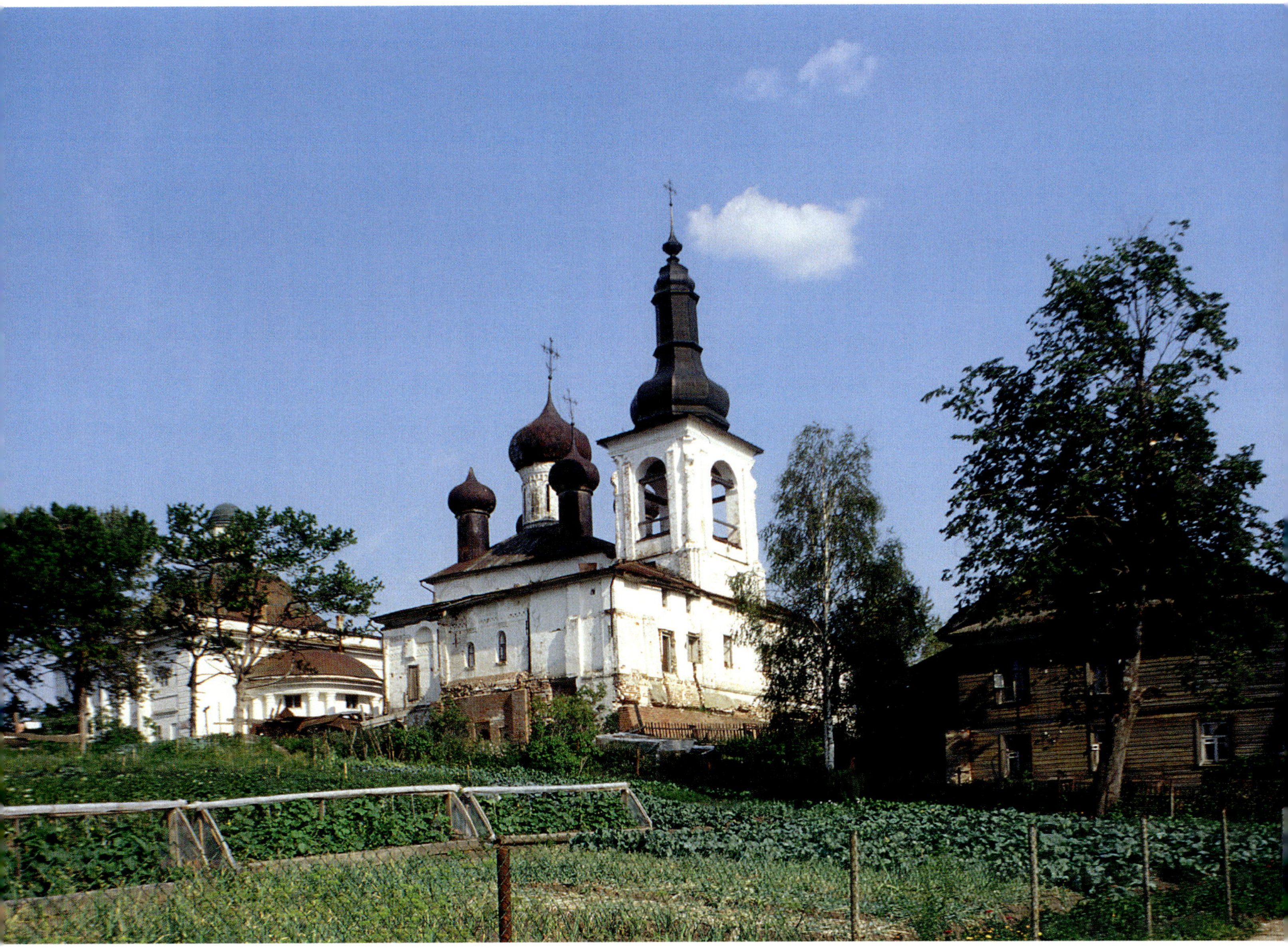

GORITSY. Bell tower and Cathedral of the Resurrection, Goritsky Resurrection Convent, northwest view. Cathedral built in 1544, with bell tower added in the eighteenth century. Left background: Trinity Cathedral (mid-nineteenth century). Photograph: July 14, 1999.

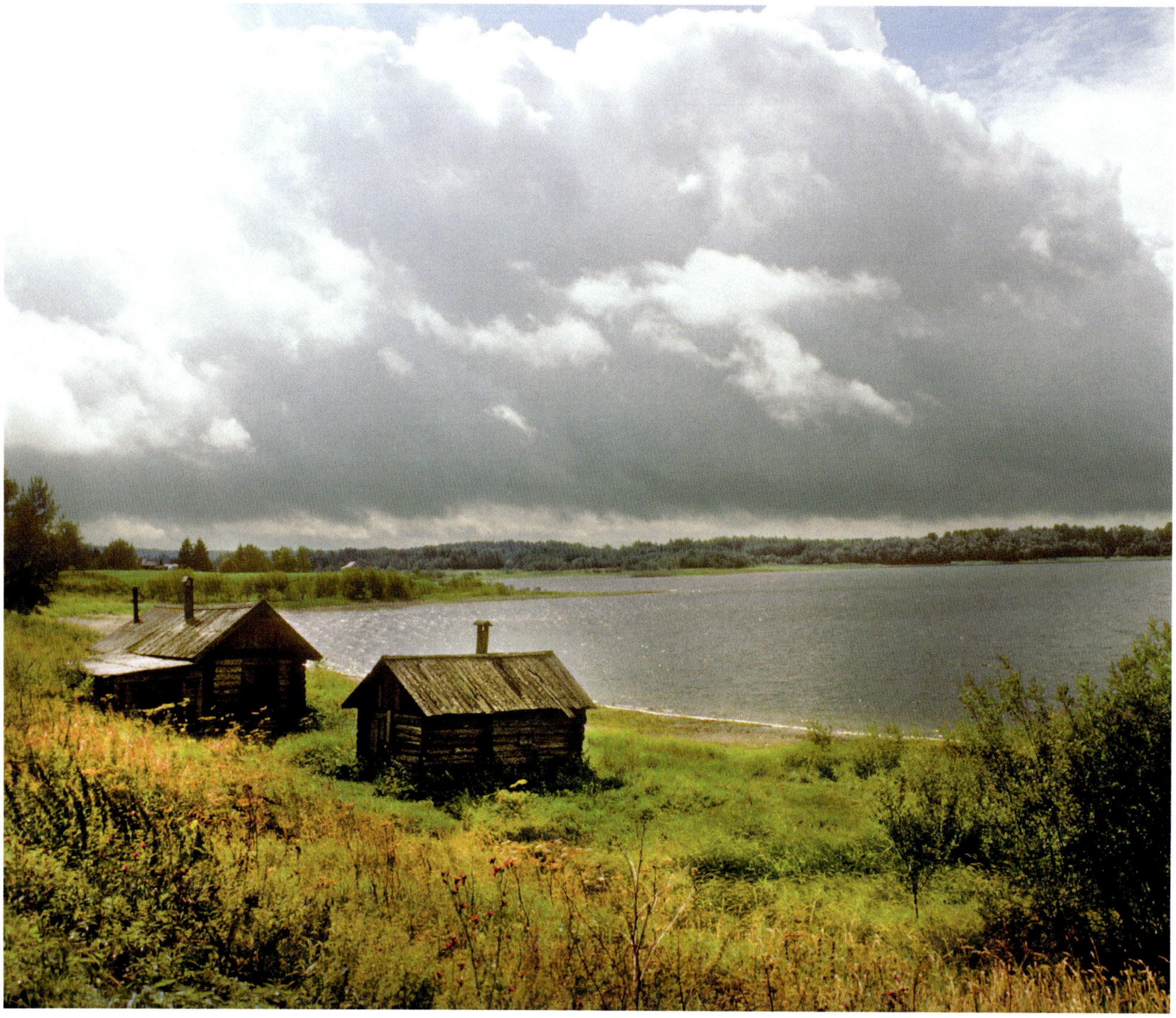

FERAPONTOVO. Log bathhouses on the shore of Lake Borodava. Photograph: August 10, 1995.

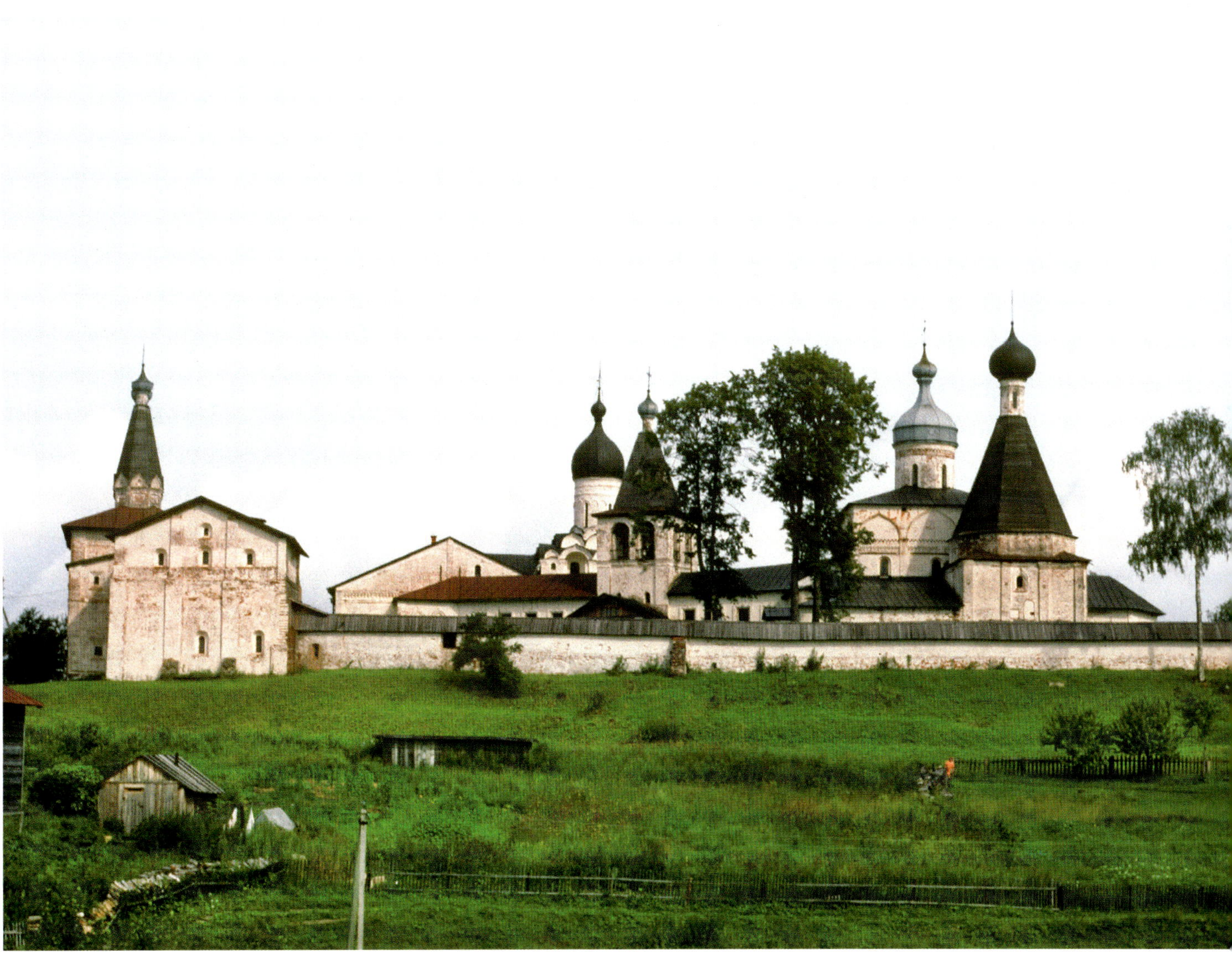

FERAPONTOVO. Ferapontov Monastery, south view across the small Paska River. From left: Gate Churches of the Epiphany and St. Ferapont (1649); refectory and Church of the Annunciation (1530–31); bell tower; Cathedral of the Nativity of the Virgin (1490); Church of St. Martinian (1640–41). Photograph: July 31, 1996.

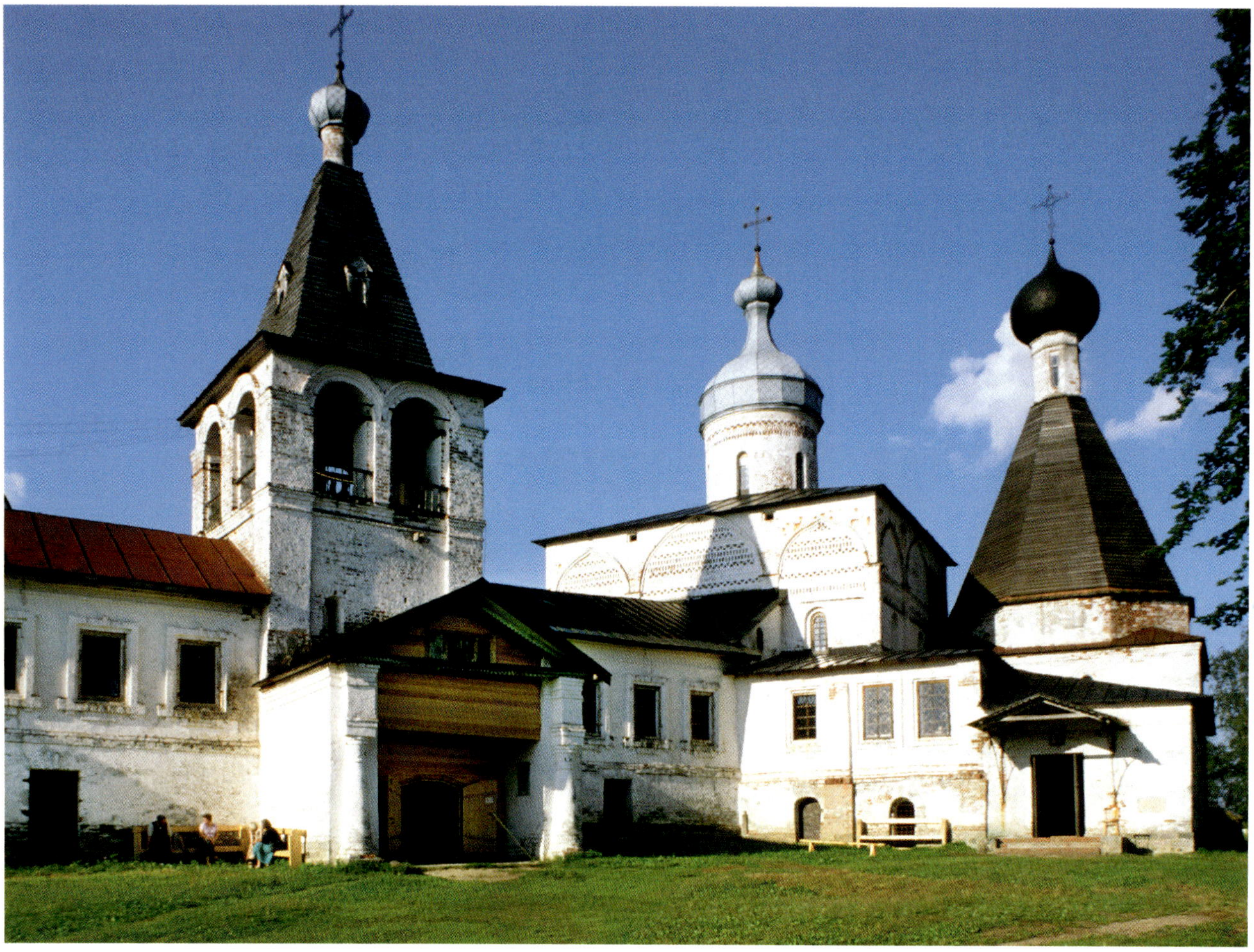

FERAPONTOV MONASTERY. From left: bell tower, Cathedral of the Nativity of the Virgin (1490), Church of St. Martinian (1640–41), southwest view. Photograph: August 2, 1998.

FERAPONTOV MONASTERY, Cathedral of the Nativity of the Virgin, interior, view northwest with northwest pier. Fresco of Christ Pantokrator in dome. Frescoes painted in 1502 by Dionisy and sons. Photograph: June 1, 2014.

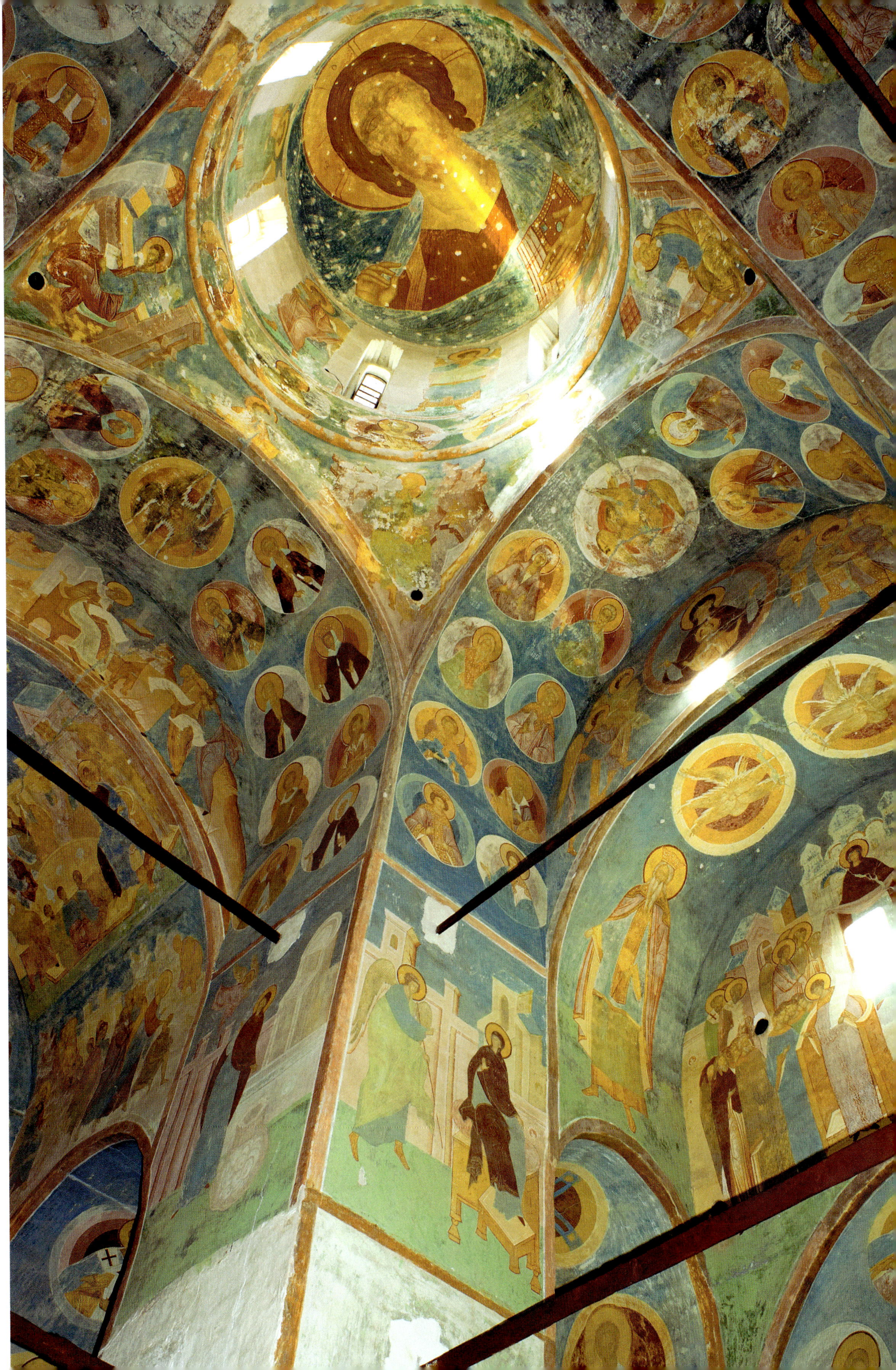

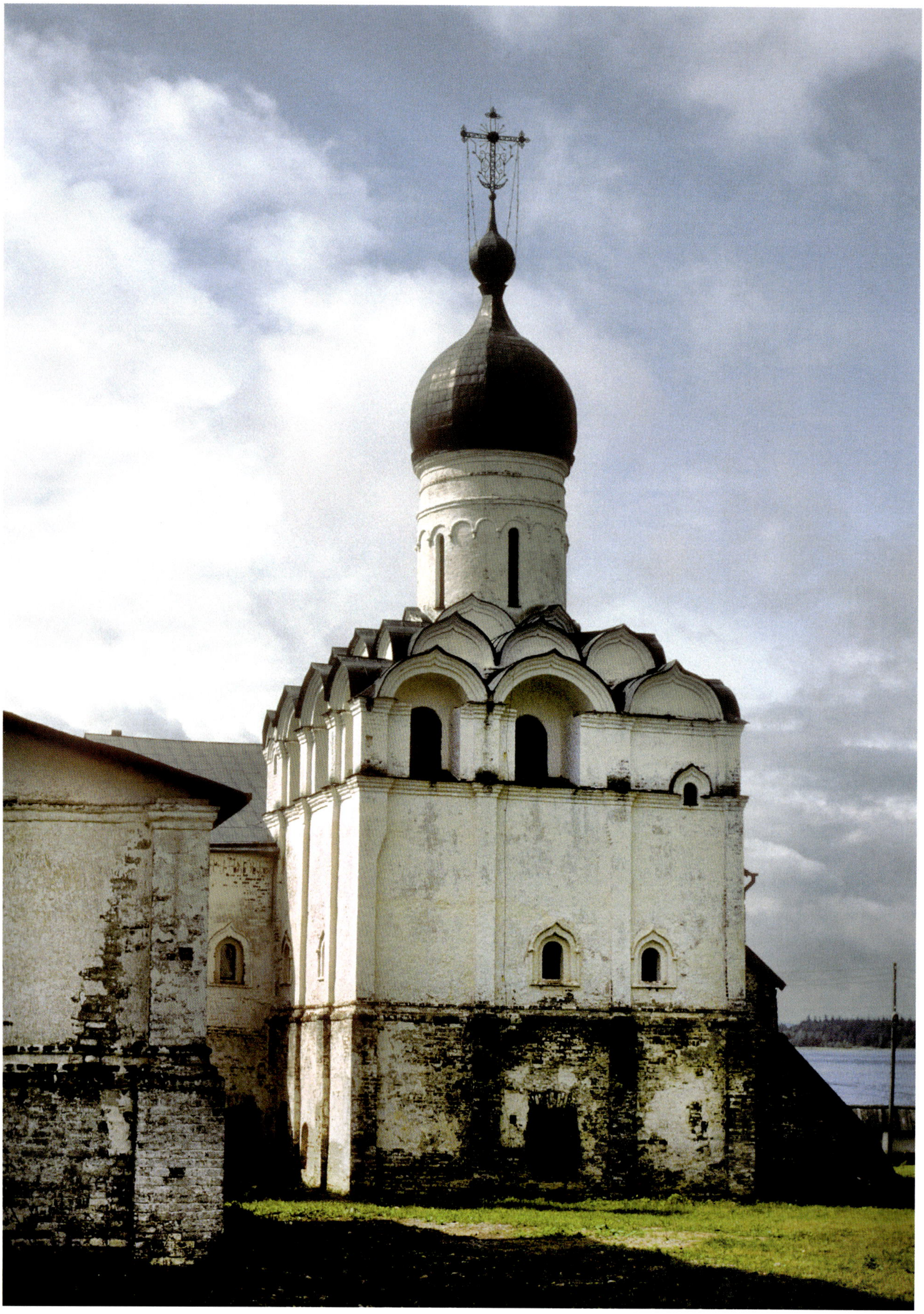

FERAPONTOV MONASTERY, refectory and Church of the Annunciation, east view.
Church built in 1530–31. Photograph: August 10, 1995.

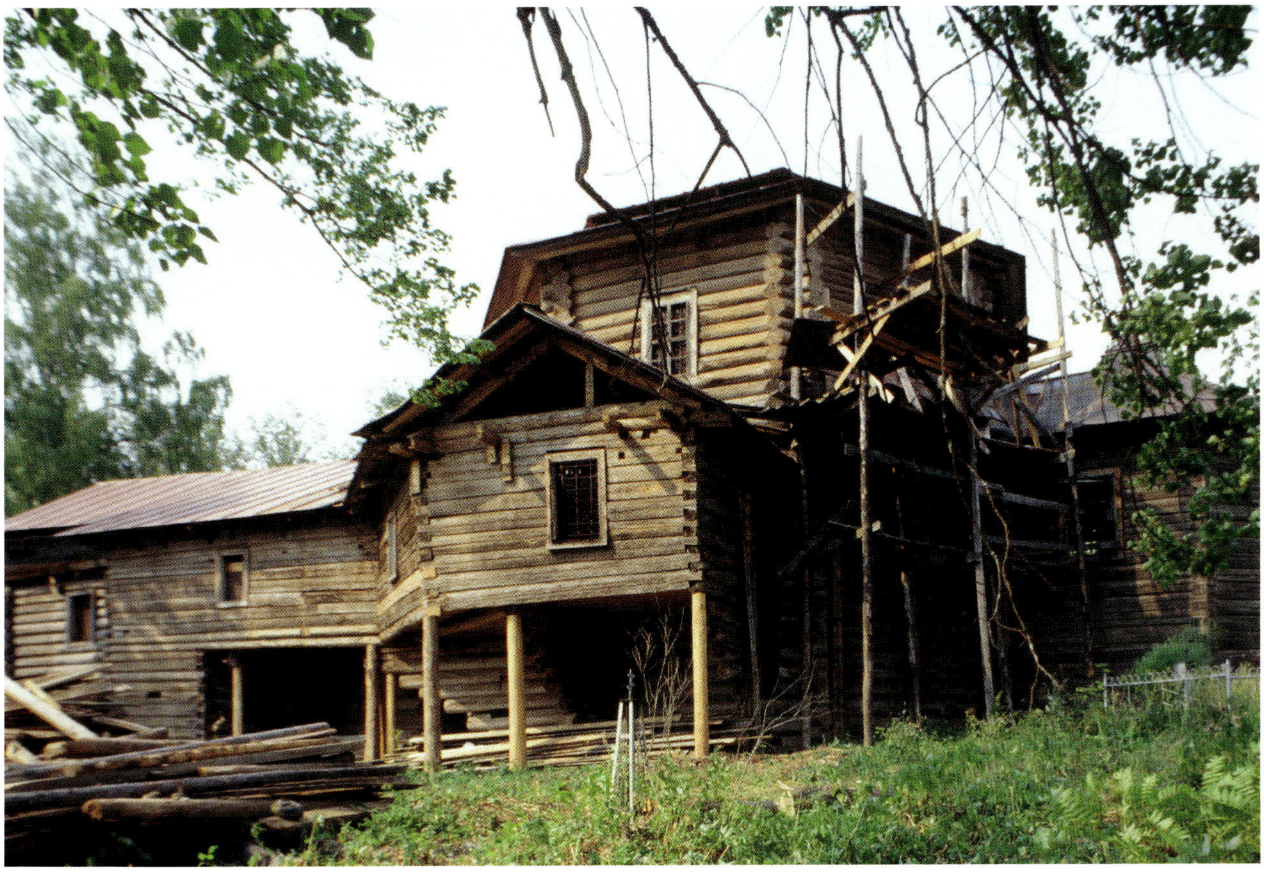

TSYPINO. Wooden Church of Elijah the Prophet. Built in mid-eighteenth century, the upper part of the abandoned church collapsed in the 1960s. This south view shows the structure as the plot was being cleared for a possible restoration, which began in 2003. Photograph: July 15, 1999.

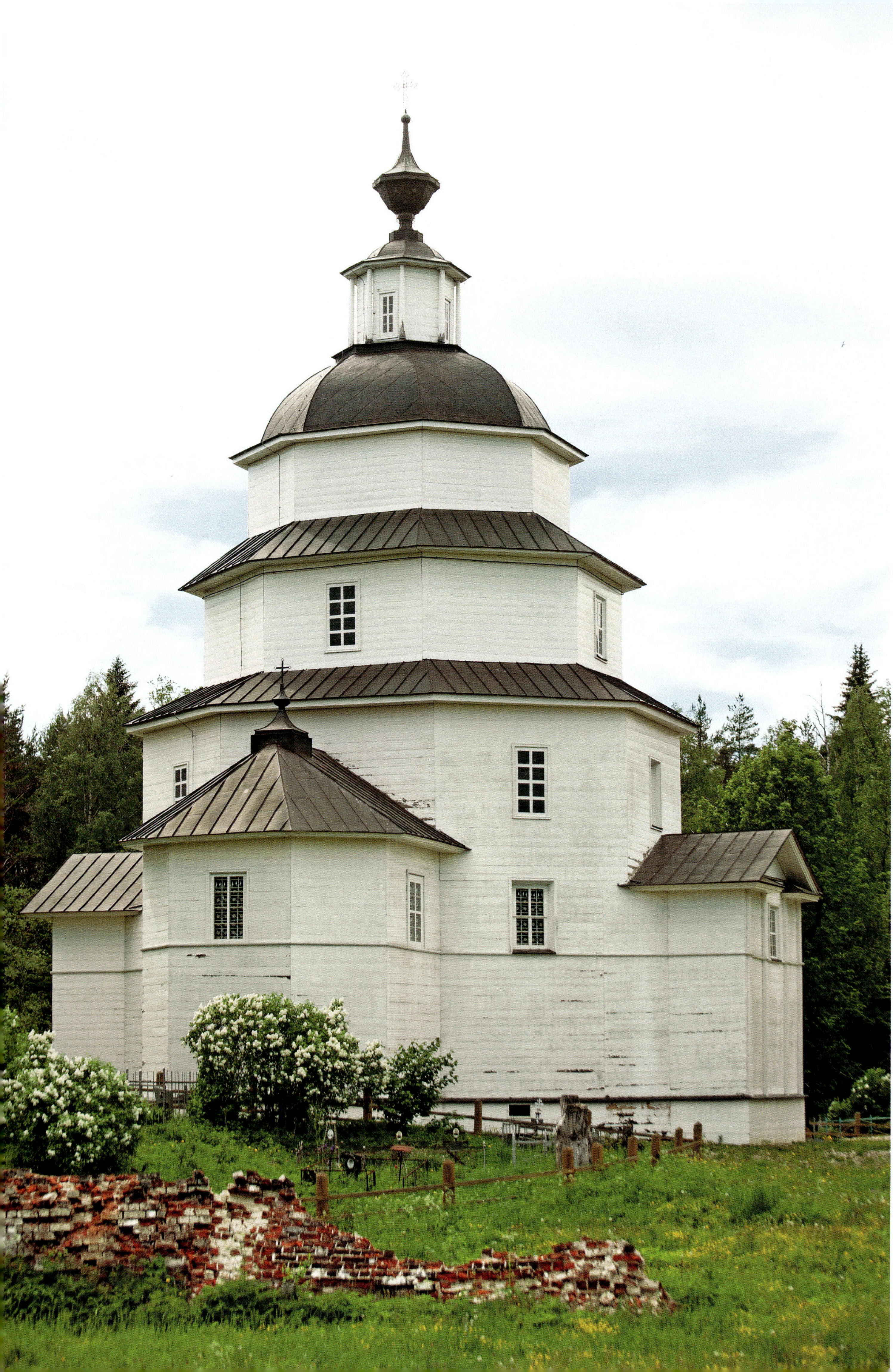

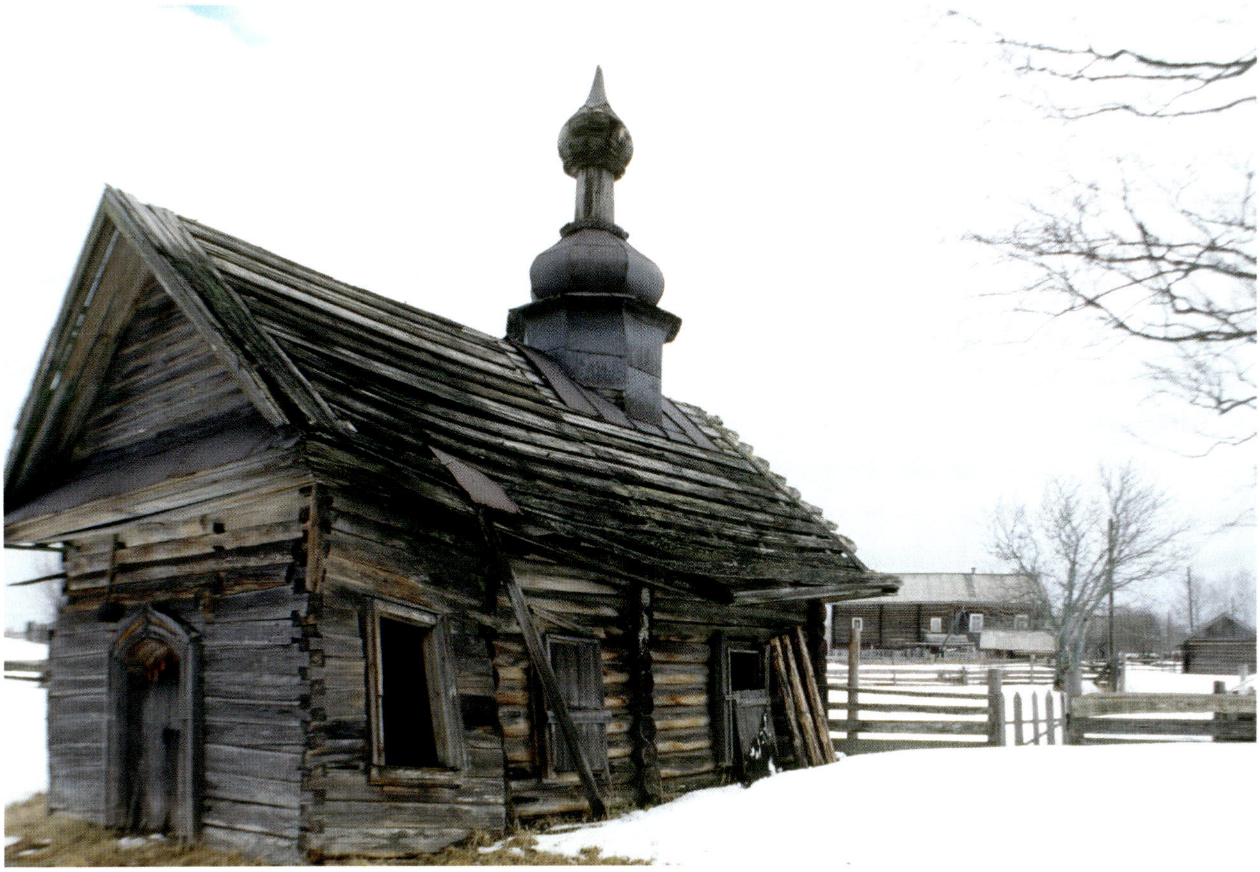

NEFEDOVSKAIA. Nineteenth-century wooden chapel, southwest view. Photograph: April 2, 2001.

TSYPINO. Wooden Church of Elijah the Prophet. This east view shows the church after restoration completed in 2010 by Alexander Popov, the leading Russian specialist in the restoration of wooden churches. Other examples of his work photographed in this book include the church at Saminsky Pogost and at Verkhniaia Uftiuga. Photograph: June 1, 2014.

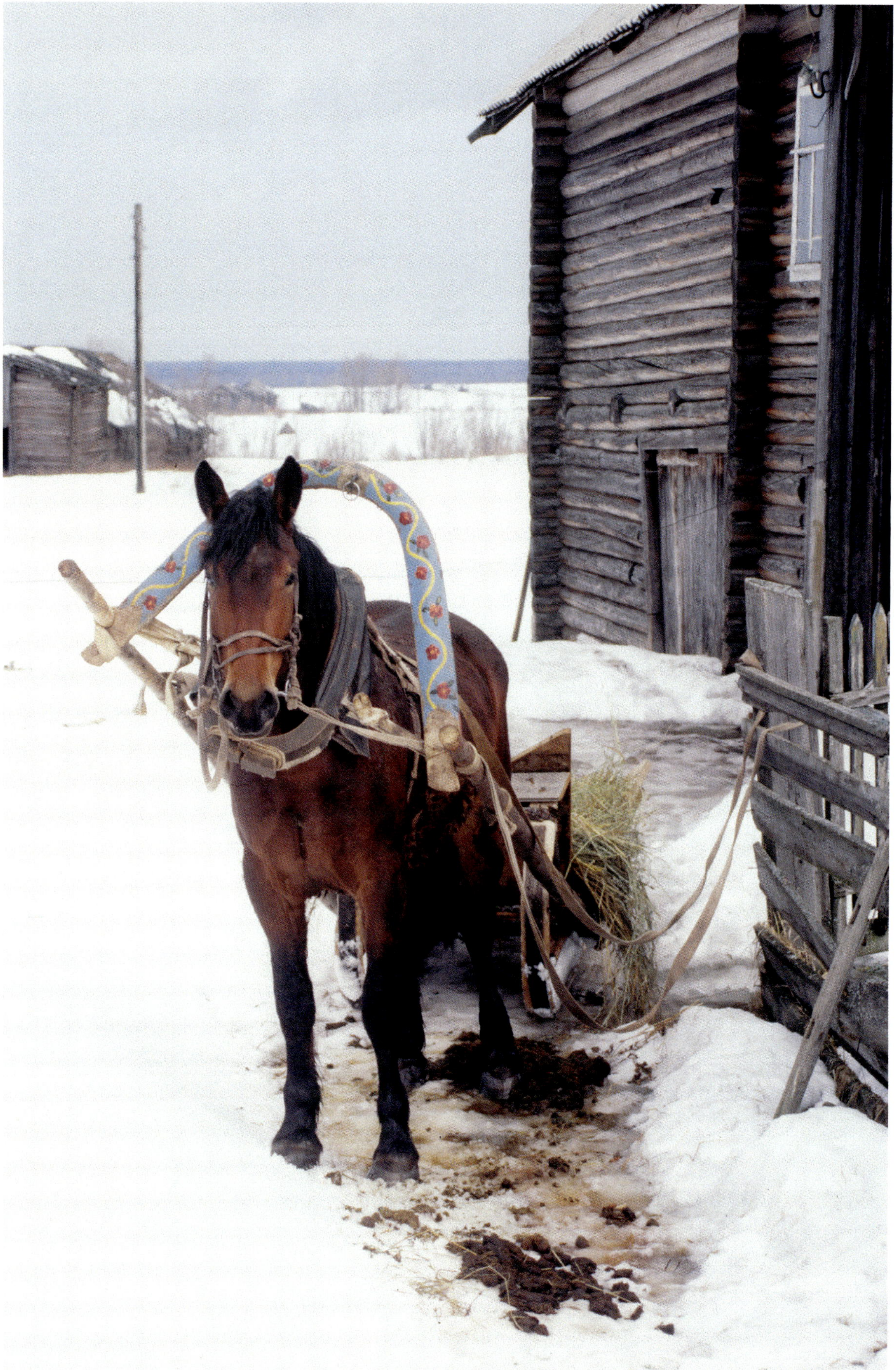

ANTSIFEROVSKAIA. Horse with painted harness next to log house and barn. Photograph: April 2, 2001.

POPOVKA-KALIKINSKAIA. Church of the Nativity of the Virgin, southeast view. Built in 1783.
Already with a visible lean, the church collapsed in 2002. Photograph: April 2, 2001.

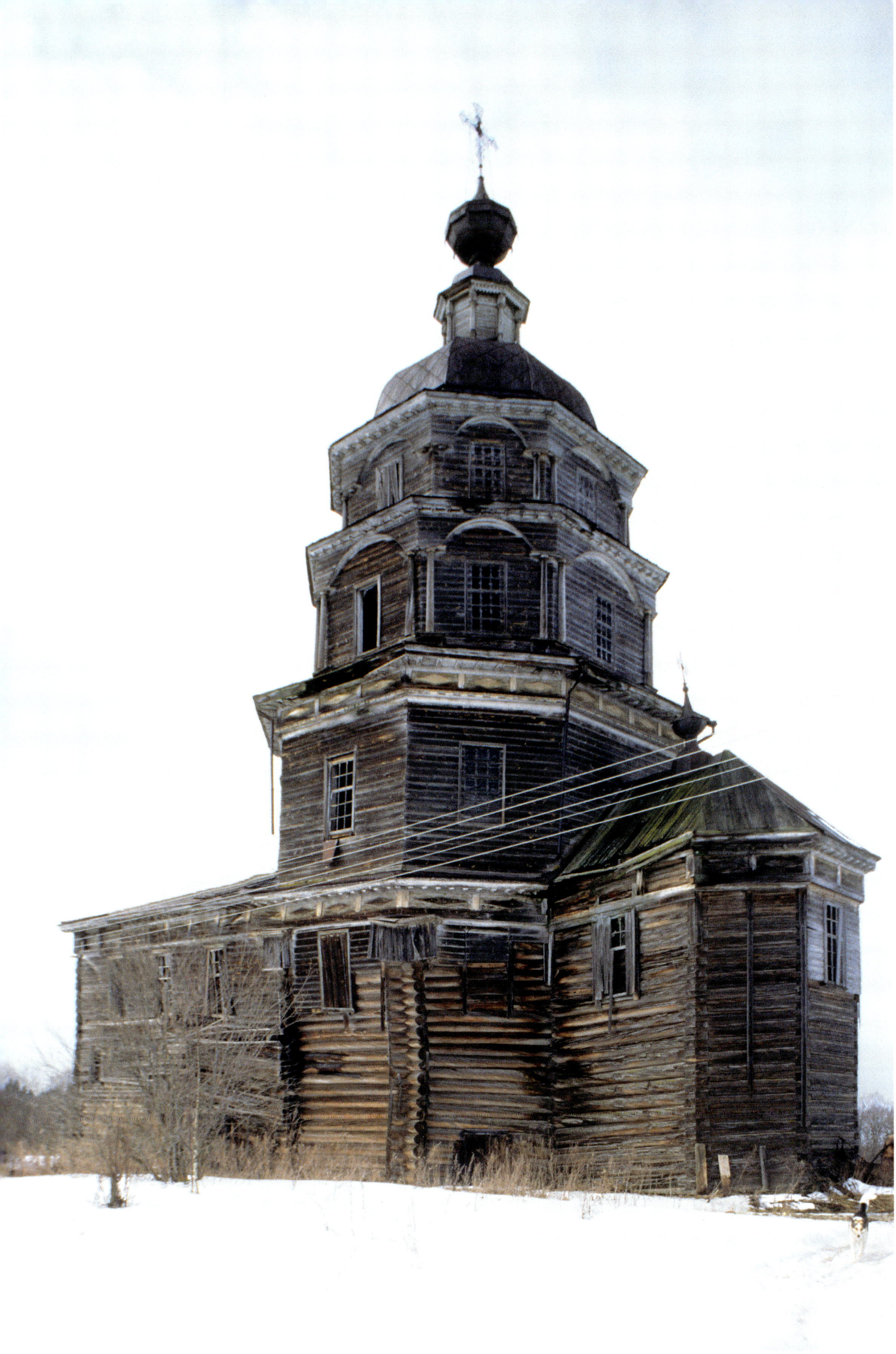

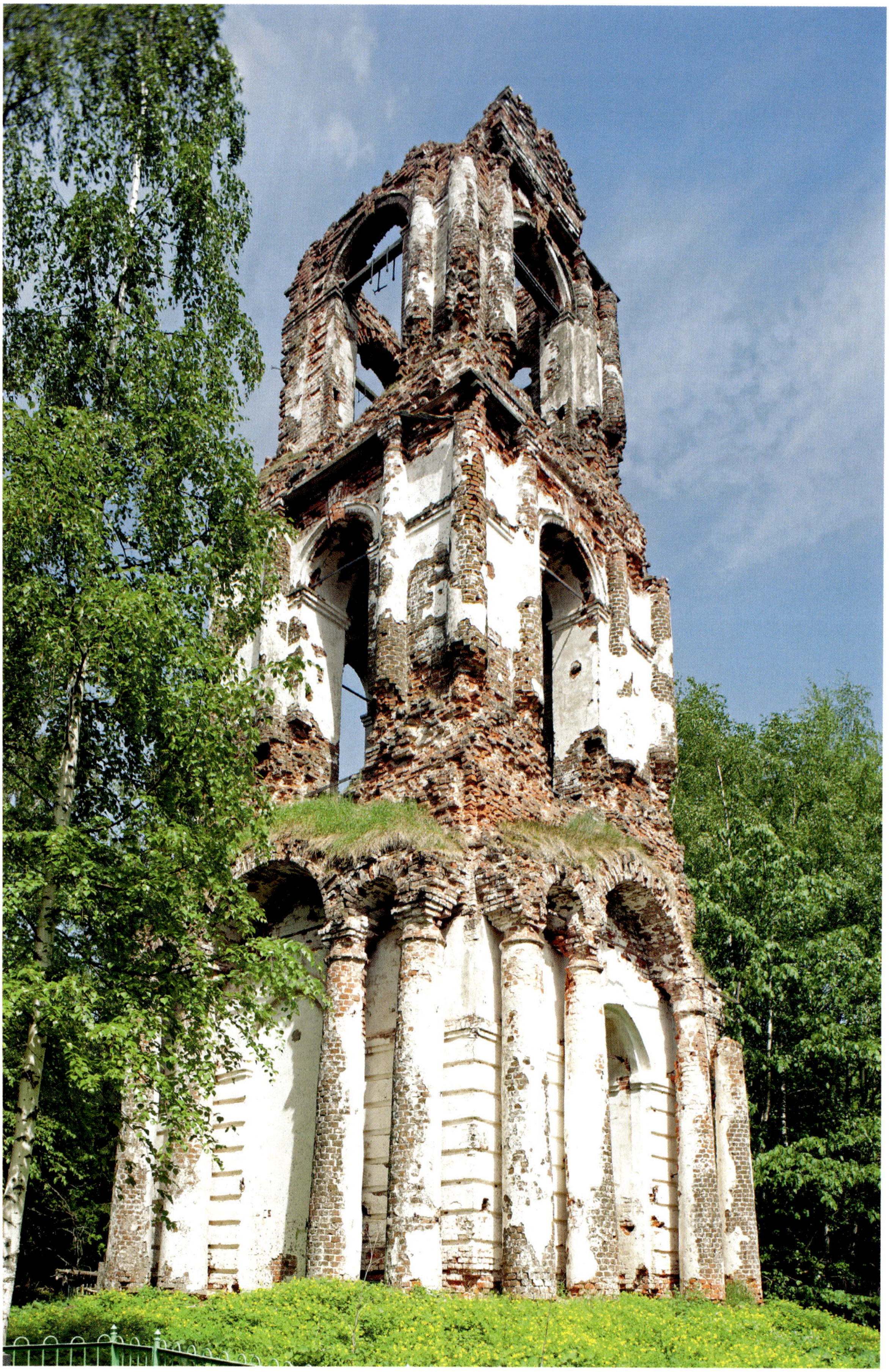

PRECHISTOE (Chud Pogost). Bell tower near ruins of Church of the Nativity of the Virgin, built between 1885 and 1893. The church was abandoned during the Soviet period, but the surrounding cemetery has continued to be maintained (top of painted grave railing visible). Photograph: June 3, 2014.

THREE *Kargopol and Its Surrounding Villages*

KARGOPOL ON LAKE LACHA

Among the many treasures of the Russian North, one of the richest is the town of Kargopol, located on Lake Lacha in the southwestern part of Arkhangelsk province. This small regional center of some twelve thousand souls was founded perhaps as early as the eleventh century. The town's numerous churches are reminders of its former wealth from the sixteenth until the nineteenth centuries, when it was part of a strategic trading route along the Onega River to the White Sea.

Kargopol's historic core approximates its boundaries in the sixteenth century, and one of its charms is the concentration of museums and architectural landmarks within an easily accessible area. The town follows a regular grid plan dating from the time of Catherine the Great, with blocks of one- and two-storied log houses, most of which are covered with plank siding. The windows display elaborately carved frames, and the eaves often have decorative cornices. In this town of merchants, craftsmen, clerics, and clerks, the carved decoration of wooden houses reflected a modest prosperity and way of life deeply rooted in tradition.

As one strolls through little streets of wooden houses, the town's dominant landmark comes easily into view: a large bell tower built in the late eighteenth century near the Cathedral of the Nativity of Christ. The main part of the cathedral itself was built of local limestone in 1552–62. With the town's revival after a devastating fire in 1765, the area around the Nativity Cathedral was cleared to form the New Marketplace, bounded in the northeast by the Church of the Nativity of John the Baptist (1740–51). The northwest part of the cathedral square was completed by the Church of the Presentation of the Virgin, built in 1802 in an archaic style.

On the eastern part of town, near the old earthen fortress, stands the large limestone Church of the Resurrection, which dates from the end of the seventeenth century in a style reminiscent of Russian cathedrals two centuries earlier. Nearby is Trinity Church, begun in 1790 and completed in 1802 in an unusual neo-Byzantine style.

The western side of Kargopol contains another group of temples, including the Church of the Annunciation, completed in 1692. Also built of local limestone, this imposing structure has tall windows framed with elaborately carved ornamental detail. Next to it is the whitewashed cube of the eighteenth-century St. Nicholas Church, missing four of its original five cupolas. These churches formed the Old Marketplace, which is further enhanced by the lyrical beauty of the Church of the Nativity of the Virgin, completed in 1680 (now one of the town's two functioning Orthodox churches). On the elevated western edge of town stands the latest of Kargopol's churches to have survived: the Church of Saints Zosima and Savvaty, completed in 1819 for a visit by Tsar Alexander I.

Like other ancient Russian towns bypassed by railroad construction, Kargopol sank into a deep torpor at the turn of the twentieth century. Despite the destruction and vandalism of a number of its churches in the Soviet era, Kargopol has succeeded to a rare degree in retaining the aura of its past.

THE VILLAGE OF LIADINY AND ITS CHURCHES

The villages of the Kargopol region have been an extraordinary source of traditional Russian art and architecture. Against formidable odds, there are villages where monuments of wooden architecture still stand despite their vulnerability to the elements and human carelessness. Yet each decade brings new losses. One of the most significant examples of that loss is the village of Liadiny, some forty kilometers from Kargopol. Although its population varies slightly between summer and winter, this hamlet of about seventy souls centered around an extraordinary architectural ensemble located on the territory of an ancient cemetery (pogost).

The Liadiny ensemble consisted of three parts: the Church of the Intercession with its soaring "tent tower" (completed by 1761; destroyed by fire in 2013); the nearby Church of the Epiphany (1793), crowned with a panoply of cupolas; and a large bell tower built in 1820. Such three-part ensembles of churches were once common in the northern farming communities, but most have long since disappeared — the villages as well as the churches.

The cluster of three derives from medieval towns such as Yaroslavl, which often had a large unheated "summer" church paired with a smaller church that could be heated for worship in the winter. At Liadiny, the Church of the Intercession had an altar on the compact ground floor that could be used in the winter. The construction of the Epiphany Church three decades later provided a larger space for worship during the long winters.

In both summer and winter, sun or windblown snow, the form of the Intercession Church produced an unforgettable visual impact. Sheathed in darkened plank siding, the structure of stout pine logs ascends to a cupola and cross at its high peak. On the interior, the ground-level chapel enclosed two massive log columns that support the floor of the main worship space above. A narrow staircase ascended to this main space, which served as a vestibule with clean whitewashed walls. All the greater was the effect of the brightly colored icon screen and the painted ceiling, or "heaven" (nebo), pitched over the worship space in an ingenious combination of art and architecture.

These "heavens" are a distinctive feature of northern Russian log churches. They have a polygonal form segmented by flat beams extending from the top of the walls to an elevated ring in the ceiling center. The beams incline upward and create a frame that is self-supporting between the walls and the ring where they meet at the center. The painted panels are in the shape of narrow triangles and are laid upon the frame without fasteners. Tension and gravity keep the panels in place.

The Kargopol area has larger examples of such painted ceilings, in particular the one in the Epiphany Church at Oshevensk (see following). But the "heaven" at Liadiny was the brighter work of art. Its twelve long triangular panels depict the four Evangelists (Matthew, Mark, Luke, and John) and seven of the eight archangels: Michael, Gabriel, Raphael, Uriel, Jehudiel, Varakhiel, and Selafiel. The main panel above the center of the icon screen depicts the Crucifixion, with Mary and other figures at the foot of the cross and Jerusalem in the background.

The archangels Michael and Gabriel were painted with an especially rich aura of beauty. Archangel Raphael is accompanied with the boy Tobias holding his fish—a Jewish legend from the apocryphal Book of Tobit and known in Renaissance painting. Within the central ring is a depiction of the Trinity: Father, Son, and Holy Spirit. The twelve seraphim at the tips of the triangles are painted with appealing female masks. This festive and personal artistic expression has been attributed to an icon painter active in Kargopol in the 1760s.

The adjacent Church of the Epiphany lost most of its interior artwork during the Soviet period. The structure itself is now being repaired under the supervision of the Kargopol Museum, which has saved it from almost certain ruin. The ceiling of its semicircular porch is painted with a starry canopy.

The two churches complement each other perfectly, with the lower silhouette of the "winter" Epiphany Church and its cupolas matched against the daring tower of the Intercession Church. The tall bell tower, with a pitched conical roof over the bell gallery, mediates between the two churches. The entire ensemble overlooks the cemetery crosses.

The Intercession Church was recently consecrated for worship when visits could be arranged with the priest in Kargopol. But on the morning of Sunday, May 5, 2013—Russian Orthodox Easter—disaster struck. By all available evidence, it seems that a strong lightning strike overwhelmed a lightning rod and started a blaze at the crown of the Intercession Church. Shortly thereafter the church was completely destroyed, with no artwork salvaged. So intense was the fire that the nearby bell tower was also consumed by flames. Only the Epiphany Church—recently restored, but with no original art—was saved through prompt efforts. That is no small consolation, but the unique treasure of the Intercession Church is forever lost.

For many decades when the Liadiny church ensemble was closed, there was another shrine, a tiny log chapel dedicated apparently to St. George and closely guarded for worship in the hamlet of Kiseleva (part of Liadiny). It, too, had its painted ceiling, and the interior was draped with votive offerings of clothing, part of an age-old folk tradition. To be admitted to the chapel was a sign of great trust.

Many of the sturdy, beautifully crafted wooden houses in Liadiny have been abandoned in a pattern of population loss long typical of the northern countryside. Life here is difficult, yet dairy farming is still possible. Despite tragic losses, the village survives.

THE VILLAGE OF OSHEVENSK AND ITS CHURCHES

Although a number of the region's architectural landmarks now exist only in photographs, there are villages within a one-hundred-kilometer radius of Kargopol that seem frozen in time. The largest and best preserved is Oshevensk, forty kilometers northwest of Kargopol on the Churyega River. On the way from Kargopol, the small road winds through fields and woods before approaching the river at a village fittingly named Reka ("river").

Near the bridge over the Churyega stands the brick Church of St. George (1890s) with its five cupolas and a bell tower. Ransacked in the 1930s and converted to farm storage, the church has been gradually restored, with the main altar reconsecrated in 2004. Reka also has appealing examples of wooden houses with painted eaves and gables.

The approach to Oshevensk is marked on the left by the remaining brick and limestone structures at the Monastery of St. Alexander Oshevensky, established by the monk Alexander in 1453 — the year Constantinople fell to the Ottoman Turks. Its founder was born with the name Aleksei to the family of a prosperous peasant, Nikifor Osheven, who encouraged his son's spiritual education.

Tonsured and given the name Alexander at St. Cyril Belozersk Monastery, the young monk followed his father's move to rich lands west of Kargopol that were owned by Novgorod, medieval Russia's leading commercial city. The monastery became a spiritual center, and Alexander (1427–79) was venerated as a "local saint." Although closed and devastated during the Soviet era, the monastery and its main Church of the Dormition (1707) are once again open for visitors and pilgrims.

Just beyond the monastery, the Churyega River is crossed by a wooden bridge that is itself a work of art. Oshevensk (or Oshevenskoe, as it is officially known) is a relatively large village with some six hundred inhabitants, a number of whom rent houses to summer visitors.

The extended linear form of Oshevensk consists of a cluster of settlements, including three hamlets picturesquely situated along the riverbank. The first hamlet is named Pogost, a name derived from a general term for sacred ground, usually containing a cemetery and church. The church in this hamlet is dedicated to the Epiphany and is one of the most extraordinary combinations of structure and art in the Russian North. Built of sturdy pine logs in 1787, the Epiphany Church culminates in a tall "tent" tower over the octagonal main structure. The church bell tower — octagonal on a square base — stands separately to the north with its own vertical cap. The two complement each other with serene harmony.

But the miracle of this church is the interior, which is one of the largest such spaces among northern log churches. Its icon screen is staggering in its extent, yet few of the icons remain. The church was closed in the 1930s, reopened during the war, and closed again in 1960 during Nikita Khrushchev's "final" campaign against religion. It was reopened for prayer and occasional services in the late 1990s. During this long period, most of the icons were taken.

No less impressive than the icon screen is the painted suspended ceiling, or "heaven," which still has most of its panels intact. The "heaven" at the Epiphany Church is uniquely large, with eighteen panel segments that show various saints, archangels, evangelists, and heavenly forms. The central ring is occupied by an image of Christ.

The main altar (behind the icon screen) is flanked on the northeast and southeast by two enclosed secondary altars that have small variants of the "heaven" painted ceilings. For heated winter worship in this severe climate, a refectory extends from the west of the main structure.

The adjacent hamlets of Pogost and Shiriaikha also have several traditional log houses, some of which have exterior painted decorations. These decorative forms often had symbolic meaning, such as the form of the solar sign.

At the far end of Oshevensk is the hamlet of Niz, whose name indicates its position at the lower end of Oshevensk. It, too, has its jewel, the miniature Chapel of St. George, built in the nineteenth century on a gentle rise as the road enters the village. The chapel has two towers, one of which serves as a belfry. Although chapels do not have altars, the Chapel of St. George has an array of icons displayed throughout the interior. And it has its small painted "heaven" with eight panels. When I visited the chapel in the winter and summer of 1998, the panels were being restored at the Kargopol Museum, and I was able to photograph the supporting structure of the "heaven."

The area north of the Kargopol region also has numerous wooden churches and chapels. Many of them are concentrated in an area around Kenozero Lake, part of the Onega River Basin. The picturesque, unspoiled qualities of the Kenozero region led to the creation of a national park in December 1991. Since that time the painstaking work of preservation, conservation, and integration of local villages into the park structure has become a major enterprise. Of particular interest is the early eighteenth-century Pochozero ensemble of two wooden churches and a bell tower at the village of Filippovskaia. Long under restoration, the ensemble has now regained its former glory, at least on the exterior.

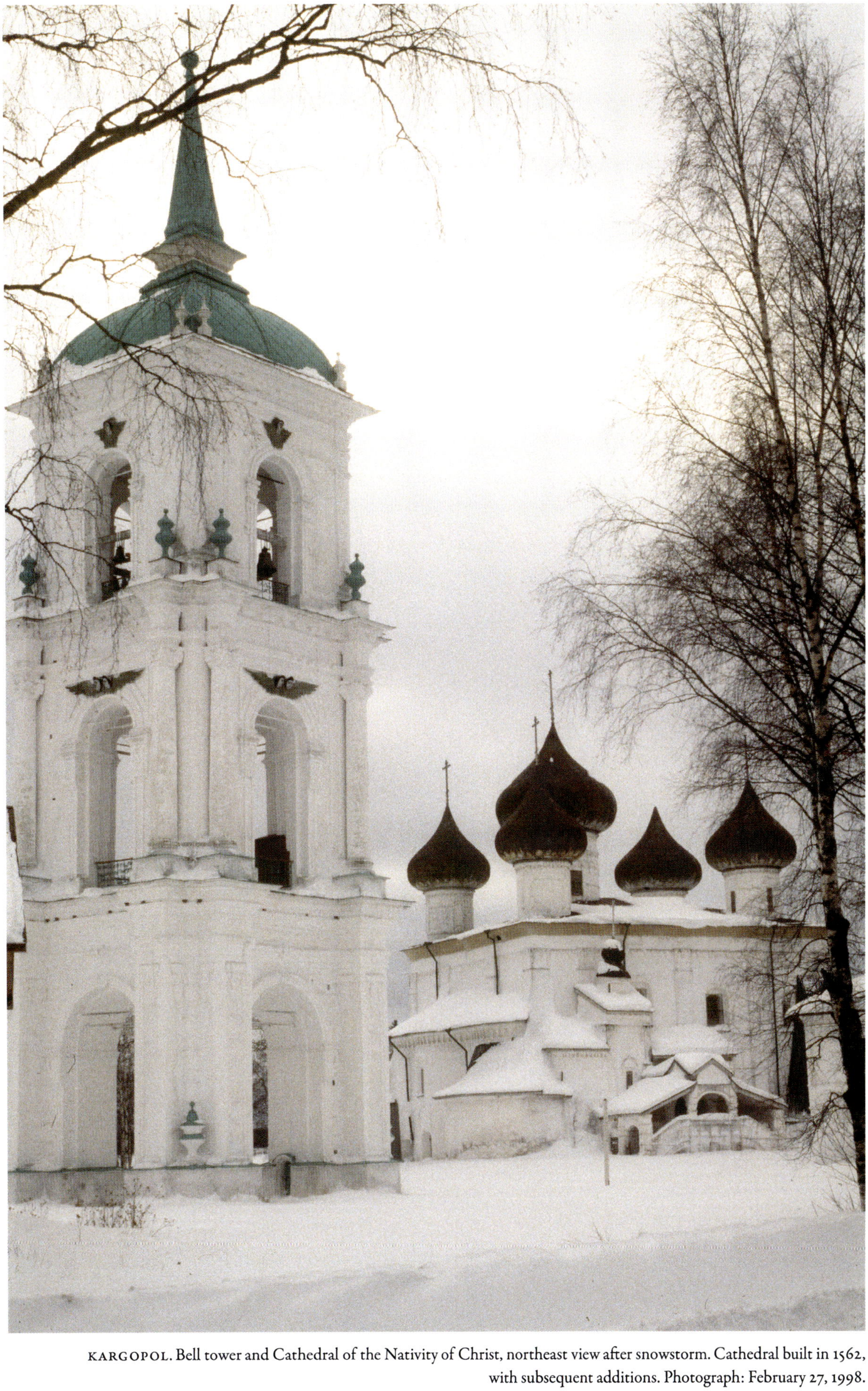

KARGOPOL. Bell tower and Cathedral of the Nativity of Christ, northeast view after snowstorm. Cathedral built in 1562, with subsequent additions. Photograph: February 27, 1998.

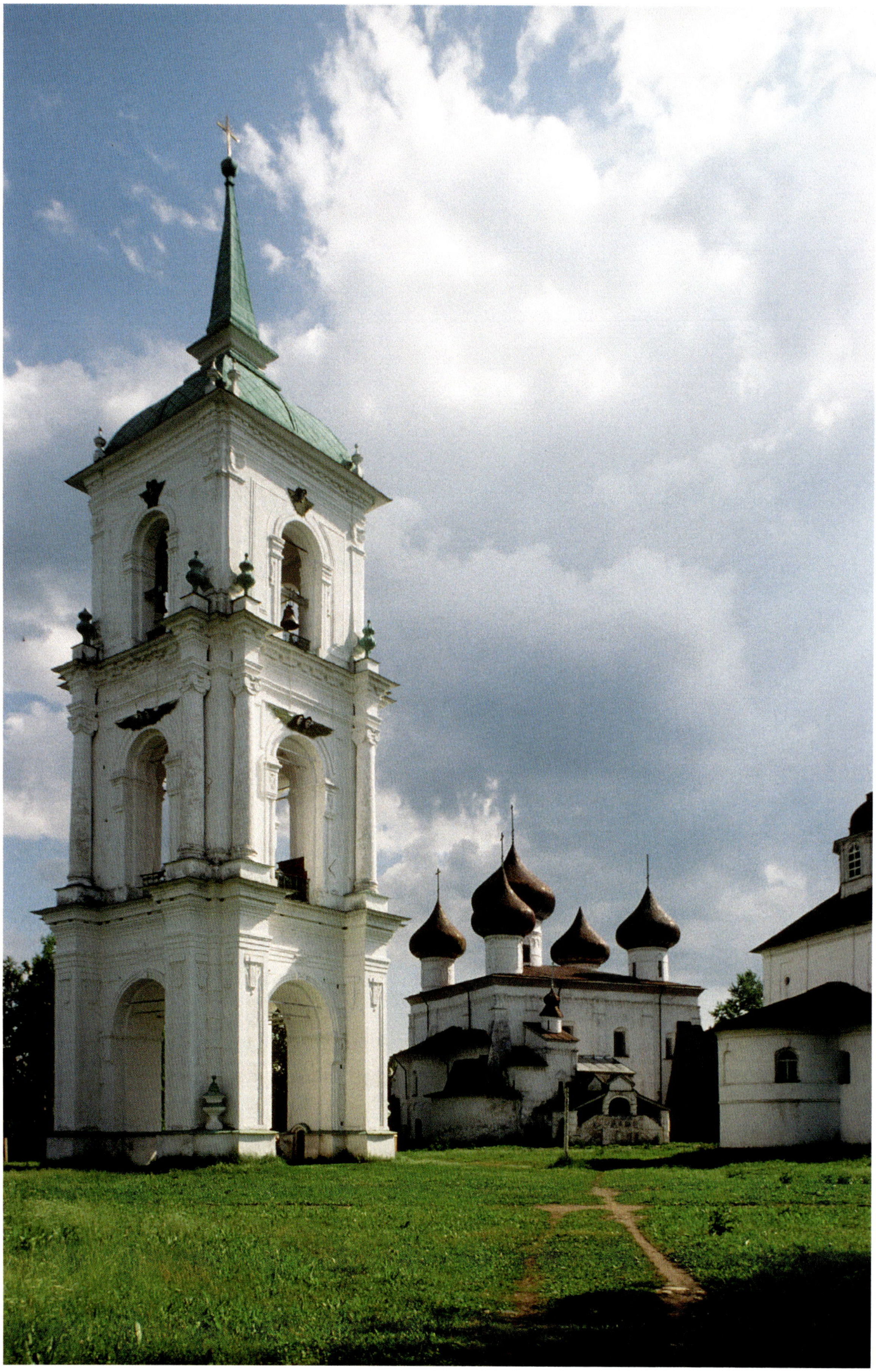

KARGOPOL. Bell tower, Cathedral of the Nativity of Christ and Church of the Presentation (1808), northeast view. Photograph: July 1, 1999.

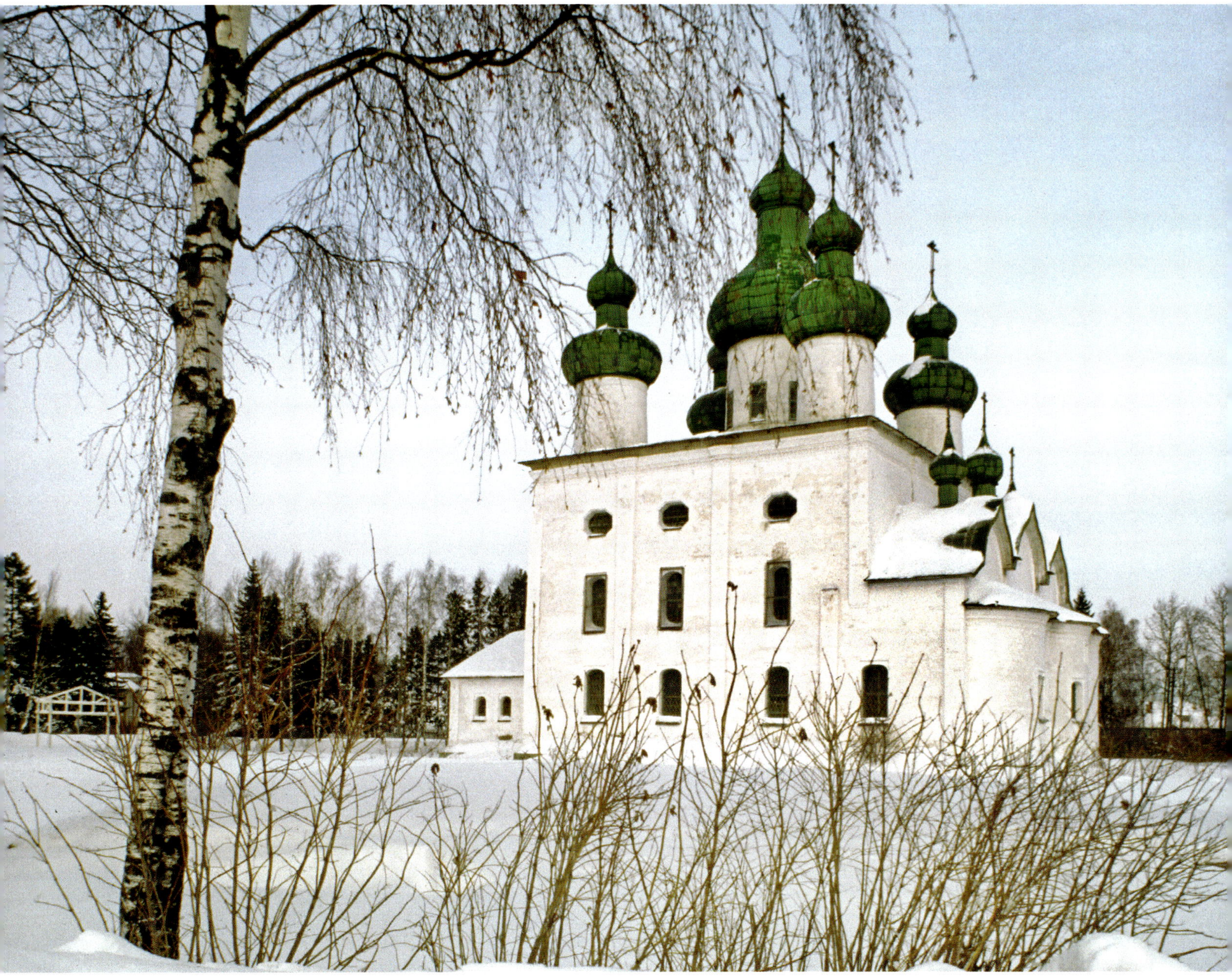

KARGOPOL. Church of the Nativity of John the Baptist, southeast view.
Church built in 1751. Photograph: February 27, 1998.

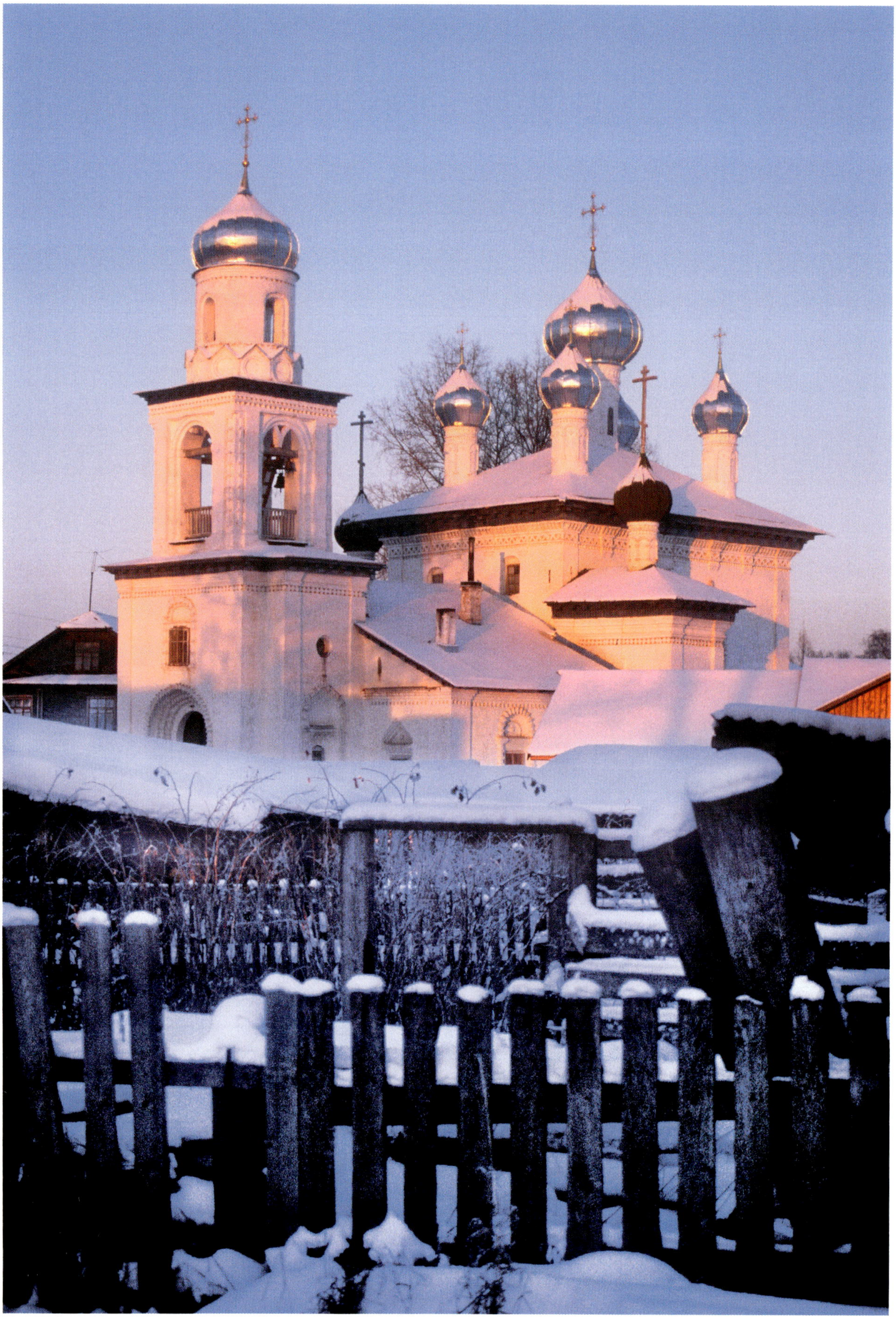

KARGOPOL. Church of the Nativity of the Mother of God, southwest view in light of setting winter sun. Church built in 1680. Photograph: November 25, 1999.

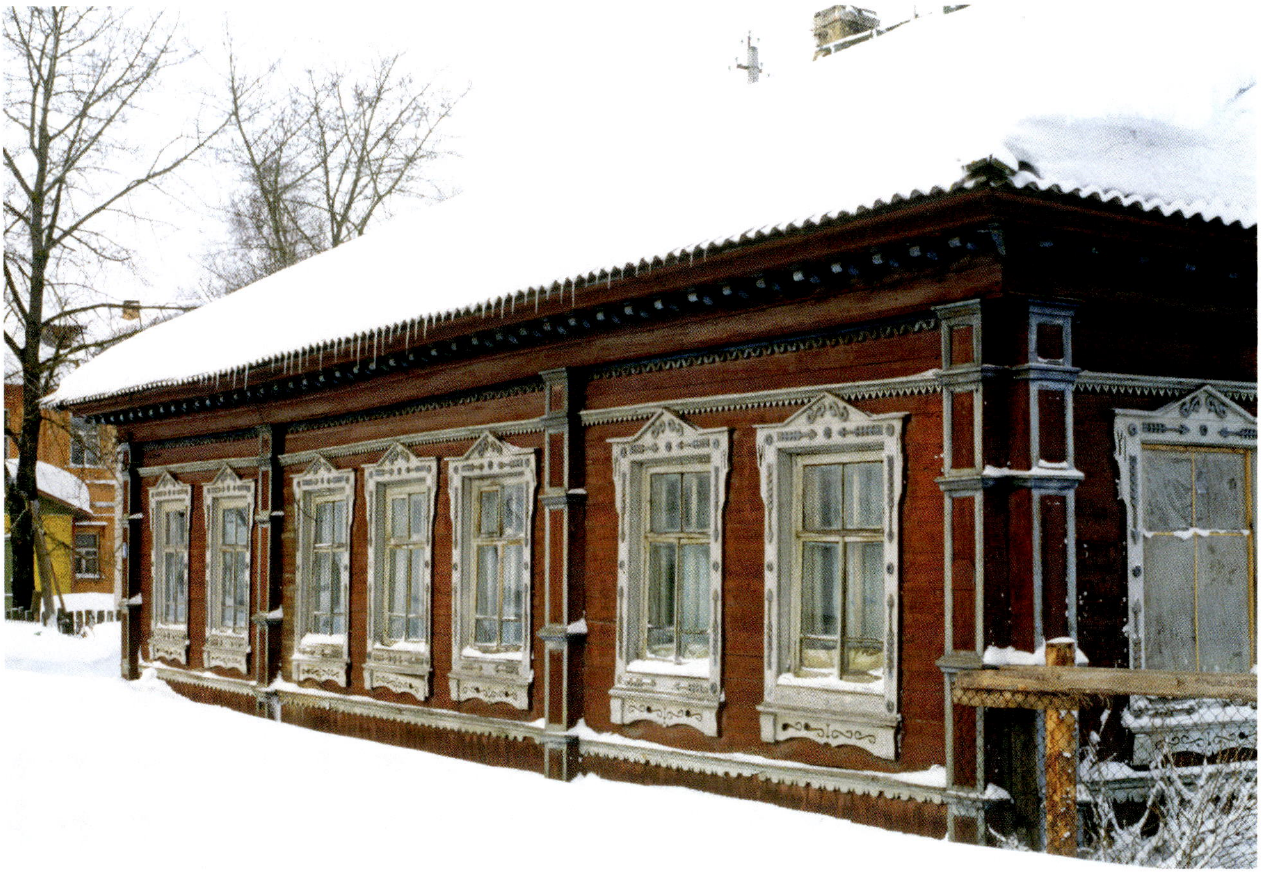

KARGOPOL. Late nineteenth-century wooden house with decorative window surrounds, Zavodskaia Street 3. Photograph: February 27, 1998.

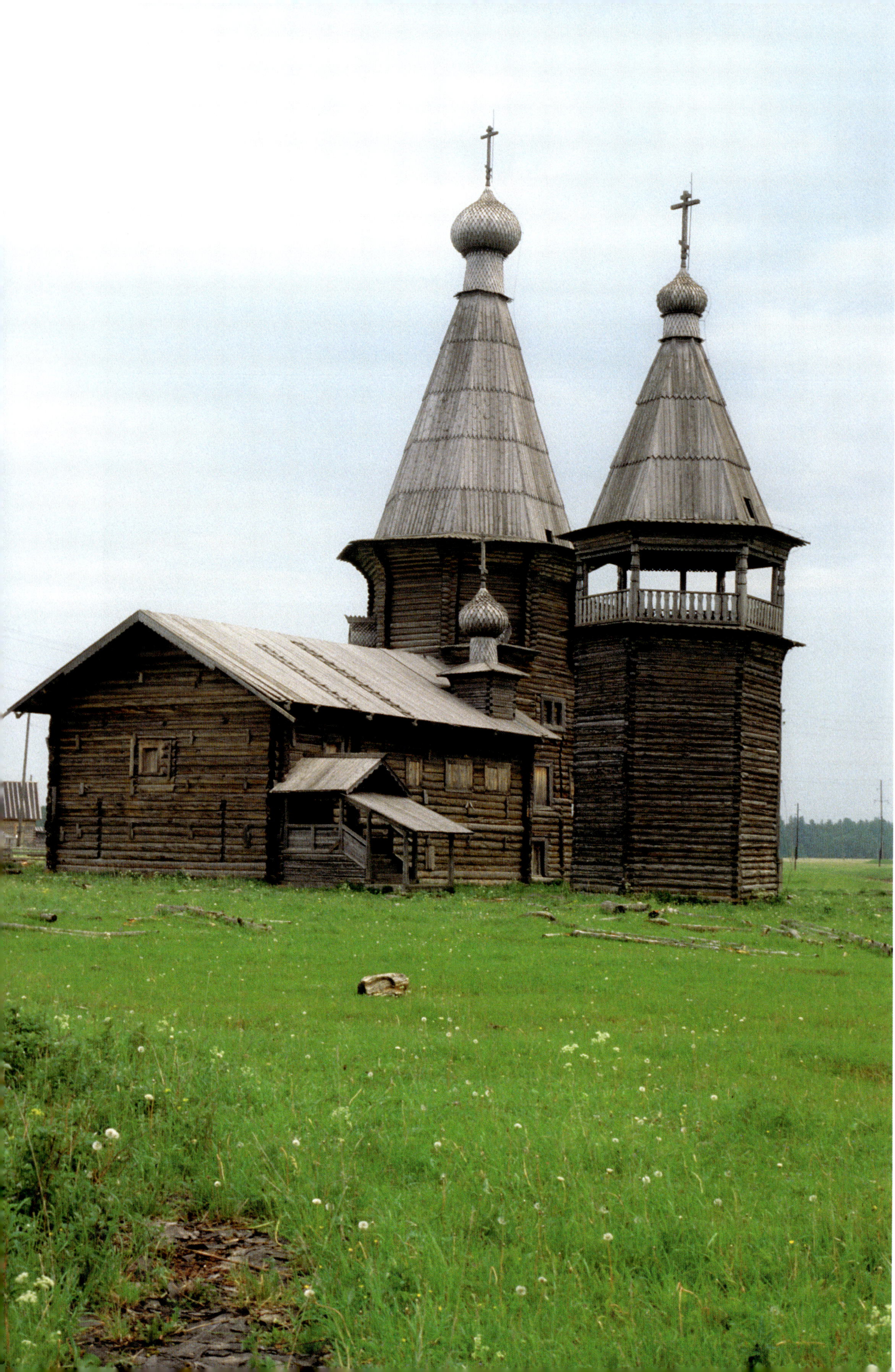

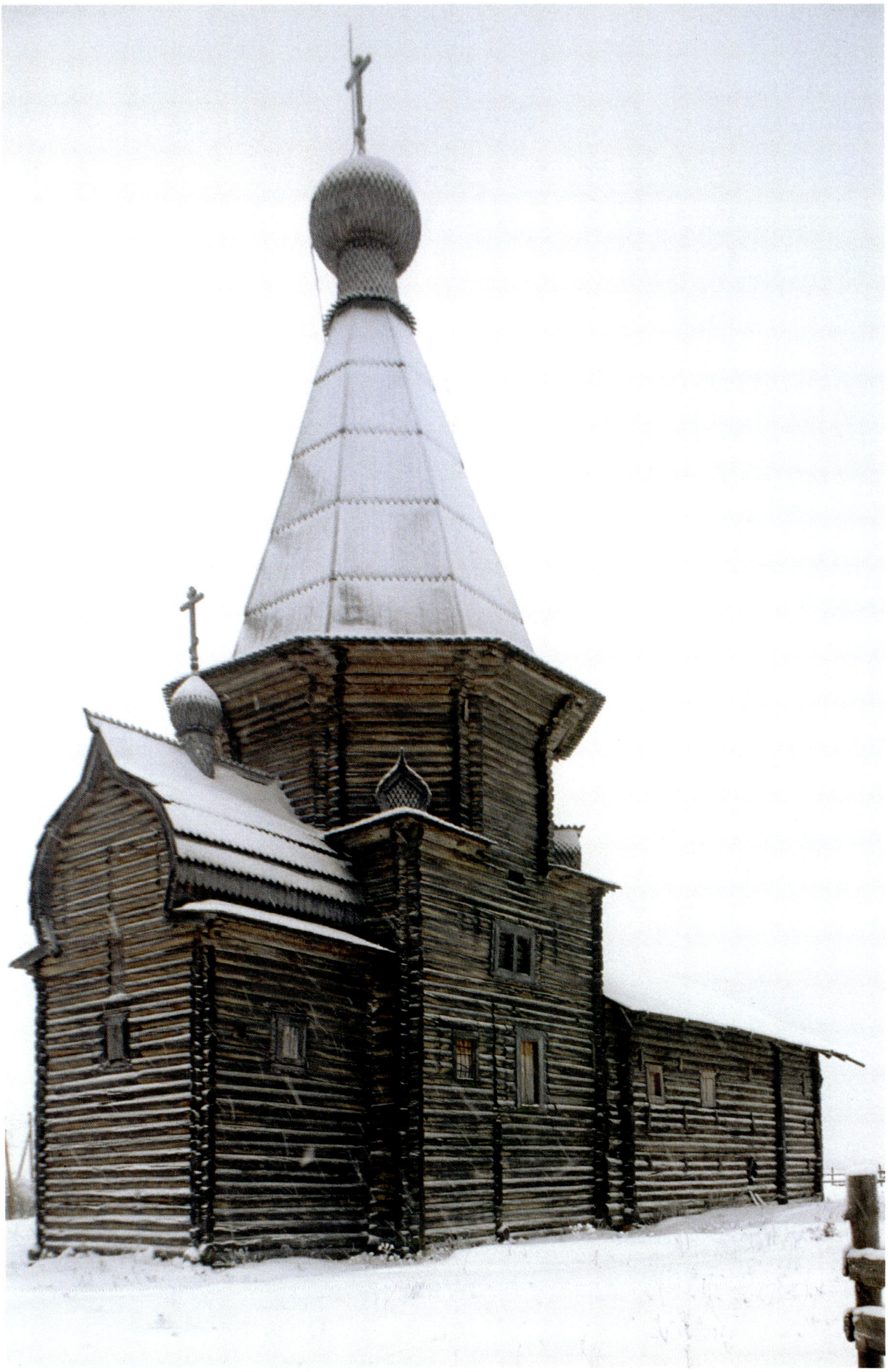

SAUNINO. Church of St. John Chrysostome, northeast view. Photograph: January 4, 1999.

SAUNINO. Wooden bell tower and Church of St. John Chrysostome, southwest view. Church built in 1665. Photograph: June 20, 1998.

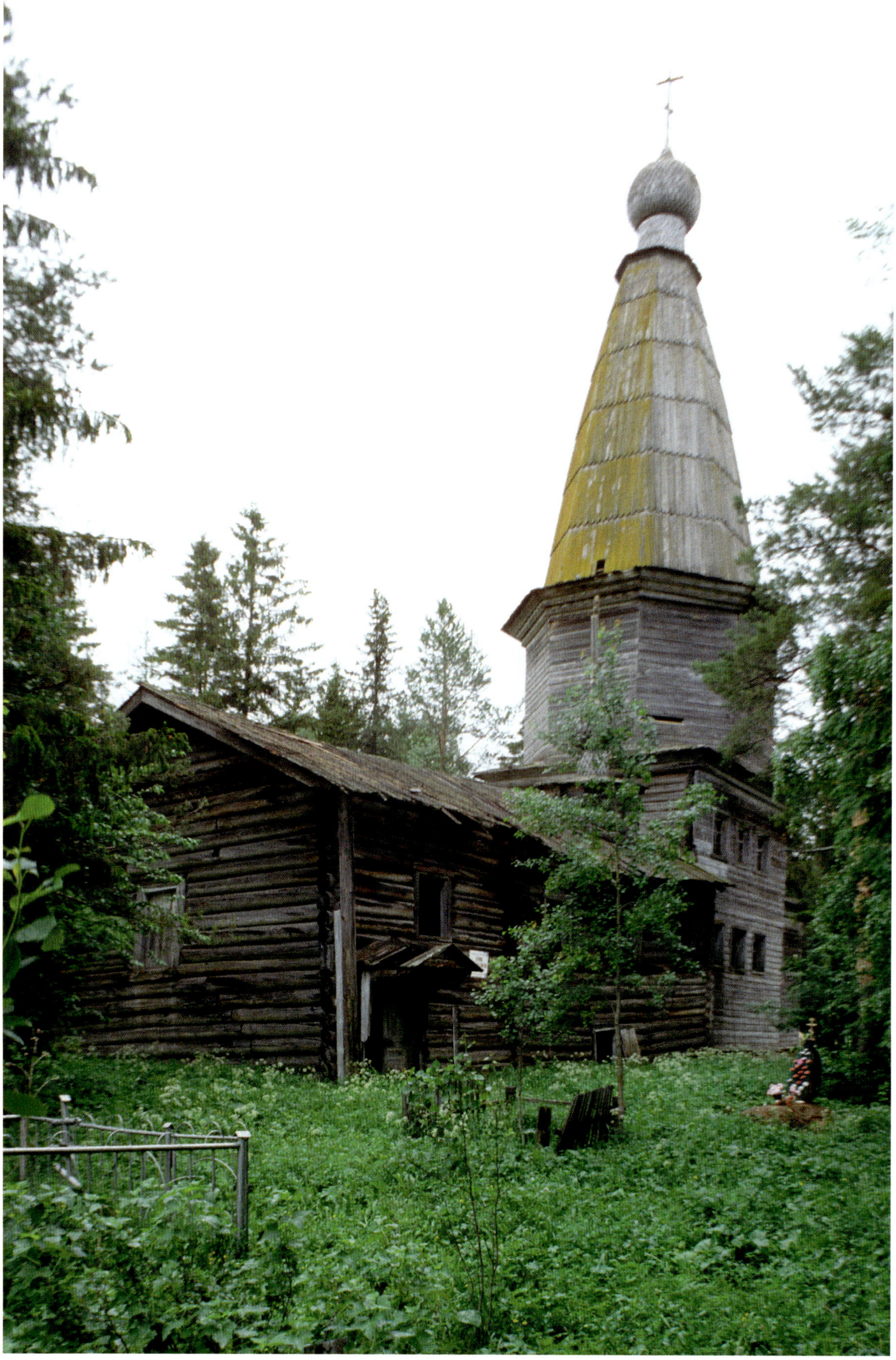

BOLSHAIA SHALGA. Church of the Nativity of Christ, southwest view. Church built in 1745. Photograph: June 23, 1998.

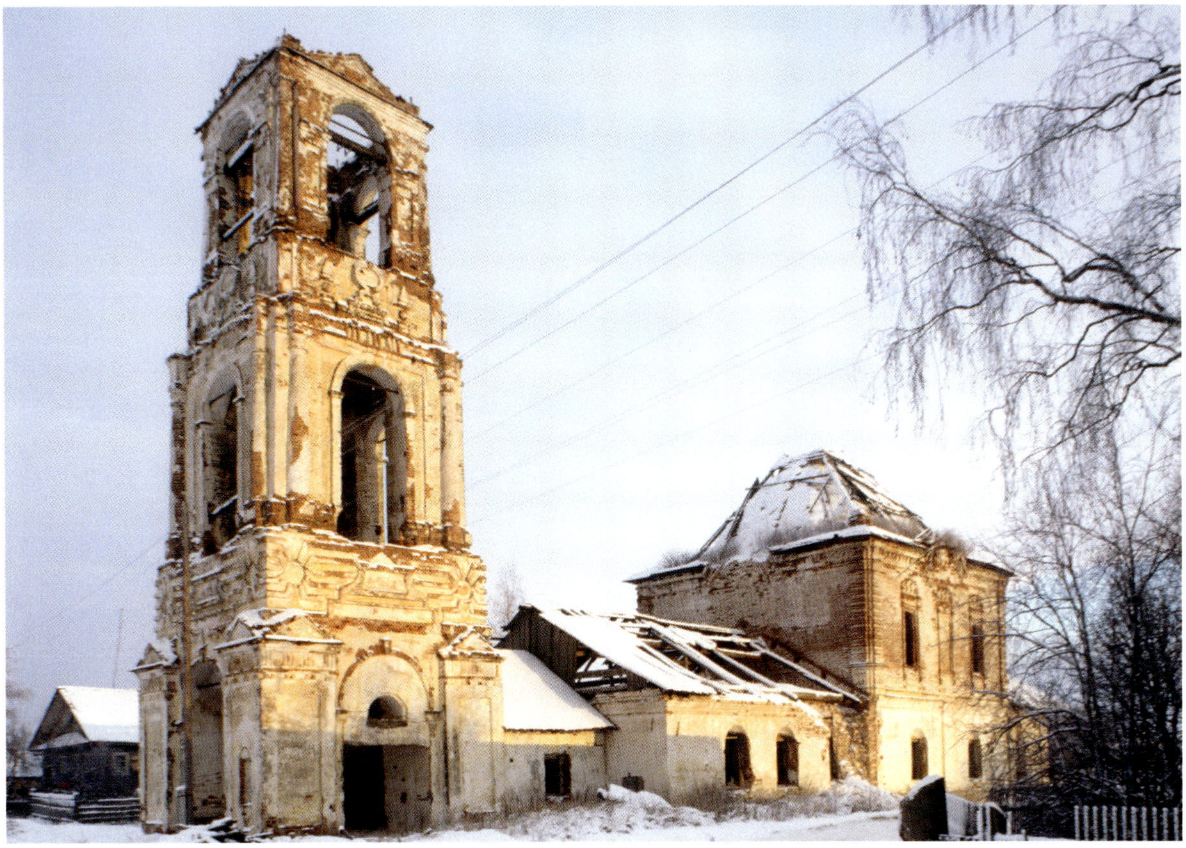

UKHTA. Church of the Trinity, southwest view. Church built in 1797. Photograph: November 26, 1999.

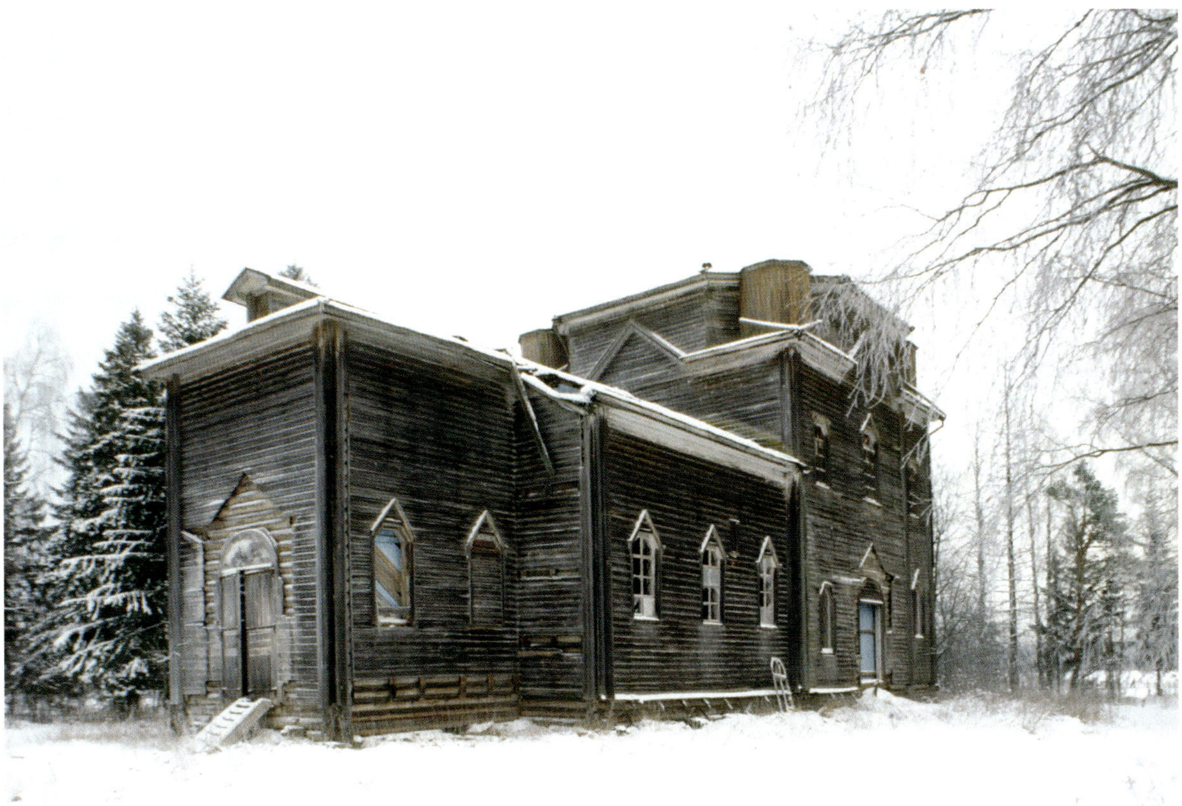

LOVZANGA. Wooden Church of St. Nicholas, southwest view. Church built in 1661. Photograph: November 26, 1999.

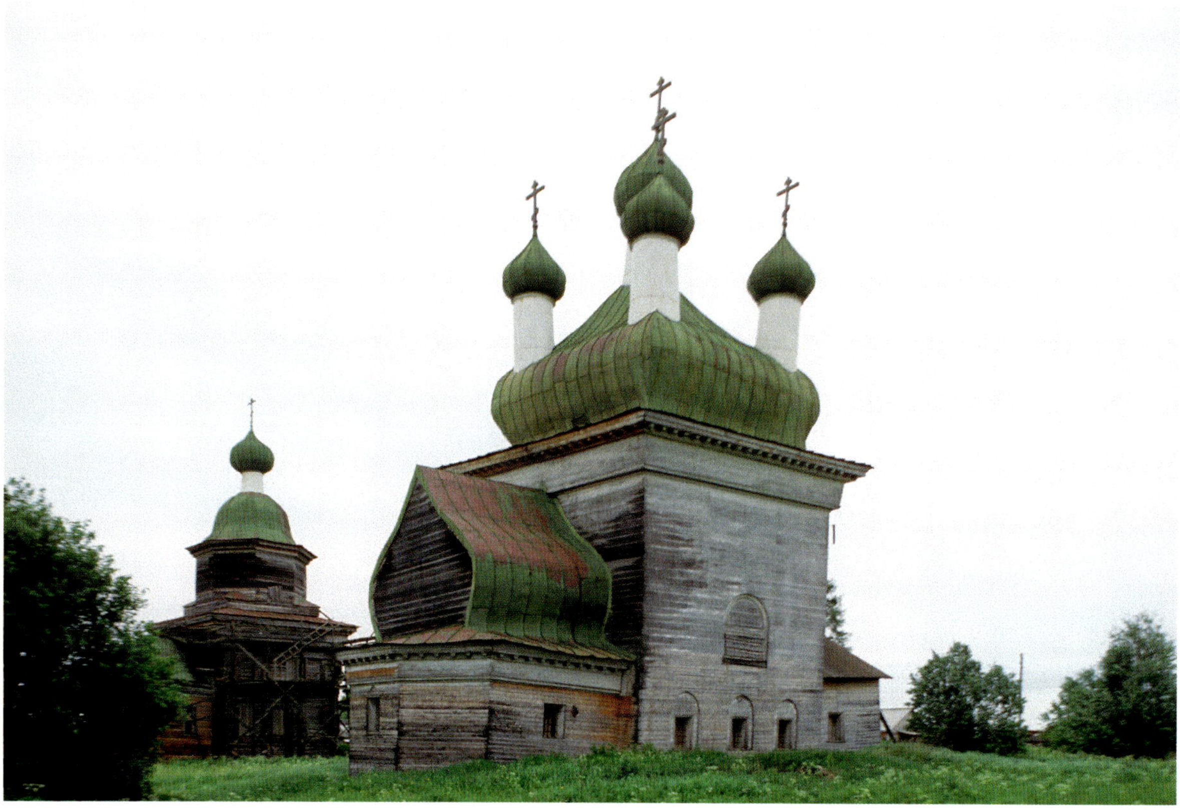

ARKHANGELO. Wooden Church of Archangel Michael (1715), northeast view. Far left: Church of the Purification, a smaller church built in 1803 for winter use. Photograph: June 22, 1998.

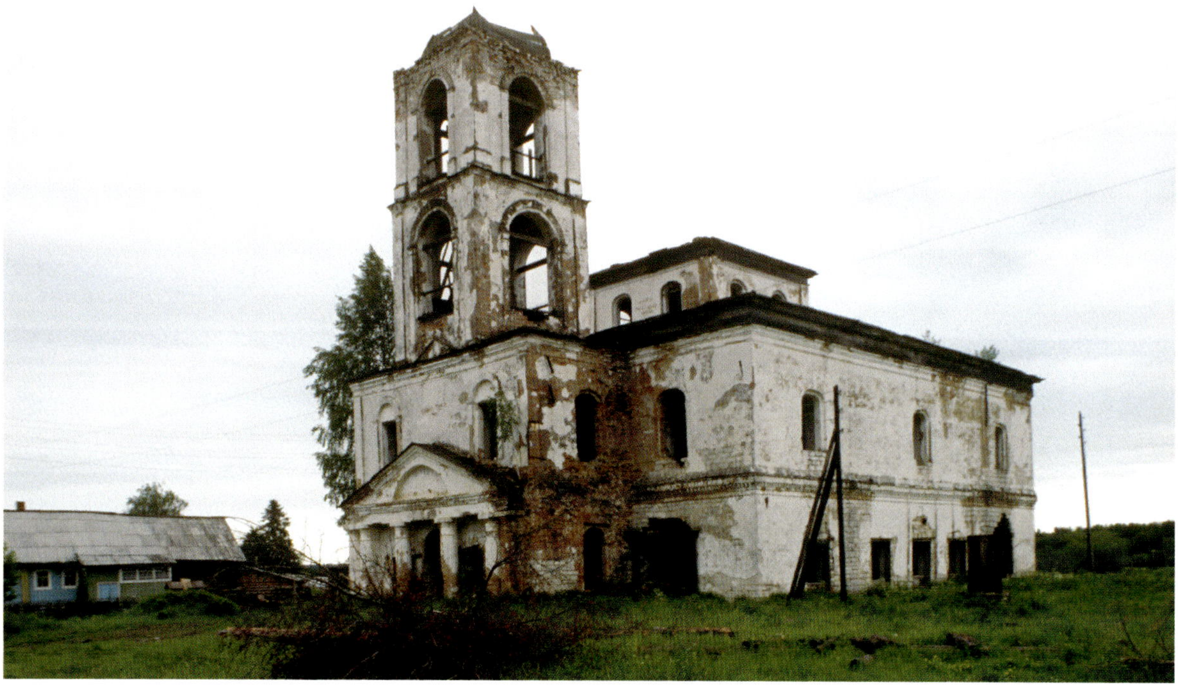

TROITSA. Church of the Trinity, southwest view. Built in late eighteenth century of locally quarried limestone. Photograph: June 22, 1998.

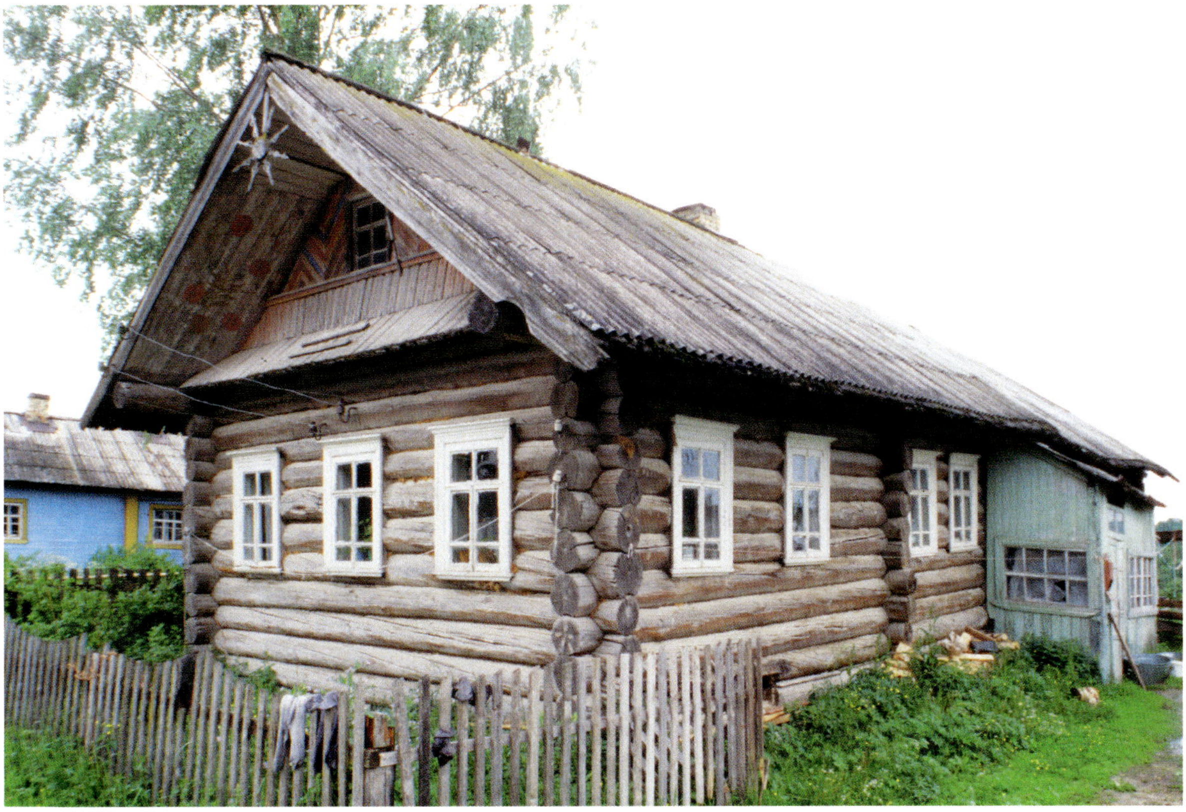

TROITSA. Log house with painted eaves, pediment, and wooden solar symbol. Photograph: June 22, 1998.

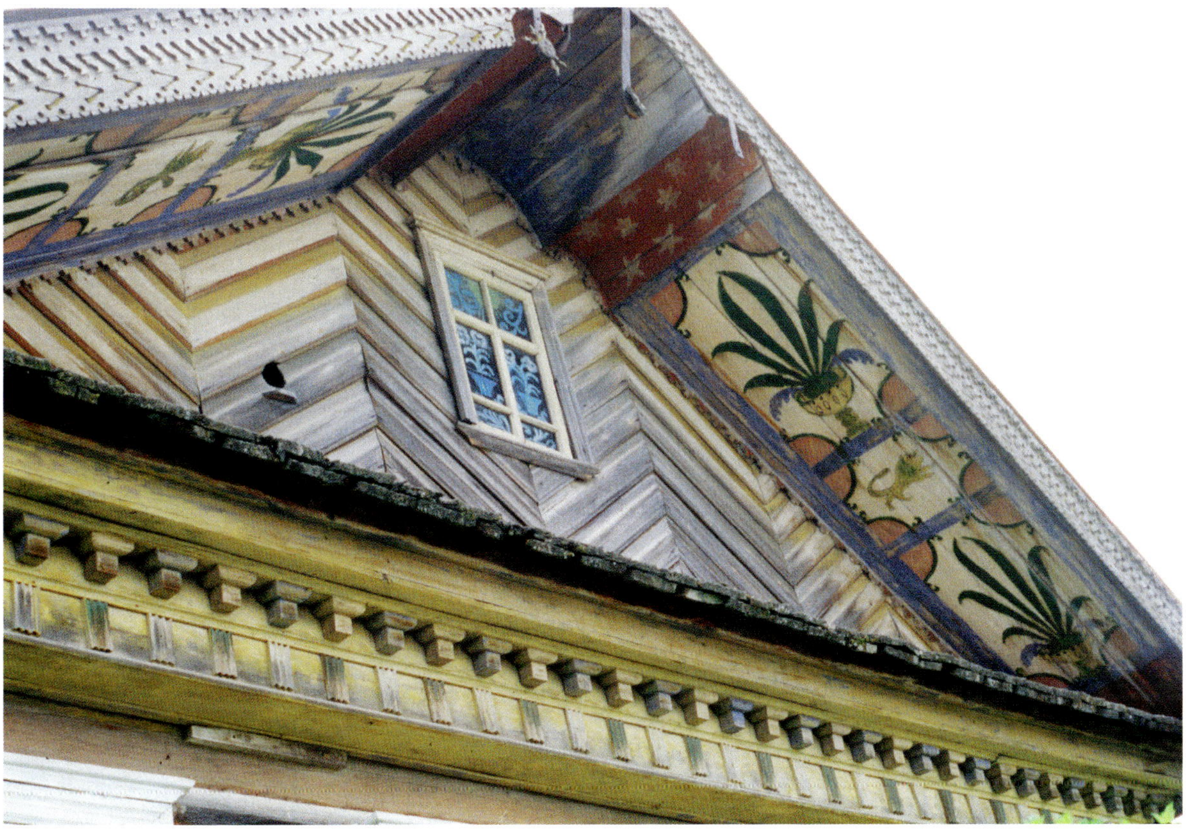

MARKOVSKAIA. Log house with painted eaves. Photograph: June 22, 1998.

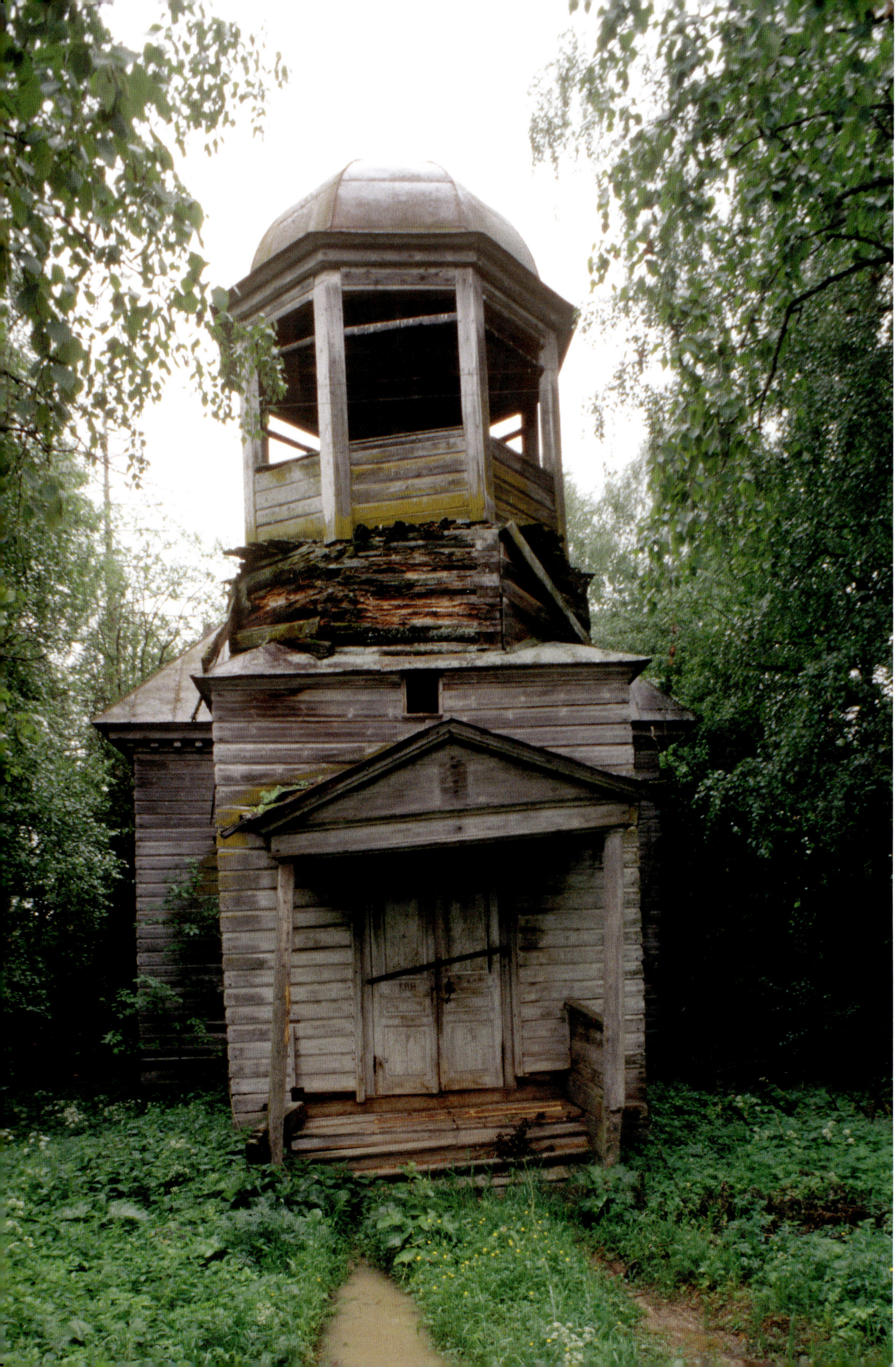

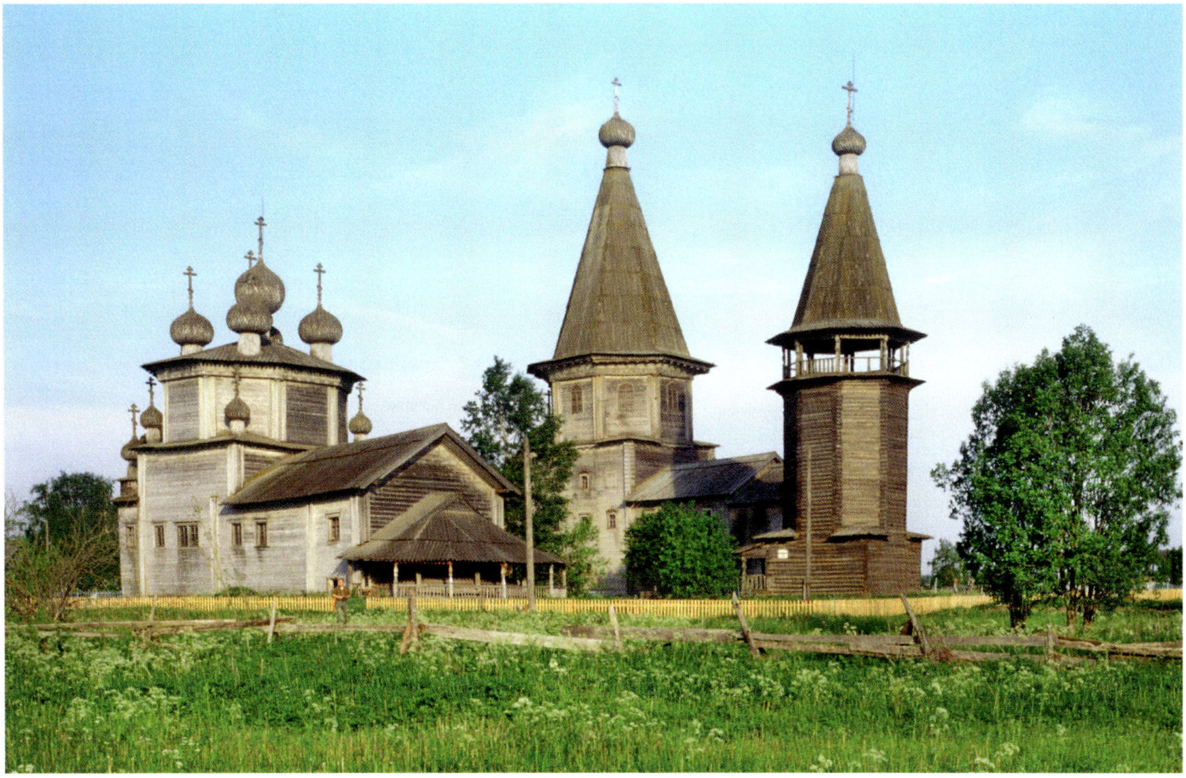

LIADINY. From left: Wooden Church of the Epiphany (1787), Church of the Intercession, bell tower, northwest view. Built in 1761, the Church of the Intercession and its priceless art were destroyed by fire (presumably from a lightning strike) on Easter morning, May 5, 2013. The fire also spread to the nineteenth-century bell tower. Photograph: June 16, 1998.

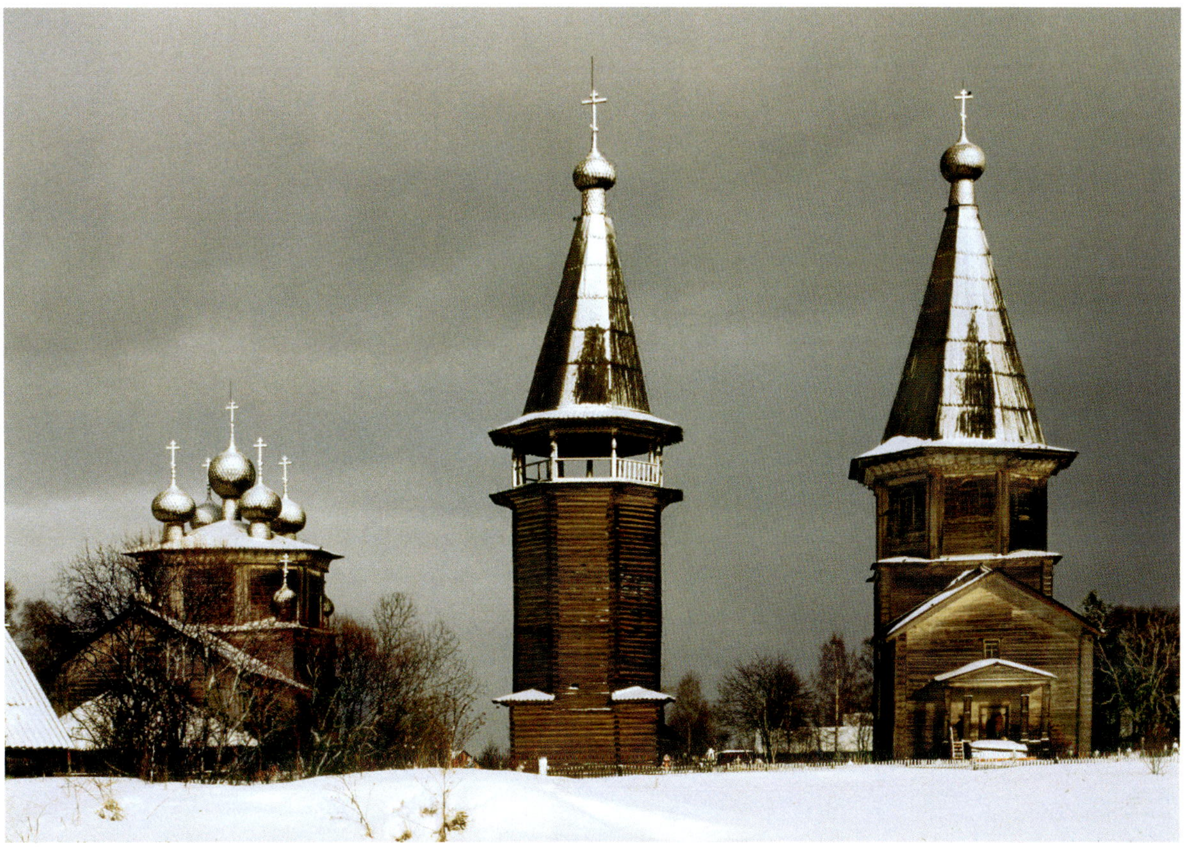

LIADINY. From left: Church of the Epiphany, bell tower, Church of the Intercession, west view after severe snowstorm that coated the vertical surfaces. Photograph: February 28, 1998.

SEMENOVSKAIA. Nineteenth-century wooden chapel, west view. This temple, located deep in the forest, is reputed to be used by the dissenting Orthodox sect known as Old Believers. Photograph: June 22, 1998.

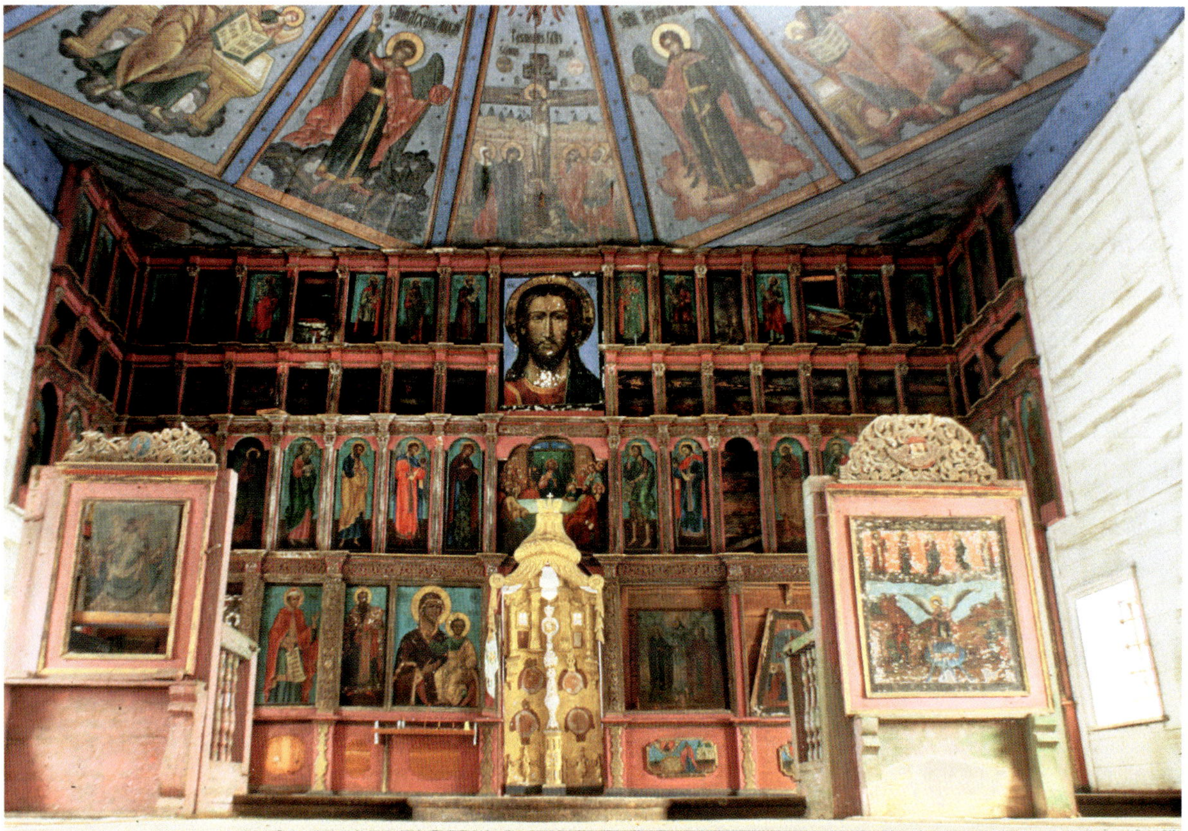

LIADINY. Church of the Intercession (not extant), interior, view east with icon screen and painted ceiling (nebo, or "heaven"). Photograph: February 28, 1998.

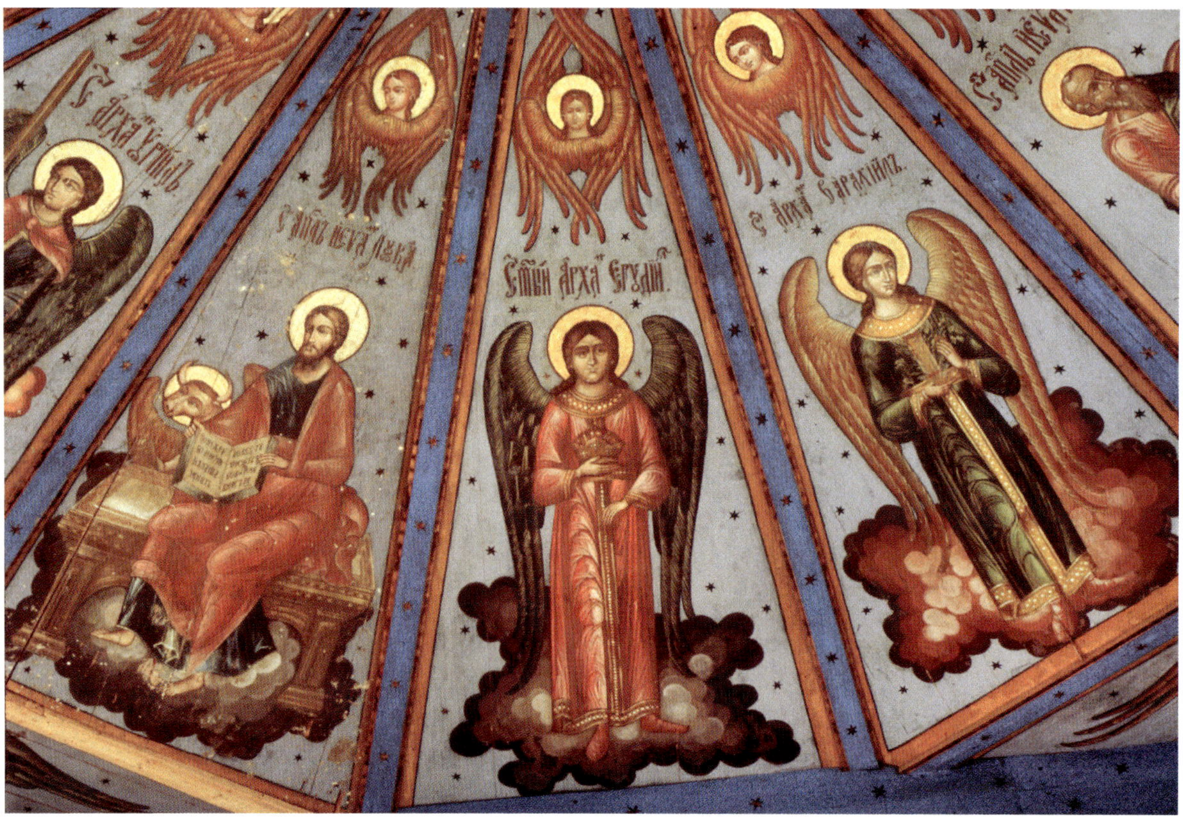

LIADINY. Church of the Intercession, interior, fragment of painted ceiling (nebo, or "heaven"). From left: St. Luke, Archangel Jehudiel, Archangel Barachiel. Photograph: July 29, 1998.

LIADINY. Church of the Intercession, interior, view east with icon screen and painted ceiling (nebo, or "heaven"). Photograph: July 29, 1998.

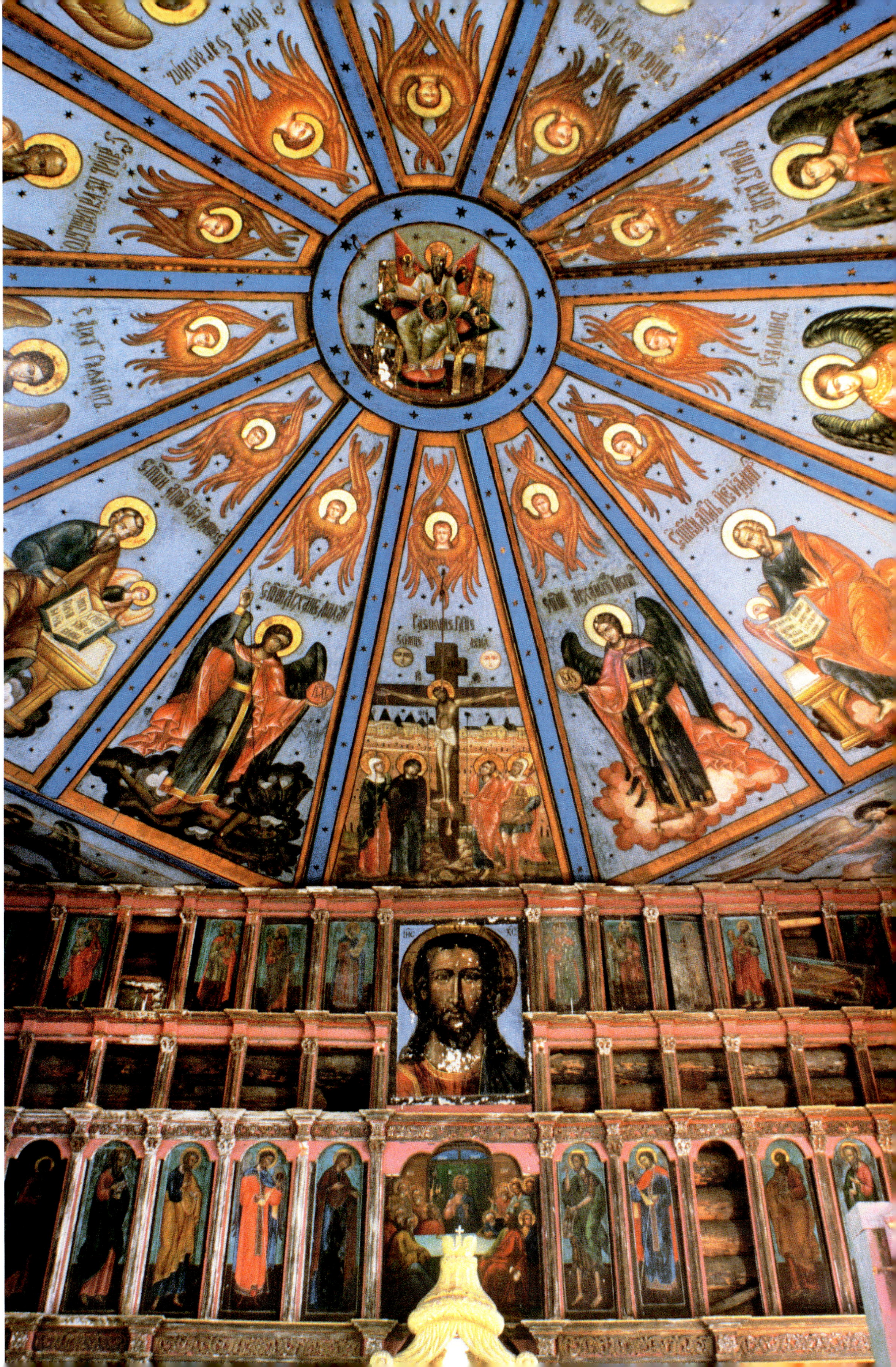

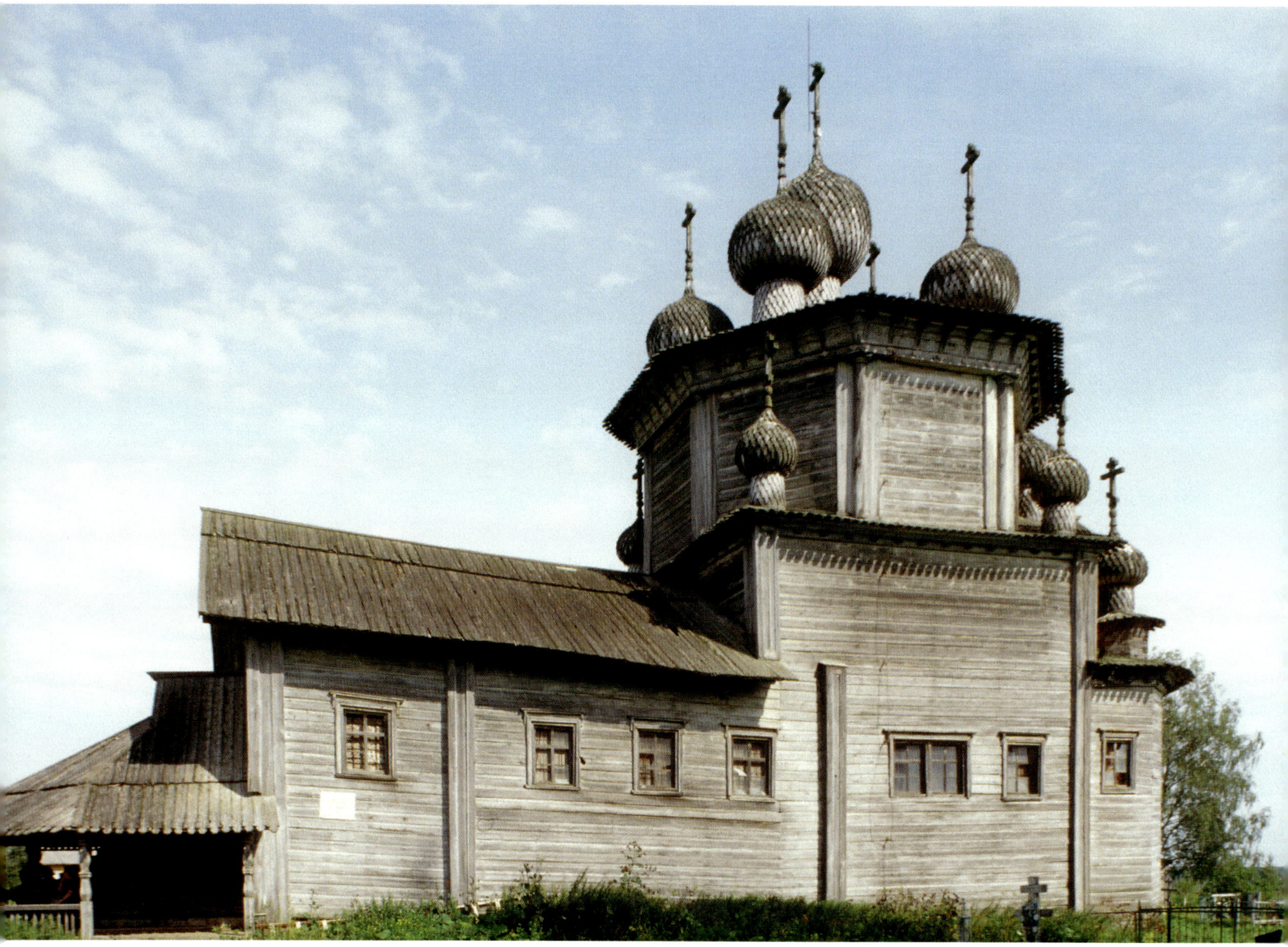

LIADINY. Wooden Church of the Epiphany, south view. Built in 1787, the Epiphany Church is the only surviving part of the pogost (church and cemetery) ensemble. Photograph: July 29, 1998.

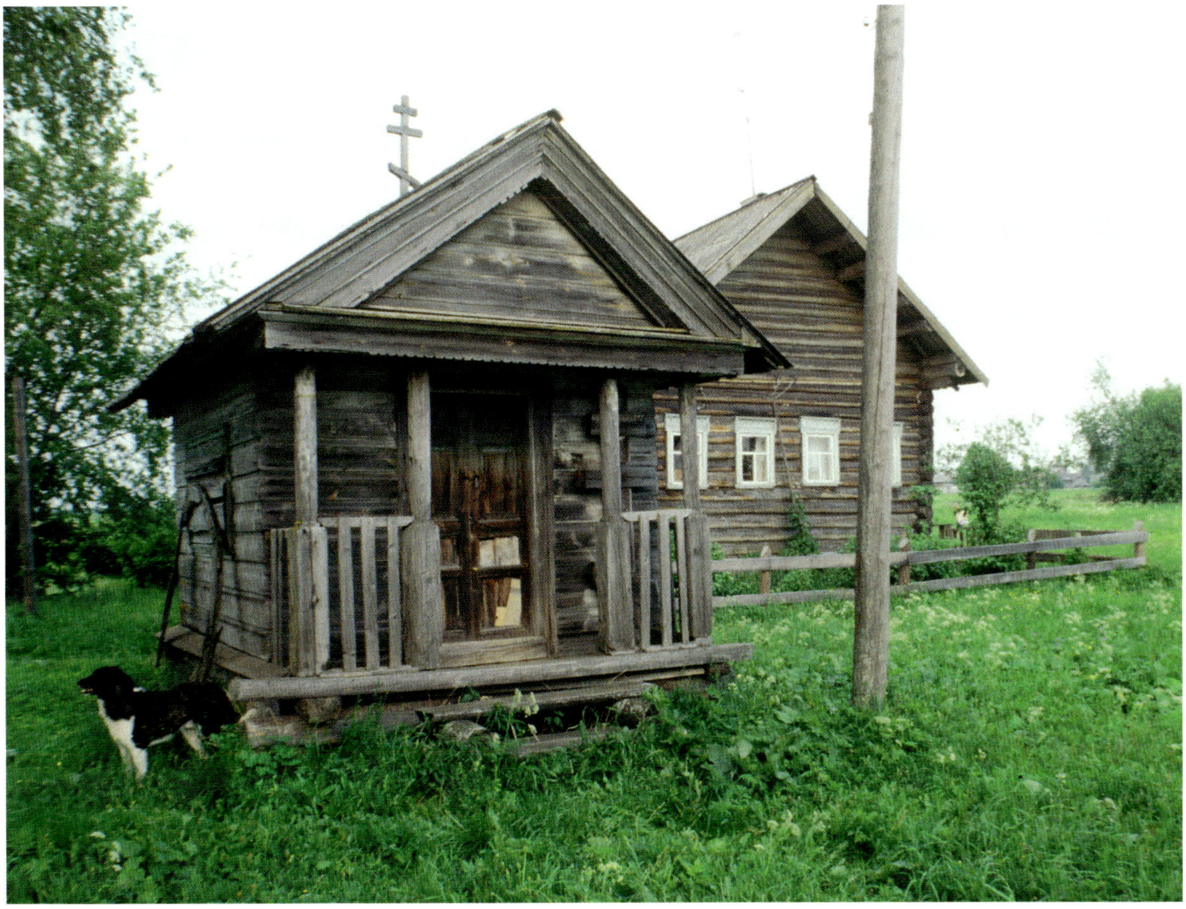

KISELEVA HAMLET (part of Liadiny). Nineteenth-century wooden chapel (St. George?). Wooden house in background. Photograph: June 16, 1998.

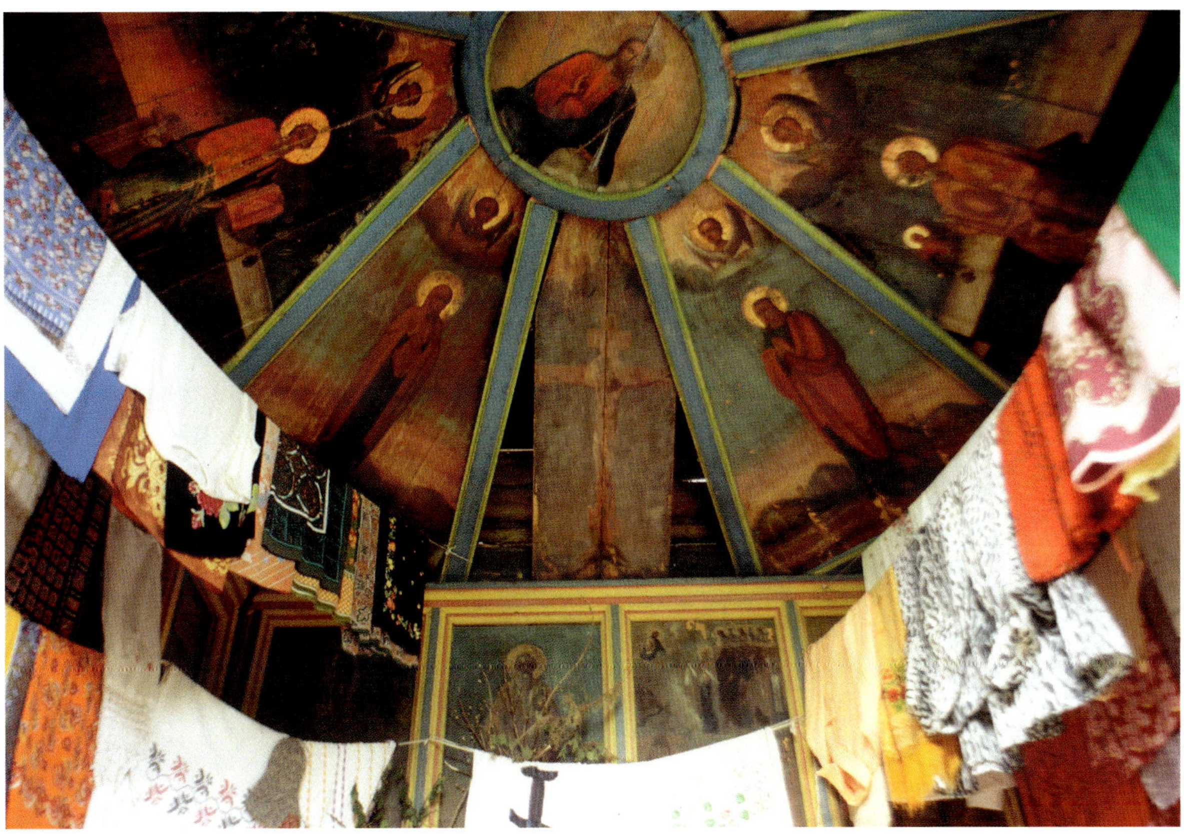

KISELYOVA HAMLET (part of Liadiny). Wooden chapel (St. George?), interior with painted ceiling and votive offerings of clothing for protection and relief from illness. Photograph: June 16, 1998.

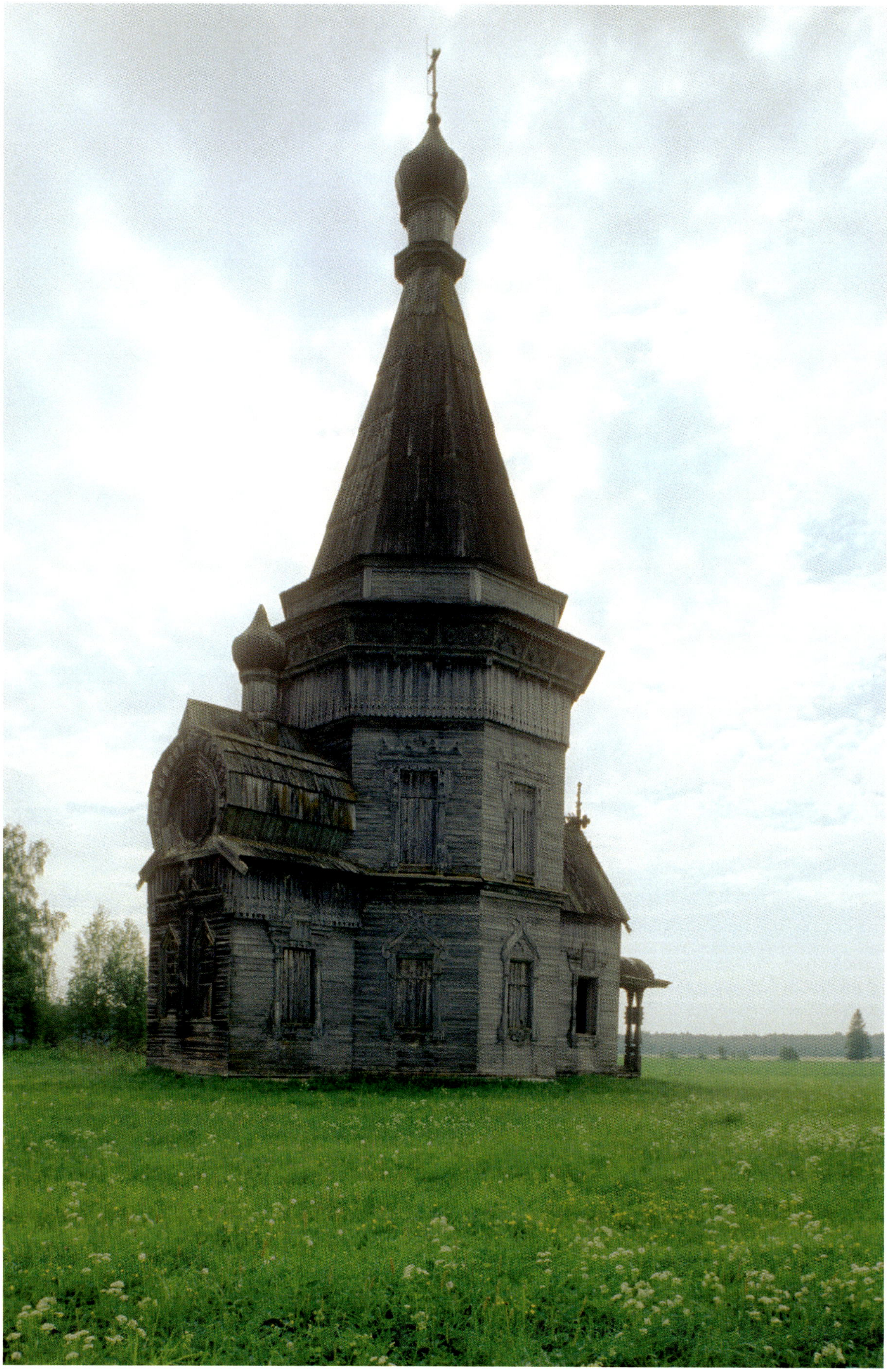

KRASNAIA LIAGA. Wooden Church of the Purification, northeast view. Built in 1655 and covered with plank siding in the nineteenth century, this "tent" tower church was once surrounded by a prosperous village. Photograph: June 20, 1998.

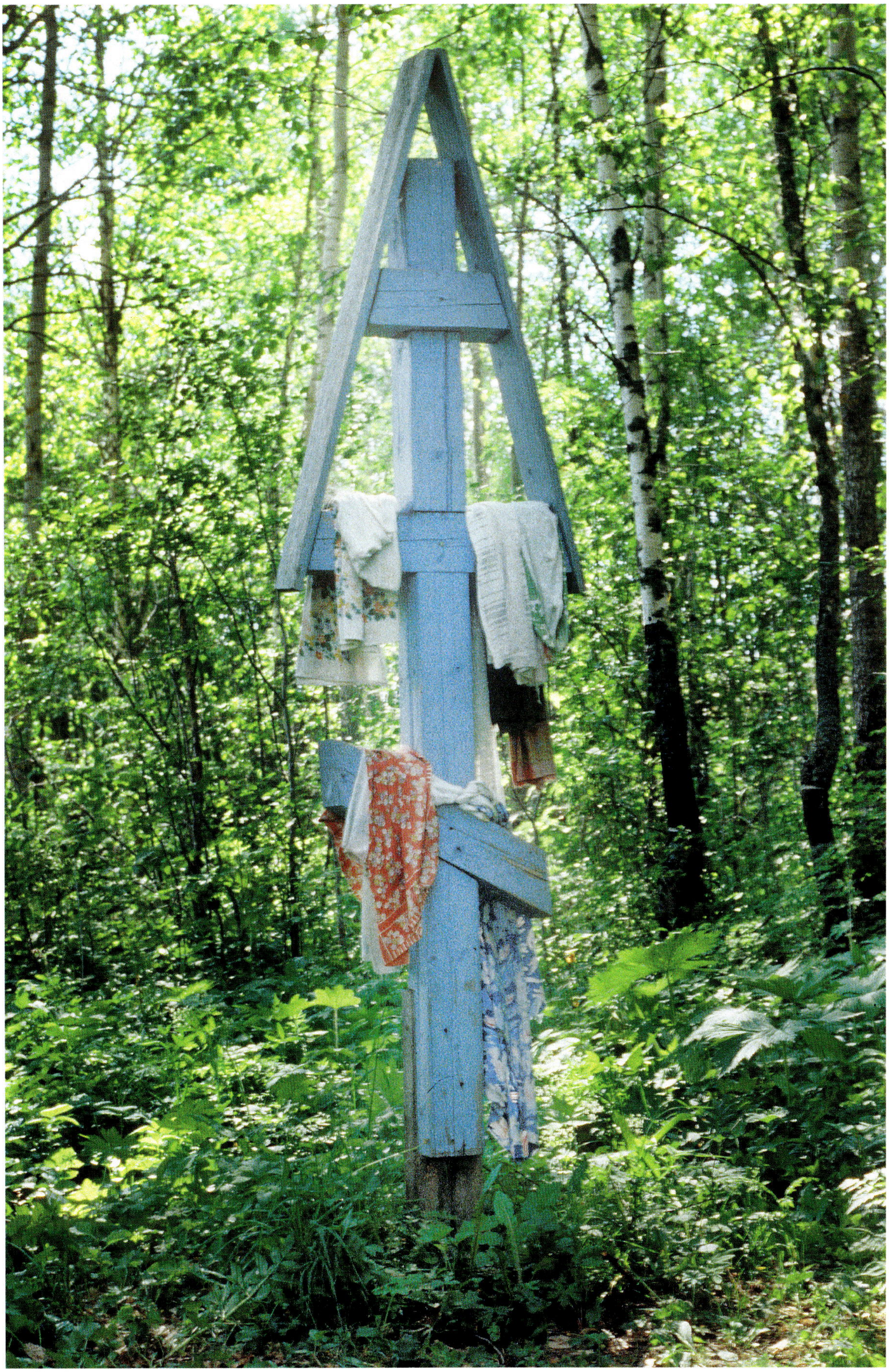

POZDYSHEVO. Hooded cross in forest, with votive offerings of clothing. Photograph: June 18, 1998.

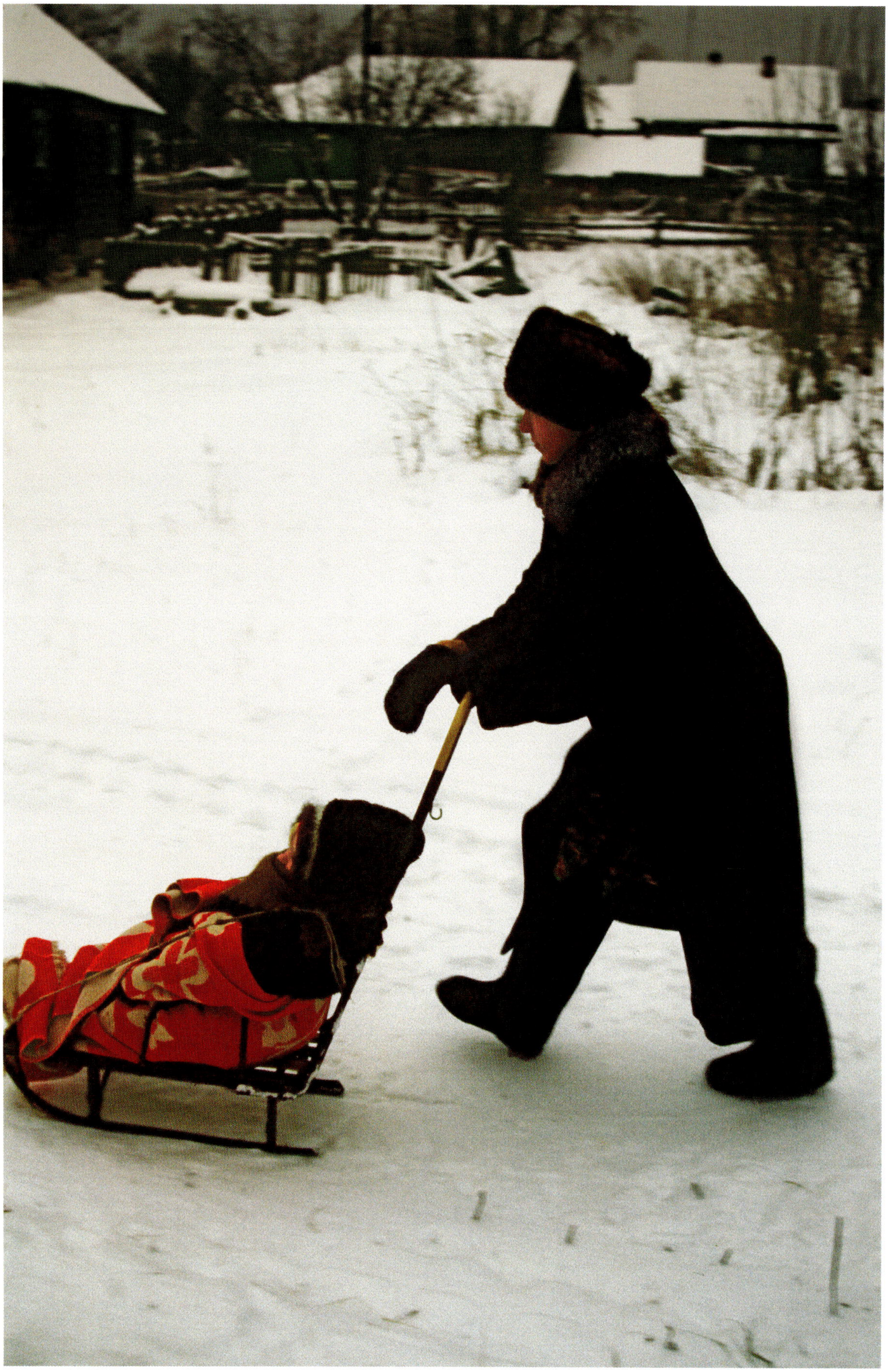

SHIRIAIKHA (Oshevensk). Village scene. Photograph: November 27, 1999.

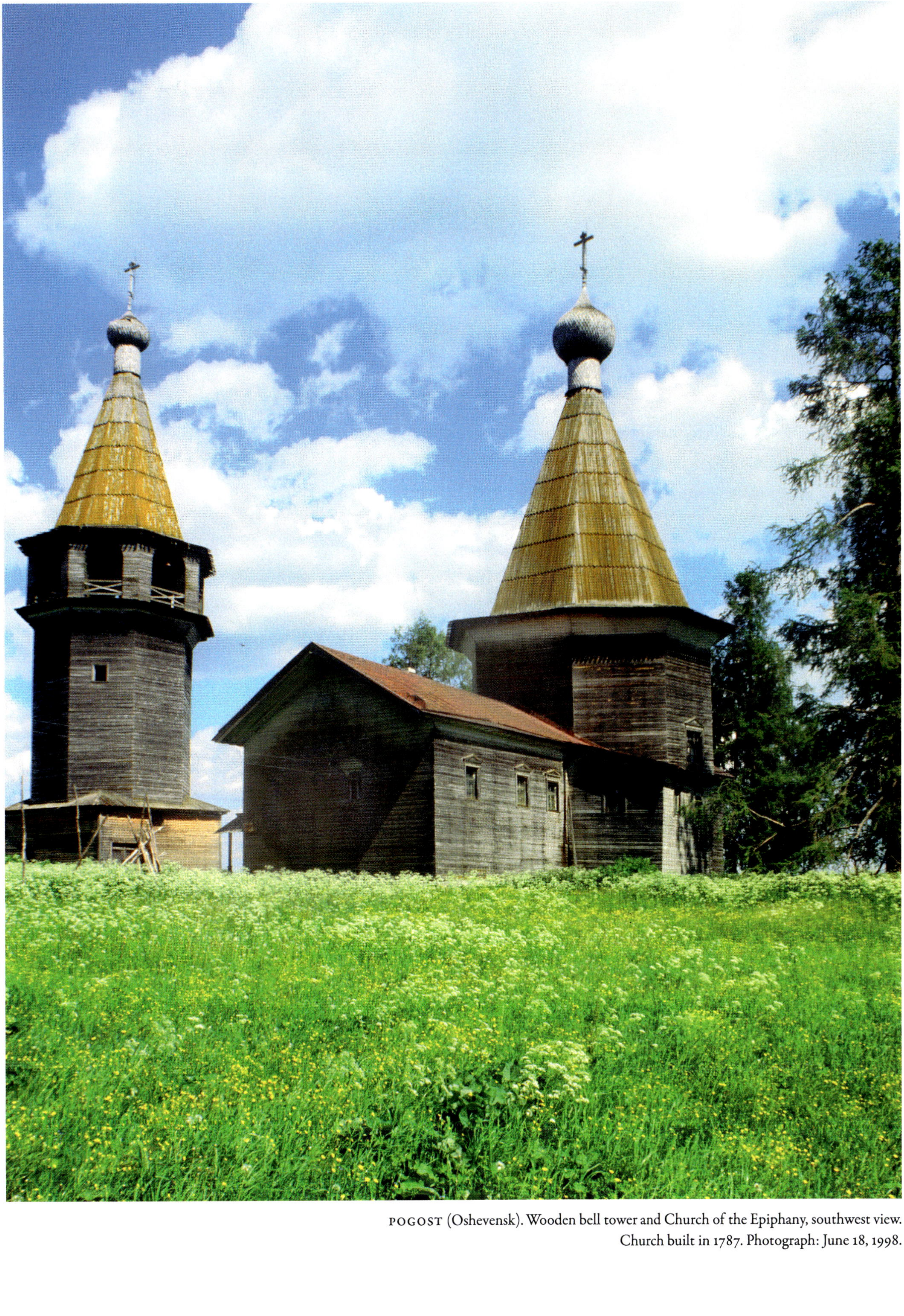

POGOST (Oshevensk). Wooden bell tower and Church of the Epiphany, southwest view.
Church built in 1787. Photograph: June 18, 1998.

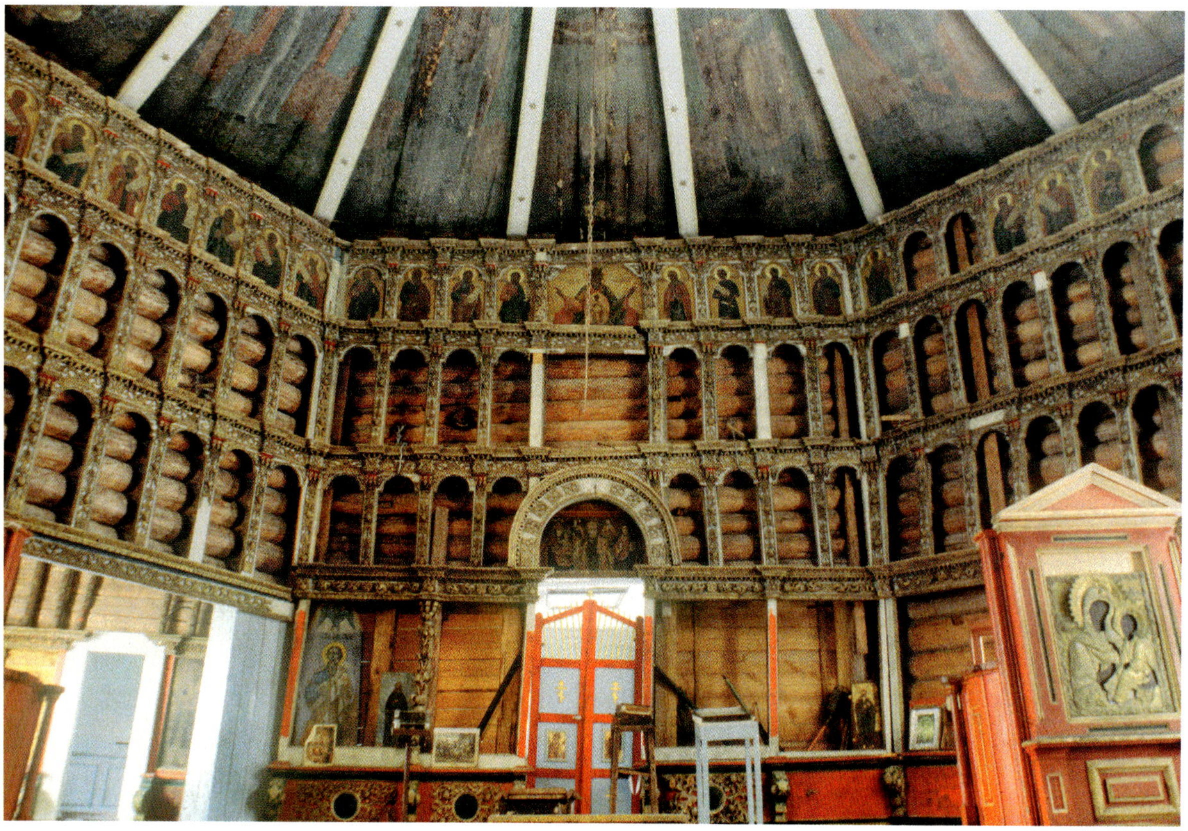

POGOST (Oshevensk). Church of the Epiphany, interior, view east toward icon screen (most icons missing). Photograph: June 18, 1998.

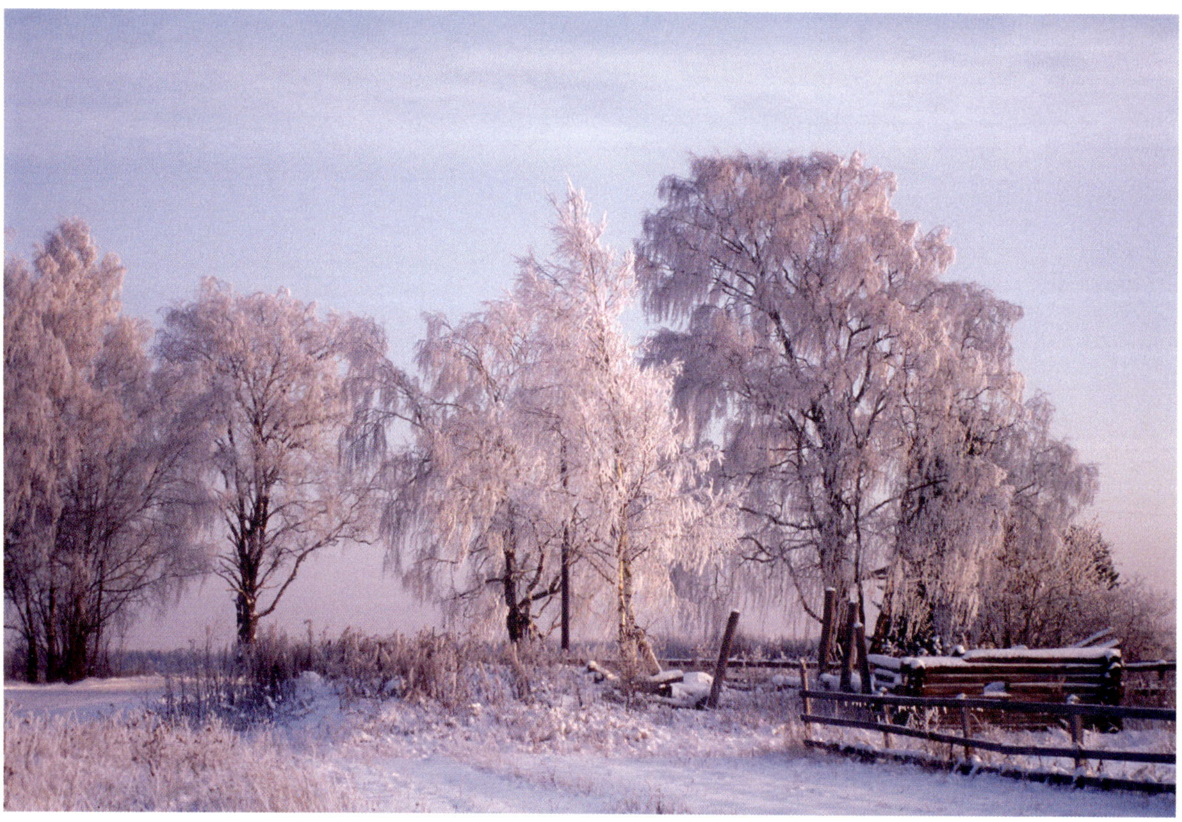

POZDYSHEVO. Evening winter light on abandoned farmstead. Snow that coated the long birch branches had slightly melted during the day and then refroze in the intense cold to create an ice sheath. Photograph: November 27, 1999.

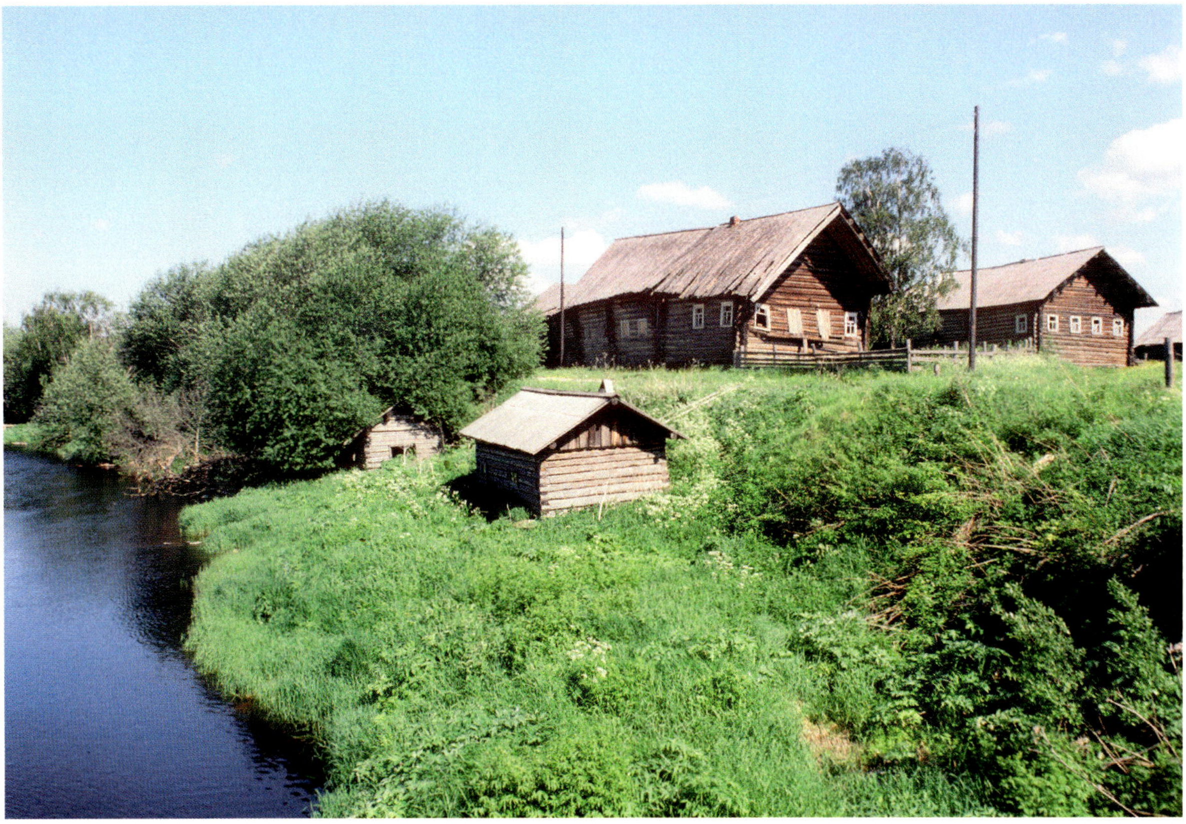

GAR. Log houses with bathhouses on Churyega River. Photograph: June 18, 1998.

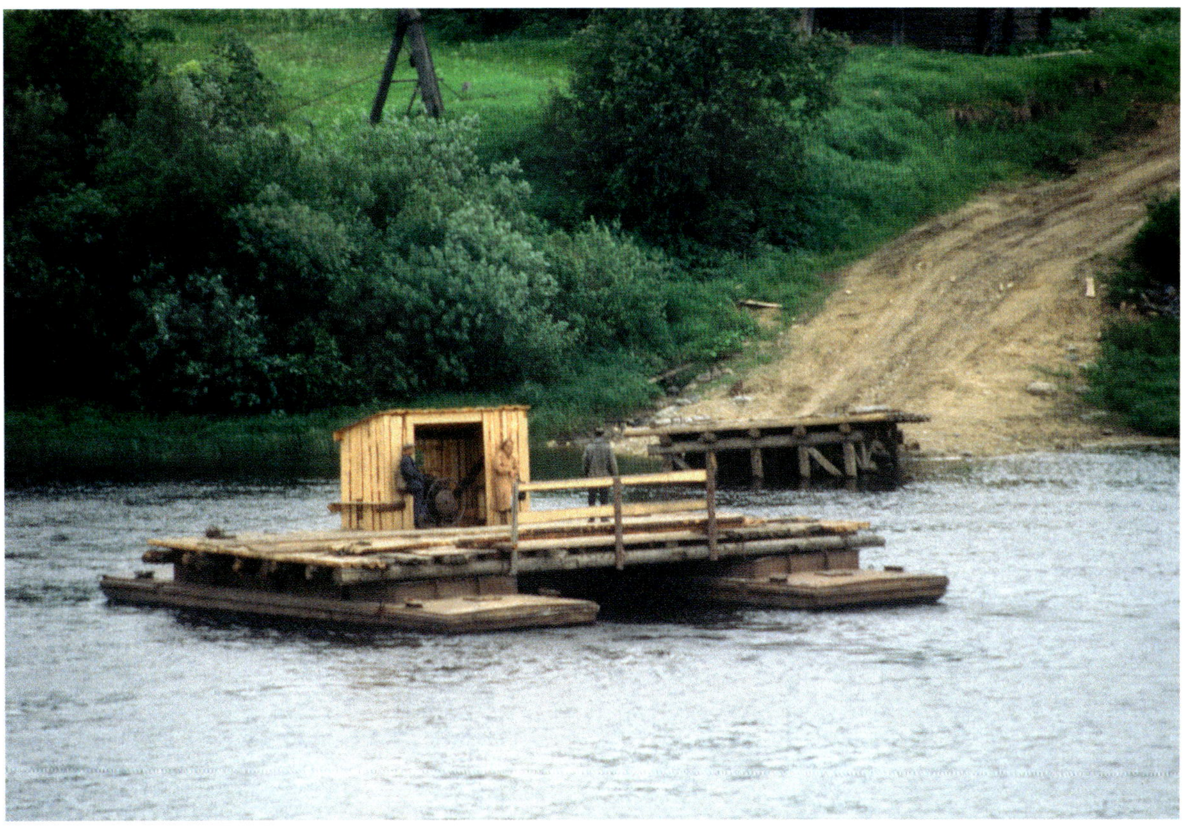

BEREZHNAIA DUBROVA. Cable ferry across Onega River. View east toward right bank. Photograph: June 22, 1998.

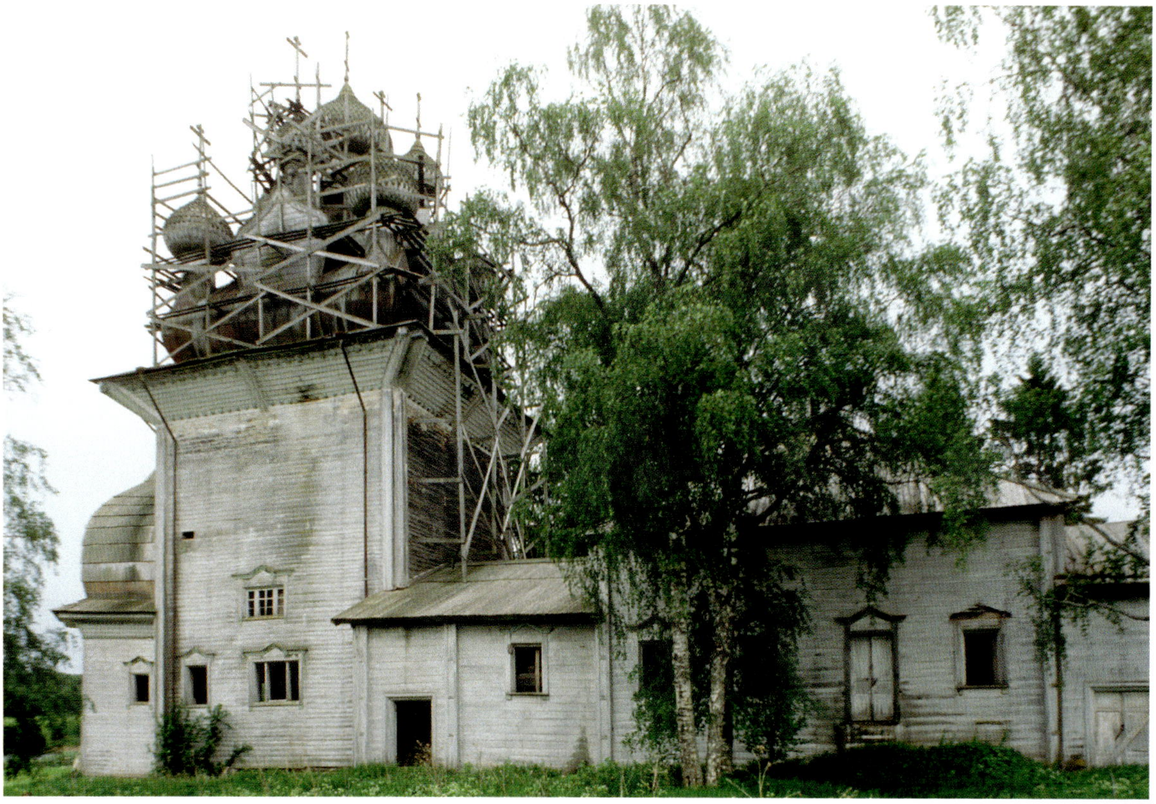

BEREZHNAIA DUBROVA. Church of the Nativity of the Virgin (also known as Church of St. Nicholas), north view. The church was originally built in 1678, with modifications in 1882. Photograph: June 22, 1998.

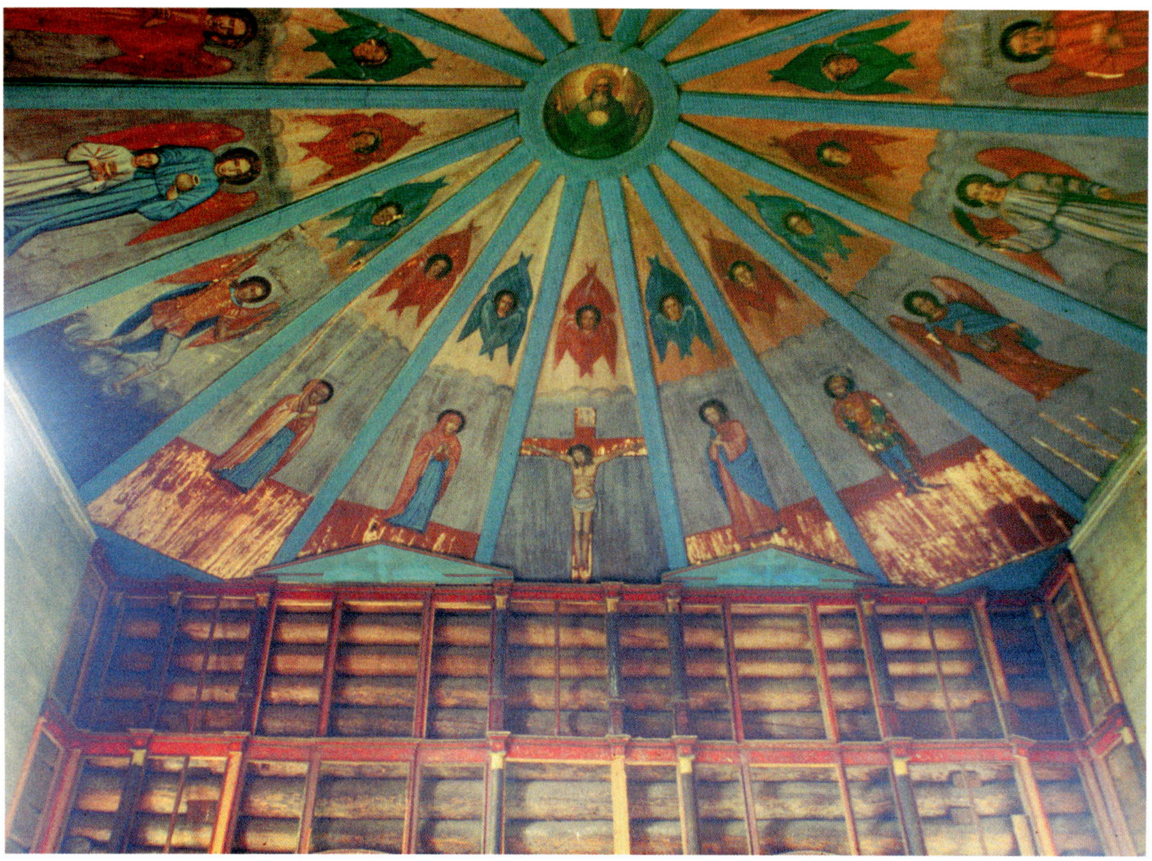

BEREZHNAIA DUBROVA. Church of the Nativity of the Virgin (also known as Church of St. Nicholas), interior, view east with painted ceiling (nebo, or "heaven"). Photograph: June 22, 1998.

VERSHININO. Nineteenth-century wooden Chapel of St. Nicholas, southwest view. On territory of Kenozero National Park. Photograph: March 1, 2000.

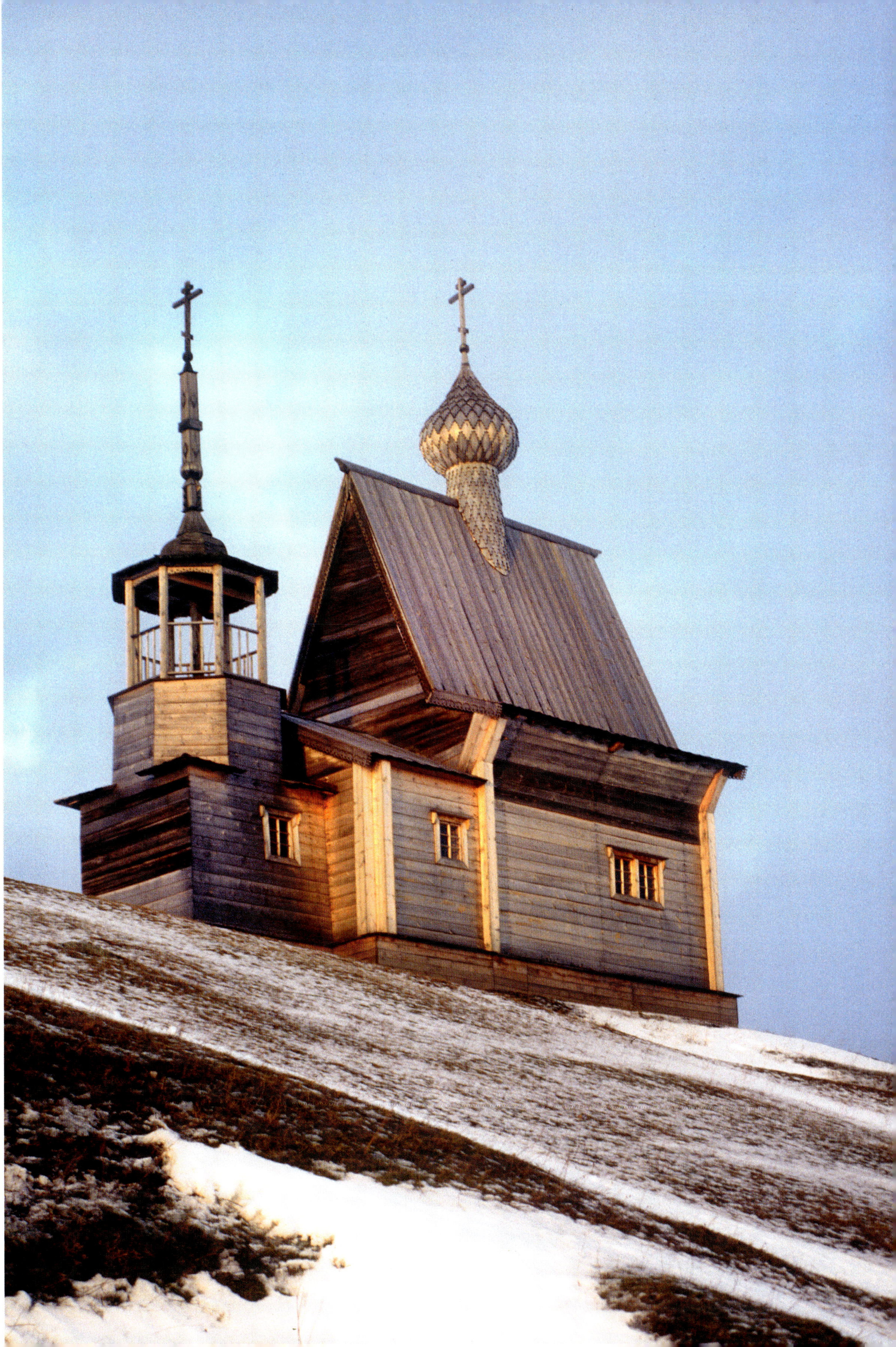

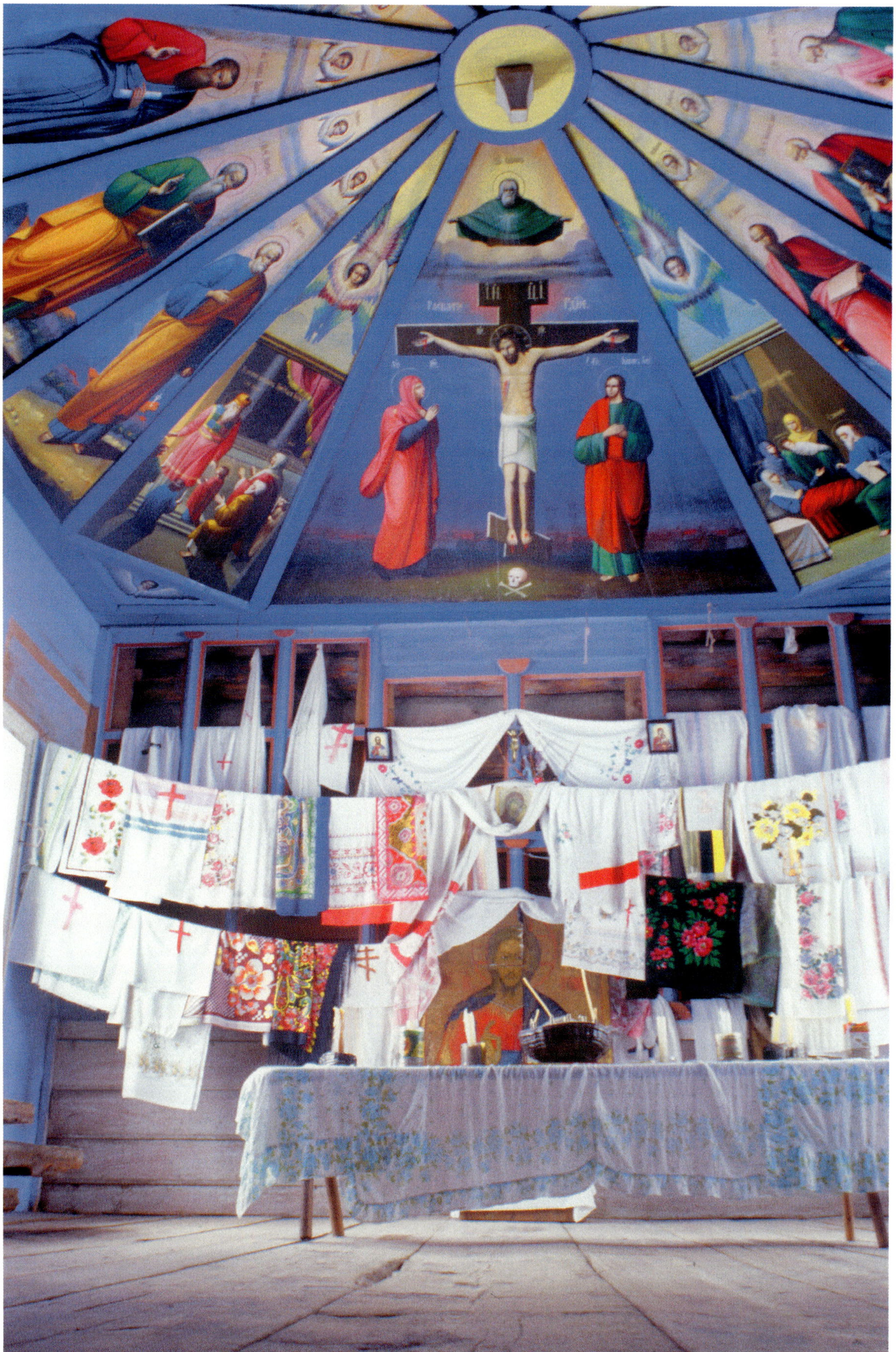

RYZHKOVO. Wooden Chapel of the Presentation, interior, with painted ceiling (nebo, or "heaven") and votive offerings of embroidered towels and clothing. Chapel built in 1801. Photograph: February 29, 2000.

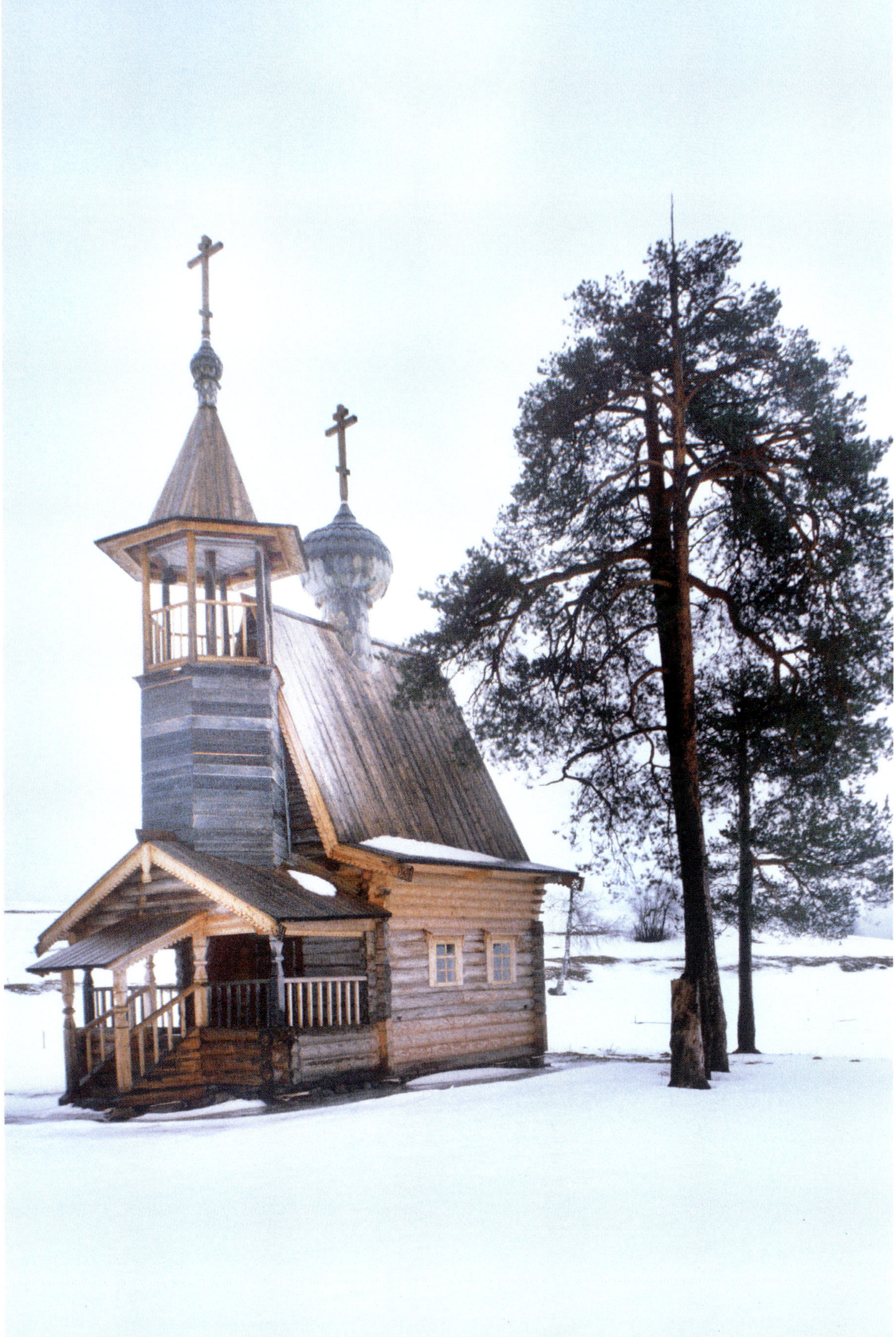

GLAZOVO. Wooden Chapel of the Descent of the Holy Spirit. Chapel built in 1805. Glazovo is part of Kenozero National Park. Photograph: February 29, 2000.

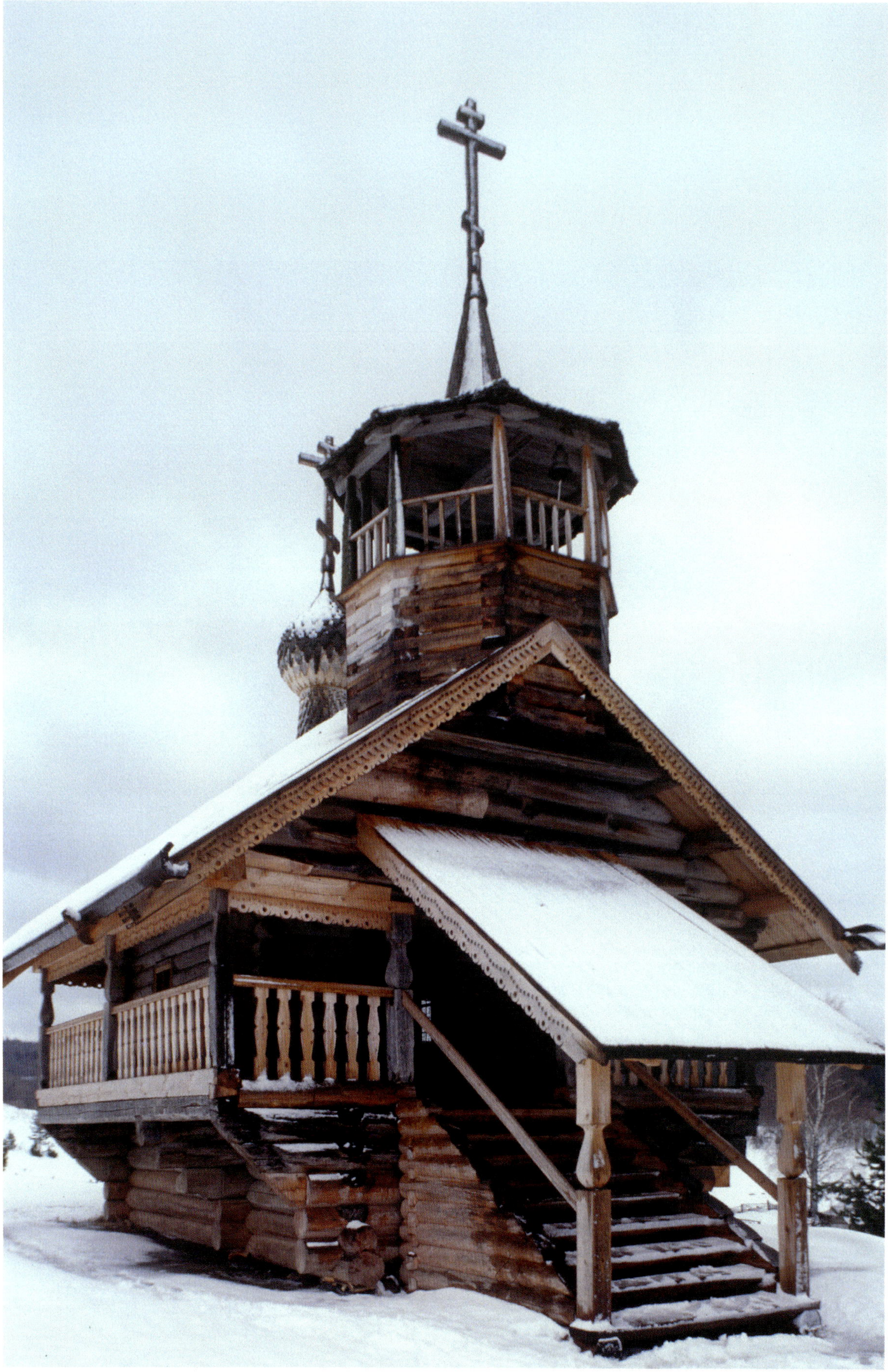

ZIKHNOVO. Eighteenth-century wooden Chapel of St. John the Divine, northwest view. Zikhnovo is part of Kenozero National Park. Photograph: March 1, 2000.

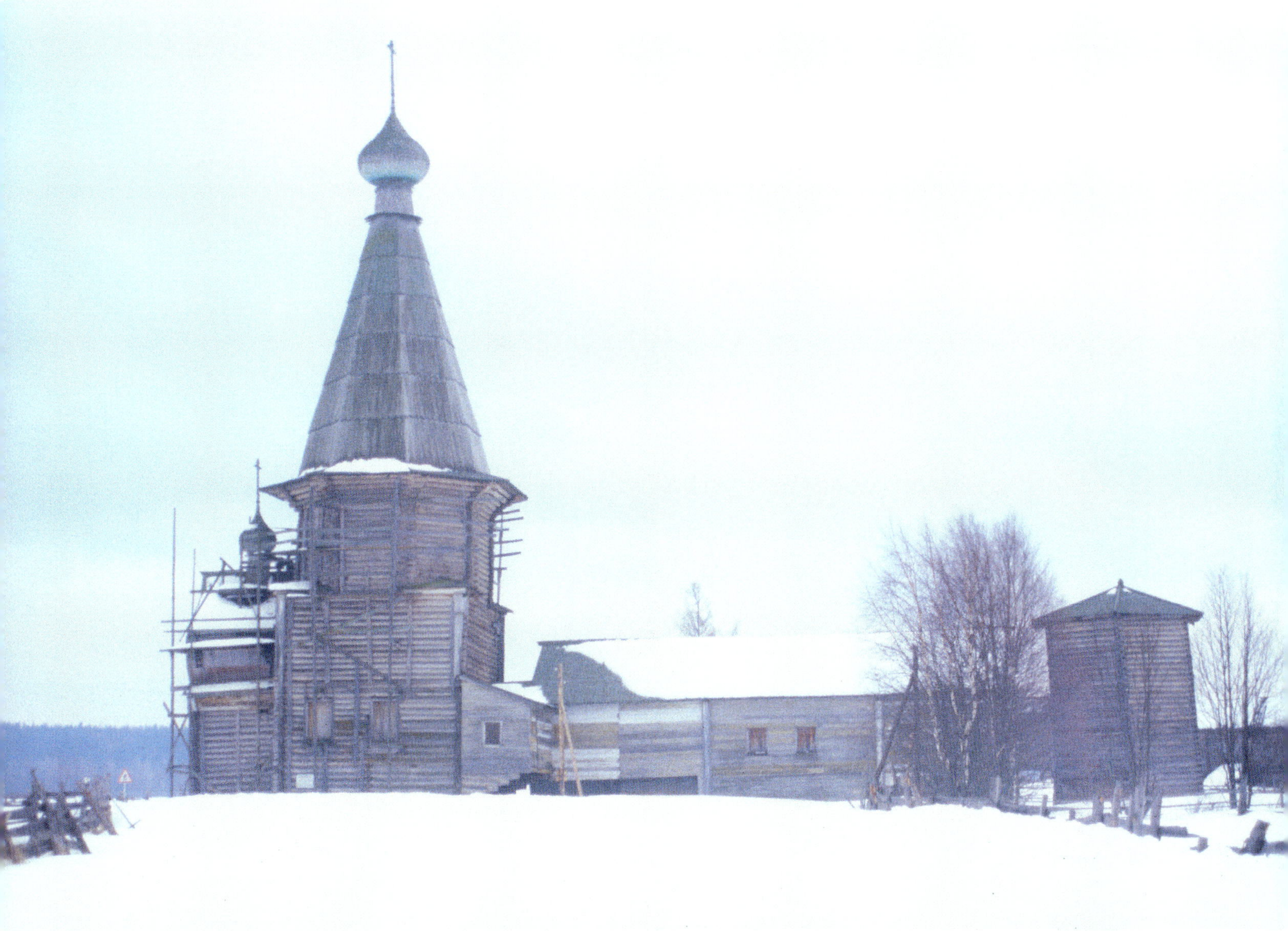

FILIPPOVSKAIA. Ensemble of wooden Church of the Procession of the Precious Wood of the Life-Giving Cross of the Lord (left), Church of the Finding of the Head of John the Baptist, and bell tower, north view. This unique early eighteenth-century ensemble of two log churches on a single axis with a bell tower in the west was under restoration at the time of this photograph, March 2, 2000.

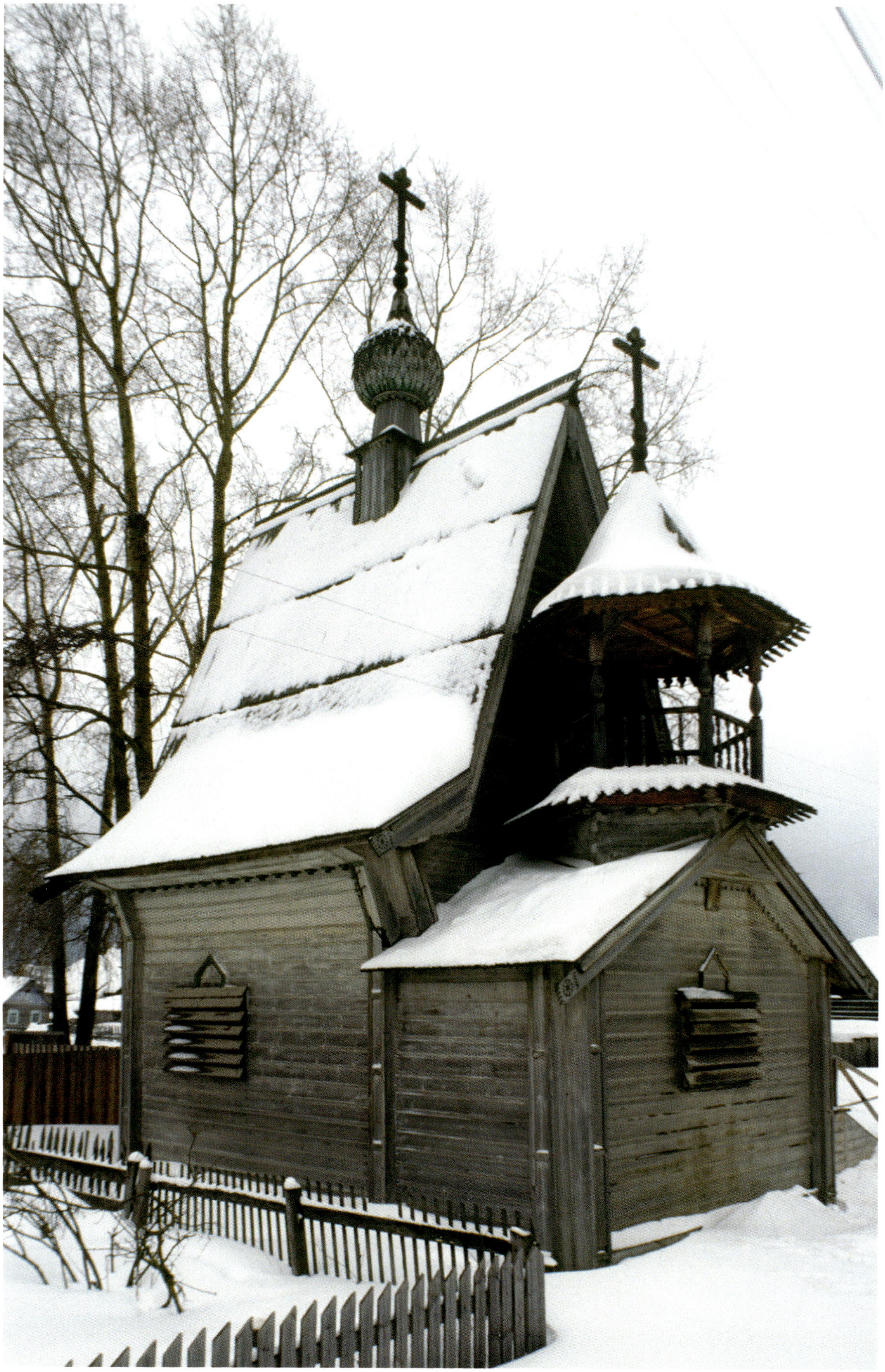

KONEVO. Chapel of the Intercession of the Virgin and St. Alexander Nevskii, northwest view.
Chapel built in first half of the eighteenth century. Photograph: February 28, 2000.

FOUR *From Vologda to Veliky Ustiug*

VOLOGDA: ARTISTIC CENTER OF THE RUSSIAN NORTH

Despite its relatively small population (slightly over three hundred thousand inhabitants), Vologda has become a significant presence in Russian culture, with an array of vibrant cultural institutions as well as many architectural monuments. Small enough to preserve a "hometown" feeling, Vologda, situated on the small Vologda River, is sufficiently distant from Moscow (470 kilometers by road to the southwest) to allow its own regional identity. With active artistic and literary groups, Vologda is also closely associated with the life and work of the writers Varlam Shalamov (1907–82) and Nikolai Rubtsov (1936–71). Its newest museum is a palatial structure devoted to the craft and art of lace making.

The "official" date of the city's founding is given as 1147 (the same year as Moscow's "founding"), yet there is no verifiable information to support that date. Indeed, no firm archeological evidence has been uncovered to confirm the Russian presence earlier than the thirteenth century. By that time the Vologda area was under the control of the city-state of Novgorod, located some five hundred kilometers to the west and one of the most important economic centers of medieval Russia.

With the growth of Moscow's power in the fourteenth century, however, Vologda was pulled into the Muscovite orbit along with the rest of the historic Russian North on the path to the White Sea. By the end of the fourteenth century, Moscow had its own representatives in the town; and a century later, after a prolonged, complicated struggle, Vologda and its surrounding territory were taken into the Moscow principality.

By the middle of the sixteenth century, Vologda had become the major trading and administrative center in northern Russia. Despite its small size, the Vologda River was linked to the Dvina River Basin to the north and was close enough for portage to the Sheksna River, linked to the Volga River Basin. Vologda thus served as the primary distribution point for rapidly increasing trade with England, and subsequently Holland, by way of the Dvina River to the port of Arkhangelsk. Although sacked and devastated by marauders in 1612 during the "Time of Troubles," Vologda retained its strategic importance until the development of St. Petersburg in the eighteenth century.

Vologda was built entirely of wood until the reign of Ivan IV (the Terrible), who in 1565 included the town in his private domain (oprichnina) and initiated construction of a masonry fortress, apparently to serve as his northern residence. After 1571 this enterprise was abandoned, and the walls were eventually dismantled. Yet one important monument from that period remains: the Cathedral of St. Sophia. Built in 1568–70, it is an excellent example of mid-sixteenth-century church architecture based on Aristotele Fioravanti's Dormition Cathedral (1475–79) in the Moscow Kremlin.

Fortunately, the Vologda Cathedral of St. Sophia has been well preserved. Its simple but imposing whitewashed brick walls lead upward to five onion domes, which provide a striking visual culmination to the structure. The interior is covered with a stunning display of late seventeenth-century frescoes by artists from the city of Yaroslavl. At the eastern end is a massive icon screen (late 1730s) that soars to the rim of the central cupola. The Sophia Cathedral interior is one of the most impressive examples of religious art in Russia.

The area adjacent to the Cathedral of St. Sophia is embellished with a tall bell tower (expanded in the nineteenth century, with an observation platform) and the secondary Cathedral of the Resurrection, built in a mixture of baroque and neo-Gothic styles in the 1770s. The cathedral ensemble leads to a walled compound popularly called the "kremlin," but informally known as the Archbishop's Court. This attractive collection of churches, residences, and service structures is now the center of the excellent Vologda State Museum.

Beyond the central cathedrals, Vologda's church architecture reveals a considerable variety of forms, but unlike other major centers to the northeast of Moscow, such as Yaroslavl and Kostroma, Vologda produced no distinctive local style. Nonetheless, there is much of interest, such as the Church of the Decapitation of

John the Baptist, located in a park in the center of the city. Dating from the early eighteenth century, its octagonal main structure is completely covered on the interior with frescoes painted in 1717 by artists from Yaroslavl.

The wealth of Vologda in the late eighteenth and nineteenth centuries is reflected in a number of houses, in both brick and wood, that have survived throughout the town. Indeed, Vologda was known for the variety and extent of its wooden housing. Neglect, indifference, and lack of resources have taken their toll on these charming wooden residences—as in so many Russian towns.

THE SAVIOR-PRILUTSKY MONASTERY ON THE VOLOGDA RIVER

During the fourteenth century, one of the most important accomplishments of the young Muscovite state was the development of monastic institutions that not only elevated the propagation of the faith and the quest for a spiritual life but also advanced the interests of the Moscow principality as the primary defender of Russian Orthodoxy. These monasteries were especially important in the sparsely settled Russian North. They were an outgrowth of principles of monastic organization defined by Sergius of Radonezh (died in 1392; canonized in 1452), the monk who founded in 1345 what became the Holy Trinity Monastery in the forests north of Moscow. Within the next century the disciples of Sergius would establish numerous monasteries in the North.

Among the earliest of the northern foundations was the Savior-Prilutsky (Spaso-Prilutskii) Monastery, picturesquely situated near a bend (*luka*) in the Vologda River to the north of the town. It was established presumably in the early 1370s (the precise year is uncertain) by the venerable Dmitry Prilutsky, who lived through most of the fourteenth century and was one of the most active proponents of Orthodoxy in the North.

Dmitry Prilutsky's childhood and youth were closely linked with the town of Pereslavl-Zalessky, where he became a monk at the Goritsky Dormition Monastery. During the 1350s he was associated both with Sergius of Radonezh and Moscow's grand prince Dmitry Ivanovich (Donskoi), who would lead Russian forces to a victory over a large Tatar army in 1380. Sensing the call to create his own spiritual retreat, Dmitry was advised by Sergius to go to the northern forests, together with the monk Pahomy, and undertake the arduous work of creating a monastic outpost.

This effort evidently had the support of Prince Dmitry Ivanovich as one of the early bulwarks of Orthodox Moscow in the northern territory around Vologda. The Prilutsky Monastery was also favored by Grand Prince Vassily III, who visited it on a pilgrimage with his wife Elena Glinskaia in 1528. A darker side of princely support was the monastery's use in the late fifteenth and sixteenth centuries as a place of imprisonment by Moscow's rulers.

The monastery's original buildings were of logs, including the main church, dedicated to the Procession of the Precious Wood of the Life-Giving Cross of the Lord. After its destruction by fire, the Savior Cathedral (its usual name) was rebuilt in brick during 1537–42 with substantial support from Moscow. In 1541 the young Grand Prince Ivan IV (later known as Ivan the Terrible) issued a decree that released the monastery from all taxes for a period of five years. Ivan first visited the monastery in 1545, and it remained under his attention thereafter.

As a result of princely favor, the Savior Cathedral at the Prilutsky Monastery became the earliest large masonry structure in Vologda. Similar in design to other provincial churches that imitated Moscow's cathedrals, the Savior Cathedral also has distinctive features that link it to late fifteenth-century northern churches such as the Dormition Cathedral (1497) at the St. Kirill-Belozersky Monastery and the Nativity of the Virgin (1490) at Ferapontov Monastery. The cathedral is elevated on a high base (*podklet*), which contained a separate church primarily for winter use — a feature of many Muscovite churches. This lower church has five altars, whose dedications include St. Dmitry and St. Sergius. The exterior walls rise to two rows of curved gables (*zakomary*) that are both structural and decorative. The structure is crowned with an ensemble of five drums and cupolas that provide a harmonious vertical accent.

The interior of the Savior Cathedral, whose whitewashed walls were never painted with frescoes, possesses an austere monumentality. Four large piers ascend to the corbelled vaults that support the cupola drums. The interior now has a new iconostasis of impressive size and scale. Its altar dedications include the Procession of the Cross and the Transfiguration of the Savior.

A raised gallery envelopes the cathedral and leads at the southeast corner to the monastery refectory and the Church of the Presentation, built in the late 1540s in a style similar to the refectory churches at the Kirillov and Ferapontov Monasteries. The church is crowned with a pyramid of decorative gables (*kokoshniki*) and a single cupola. The central monastic ensemble is completed by a bell tower, rebuilt in 1729–30 on a seventeenth-century base.

On the north side of the monastery is the Gate Church of the Ascension, built in 1584–90 and originally dedicated to St. Theodore Stratilates, the patron of Tsar Fyodor, who ruled from 1584 to 1598. With Fyodor's death the Riurikovich dynasty came to an end and Boris Godunov took power with the intent to found a new dynasty. The death of Boris in 1605 and the subsequent murder of his family ushered in an interregnum and the Time of Troubles, which continued even after the election of Mikhail Romanov as tsar in 1613.

During this period the Savior-Prilutsky Monastery made many contributions to the restoration of legitimacy and order, but it also suffered greatly. In 1612 it was sacked by Polish forces and rogue Cossacks. Further raids occurred in 1615 and 1619. With these memories in mind, the Prilutsky Monastery received state funds to build massive brick walls and five towers, completed in 1656. In the eighteenth and nineteenth centuries, other churches, cloisters, and an infirmary were built within the monastery walls.

In 1924 the Savior-Prilutsky Monastery was closed as a result of the general campaign against religion. During the 1930s the monastic grounds became a crowded detention center for peasants dispossessed during the collectivization of agriculture and shipped to harsh "resettlement" in the North. Following the death of Stalin (1953), the monastic ensemble was gradually restored as a cultural and historical monument. In 1979 it became a part of the Vologda State Museum.

The monastery gained a stunning addition in 1962 with the reconstruction of the ancient log Church of the Dormition from the long-abandoned Alexander Kushtsky Monastery, located near Kubenskoe Lake in Vologda Province. Although manuscript references lead some to state that the structure dates from 1519, other specialists assume that its existing form was frequently rebuilt and more probably dates from the late seventeenth century.

In 1990–91 the Savior-Prilutsky Monastery was returned to the Orthodox Church, which carefully maintains the historic buildings. The monastery now plays an active role in the spiritual life of the Vologda region, even as it remains one of the cultural and architectural treasures of the Russian North.

TOTMA ON THE SUKHONA RIVER

There are many settlements in the Russian North whose architectural monuments reflect an earlier economic vitality and strategic importance. Among the most distinctive of these towns is Totma. Located on the Sukhona River midway between Vologda and Veliky Ustiug, Totma is today a small town (population around ten thousand), and yet it contains some of the most dramatic forms of church architecture to be found in Russia. Impressive in all seasons of the year, the towers of Totma's churches are especially evocative in the winter, when they reach above the plumes of ice haze and smoke from surrounding snow-draped wooden houses.

The earliest known mention of Totma is 1137 — ten years earlier than the first recorded reference to Moscow. Originally located at the Totma River, which flows into the Sukhona some seventeen kilometers downriver (i.e., to the northeast), the settlement was apparently sacked in 1539 by Kazan Tartars. The survivors relocated to a more favorable site upriver near salt springs and mineral deposits that would form a major source of the region's wealth.

By the middle of the sixteenth century, Totma had become a center of salt refining, developed by certain monasteries in the Vologda region. In return for their efforts in producing that essential commodity, the monasteries received tax exemptions. The Savior-Prilutsky Monastery near Vologda sent one of its monks, Feodosy Sumorin, to supervise salt production in Totma. As a result, in 1554 he founded a monastery dedicated to the Transfiguration of the Savior on the small Pesya Denga River.

The Savior-Sumorin Monastery soon became one of the North's wealthiest Orthodox institutions, even though it consisted of log structures until the end of the eighteenth century. In the early nineteenth century, the monastery began a magnificent building campaign whose results impress even in their current semi-abandoned state. A modest hostel in one of the former monastery cloisters allows travelers to rest in a bucolic setting.

The other major force in the development of Totma's lucrative salt works was a Stroganov family branch headed by Afanasy and his son Grigory. As elsewhere in the North, the Stroganovs gained a near monopoly on salt production by undercutting any possible competition (with the exception of the protected monasteries), and by rendering valuable services to the Muscovite tsar. Indeed, Tsars Ivan the Terrible and Peter the Great visited Totma numerous times—a sign of its economic and strategic significance in the northern territories.

Salt was not the only source of wealth for the Totma region. Fur-producing animals also played a significant role. The importance of the fur trade to the local economy is indicated on the town's official seal, which displays a black fox on a gold background. As trade with England and Holland developed through Arkhangelsk on the White Sea, Totma became a major river port and trading center. Its extensive warehouses also served the growing trade with Siberia through river networks pioneered by the Stroganovs.

With the founding of St. Petersburg in 1703, Peter changed the direction of trade between Russia and the West. Nonetheless, northern towns retained their commercial importance. During the eighteenth century, certain local merchants such as the Panovs showed vigorous enterprise in exploring distant territories, and by the end of the century, a number of expeditions to Alaska were funded in Totma. Moreover, a Totma resident named Ivan Kuskov founded California's Fort Ross in 1812 and served as its first commandant. His grave is now carefully maintained at the Savior-Sumorin Monastery, and his modest log house has been preserved as part of the excellent Totma Regional History Museum.

The wealth that flowed into this community during the eighteenth century supported the building of a number of brick churches of striking design, with large bell towers and baroque decoration in a distinctive "cartouche" pattern formed in brick. These churches, and the nearby Savior-Sumorin Monastery, were designed to present an imposing view to the river, rising as they did above the wooden settlements around them.

The most imposing of the monuments, the Church of the Entry of Christ into Jerusalem, was erected in 1774–94 with funds provided by the brothers Grigory and Peter Panov, merchants who were involved in the trade with "Russian America." This church follows the northern practice of "stacking" two places of worship, the lower of which was used in winter and the upper in the summer. A number of Totma's eighteenth-century churches had long gestations: first the lower church was built, then the upper part as further funds appeared. In an ingenious approach the walls of the lower structure were properly calculated to support the hoped-for addition years ahead.

Equally impressive is the soaring tower of the Church of the Nativity of Christ, whose lower space was built in 1746–48, with the upper church added in 1786–93. Although most of these architectural monuments have survived, Totma's churches were thoroughly desecrated during the Soviet period. Almost nothing remains of their once-splendid baroque interiors. Three of them are being restored (two for the parish and one for the local museum), but the glorious craftsmanship that once decorated these spaces is visible only in archival photographs.

As in other northern Russian towns, the preservation of log houses in Totma has often yielded to the construction of monotonous brick apartments. Fires have also taken their toll. Yet Totma is better preserved than most northern towns, partly because of nineteenth-century economic stagnation compounded by the lack of a rail link. With an economy based primarily on farming, the small town retained its harmonious relation to the surrounding landscape.

Tourism is gradually becoming an economic factor in contemporary Totma, and the construction of a major pipeline nearby provides additional resources. Yet coordination among many groups is necessary if Totma is to preserve the legacy of its commercial ingenuity, which spanned continents from the European North through Siberia to the American West.

THE VELSK REGION ON THE VAGA RIVER

Traditional culture in the Russian North has often been associated with once prosperous villages where folk crafts flourished. The pace of modern development has severely depleted such villages, and regional centers such as Velsk have attempted to gather the fragments. Although its livelihood depends primarily on modern transportation and forest development, the northern town of Velsk (current population about 23,500) has become an important center for the study of traditional arts and crafts. Indeed, its regional history museum is considered one of the best in Russia's provinces.

The oldest known reference to Velsk dates to 1137. Yet it is likely that a settlement existed much earlier near the point where the small Vel River flows into the Vaga (now in the extreme southern part of Arkhangelsk Province). As an important left tributary of the Northern Dvina, the Vaga River offered a favorable connection to vast reaches in the North. The area's many small rivers and lakes also provided an ample source of fish and wildlife.

Like most settlements in the North during the early medieval period, Velsk fell within the orbit of the major commercial center of Novgorod. By the late fifteenth century, however, the region was absorbed into the rapidly expanding territory of Muscovy during the reign of Ivan III (the Great). Velsk and its forests soon proved a reliable source of income for Moscow's princes.

In the early seventeenth century, this prosperity vanished during the Time of Troubles. Like many northern communities, Velsk provided support to expel Polish forces from Moscow in 1613. But Velsk itself was left vulnerable to marauders who overcame a nearby fort and sacked the settlement and its Church of St. John the Merciful.

Gradually, the settlement revived through the ample resources of local forests. Especially valuable was the extraction of pitch, or pine tar, obtained by reducing pine wood under high temperature to charcoal and resin. Pitch was essential in many ways, including the sealing of boats, barrels, and other vessels. It became one of Russia's main northern exports, primarily to England, where it was called "Archangel tar" (after the port of Arkhangelsk). Production of pitch began in Velsk in the sixteenth century and grew steadily thereafter. Its importance to the local economy was officially acknowledged during the reign of Catherine the Great, when Velsk—like many other Russian towns—gained a coat of arms. Its shield proudly displays a barrel, with black pitch spilling from the top.

During the nineteenth century, the Velsk region was included in the Crown

Estates, managed especially for the imperial family. This gave a relatively favorable status to the peasants who lived and worked on the land. Velsk also benefited as an important way station on the Moscow–Arkhangelsk Road. With modest prosperity, this provincial corner gained a pleasant appearance that included a number of well-built wooden houses for merchants and officials. Fortunately, a number of these houses have survived. The center of town had its commercial buildings, one of which—the redbrick Sobolev Building (1913)—has been converted for use by the Regional History Museum. Like many northern towns, Velsk also served as a place of political exile.

Among the churches of Velsk in the early twentieth century, one has survived with little change: the wooden Church of the Dormition, built in the 1790s at the town cemetery. Velsk also had a large Cathedral of the Transfiguration, begun in 1898 and consecrated in 1913. Closed after the establishment of Soviet power, the structure was substantially remodeled in the 1930s to serve as a House of Culture. There are now proposals to restore it for church use.

Following the turbulence of the revolutionary years, the forests once again provided the basis for economic revival in the early 1930s. During the same period, the Velsk region became one of several northern relocation areas for peasants who had been forcibly uprooted during the collectivization of agriculture. Their existence was harsh and often amounted to little more than forced labor.

Transportation links through Velsk improved dramatically with the completion in 1942 of a rail line extending from Konosha, some 120 kilometers to the west (on the main line to Arkhangelsk), to Kotlas on the Dvina River, 270 kilometers to the east. From Kotlas the rail line extended almost 1,200 kilometers northeast past Pechora to the coal mines of Vorkuta.

Today Velsk continues to play an important transportation role. The region's forest products are shipped out by rail, and the town remains a major stop on the long Moscow–Arkhangelsk highway. At Velsk the road turns north for the final leg to Arkhangelsk—some 510 kilometers distant. Another road winds eastward 400 kilometers through forest and swamp to Kotlas. (The direct rail line is much shorter.)

Nearby villages continue to feel the impact of demographic shifts that have led in some cases to depopulation. Nonetheless, memories of old traditions remain, along with a few parish churches—most in an abandoned state. One historic village, Bereznik, is picturesquely located on the Vel River and is partially maintained by the Velsk Regional History Museum. In addition to a wooden firehouse and tower built in the early twentieth century, Bereznik has a large two-story log dwelling that dates from the late eighteenth century. This *kurnaya izba* was built for use during the long winters and has been remarkably well preserved as part of a functioning farmstead.

The upper reaches of the Vaga River are fed by a web of streams and small rivers such as the Kuloi, Vel, Ustye, Pezhma, Shadrenga, and Kokshenga. This aquatic network is nestled among gentle, rolling hills that form some of the most picturesque landscapes in the North. The center of the upper Vaga region is the town of Verkhovazhye (population five thousand), located in the northernmost part of Vologda Province. Its name, not surprisingly, means "upper Vaga." First mentioned in the early seventeenth century, the settlement struggled for existence in its remote location.

Later in the eighteenth century, the position of Verkhovazhye improved with the development of the Vologda–Arkhangelsk post road, which skirted the settlement to the north. A symbol of its status was the brick Cathedral of the Dormition of the Virgin, begun in 1755 to replace a wooden church. Completed ten years later, the Dormition Cathedral was expanded in the mid-1770s with a western extension that could be heated for worship during the winter.

During the nineteenth century, a few imposing brick buildings were erected in the neoclassical style, but the small town — formally a "village" — was built largely of wood. During the mid-nineteenth century, it was widely known for its annual St. Aleksy Fair, which attracted hundreds of merchants and peasants. In the summer of 1858, Tsar Alexander II passed through Verkhovazhye as part of his tour of the Russian North.

A devastating fire in 1879 reduced much of Verkhovazhye to ruins, and it never regained the active market life of the mid-nineteenth century. Nonetheless, a gradual rebuilding resulted in a number of appealing wooden houses that exist to this day — including a two-story structure that houses an interesting local history museum.

During the late 1930s, what remained of the Dormition Cathedral was closed, vandalized, and used for secular purposes, including a club and a gym. Its cupolas were destroyed, and over the next half century its interior art vanished. Fortunately, plans to raze the church were not implemented, and during the 1990s it was reconsecrated for worship.

Verkhovazhye continues its sleepy existence as a modest administrative center in the Vologda hinterlands. The nearest rail station is at Velsk, forty kilometers to the north. Improvement of the Moscow–Arkhangelsk highway (M-8) in the late 1980s led to an increase in highway traffic and a modest boost to the local economy.

Those interested in traditional Russian art will find obscure treasures in villages scattered throughout the Verkhovazhye region and the adjacent Velsk region, to the north in Arkhangelsk Province. The area has its brick churches, a few of which have been partially restored. Notable examples include the Church of the Epiphany in Pezhma (1806) and the early nineteenth-century Church of the Resurrection at Smetanino.

But the traditional culture of the upper Vaga region is most distinctively expressed in wooden houses and churches. Some of the houses are in perilous state, located in villages that have been nearly abandoned. Nonetheless, there are surviving houses with unique decorative paintings on both exterior and interior. A good example is a rambling log dwelling in the hamlet of Ostrovskaya. Particularly notable here is the lion motif, symbolizing power and yet delightfully playful in this folk painting. In rare cases some of the house interiors still preserve chromolithograph posters from the early twentieth century.

The pervasive presence of painting in this environment is also evident in the remains of wooden chapels that dot the landscape near villages such as Fedkovo, Nikiforovo, Selivanovo, and Seredniaia. Abandoned and weathered by the elements, these lyrical remnants of folk culture still have fragments of paintings and decorative art within them.

Of equal interest are the area's wooden churches, such as the large Church of the Resurrection at Kozlovskoe, built in 1791 near the Kokshenga River just north of the border between Vologda and Arkhangelsk Provinces. In a recent restoration the plank siding of the church has regained its white color. These capacious houses of worship show a more expansive sense of space than the traditional log churches of an earlier period, with their dramatic tower forms. The increased size and simpler forms of churches such as the one at Kozlovskoe suggest a wide and active participation in religious observances in large northern villages. This is a little-studied aspect of Russian spiritual life before the cataclysms of the twentieth century.

VELIKY USTIUG: THE END OF THE SUKHONA RIVER AND THE BEGINNING OF THE NORTHERN DVINA

The Vologda territory in the Russian North possesses a special charm, with its forested landscape and old towns along river trading networks that once carried Russia's wealth to the West and to Siberia. The faded glory of these historic settlements is still evident in the churches, great and small, that dot the countryside.

Among these towns, Veliky Ustiug has a particularly rich history and culture.

It is located in the northeastern corner of Vologda Province at the confluence of the Sukhona and the Iug, which merge to form a third river—the Northern Dvina. This network of three navigable rivers spread throughout northern Russia in a major transportation route that attracted the earliest Russian settlers here, apparently by the middle of the twelfth century. The mercantile city of Novgorod sent its pioneering traders to the region and lay claim to the area until the middle of the fifteenth century. Veliky Ustiug ultimately cast its lot with Moscow and became an important military post.

Veliky Ustiug also witnessed the vigorous development of the Orthodox Church. One of its most remarkable spiritual leaders, St. Stephen of Perm, began missionary activity as early as 1379 among non-Russian indigenous tribes eastward to the Ural Mountains. Stephen subsequently became a bishop and was eventually canonized by the Russian Orthodox Church.

Despite the severe northern climate and the great distances between major settlements, Ustiug grew and thrived in the sixteenth century, especially with the development of trade between Russia and England and Holland during the reign of Ivan the Terrible. After the return to prosperous trade with western Europe in the seventeenth century, Ustiug's merchants and artisans flourished. In particular its silversmiths developed specialized skills in the *niello* technique, and their work was in demand not only in the North but also in St. Petersburg, including at the imperial court. These commercial ties to cities such as St. Petersburg led to a familiarity with the lavish decorative forms of eighteenth-century religious art. Consequently, a number of Ustiug's churches had gilded icon screens that display a northern interpretation of the European baroque style.

At the center of town is the Cathedral of the Dormition of the Mother of God, whose form dates primarily from the seventeenth and eighteenth centuries. The Dormition Cathedral is surrounded by six other churches to form an ensemble known as Cathedral Court and the adjacent Archbishop's Court. Together with the cathedral bell tower, they are dramatically situated on the high left embankment of the Sukhona River and form the dominant feature in the town's landscape. Cathedral Court is the appropriate place to begin a walking tour of Ustiug, with its quiet streets, neighborhood churches, and the Archangel Monastery, with its rich church art. But the most remarkable example of the late baroque in Ustiug is contained at the Trinity-Gleden Monastery, on the opposite side of the Sukhona River.

THE VILLAGE OF GLEDEN AND ITS TRINITY MONASTERY

On the lower reaches of the right bank of the Sukhona River, near its confluence with the River Iug, is the ancient settlement of Gleden. Less known than the town of Veliky Ustiug, just across the Sukhona, Gleden is the site of the Trinity Monastery. The main church of that monastery contains an icon screen that is one of the great works of baroque religious art in Russia. Statues of angels, putti, and divine figures hover around elaborately carved frames for dozens of icons painted in the style of the Italian Renaissance. This miraculous display originated in the wealth of local merchants who made substantial donations to Ustiug's monasteries.

Established at the ancient settlement of Gleden no later than the middle of the thirteenth century, the monastery consisted of wooden structures (including three log churches) for the first four centuries of its existence. The monastery's earliest masonry structure was the rebuilt Trinity Cathedral, begun in 1659 with donations by Sila and Ivan Grudtsyn, among Ustiug's wealthiest merchant families. Financial and legal difficulties after the death of the brothers halted construction for much of the 1660s until 1690. The structure, with its five cupolas and a separate bell tower in the west, was finally completed at the end of the seventeenth century.

The exterior is austere, without the elaborate facade ornaments typical of many seventeenth-century Russian churches. The design of the interior is also restrained, with no frescoes and only two massive piers (instead of the usual four) supporting the ceiling vaults and domes. The icon screen, however, is a wonder to behold. Framed with five rows of intricately carved and gilded wood, it took almost a decade to create, from 1776 to 1784. The soaring wooden structure rises to a crescendo at its center, with flanking "wings" on either side. From left to right these three parts form a seamless whole, behind which is the altar space in the apse.

The masterful carving includes extensive statuary that amplifies the church's guiding motif, dedicated to the ministry and Passion of Christ. The style of the icon painting imitates that of Italian masters, particularly noticeable in depictions of the Virgin. To the right of the Royal Gate (to the altar) is a large icon of the Old Testament Trinity—to which the monastery is dedicated.

The ultimate source for this combination of florid baroque and classical elements is St. Petersburg, yet numerous other eighteenth-century Russian churches displayed a similar style. For example, the town of Totma, located on the Sukhona River some two hundred kilometers to the southwest of Veliky Ustiug, was known as a center of "northern baroque." Indeed, the contract for the icon screen at the Trinity Monastery identifies the primary master craftsmen as residents of Totma. But even Totma, whose baroque church interiors were ransacked during the Soviet era, lacked the complexity of the iconostasis at the remote Trinity-Gleden Monastery.

Within the Trinity Monastery's unfinished brick walls there are two other churches: the refectory and Church of the Presentation, completed in the 1740s; and the infirmary Church of the Dormition, built in the 1740s over the monastery's west gate. In 1841 the small, secluded monastery with its unimaginably beautiful treasure was closed, only to be reopened in 1912 as a convent. After the revolution the nuns existed precariously as an agricultural commune until the convent was disbanded in 1925. In the aftermath of social chaos, the former monastery served various uses, including a refuge for orphans and a detention center for juvenile delinquents. From the 1930s it was also used to house exiled peasant families and indigent elderly. The interiors of the Churches of the Presentation and Dormition were completely vandalized.

Throughout these cataclysms the Trinity Cathedral remained locked and protected until the 1980s, when the entire ensemble was deeded to the Veliky Ustiug Museum. With limited resources, the museum has carefully preserved what time and fate have left. Thus the magnificent baroque icon screen at the Trinity-Gleden Monastery embodies two miracles—that of its creation and that of its improbable survival in the twentieth century.

To the north of Gleden is the village of Dymkovo, with its well-preserved wooden houses and two churches—St. Sergius of Radonezh (1739–47) and the larger St. Dmitry (1700–1709)—located on the right bank of the Sukhona opposite Cathedral Court. Either side of the river offers excellent views of churches and houses on the other bank—an example of the sense of ensemble that characterizes the unique environment of historic Ustiug.

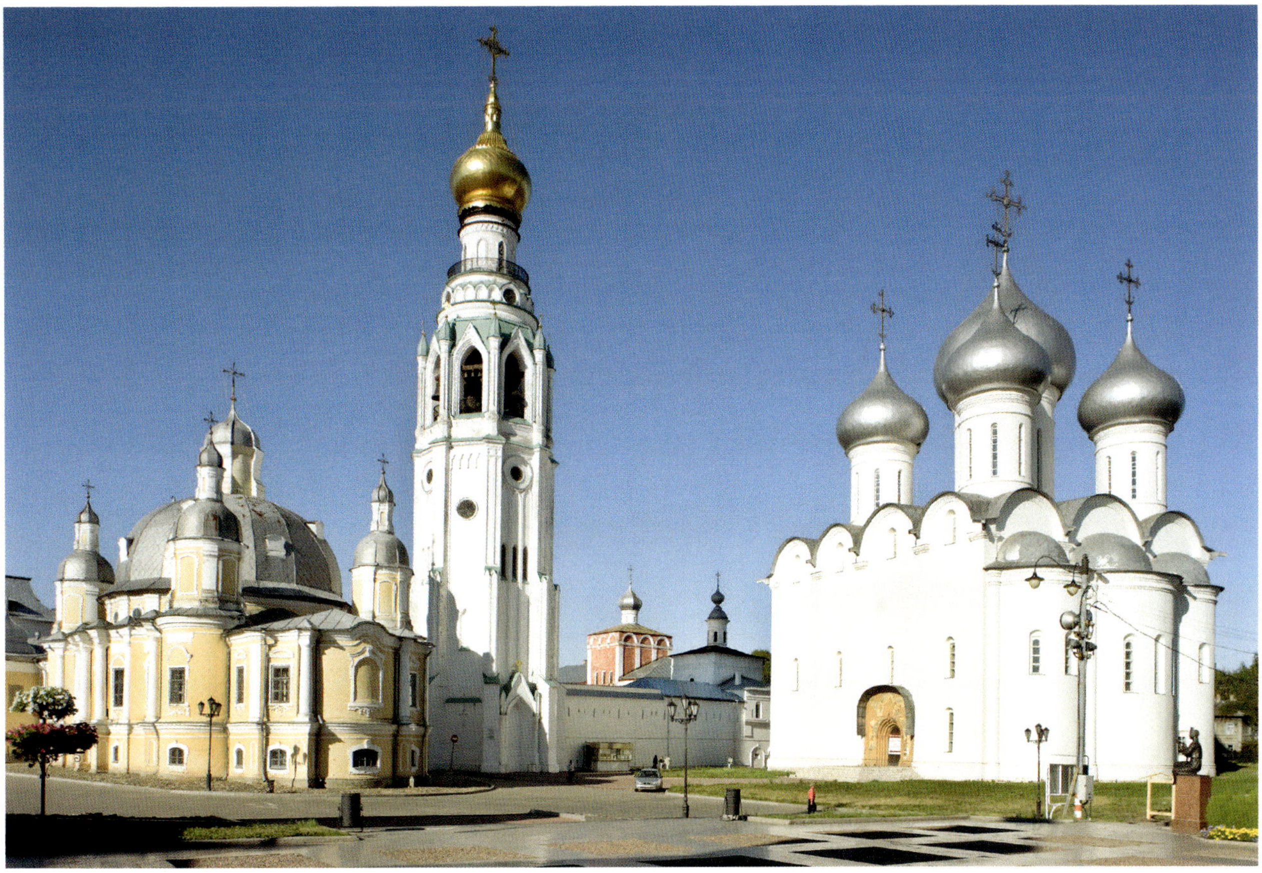

VOLOGDA. Cathedral Square. From left: Cathedral of the Resurrection (1772–76); bell tower (seventeenth century; enlarged in nineteenth century); walls of Archbishop's Court; Church of the Nativity of Christ in Archbishop's Court (1667–70); Church of the Elevation of the Cross over the Holy Gate (1687–92); Cathedral of St. Sophia (second half of sixteenth century), southeast view. Photograph: August 3, 2011.

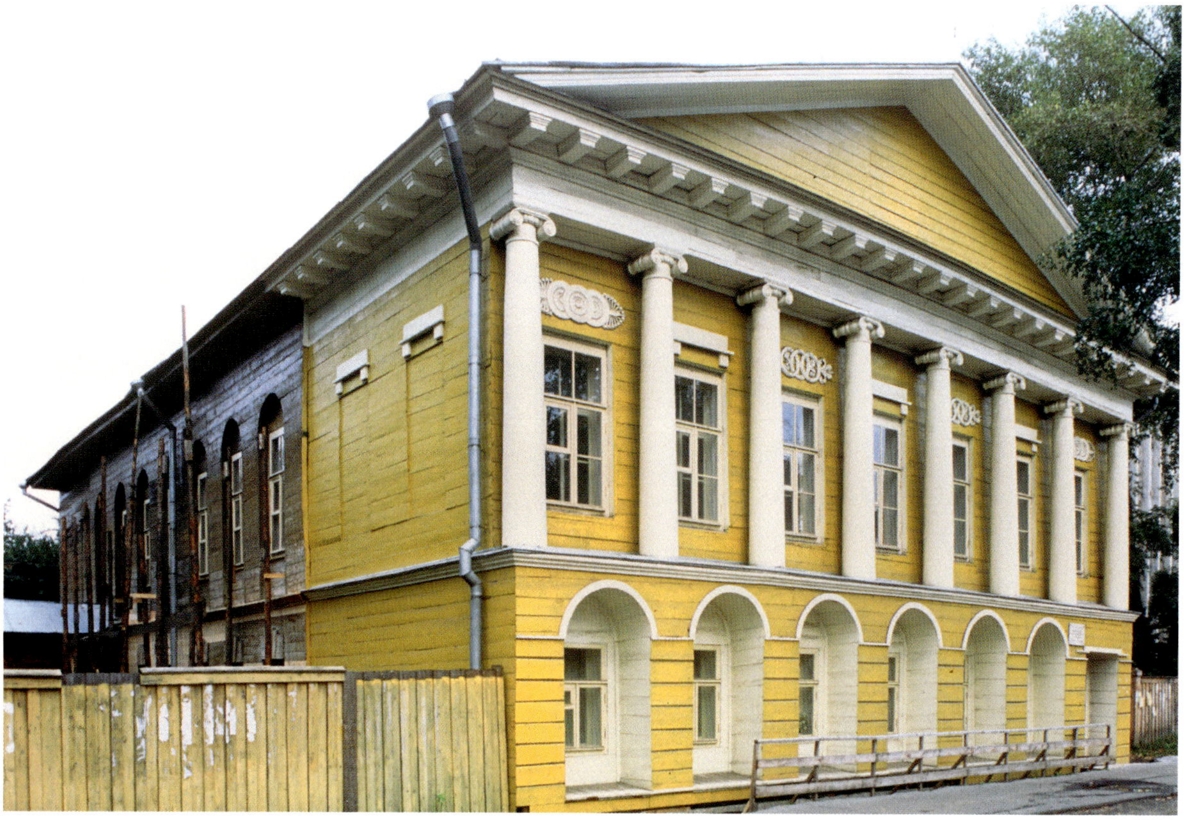

VOLOGDA. Levashov house, early nineteenth century, Herzen Street 37. A superb example of the neoclassical Empire style applied to a large log structure in the Russian provinces. Photograph: August 22, 2004.

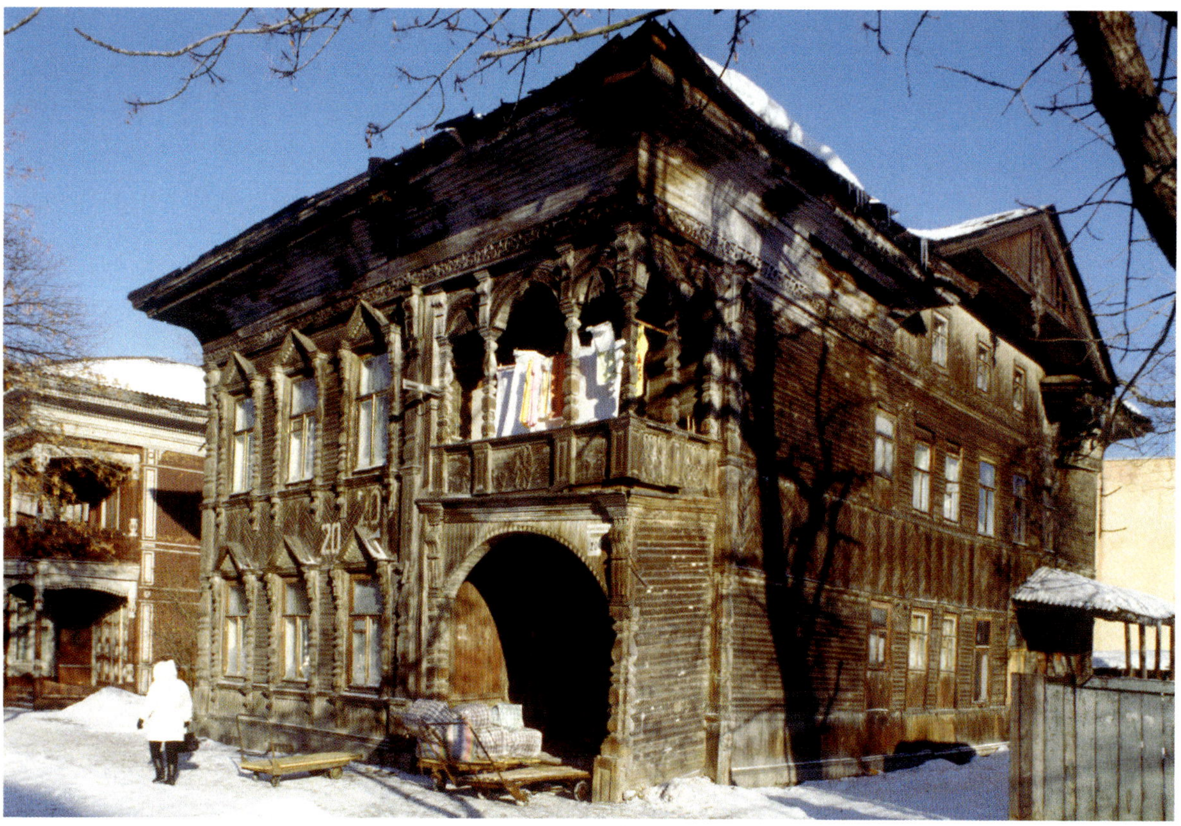

VOLOGDA. Kirkhoglanin house, Annunciation Street 20. Built at the turn of the twentieth century, this house displays the exuberant decoration typical of merchant houses. Photograph: February 26, 1998.

VOLOGDA. Cathedral of St. Sophia (Divine Wisdom), east view. Begun by Ivan the Terrible around 1568, the basic structure was completed in the early 1570s. Photograph: August 3, 2011.

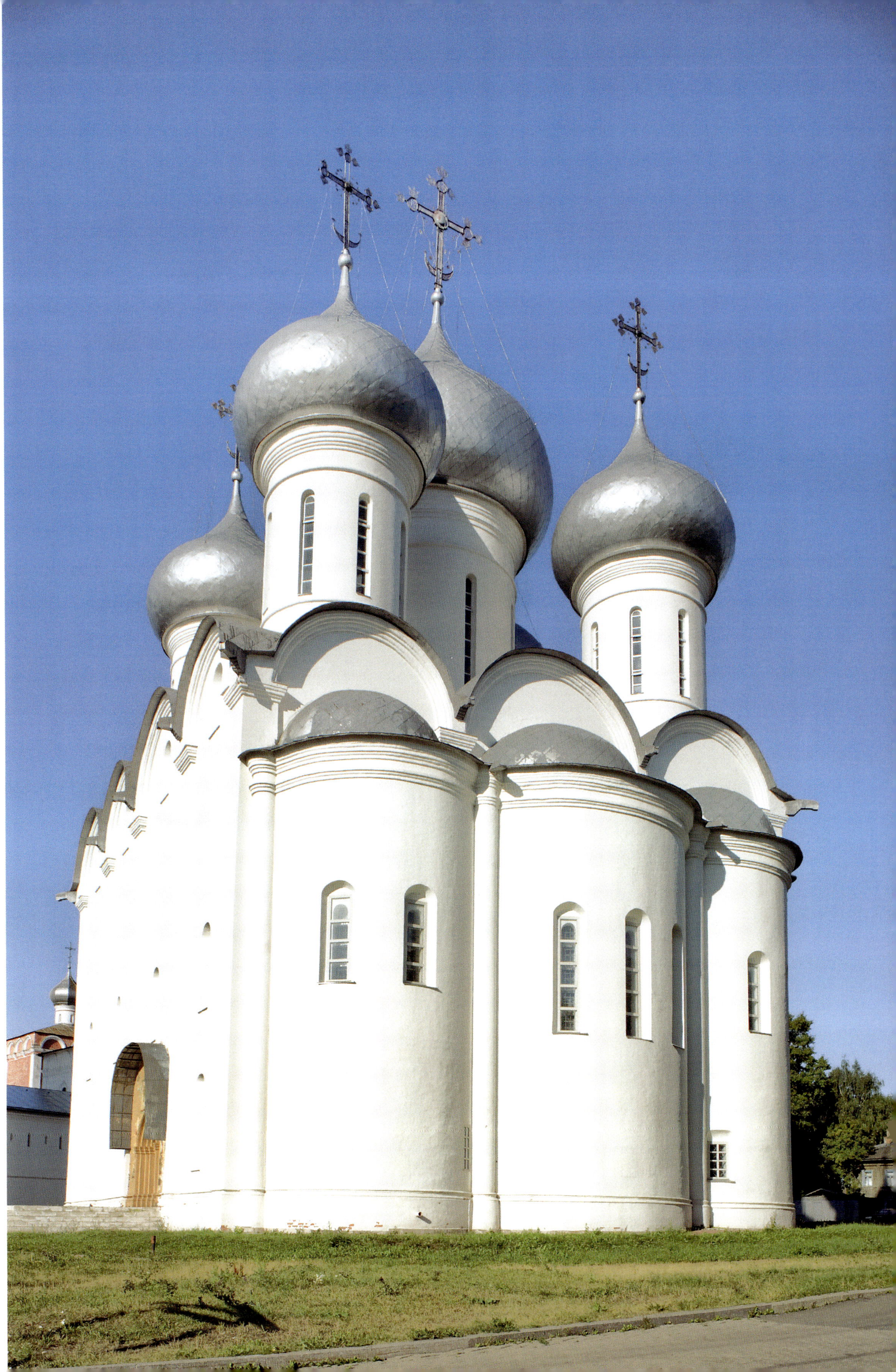

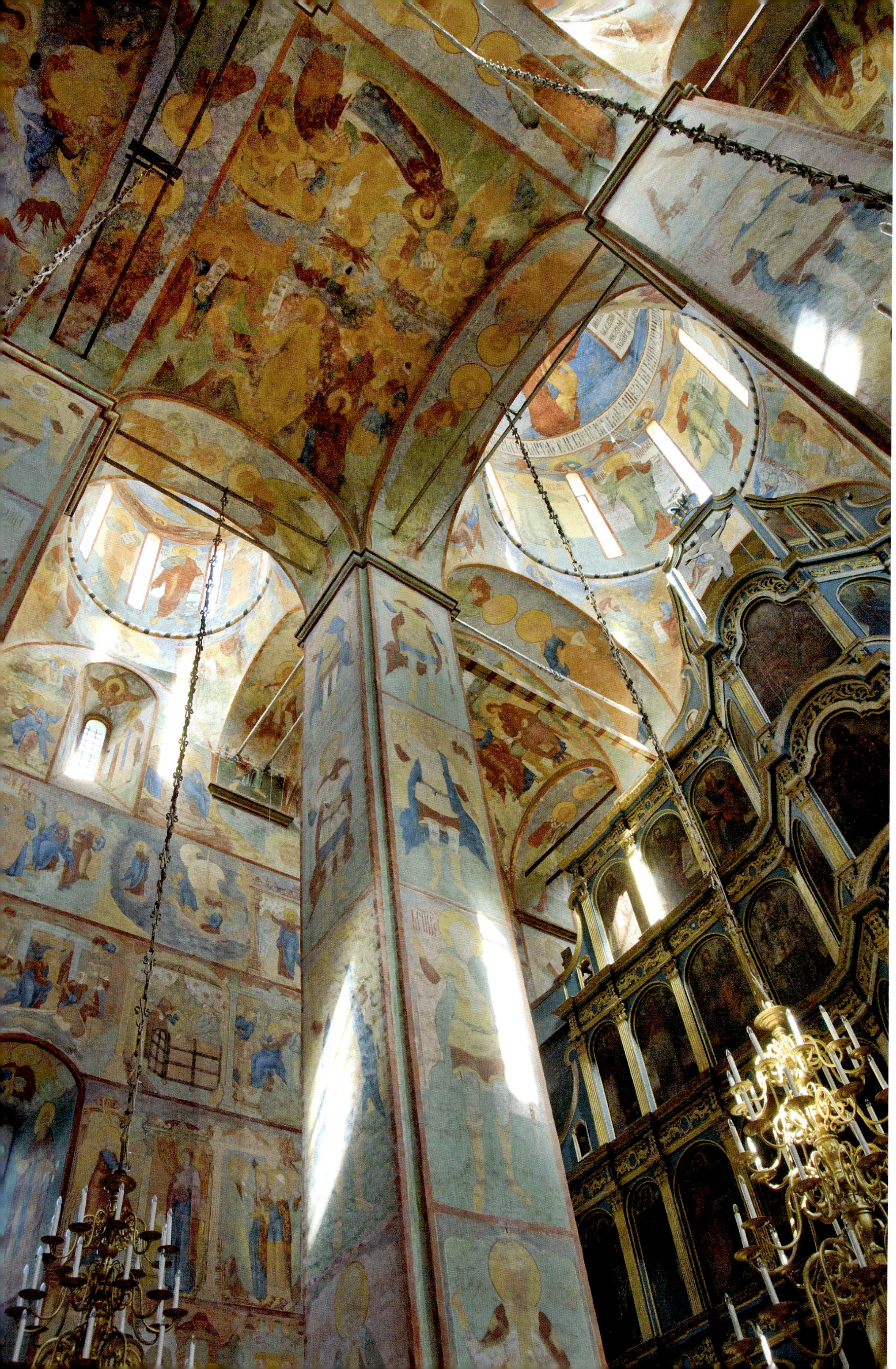

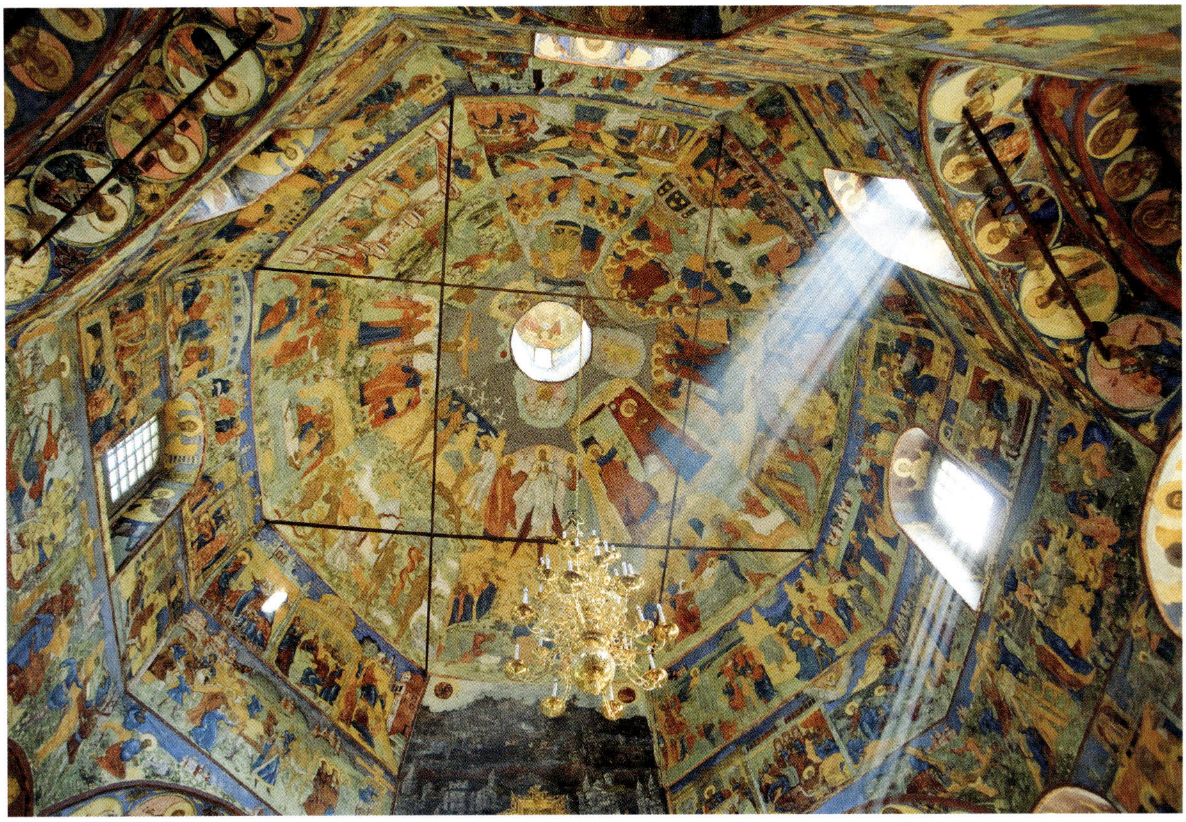

ROSHCHENYE. Church of the Decapitation of John the Baptist, view toward dome. Church construction begun in 1710. Interior covered with wall paintings in 1717. Photograph: July 24, 2011.

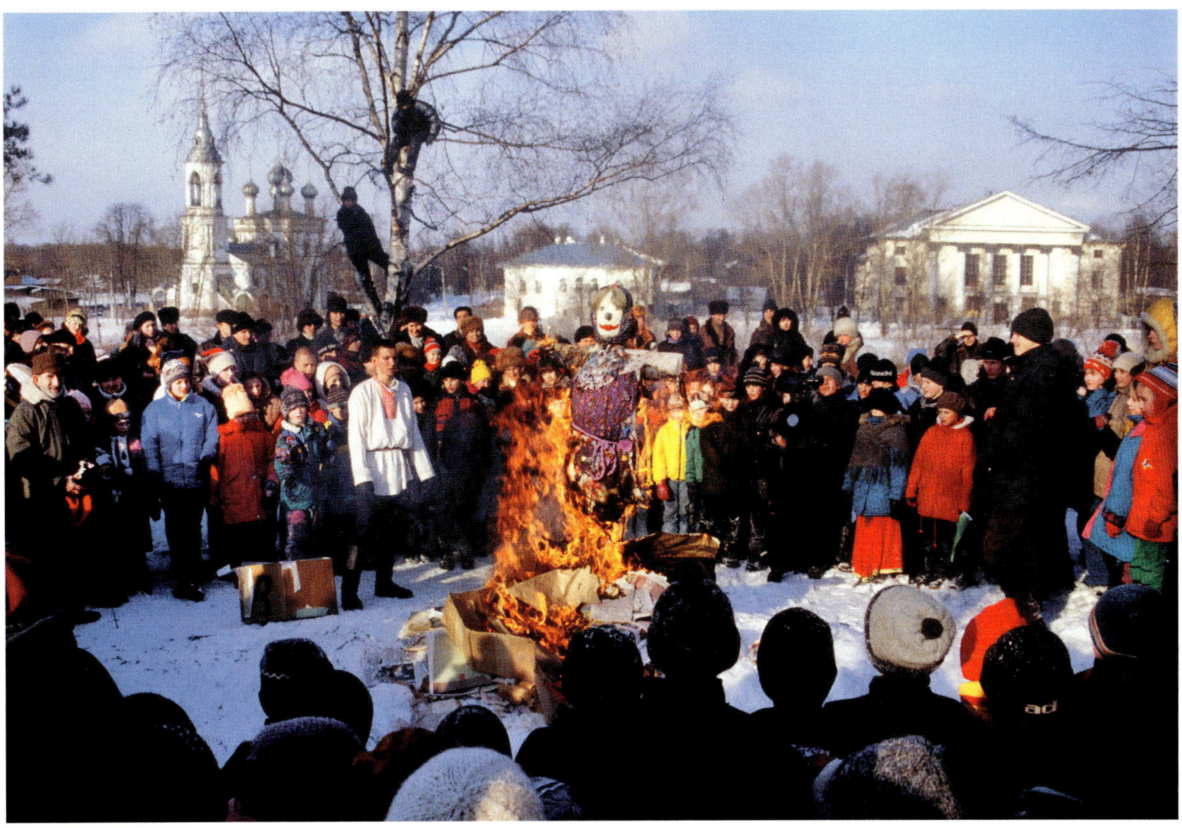

VOLOGDA. Maslennitsa (Shrovetide) festival. Burning of rag doll symbolizing the passage from winter to spring. Left, on opposite bank of Vologda River, Church of the Purification. Photograph: March 12, 2000.

VOLOGDA. Cathedral of St. Sophia (Divine Wisdom), interior, view northeast with northeast pier and icon screen; ceiling vault with frescoes of Dormition and Descent into Hell. Photograph: July 20, 2011.

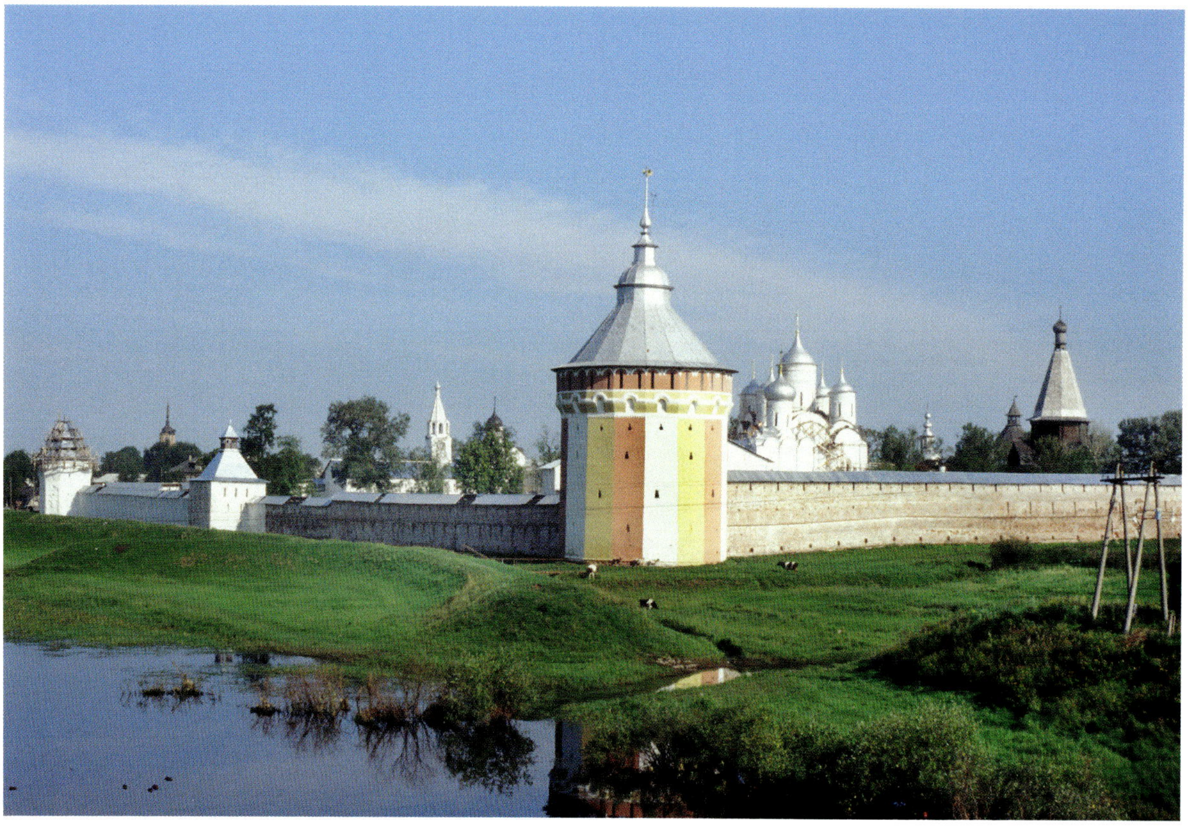

PRILUKI. Savior-Prilutsky Monastery, southwest view from Vologda River railroad bridge. Photograph: August 1, 1998.

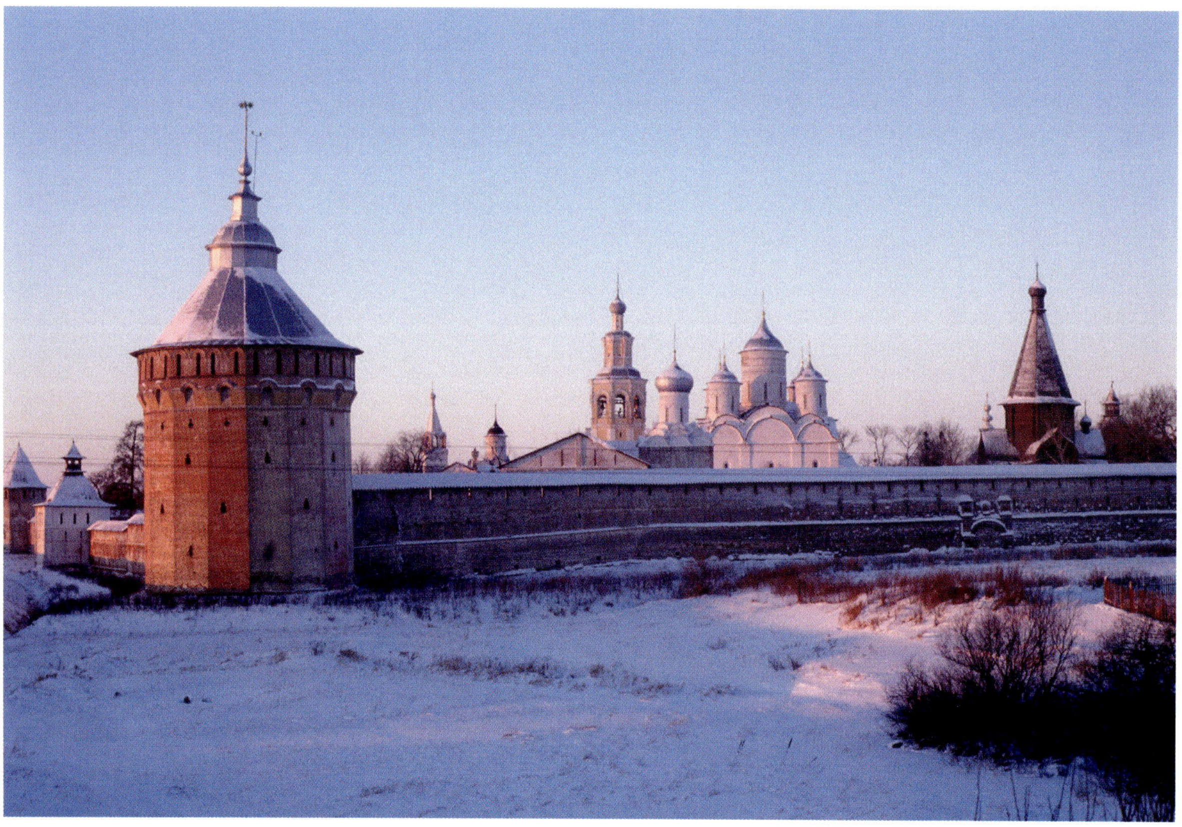

PRILUKI. Savior-Prilutsky Monastery, southwest corner, walls and tower, south view at winter sunset from railroad embankment. Photograph: January 4, 1997.

PRILUKI. Cathedral of the Procession of the Precious Wood of the Life-Giving Cross of the Lord, with bell tower. Also known as the Transfiguration of the Savior, this main monastery church was built in 1537–42. Savior-Prilutsky Monastery, southwest view. Photograph: February 23, 1998.

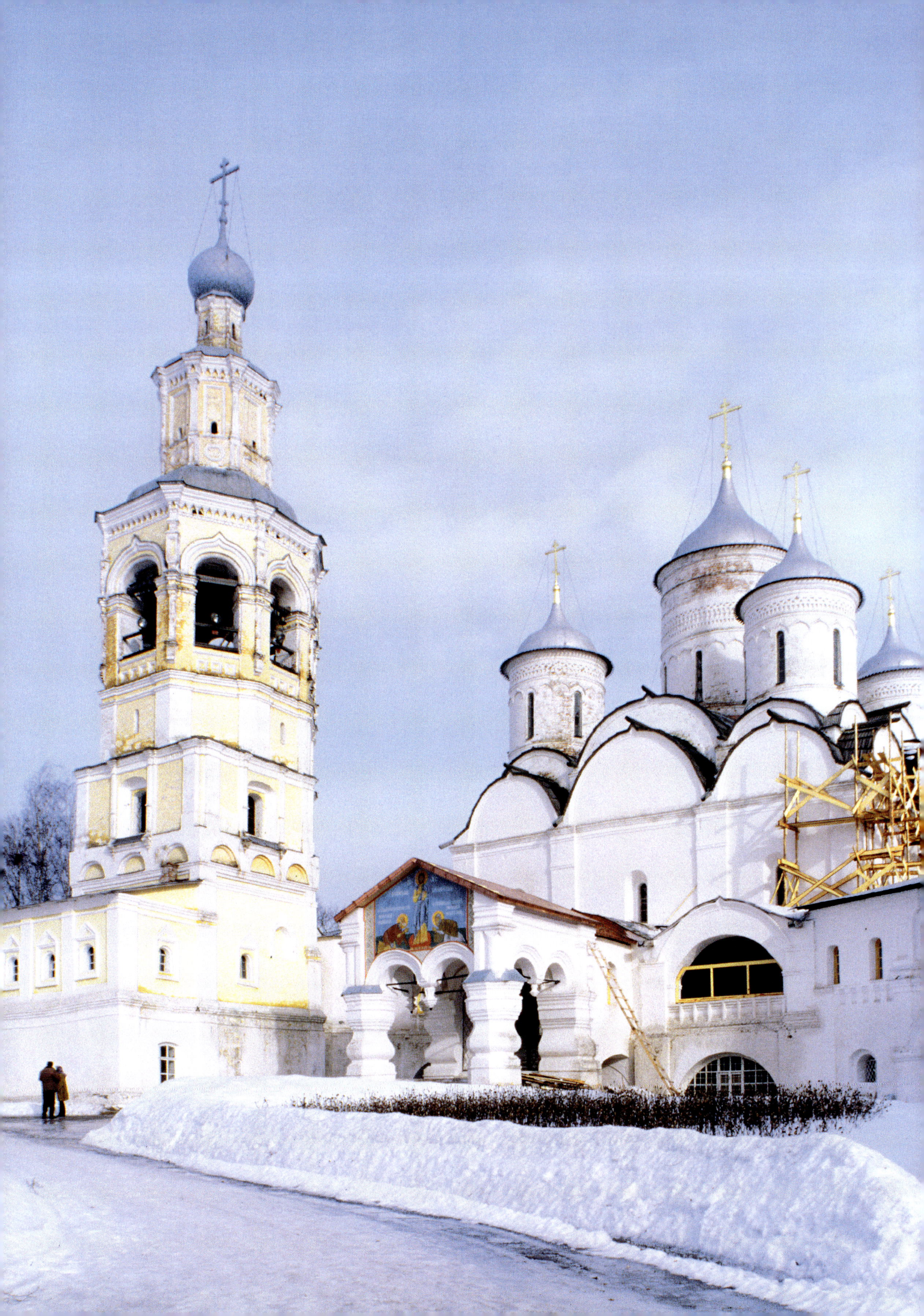

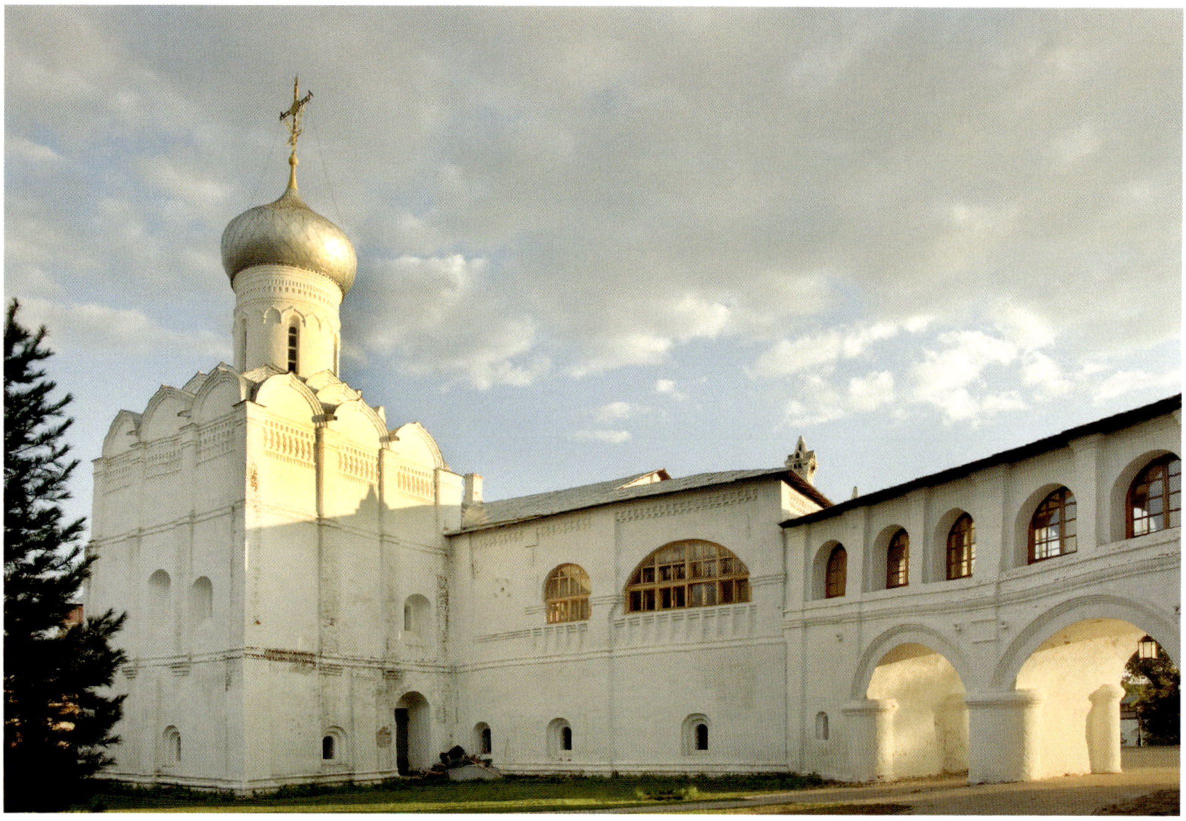

PRILUKI. Refectory and Church of the Presentation, Savior-Prilutsky Monastery, northeast view. The church and refectory were built in the late 1540s, with a covered gallery to the cathedral built in 1623. Photograph: August 13, 2010.

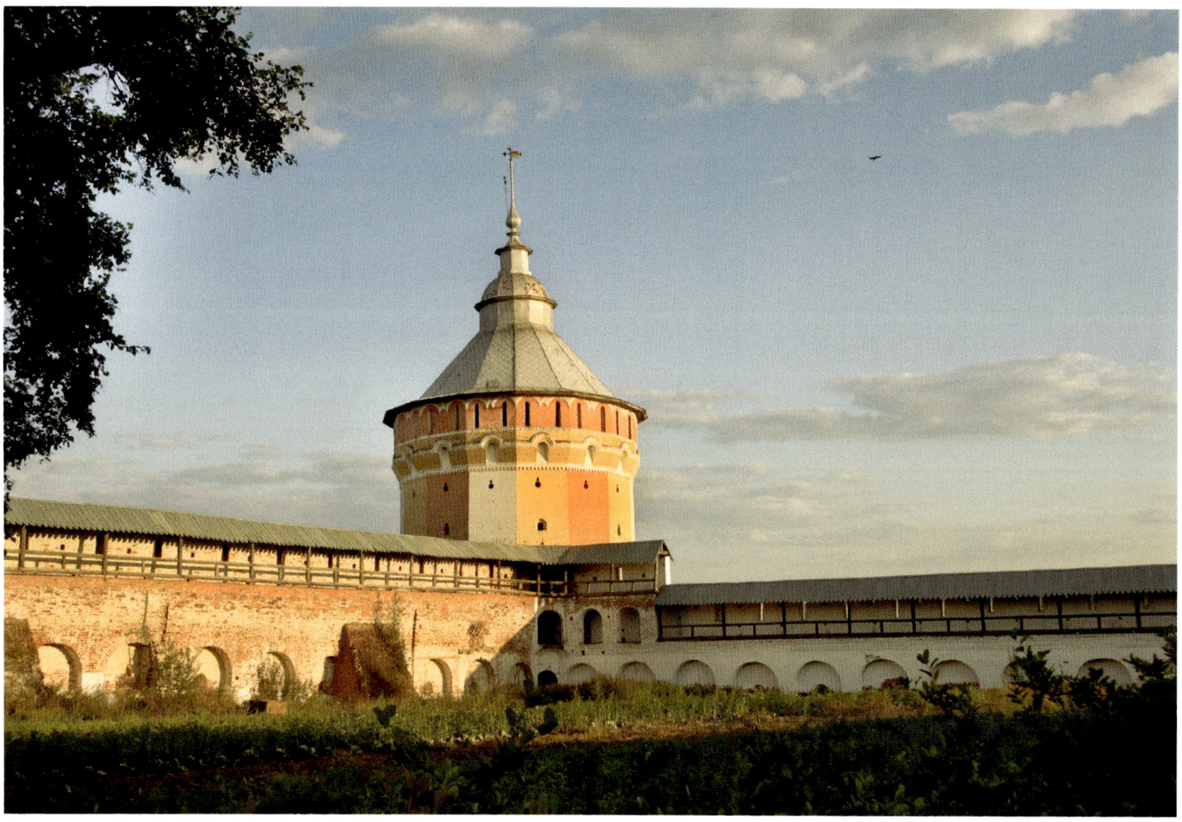

PRILUKI. Savior-Prilutsky Monastery, southwest corner, walls and tower, northeast view. Photograph: August 13, 2010.

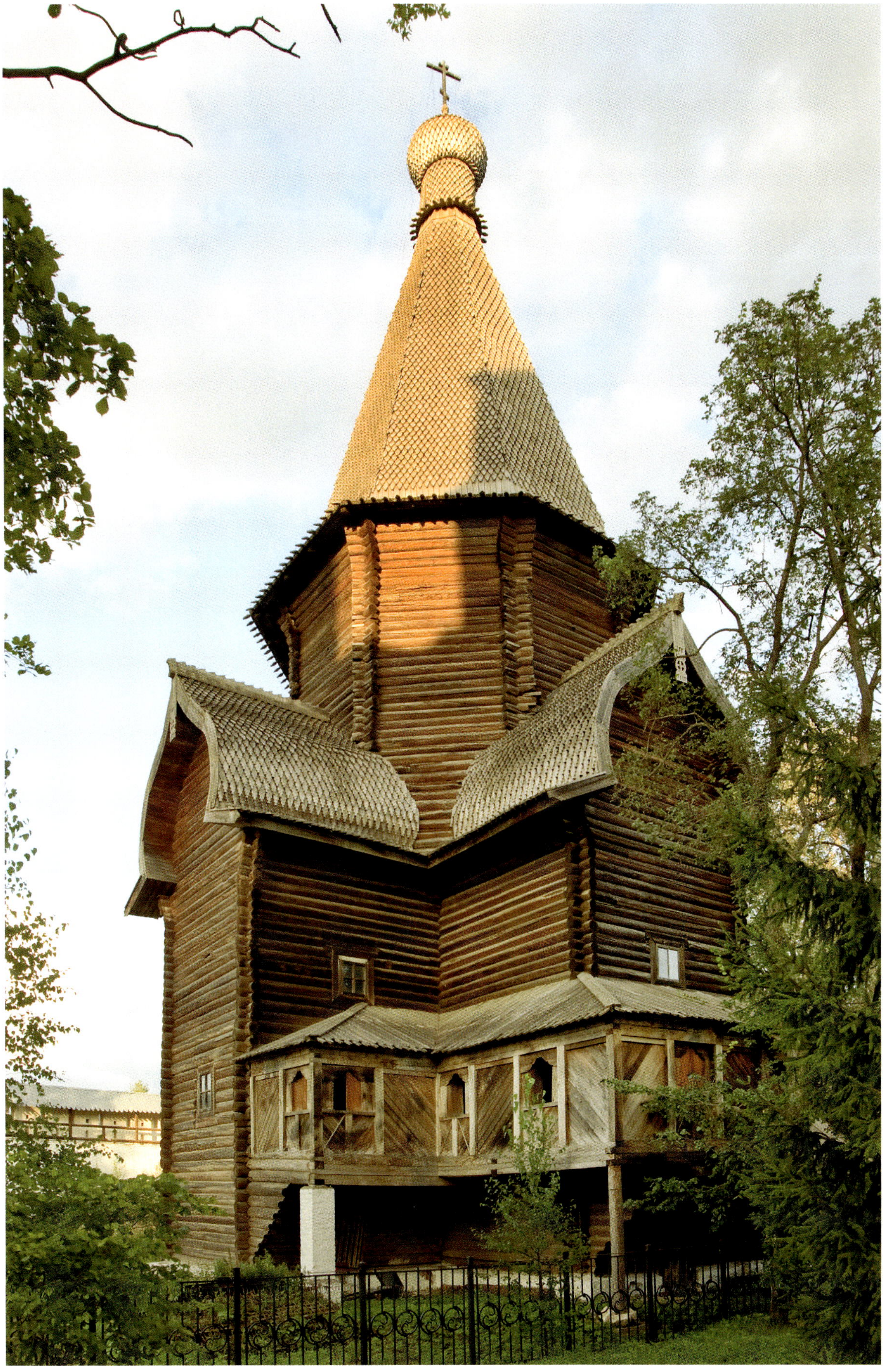

PRILUKI. Wooden Church of the Dormition, brought from Alexander Kushtsky Monastery in the 1960s. The basic structure of this log church is dated, with much question, to 1519. Although not used for worship, the church is now considered an integral part of the Savior-Prilutsky Monastery. Northwest view. Photograph: August 13, 2010.

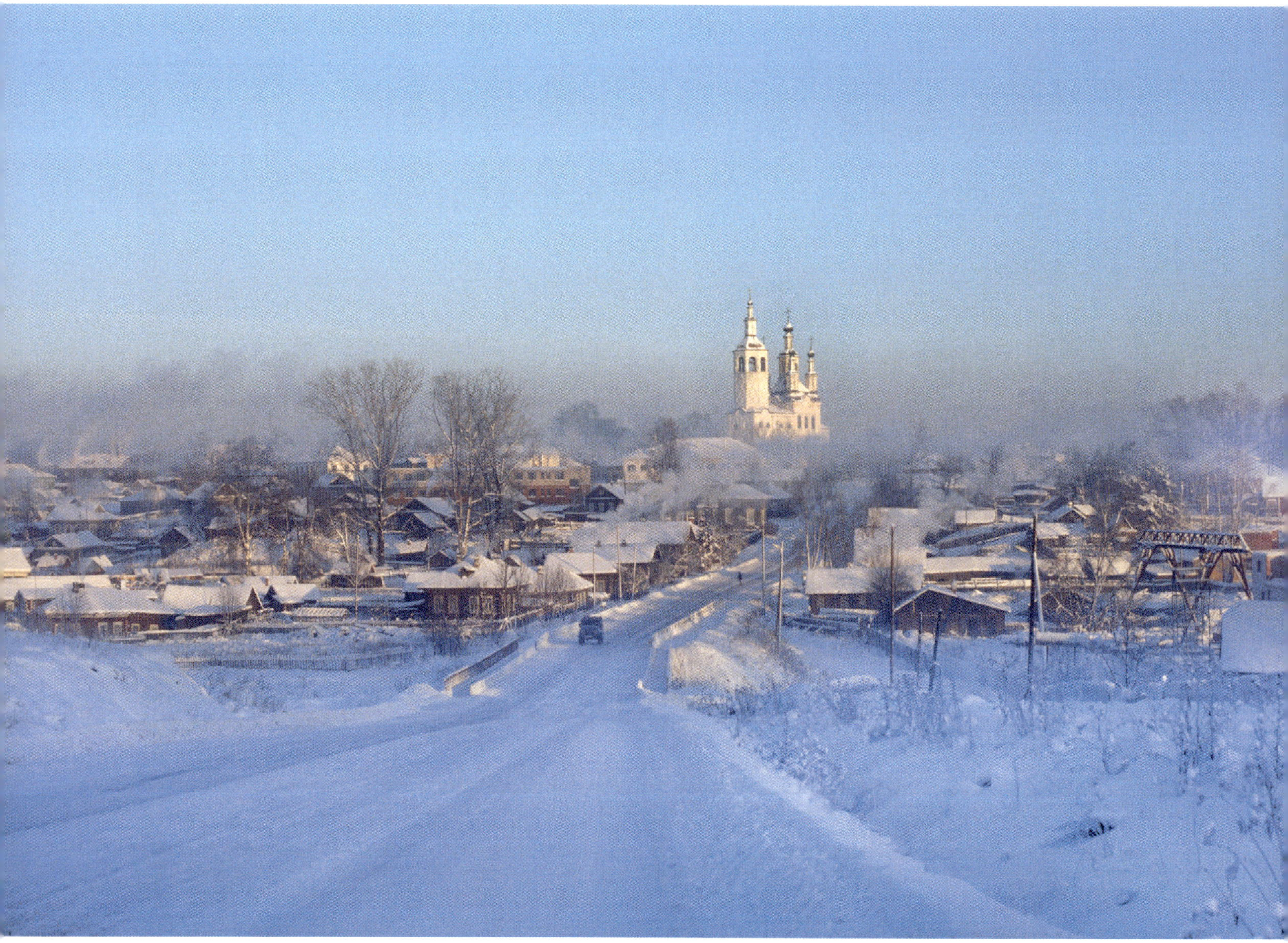

TOTMA. Panorama, with Church of the Entry of Christ into Jerusalem, southwest view. Photograph: January 5, 1997.

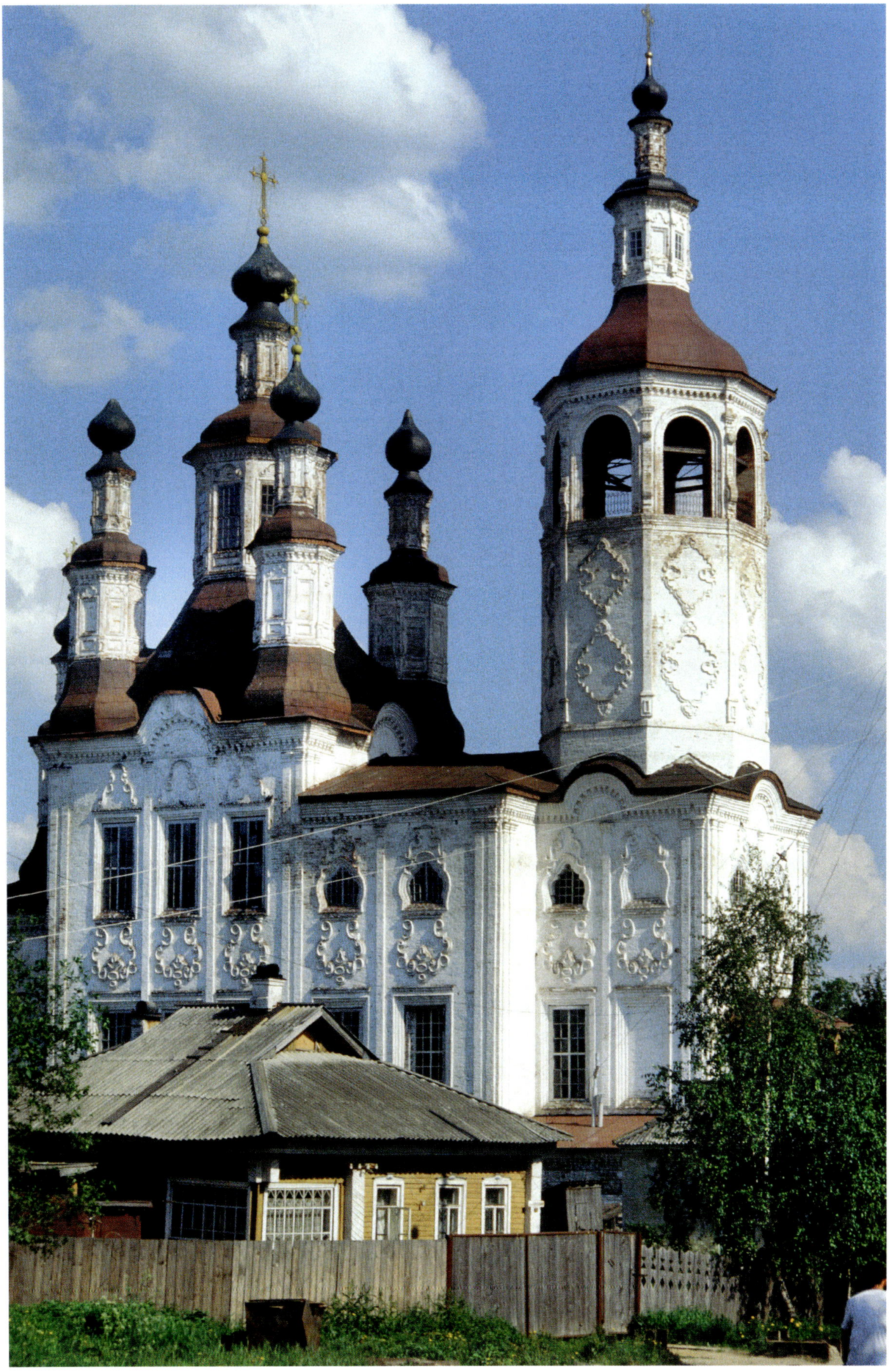

TOTMA. Church of the Entry of Christ into Jerusalem, northwest view. Church built in two stages, completed in 1794. Photograph: June 12, 1998.

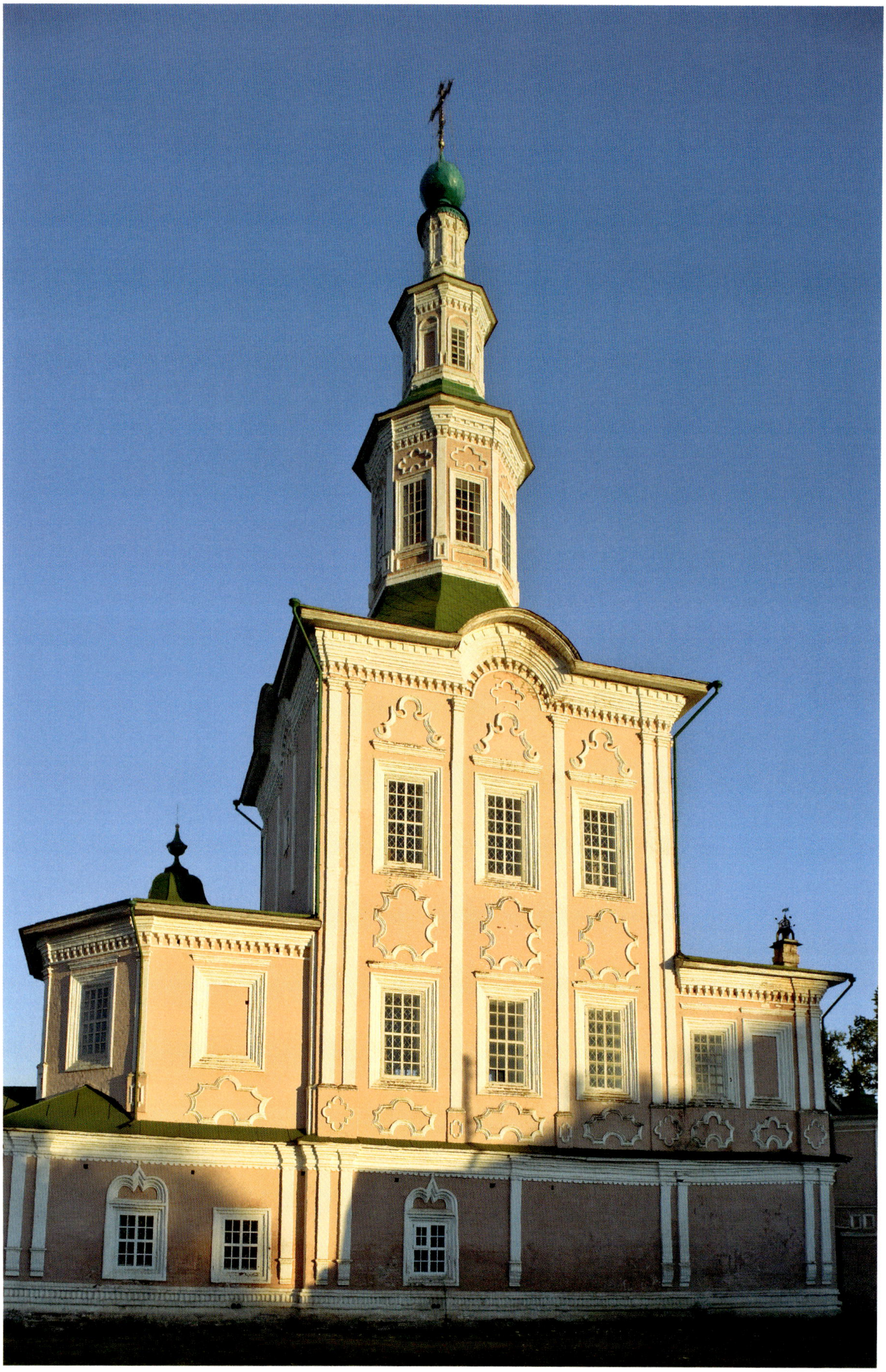

TOTMA. Church of the Nativity of Christ, north view. Church built in two stages: lower church in 1746–48; upper in 1786–93. Photograph: August 2, 2011.

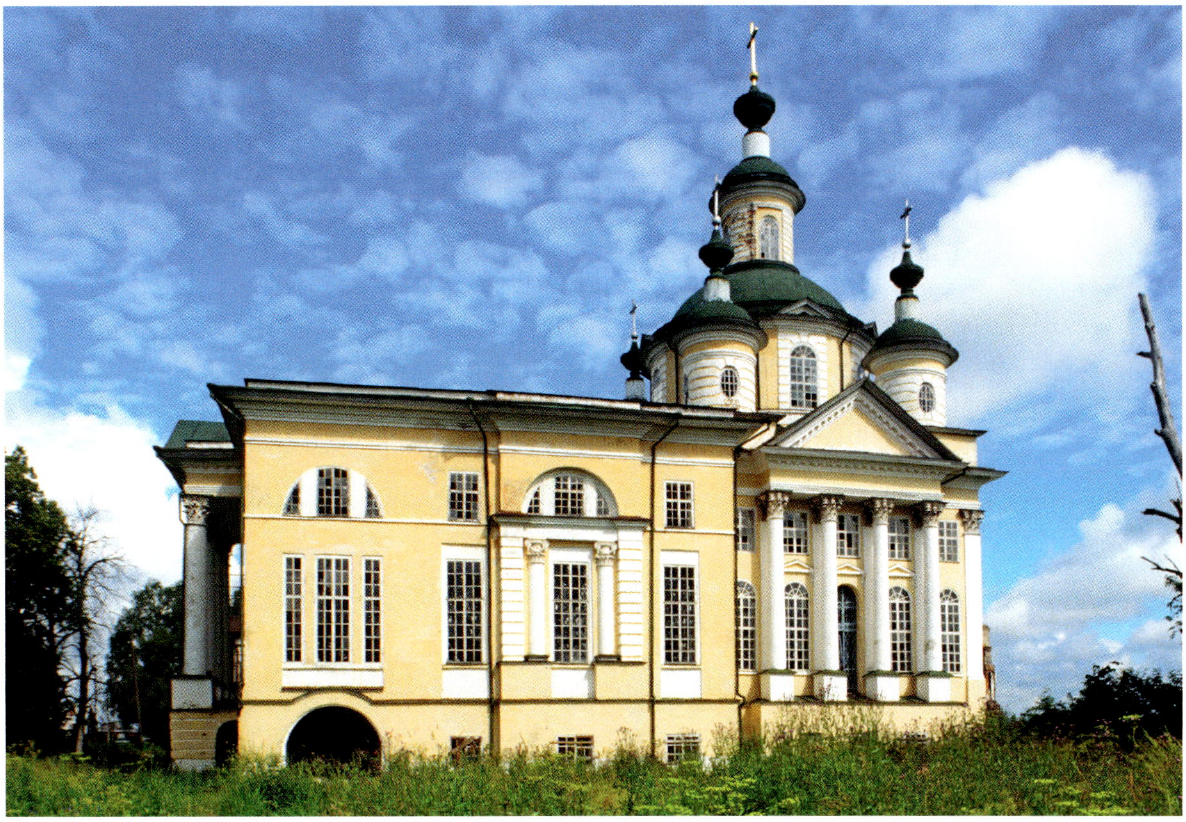

TOTMA. Cathedral of the Ascension, Savior-Sumorin Monastery, south view. Built between 1796 and 1801, this imposing neoclassical church has been partially restored but subject to petty vandalism. Photograph: July 25, 1996.

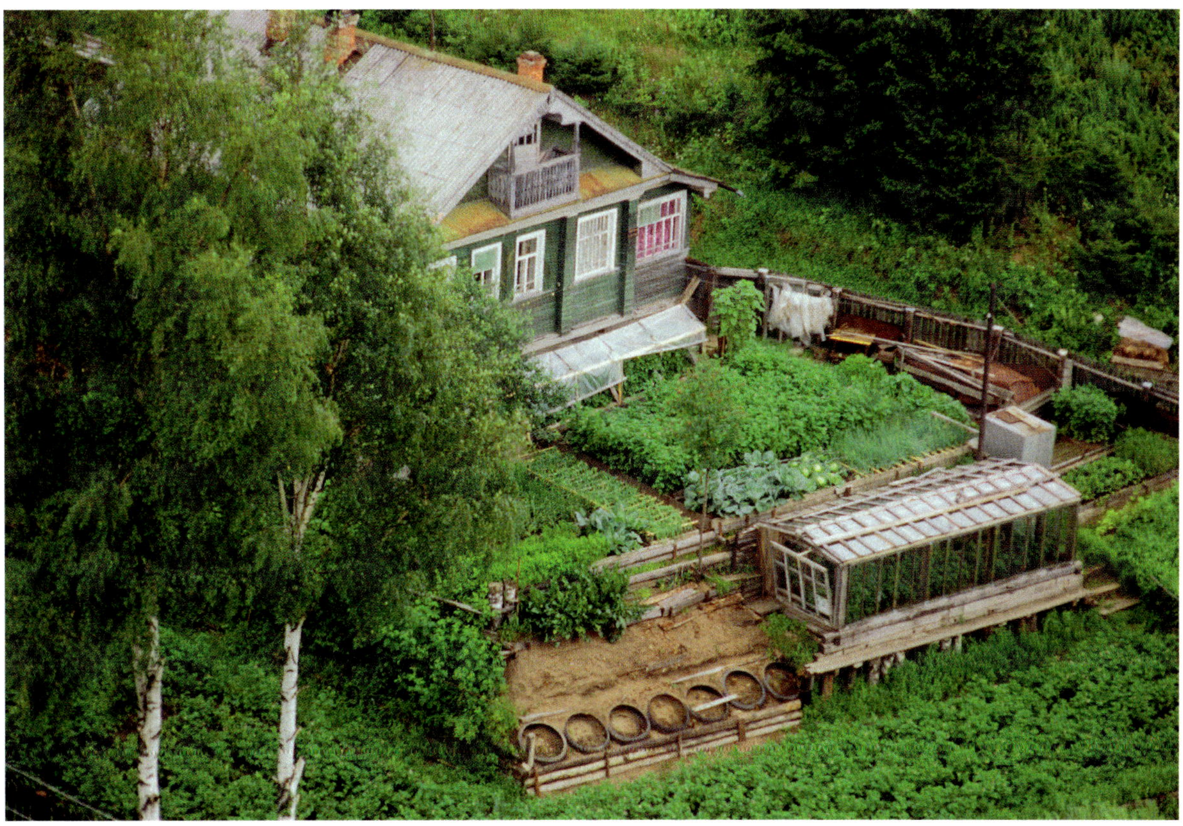

TOTMA. Wooden house surrounded by birch trees and flourishing garden, with potatoes, cabbage, tomatoes, carrots, all maturing for winter canning. View from Dormition Church bell tower. Photograph: July 25, 1996.

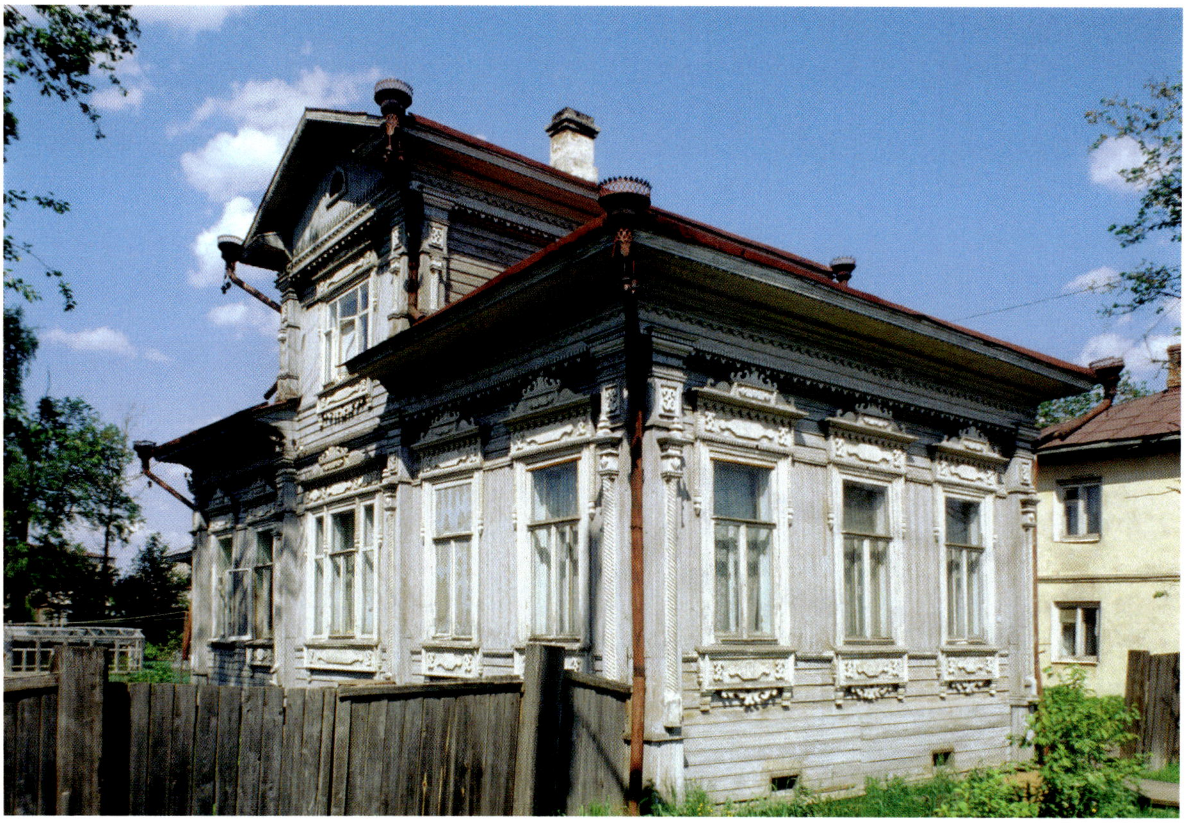

TOTMA. Late nineteenth-century wooden house, Lenin Street 41. Photograph: June 21, 1998.

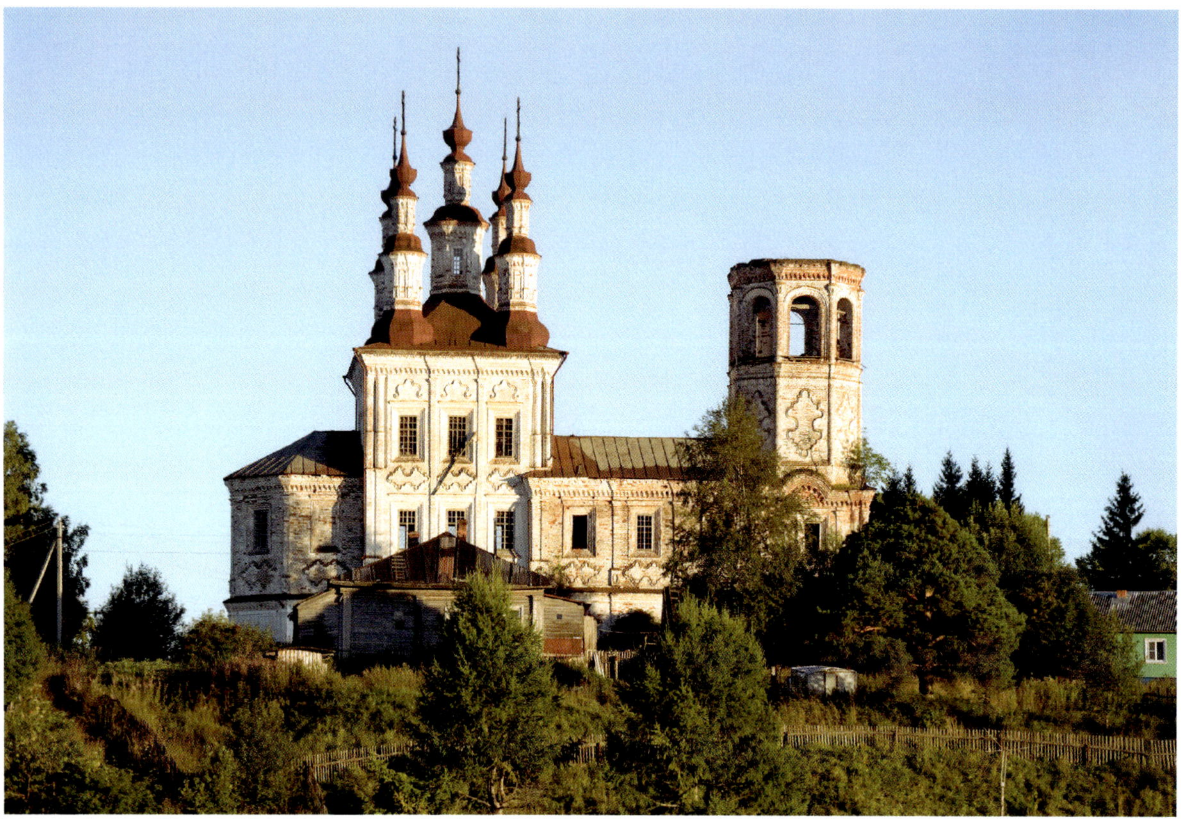

TOTMA. Church of the Resurrection at Varnitsy, north view. Church built in two stages: begun in 1743 and completed in 1775. Photograph: August 4, 2011.

MEVEDEVO. Church of the Resurrection, southeast view. Built in 1756. Photograph: August 4, 2011.

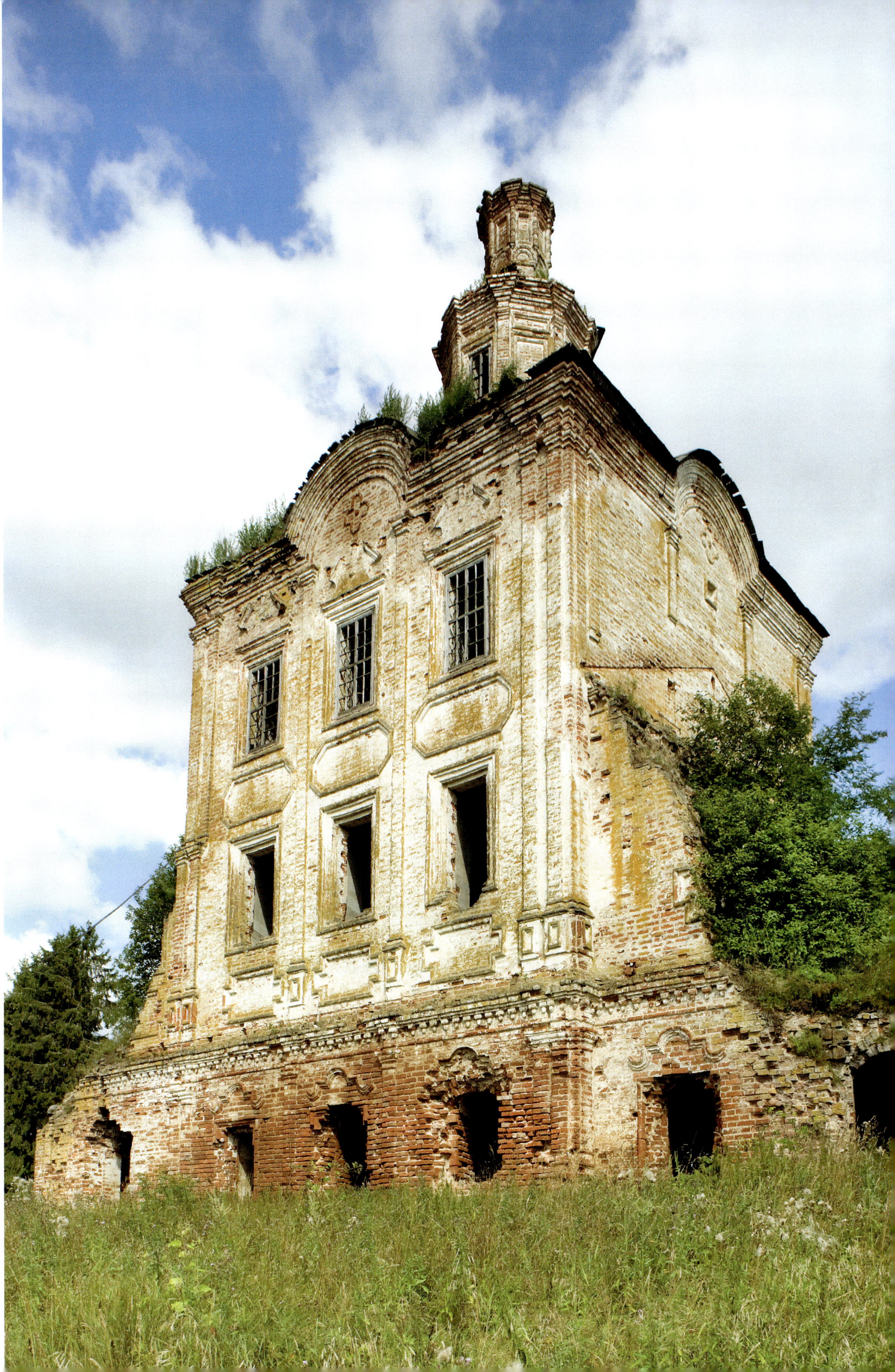

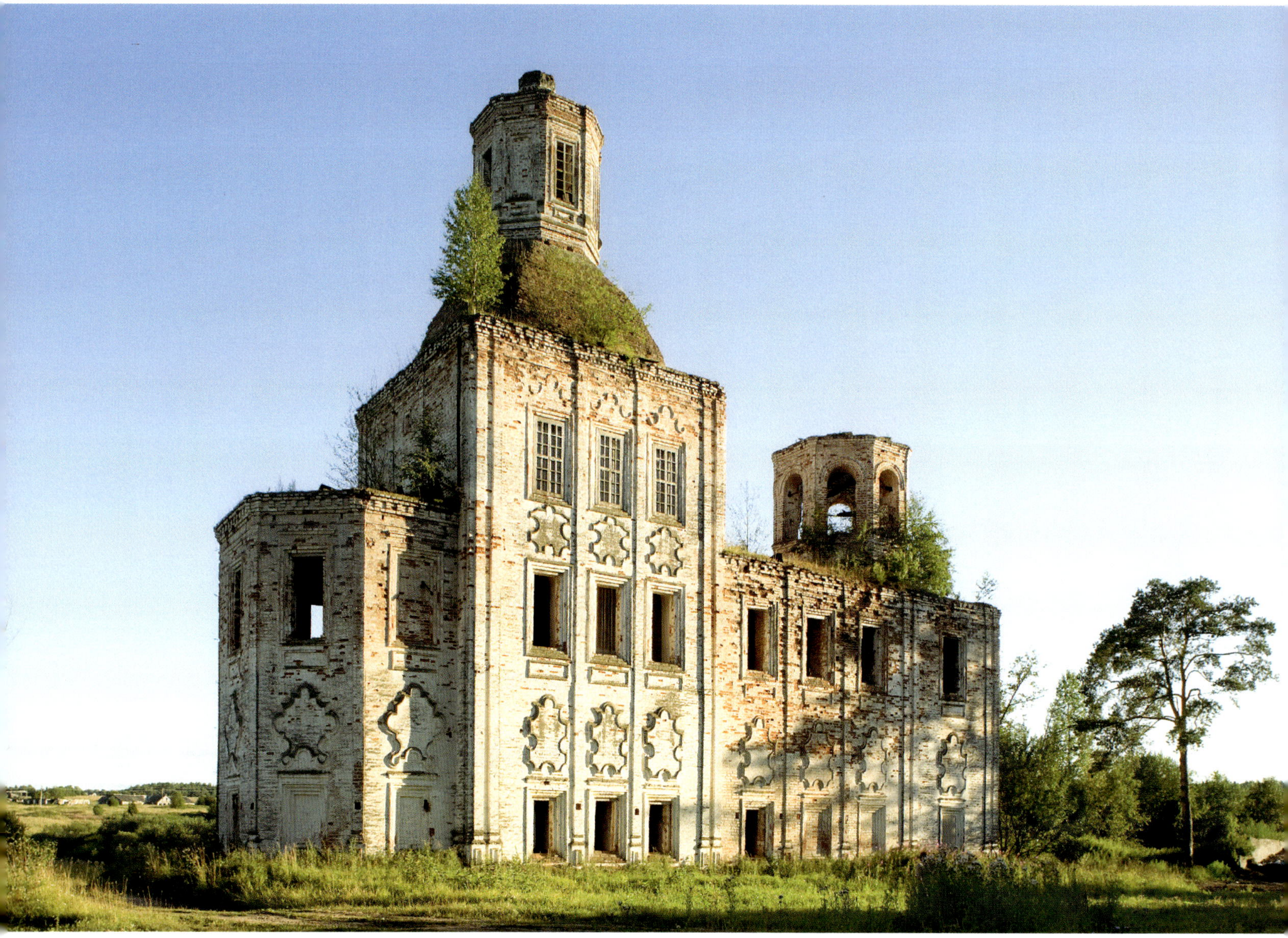

VERKH-EDENGA (Matveevo). Church of St. Nicholas, northeast view. One of the best examples of the "Totma baroque," this church was completed in 1796. Photograph: August 4, 2011.

USTYE-PECHENGSKOE. Church of the Dormition, southwest view. Church built in 1782, with bell tower added in 1890. Photograph: August 4, 2011.

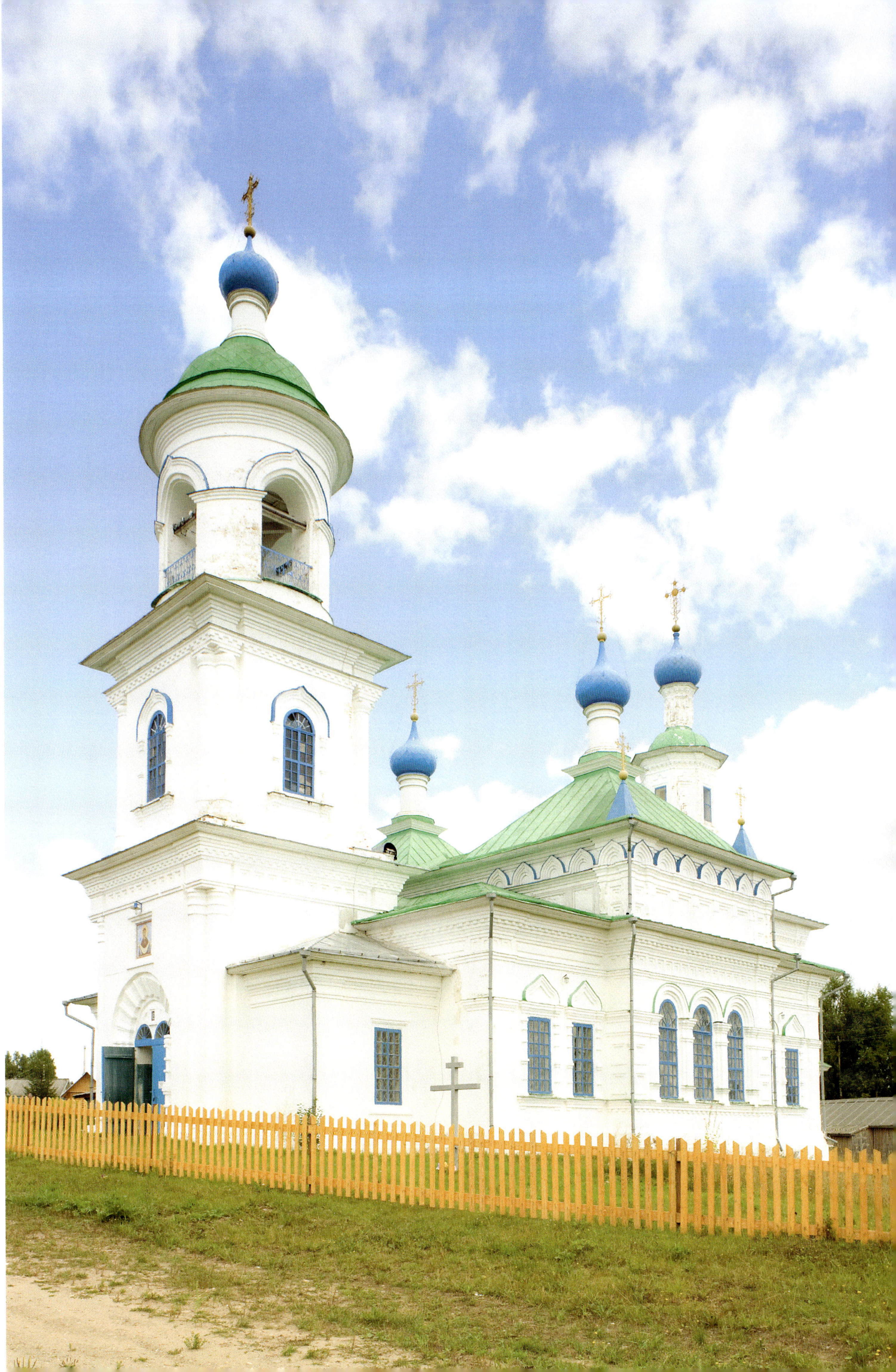

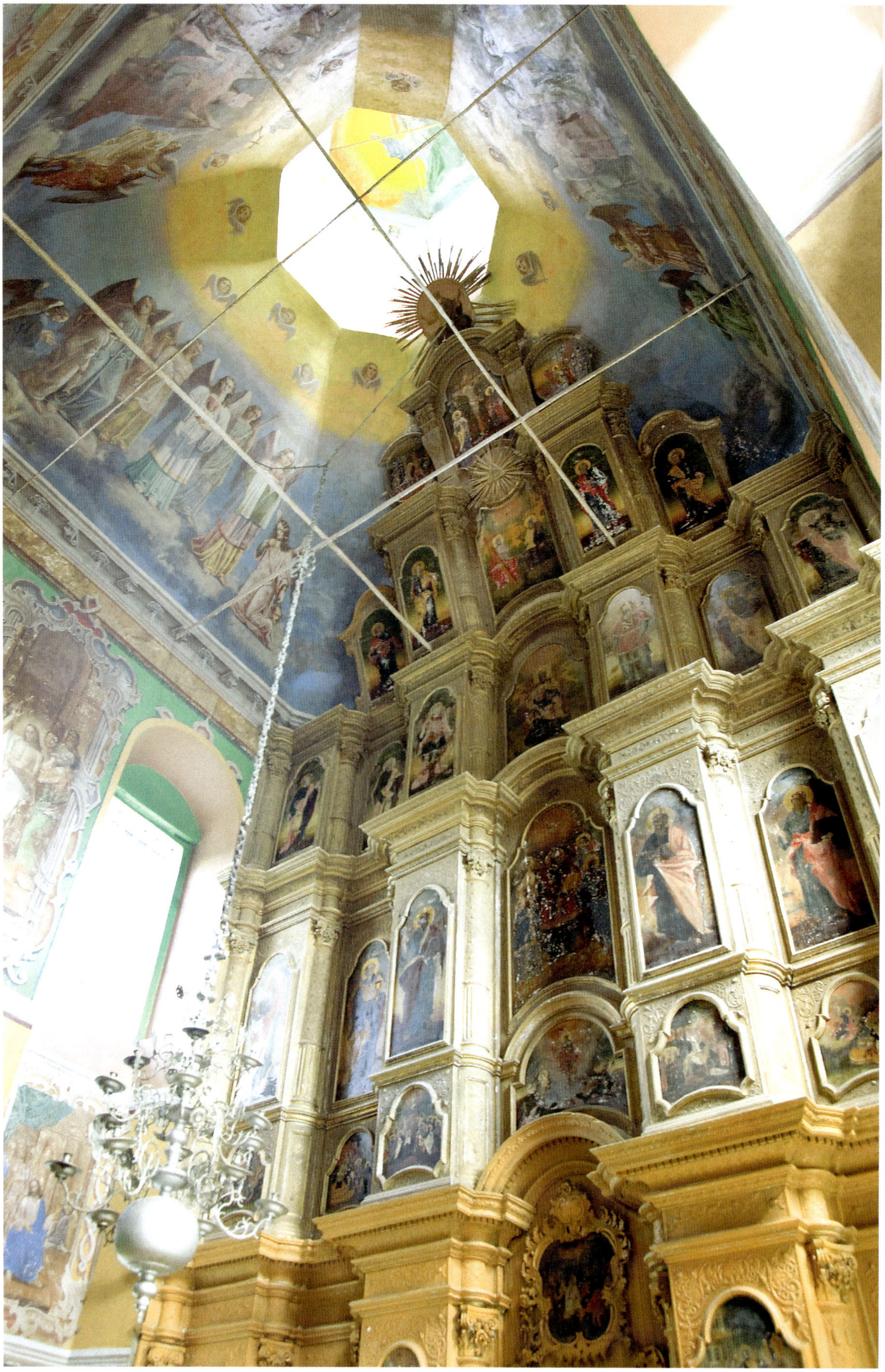

USTYE-PECHENGSKOE. Church of the Dormition, interior, view northeast with icon screen (late nineteenth century). Photograph: August 4, 2011.

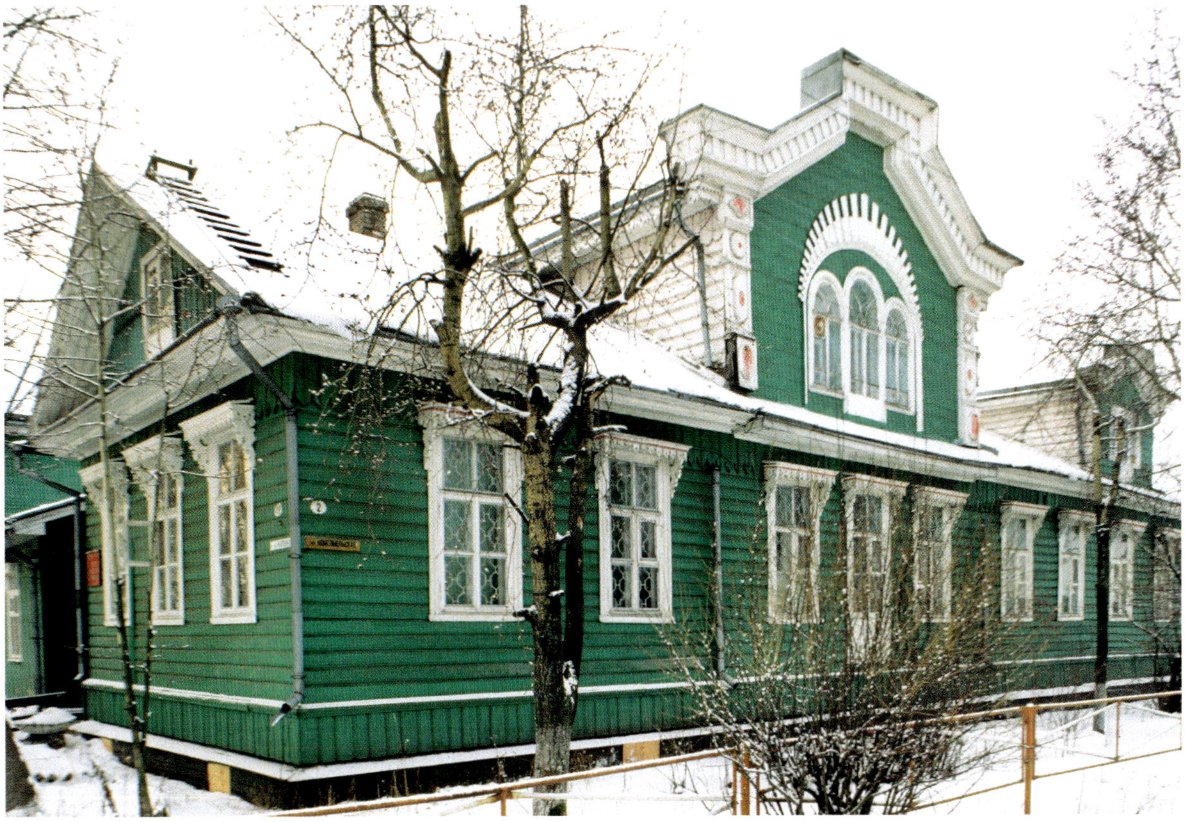

VELSK. Astafyev house, Embankment Street 49. Photograph: December 6, 1999.

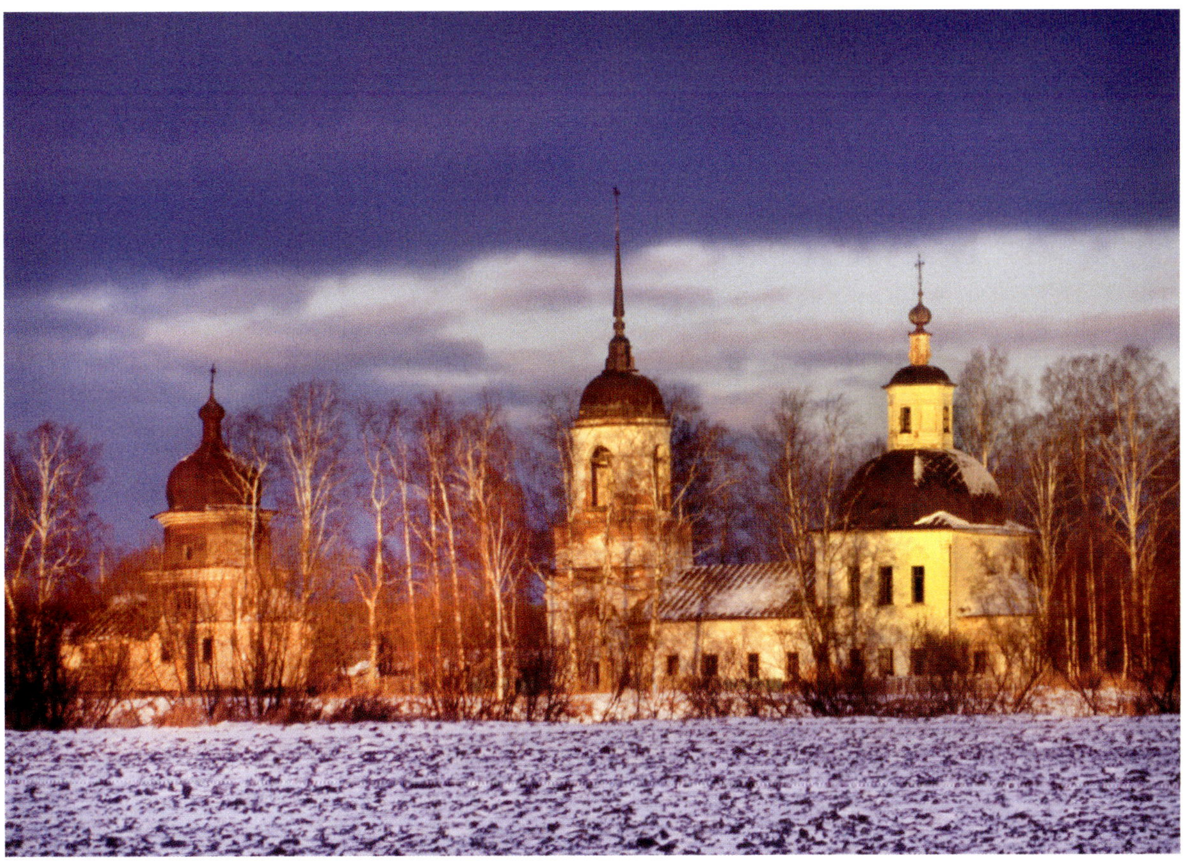

ROSTOVSKOE. Wooden Church of Elijah the Prophet (1756) and Church of the Ascension (1805), south view across the Vel River. Photograph: December 6, 1999.

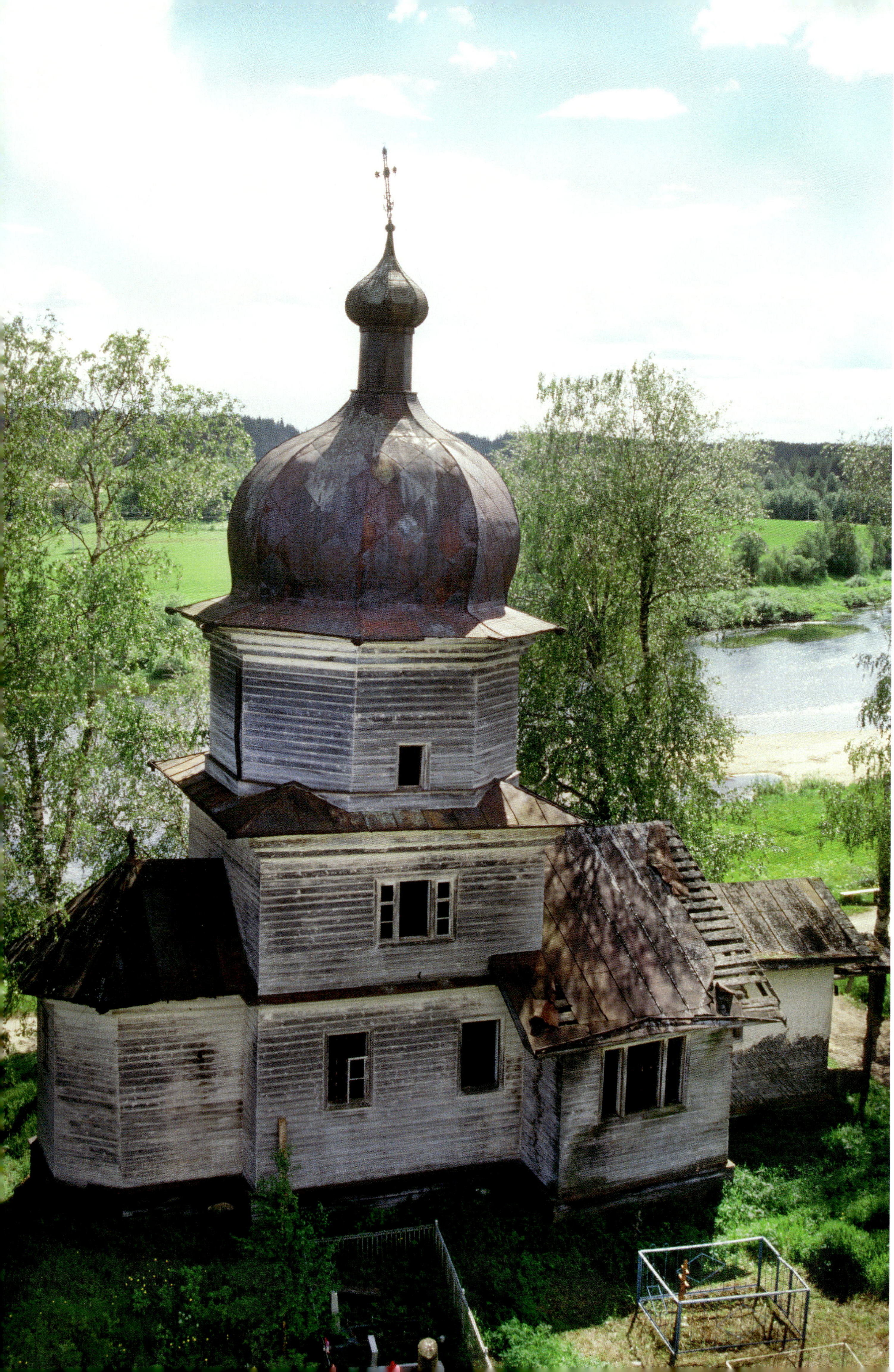

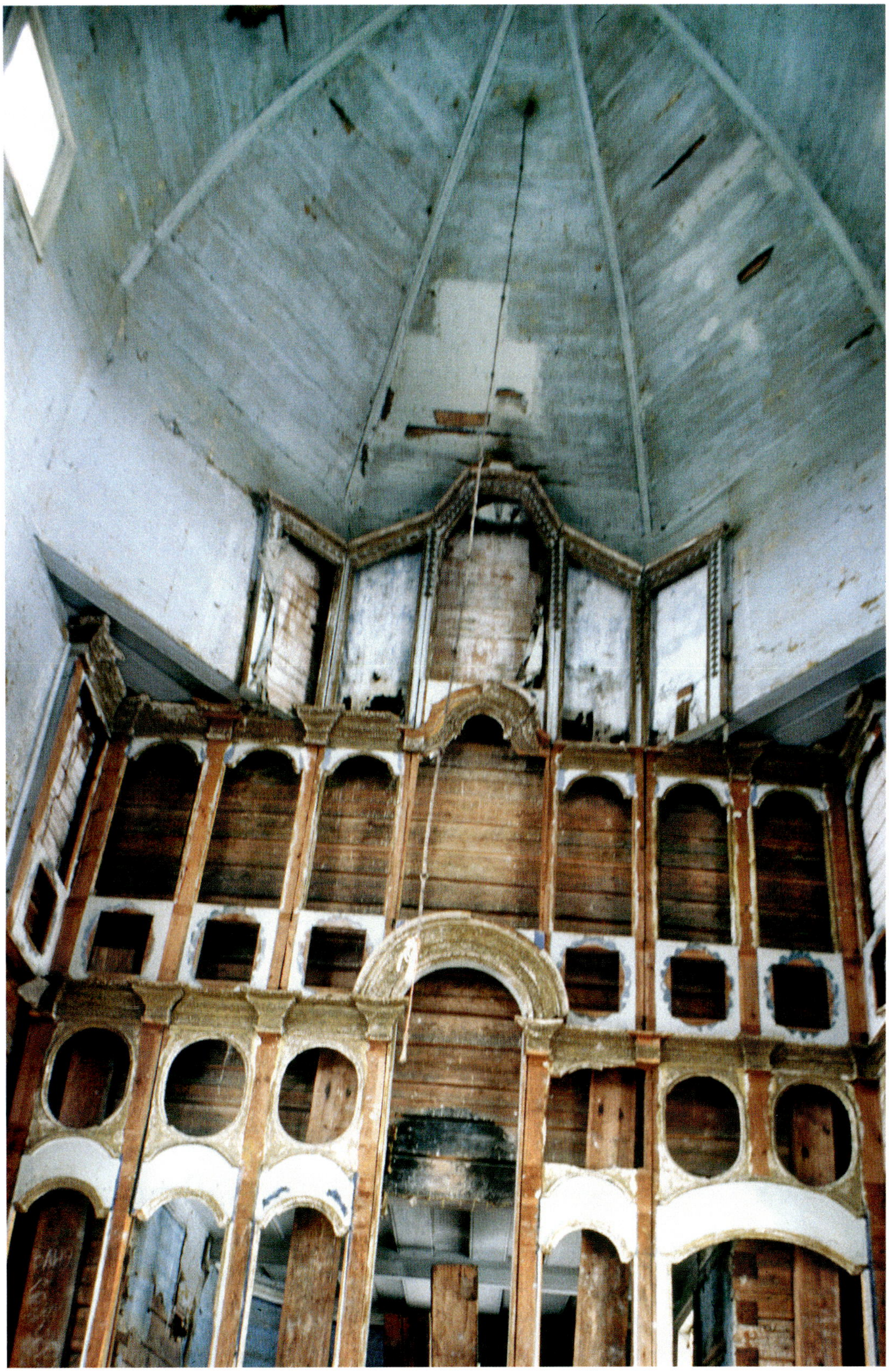

ROSTOVSKOE. Church of Elijah the Prophet, interior, view east with remains of icon screen. Photograph. December 4, 1999.

ROSTOVSKOE. Wooden Church of Elijah the Prophet, north view from bell tower of Church of the Ascension. Photograph: June 16, 2000.

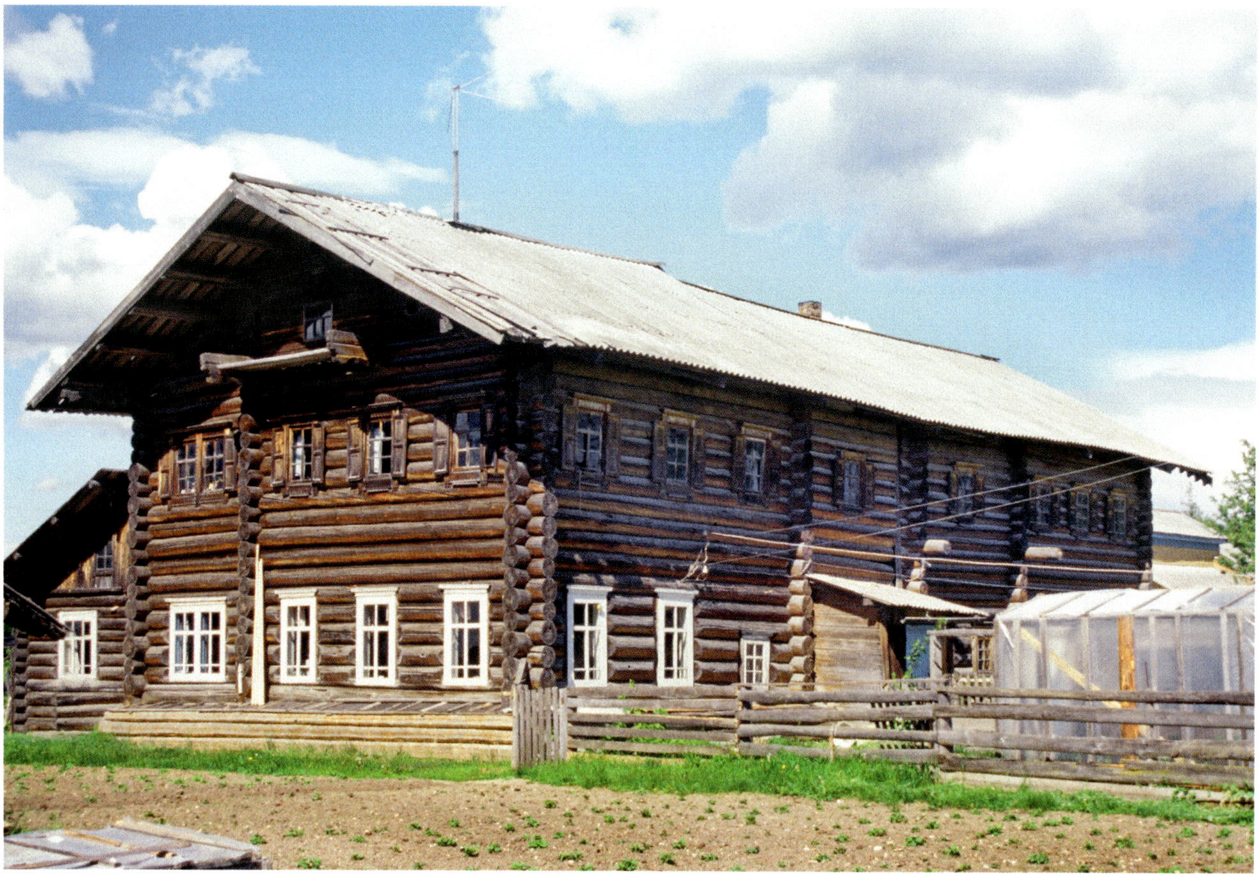

BEREZNIK. Log house (kurnaya izba), river facade. Photograph: June 17, 2000.

NIKIFOROVO. Wooden Church of the Nativity of the Virgin (Elijah the Prophet), southeast view. Built in 1767. Photograph: December 3, 1999.

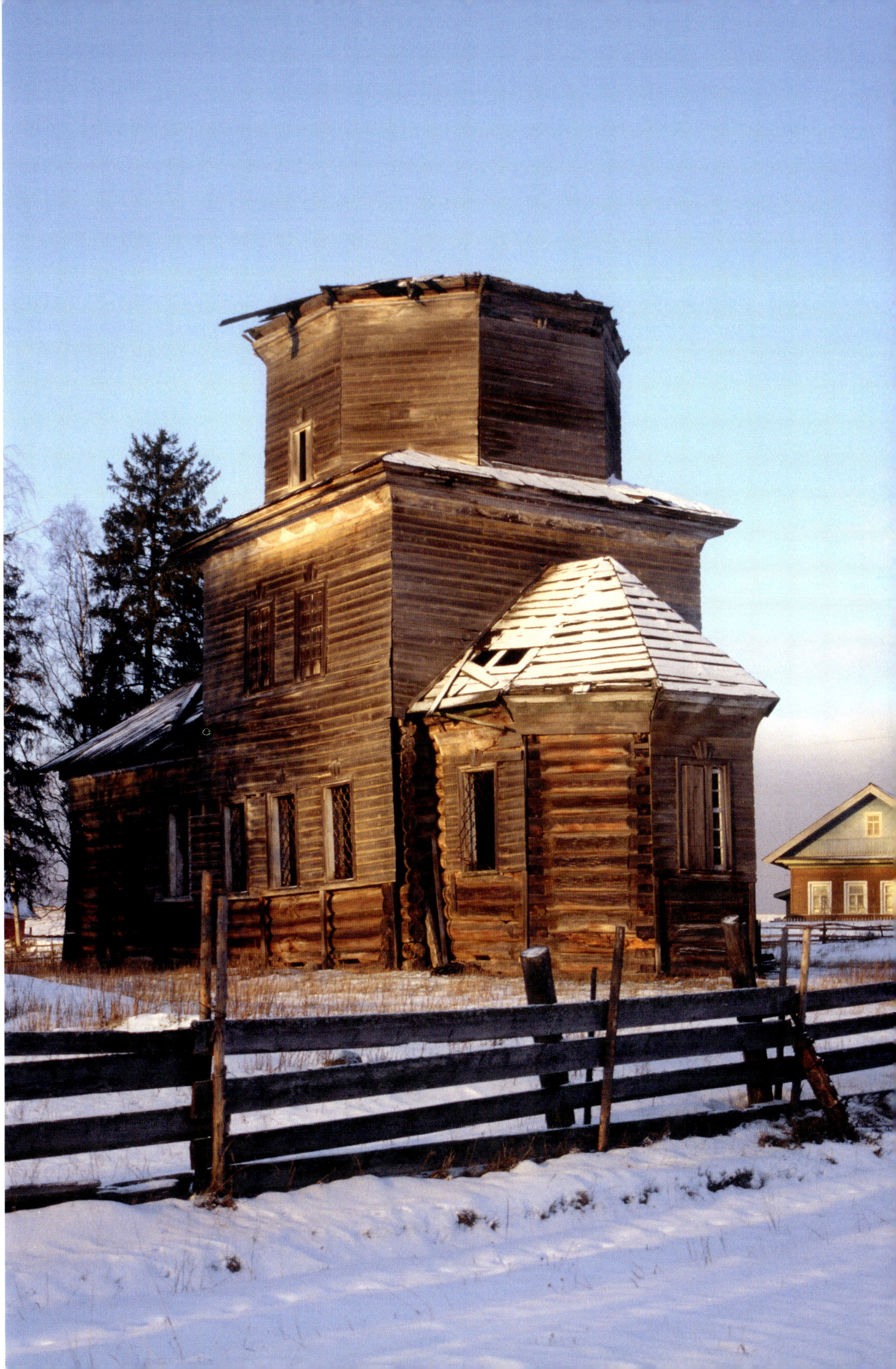

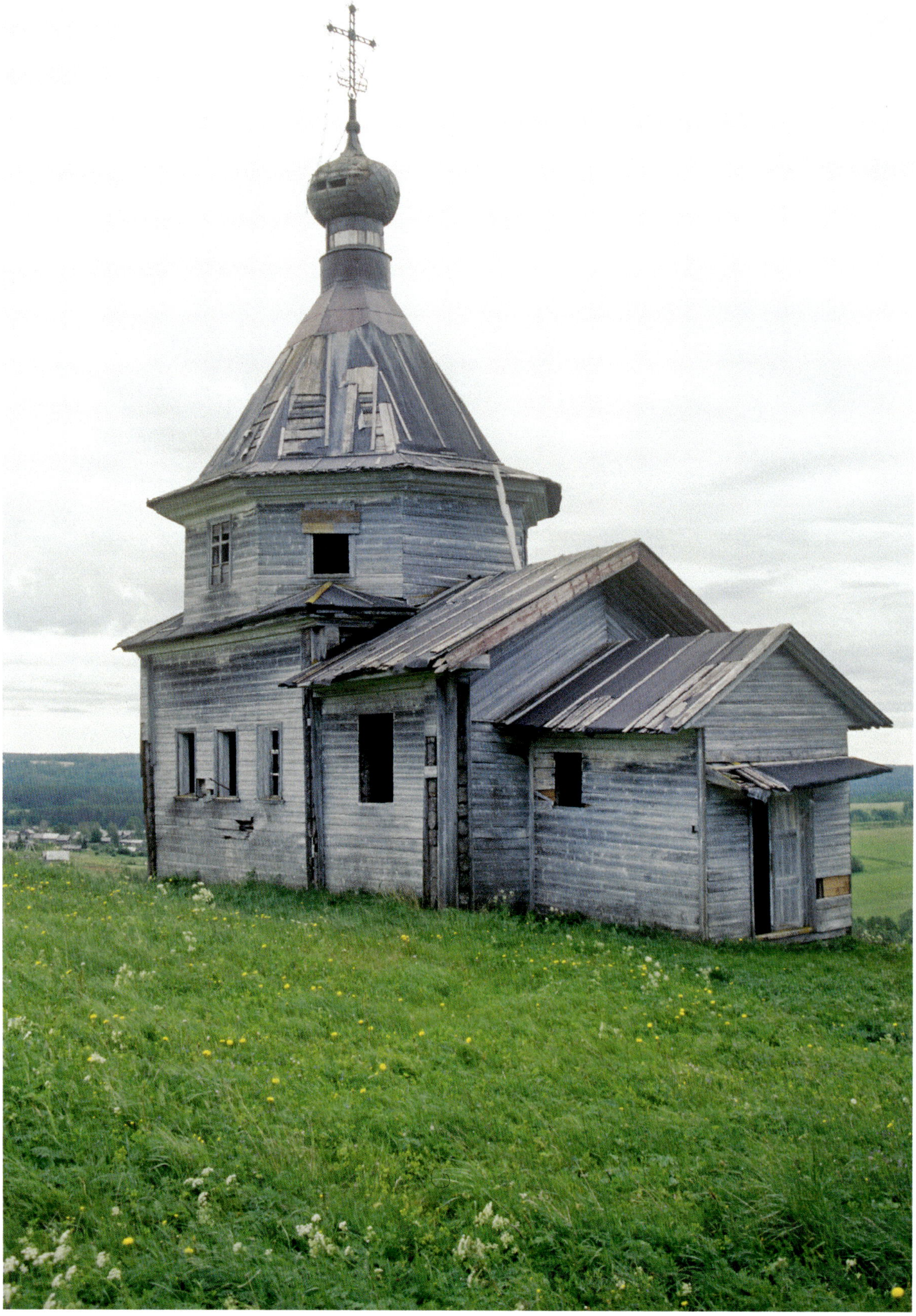

SEREDNIAIA (Yakovlevskaia). Chapel of Saints Zosima and Savvaty, northwest view. Chapel built in late eighteenth or early nineteenth century. Photograph: June 14, 2000.

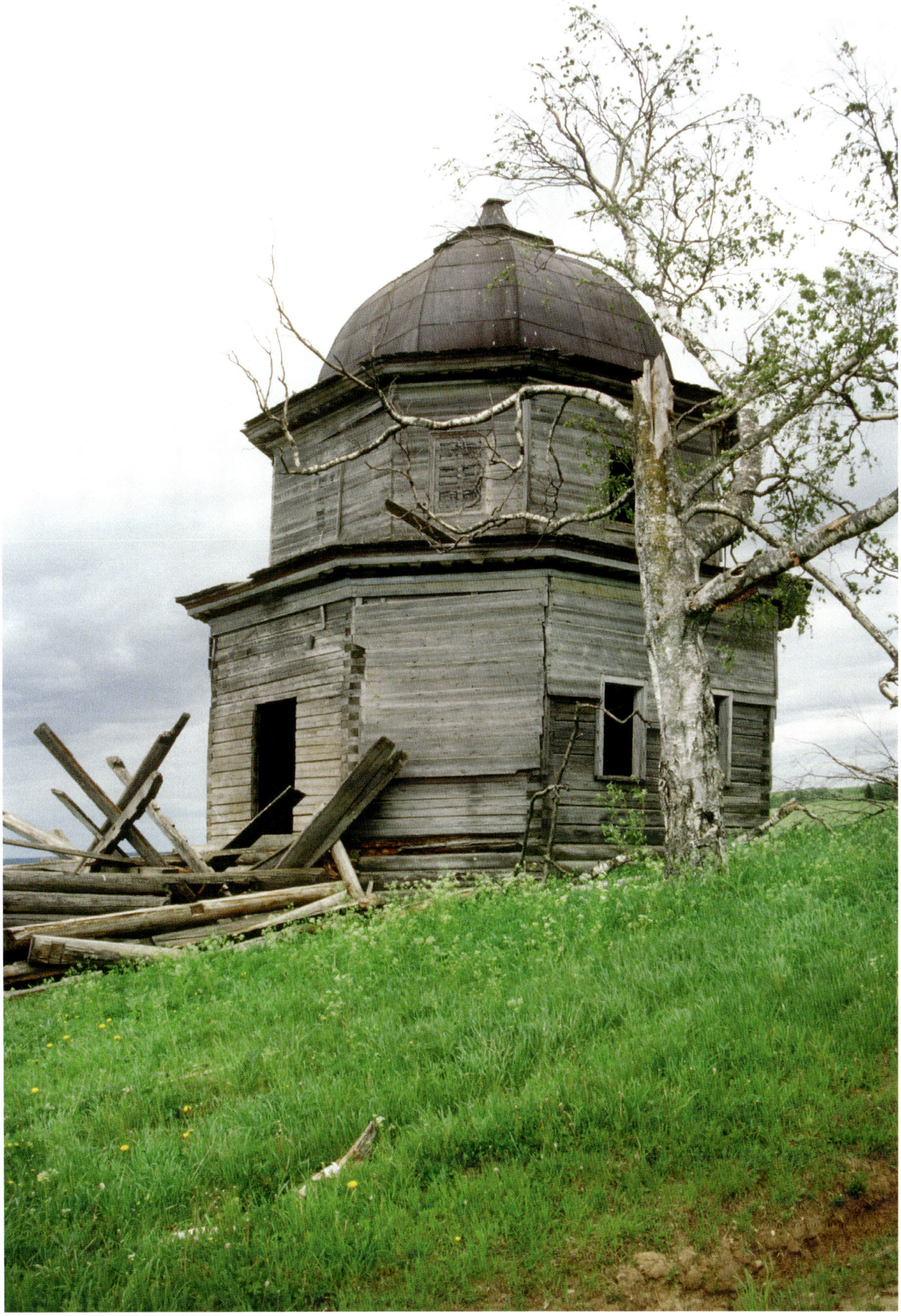

FEDKOVO. Chapel of Saints Quiricus and Julietta, southwest view. Built in late nineteenth century. Photograph: June 14, 2000.

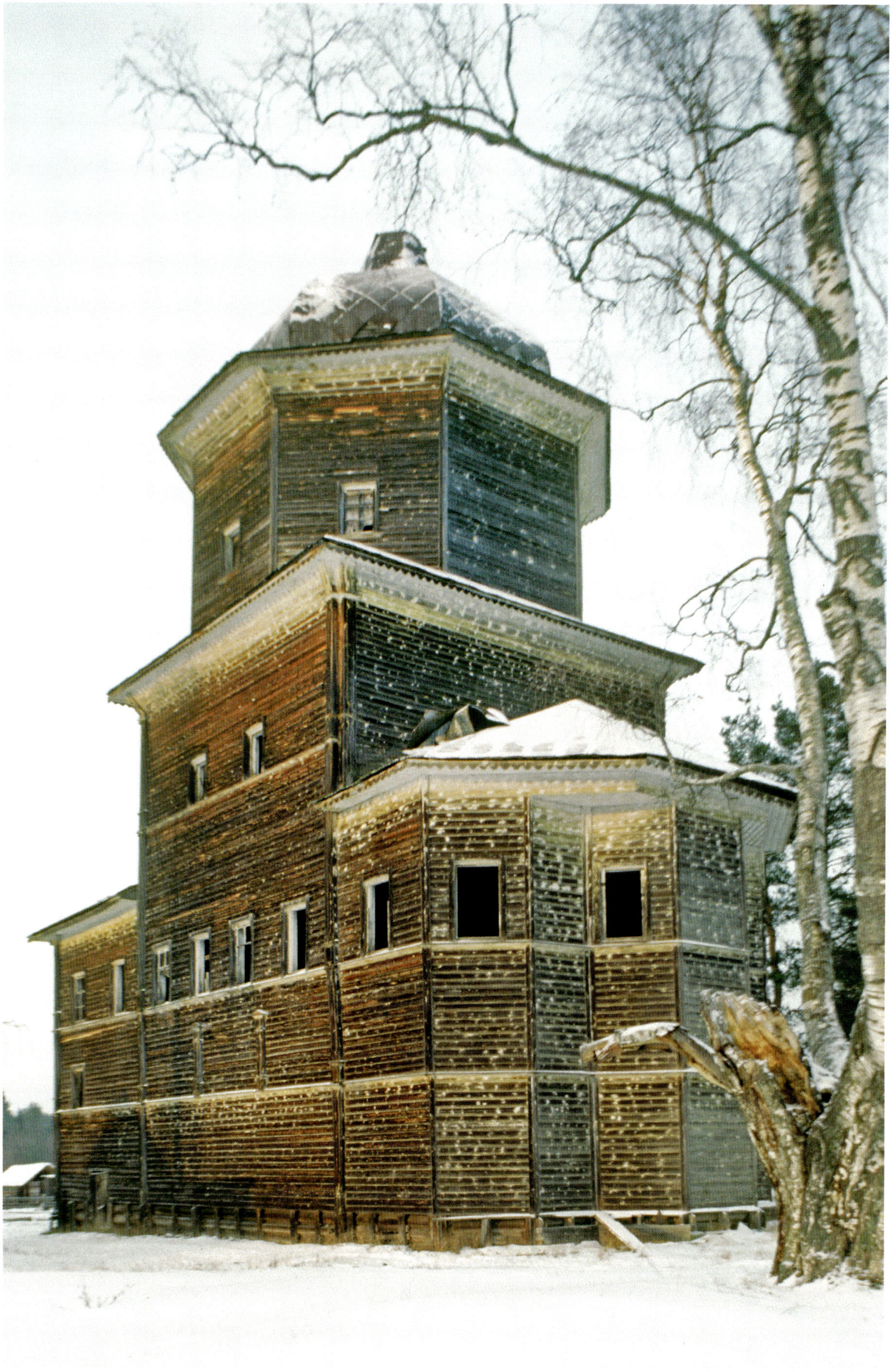

KOZLOVSKOE. Wooden Church of the Resurrection, southeast view. Built in 1791. Photograph: December 5, 1999.

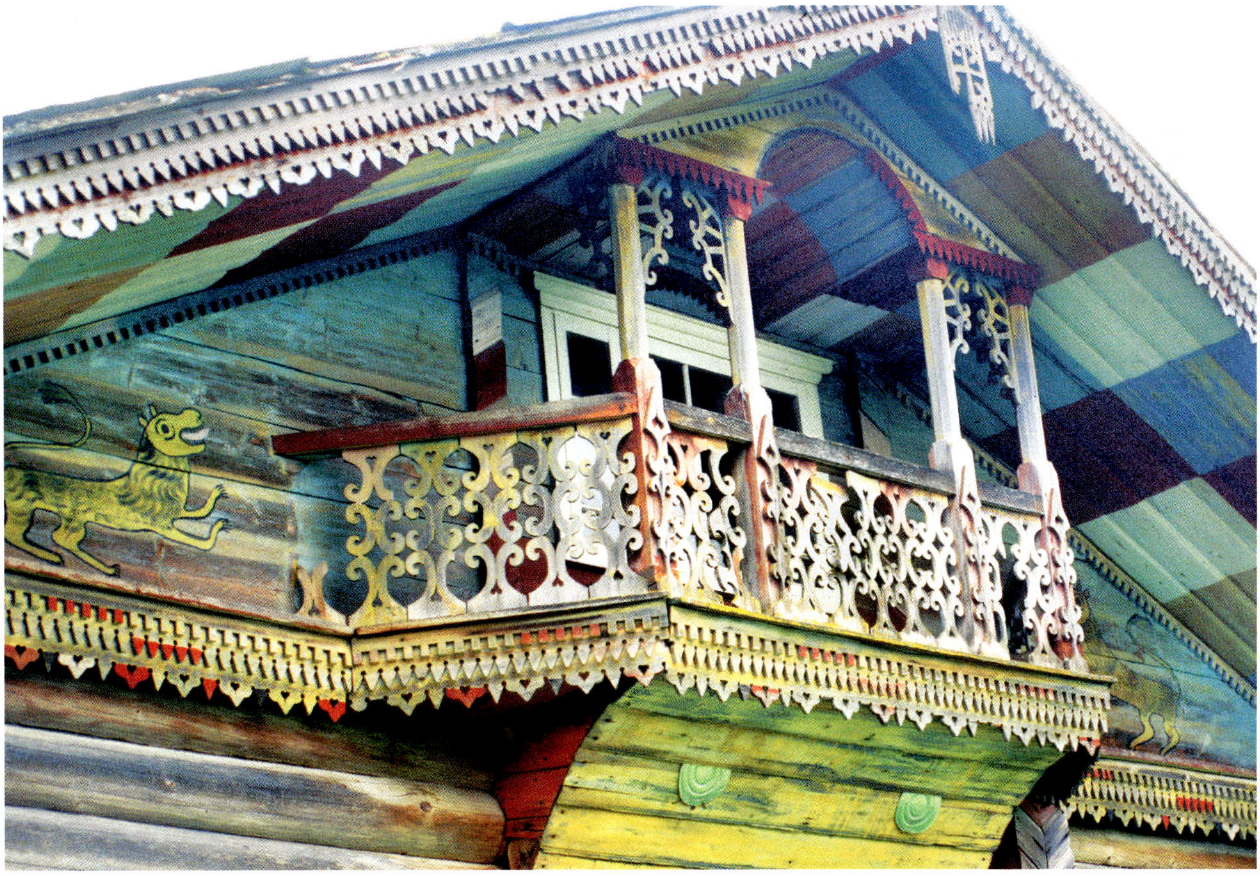

OSTROVSKOE. "House of Lions." Facade with painted eaves, balcony, and ornamental gable. Built in late nineteenth century. Note decorative use of tops from large cans of sardines under the balcony. Photograph: June 13, 2000.

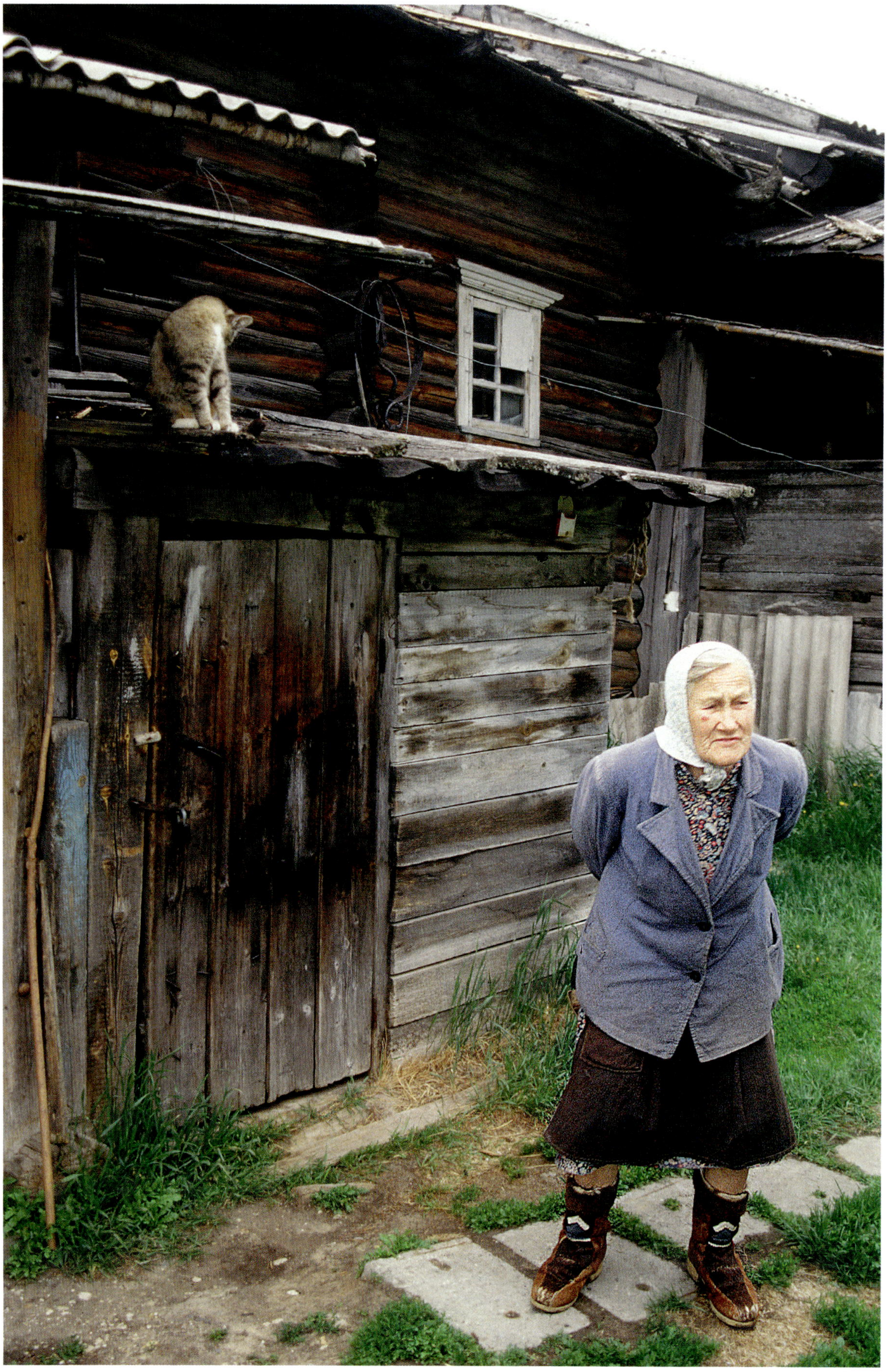

OSTROVSKOE. Marfa Martynova, owner and sole remaining resident of "House of Lions" (seventy-two years old at the time of this photograph). Photograph: June 13, 2000.

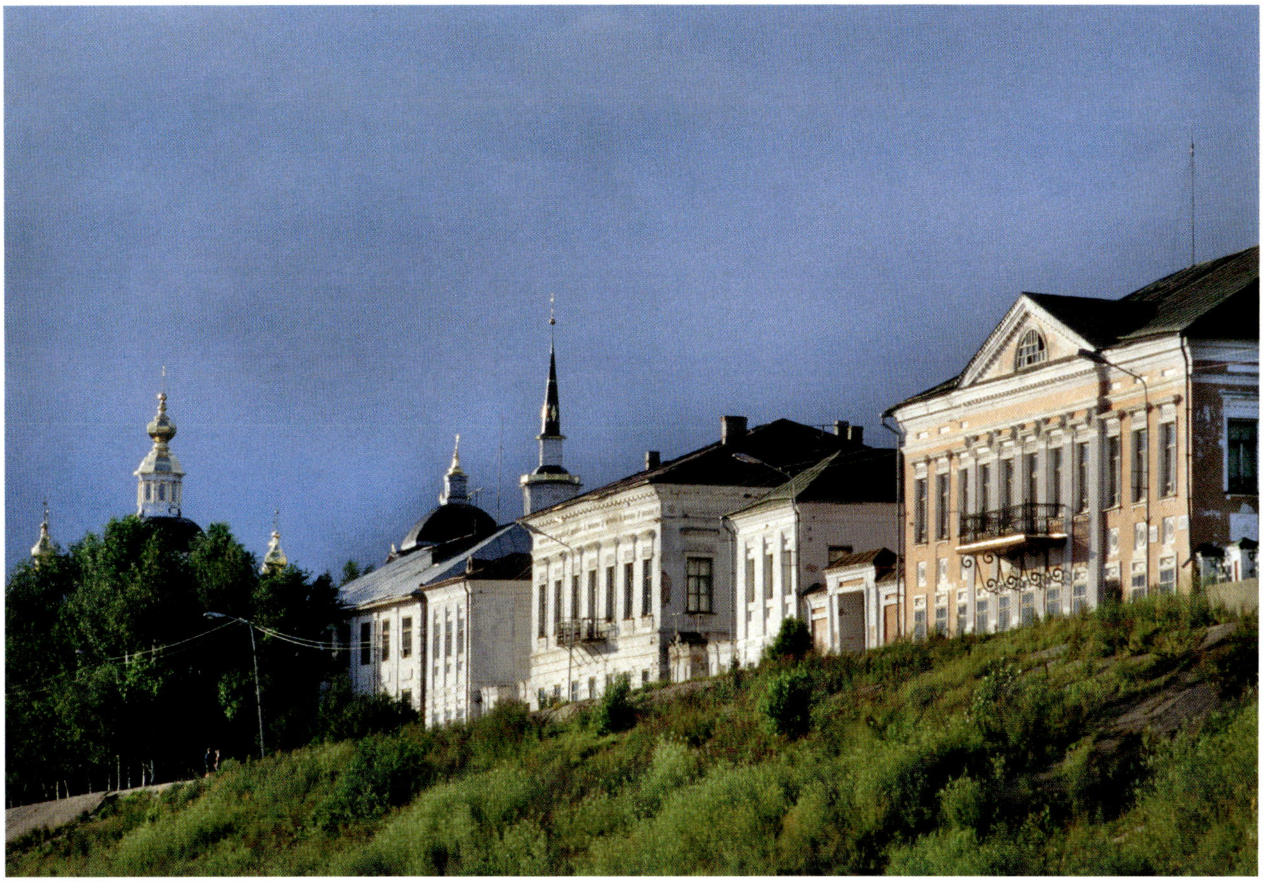

VELIKY USTIUG. Sukhona River embankment, with Usov mansion (right). Photograph: July 26, 1996.

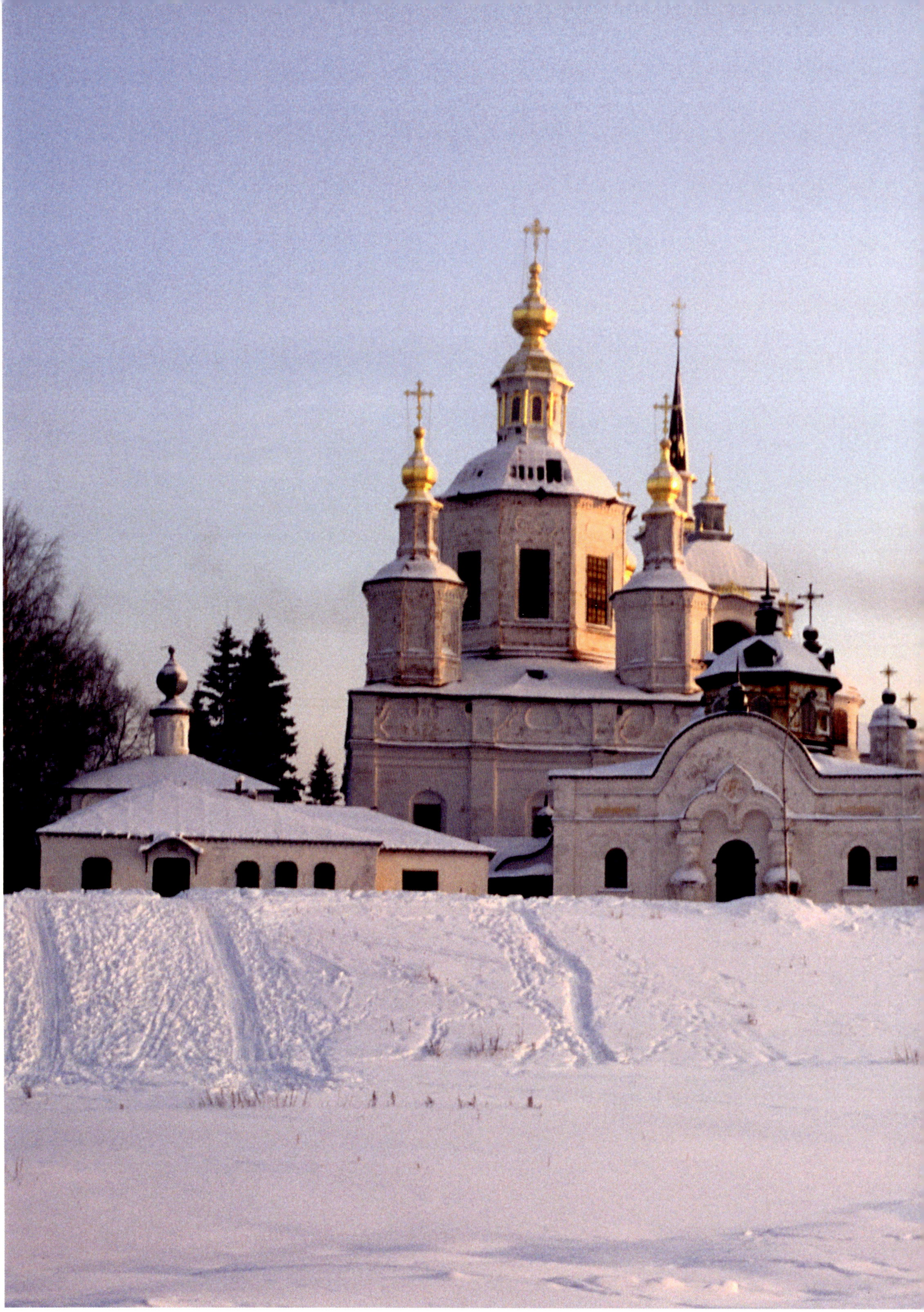

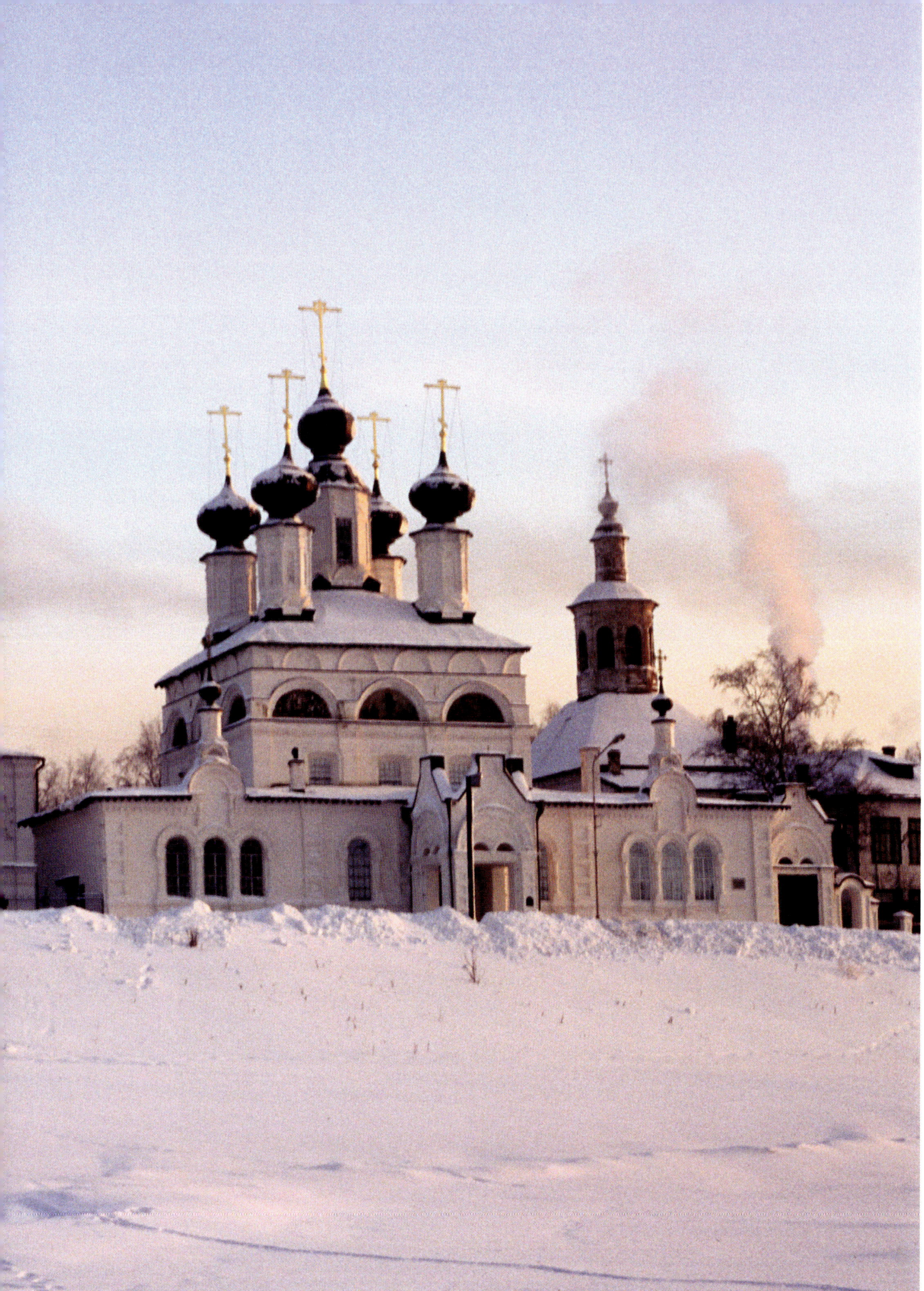

VELIKY USTIUG. Cathedral ensemble, west view from frozen Sukhona River. From left: Cathedral of St. John of Ustiug (1656–63), Dormition Cathedral (seventeenth century), Cathedral of Prokopy of Ustiug (1668). Photograph: January 6, 1997.

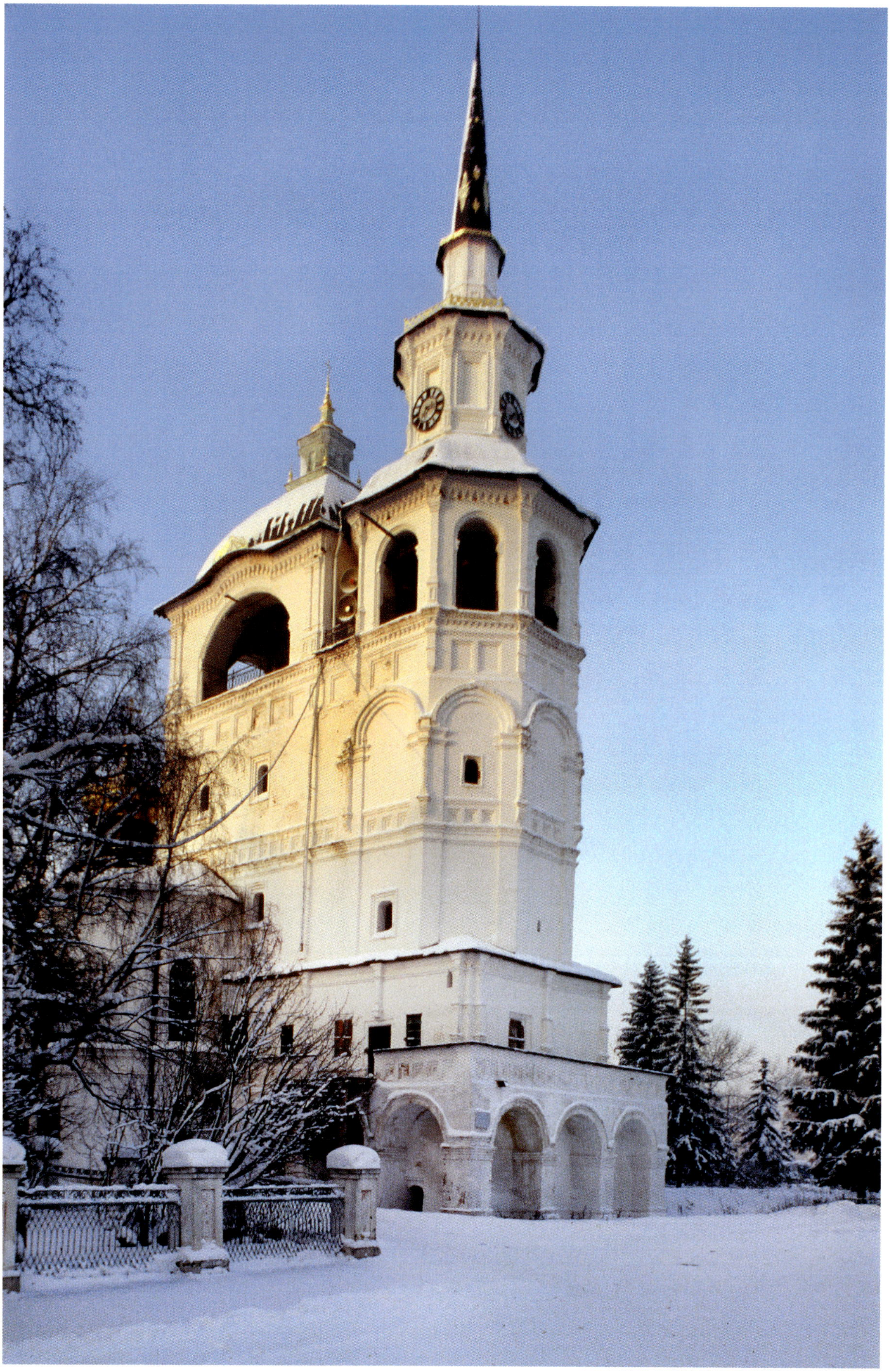

VELIKY USTIUG. Bell tower, Cathedral of the Dormition, southeast view. Photograph: January 6, 1997.

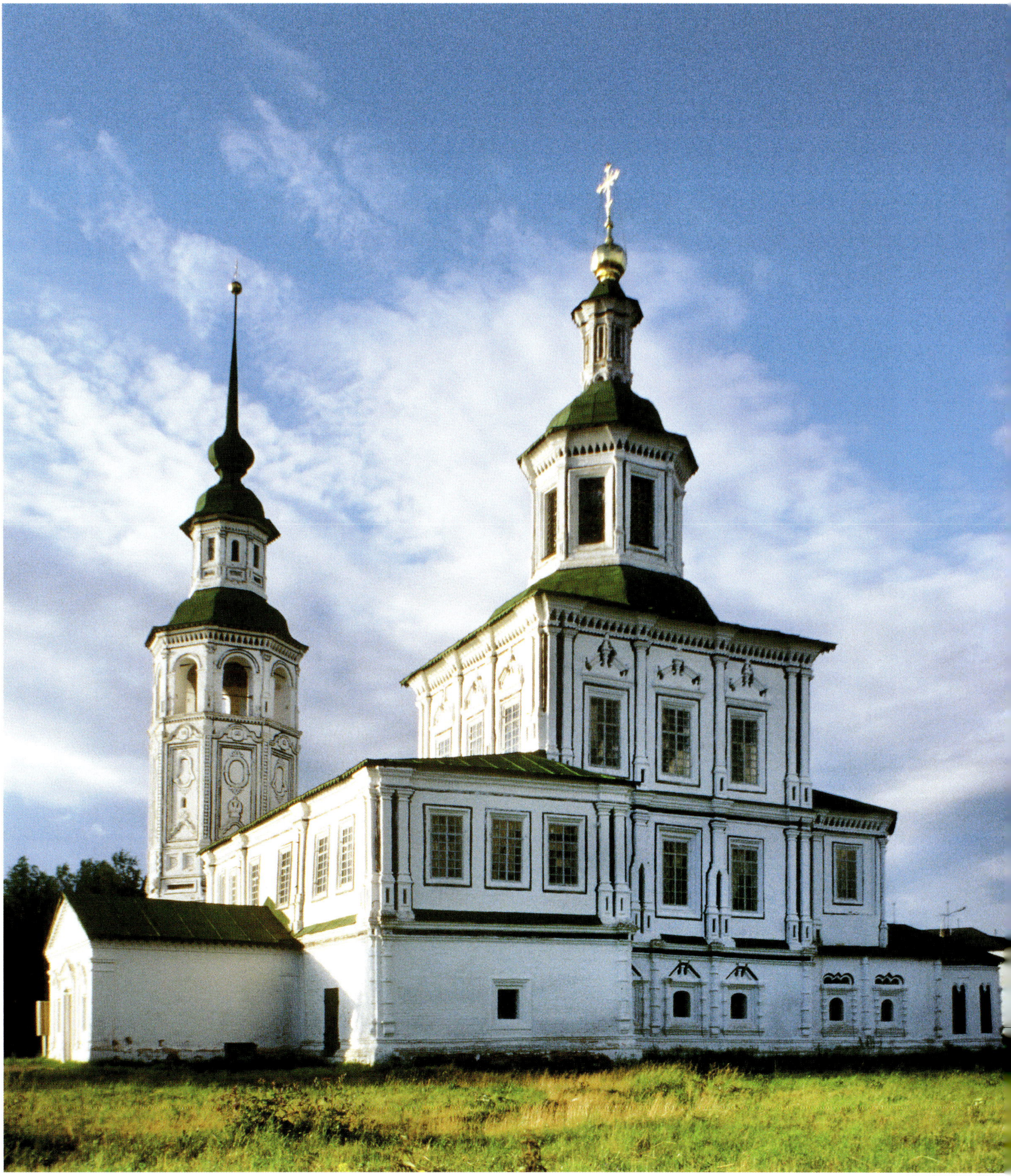

VELIKY USTIUG. Church of St. Nicholas and bell tower, southwest view from Sukhona embankment. Built in late seventeenth/early eighteenth century. Photograph: July 26, 1996.

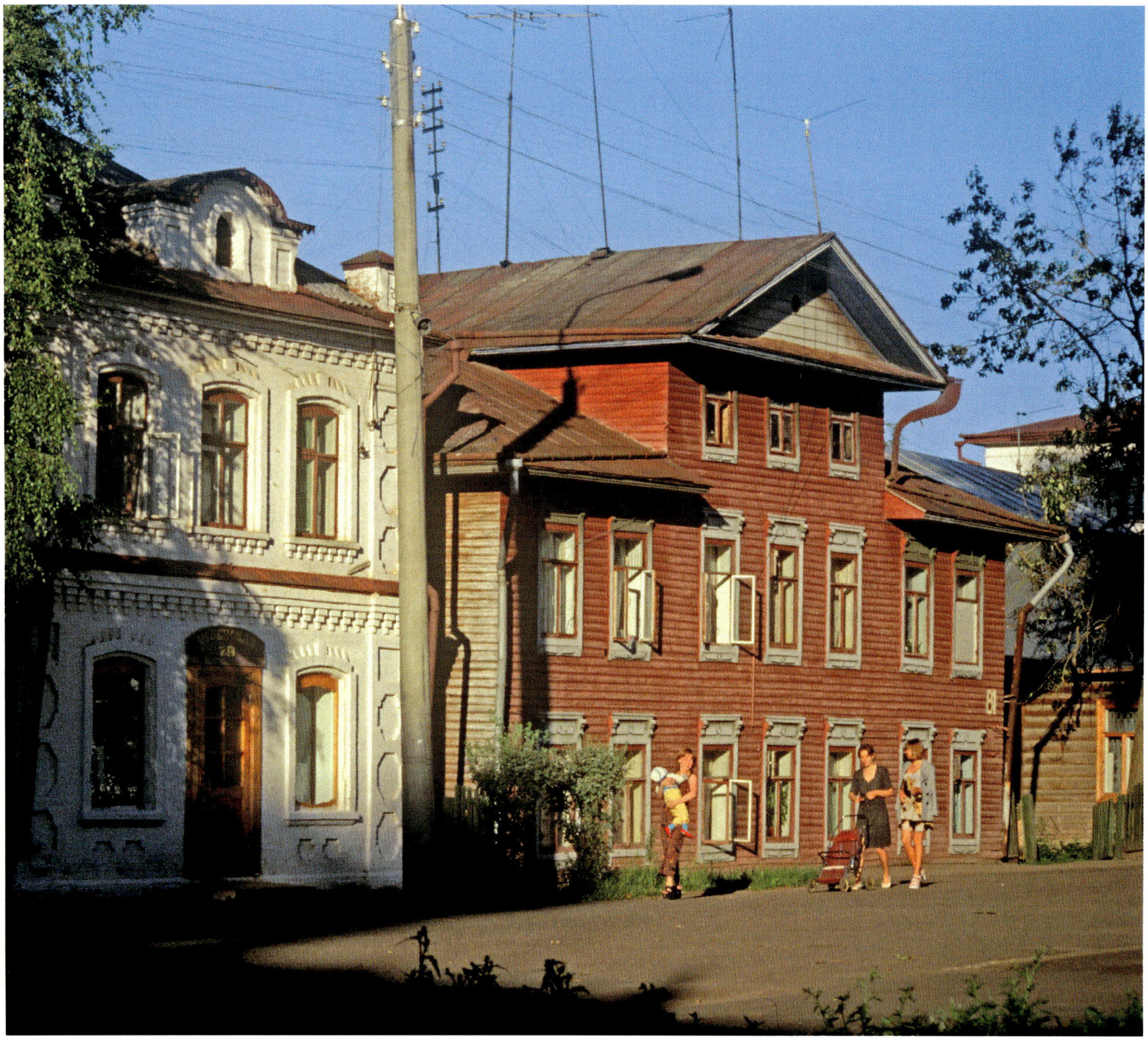

VELIKY USTIUG. Nineteenth-century houses, Dormition (Soviet) Street. Photograph: July 18, 1999.

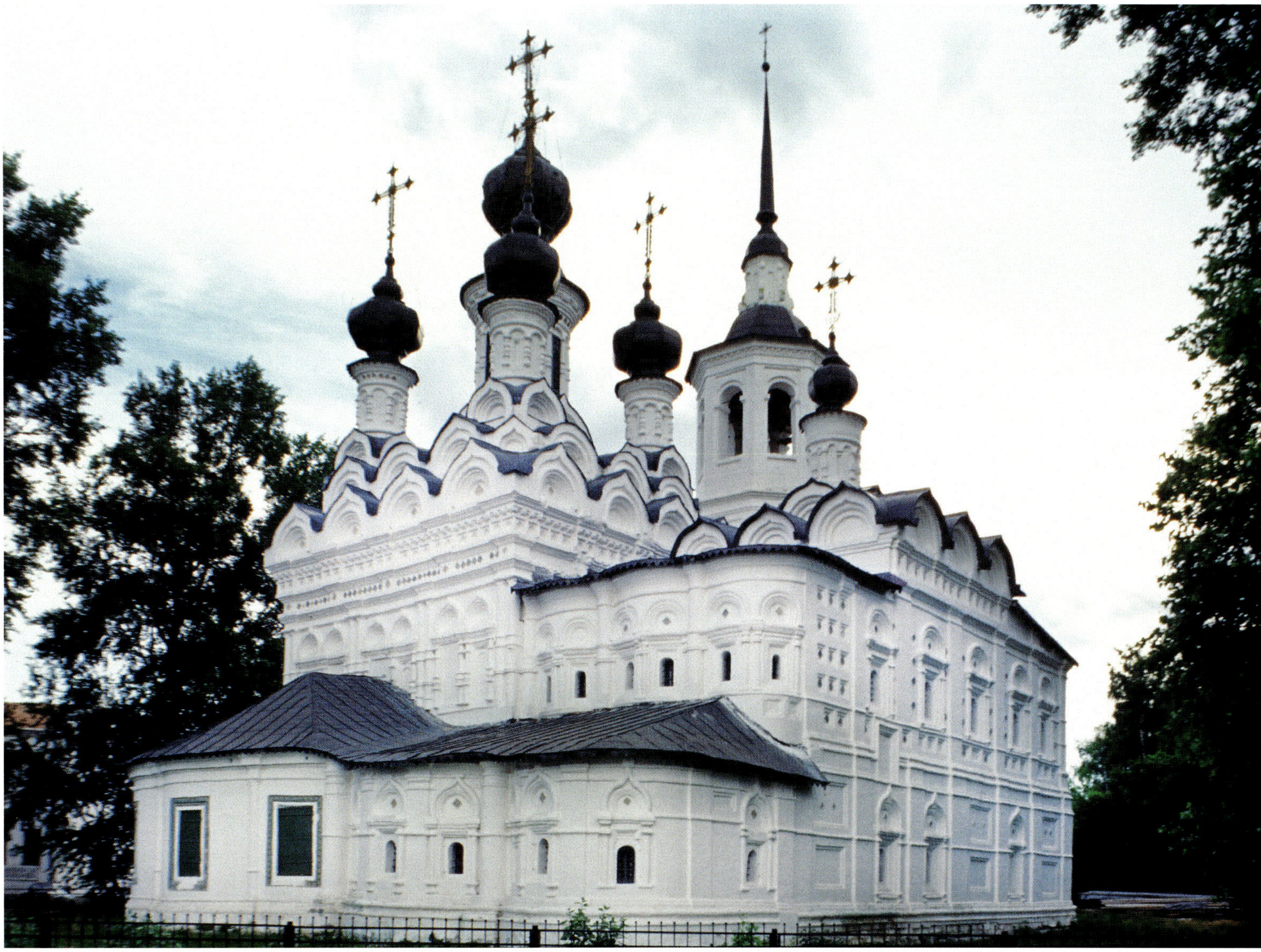

VELIKY USTIUG. Church of the Ascension, with Resurrection Chapel attached on the right, northeast view. This seventeenth-century jewel reflects the ornamental style prevalent in Moscow at that period. Main structure built in 1648. Photograph: July 18, 1999.

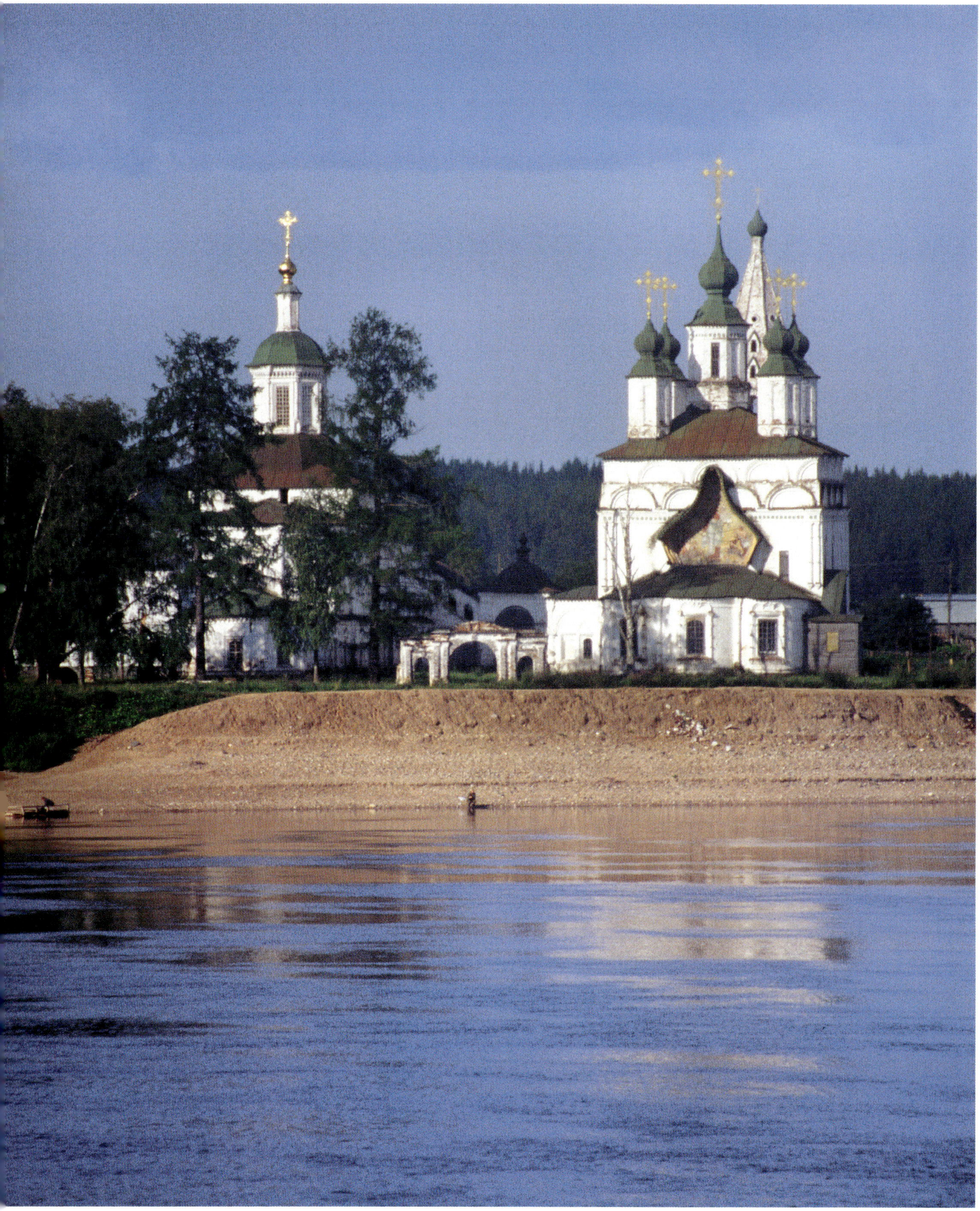

DYMKOVA SLOBODA. Paired Churches of St. Sergius of Radonezh (1739–47) and St. Dmitry (1700–1709), across the Sukhona River from Veliky Ustiug. Photograph: July 23, 1998.

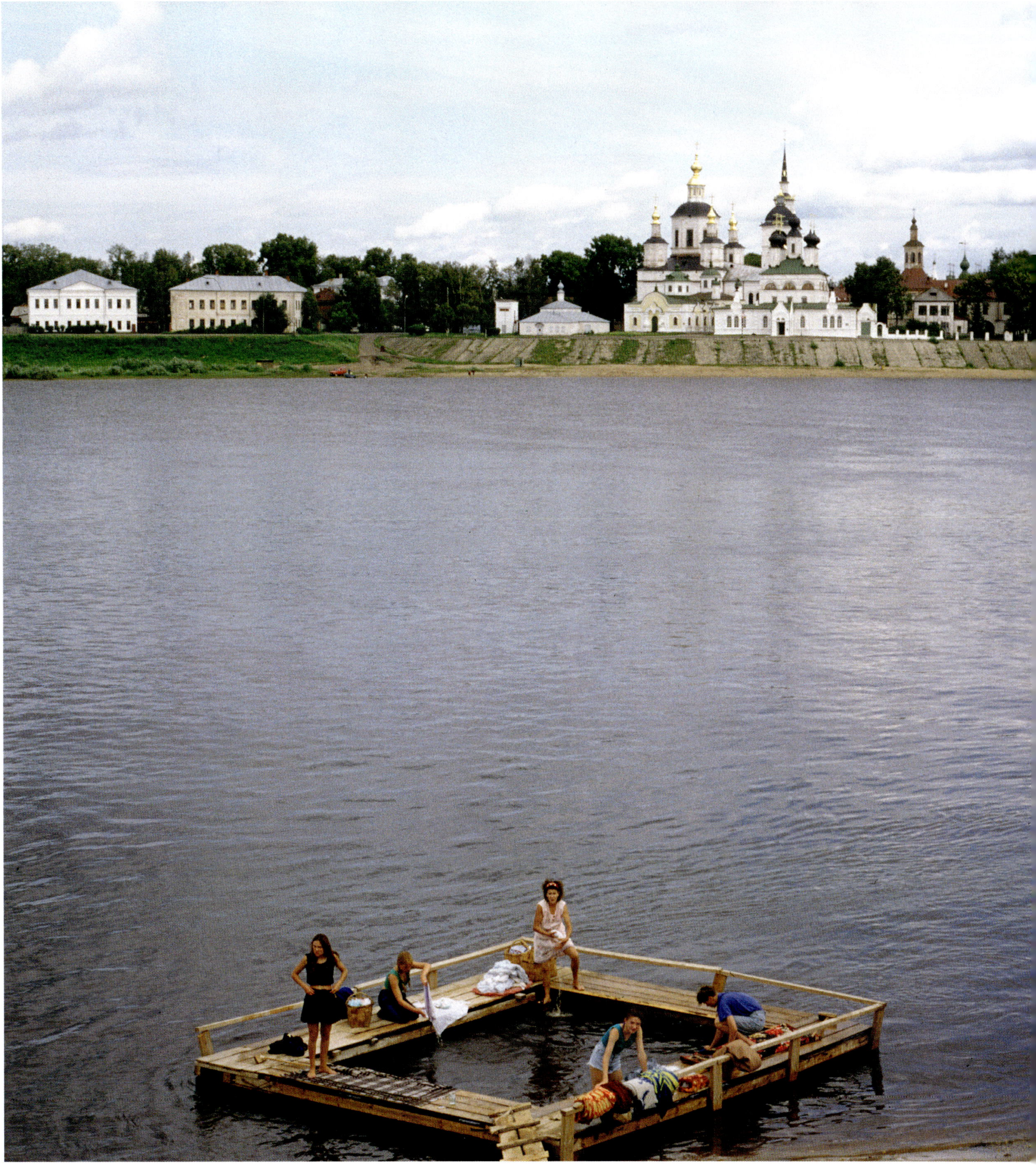

DYMKOVA SLOBODA. Wash day on Sukhona River, with Veliky Ustiug cathedral ensemble on opposite bank. Photograph: July 23, 1998.

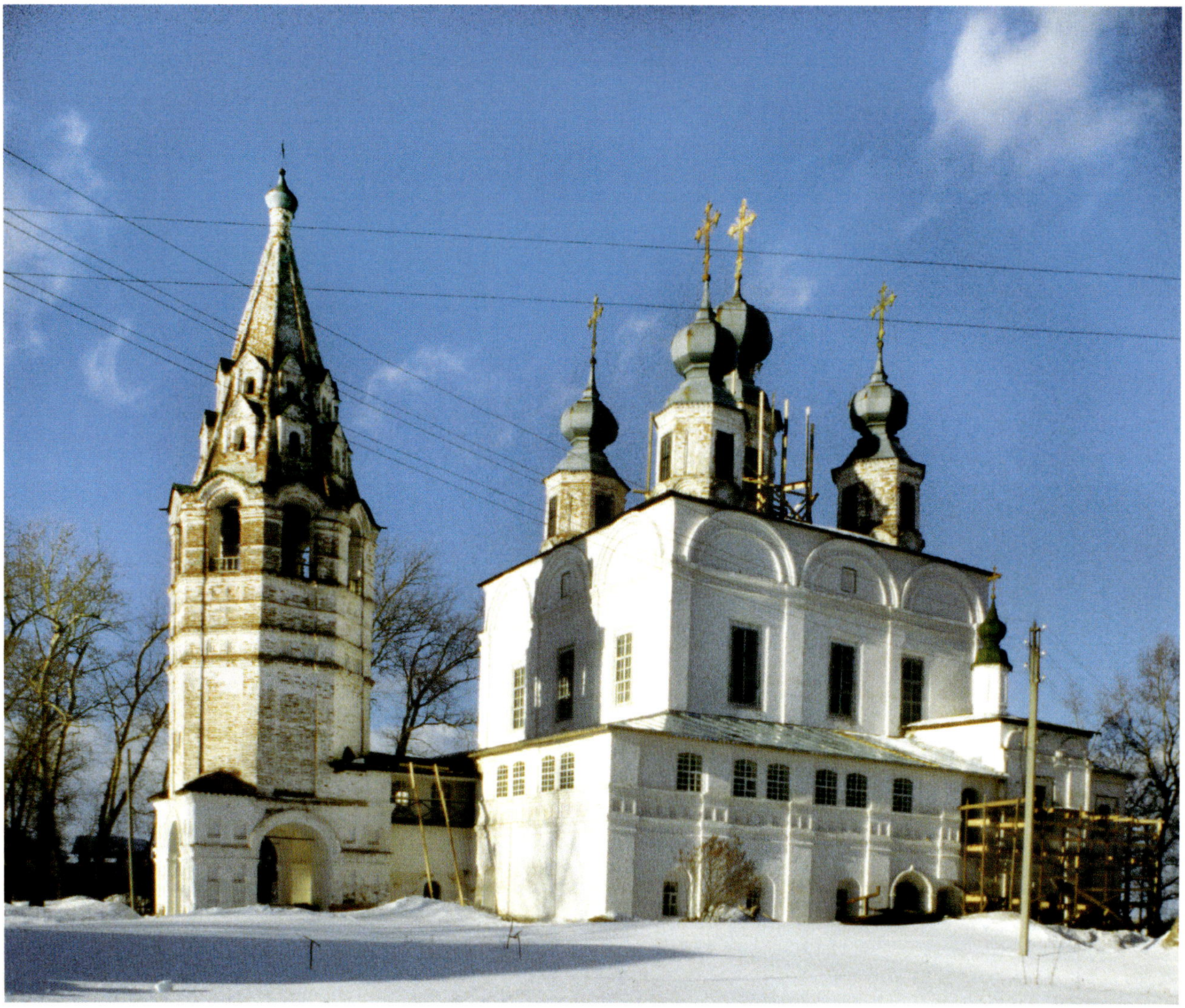

MOROZOVITSA. Trinity Cathedral and bell tower, Trinity-Gleden Monastery, southwest view. Construction began in 1659 but was completed only in the 1690s. Photograph: March 7, 1998.

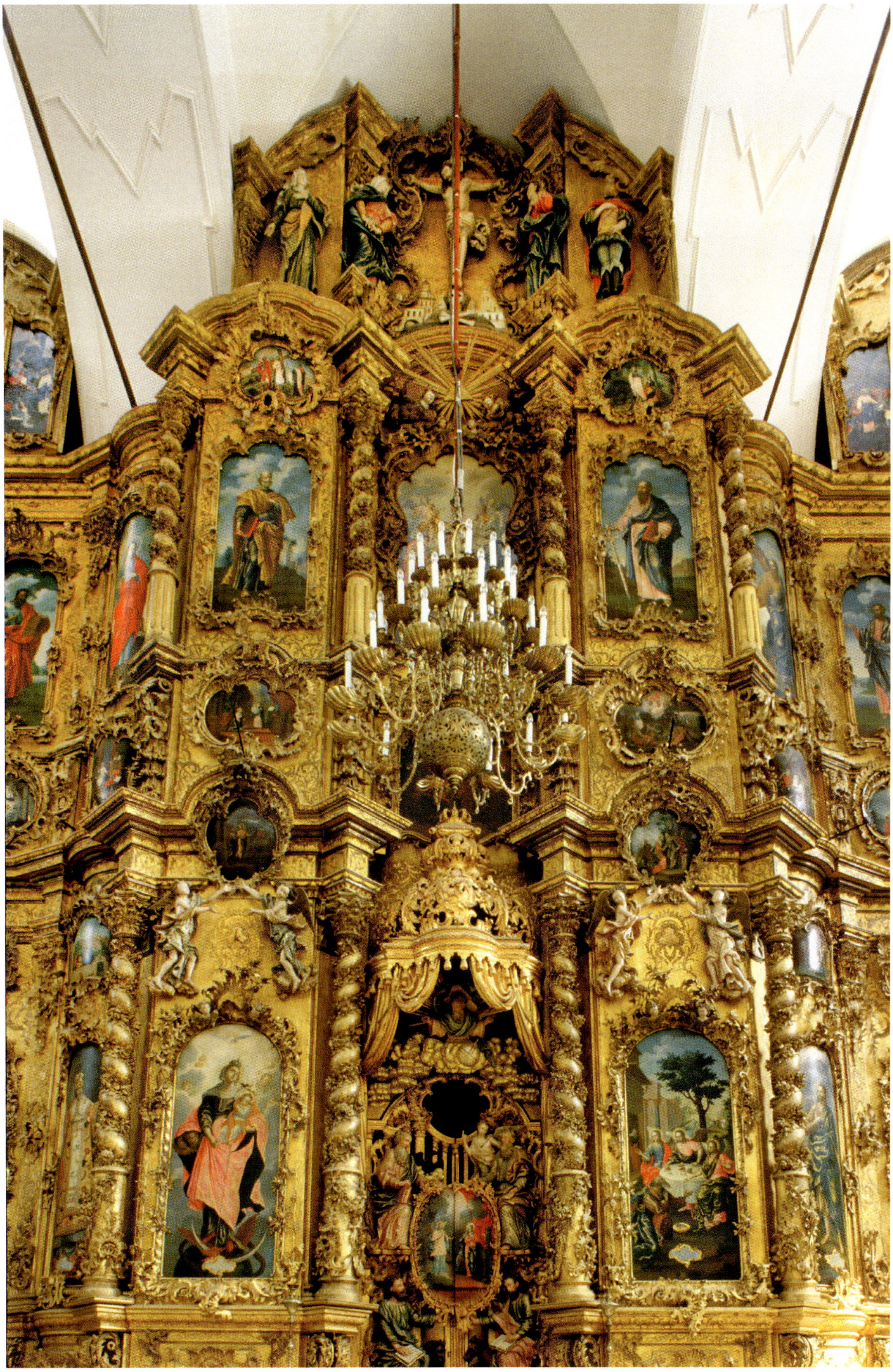

MOROZOVITSA. Trinity Cathedral, Trinity-Gleden Monastery, icon screen. Created in 1776–84, one of the best examples of baroque church art in Russia. Photograph: July 23, 1998.

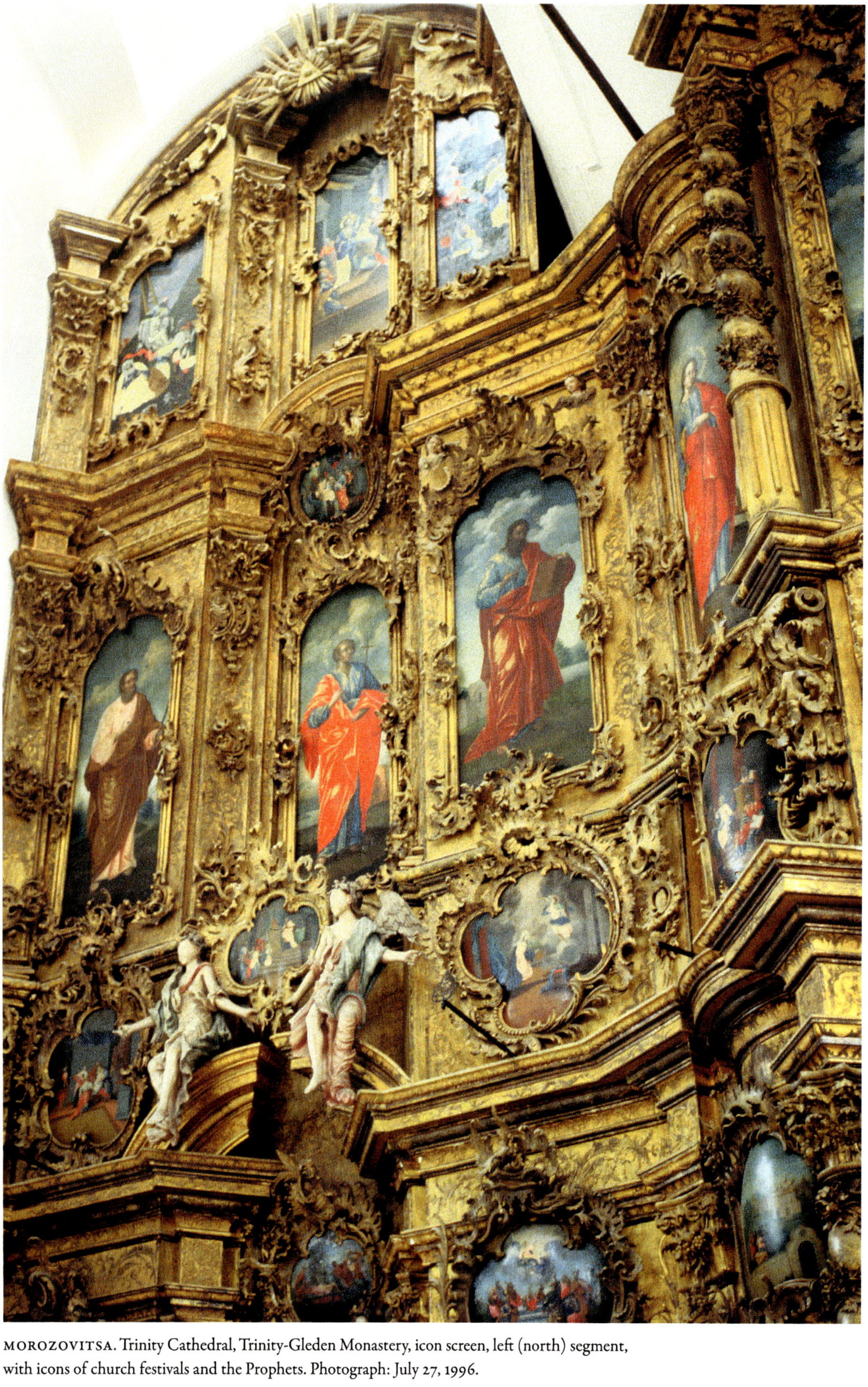

MOROZOVITSA. Trinity Cathedral, Trinity-Gleden Monastery, icon screen, left (north) segment, with icons of church festivals and the Prophets. Photograph: July 27, 1996.

MOROZOVITSA. Church of the Descent of the Holy Spirit at Gleden, southeast view. Built between 1760 and 1764, this small church collapsed in 1999. Photograph: July 27, 1996.

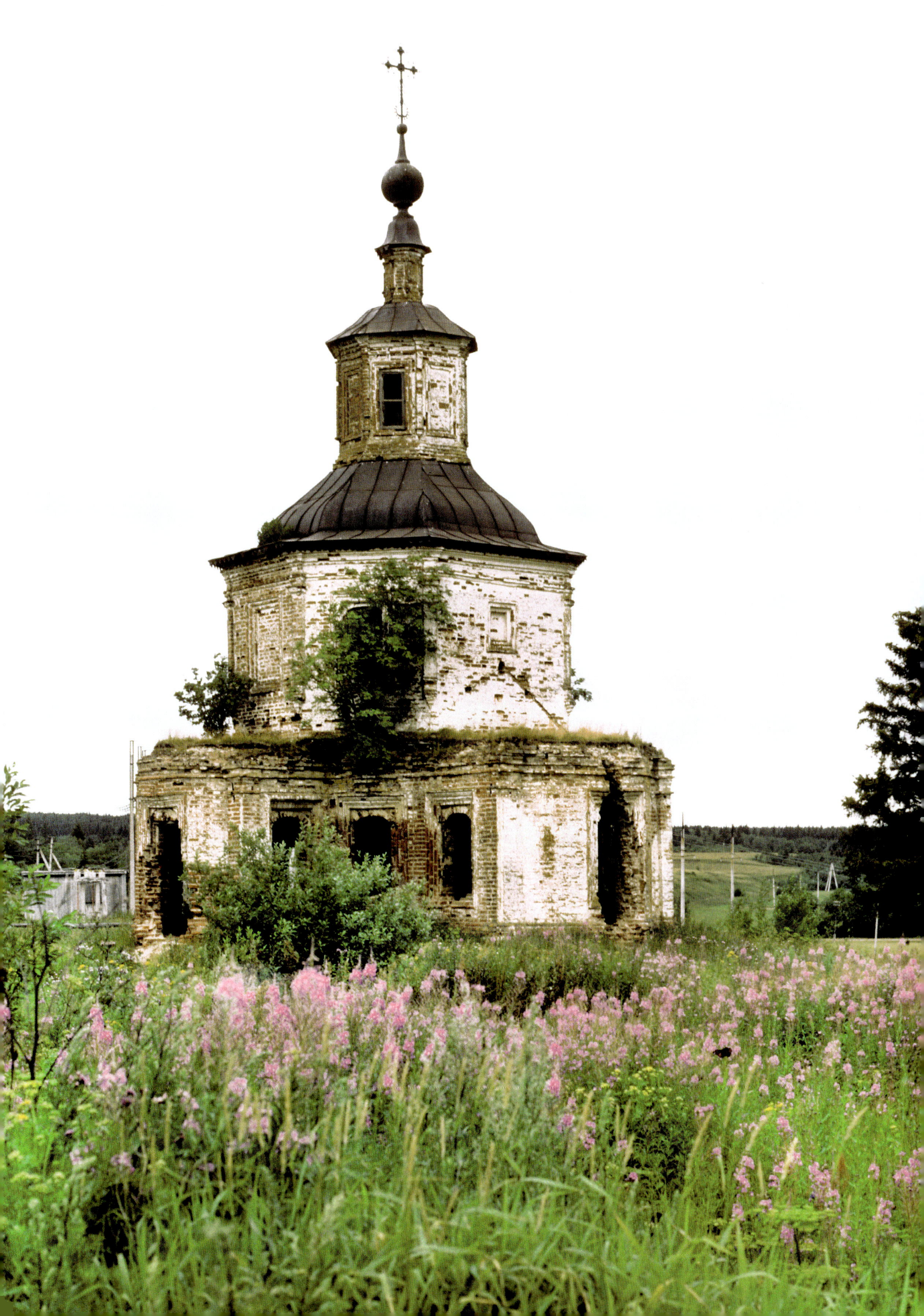

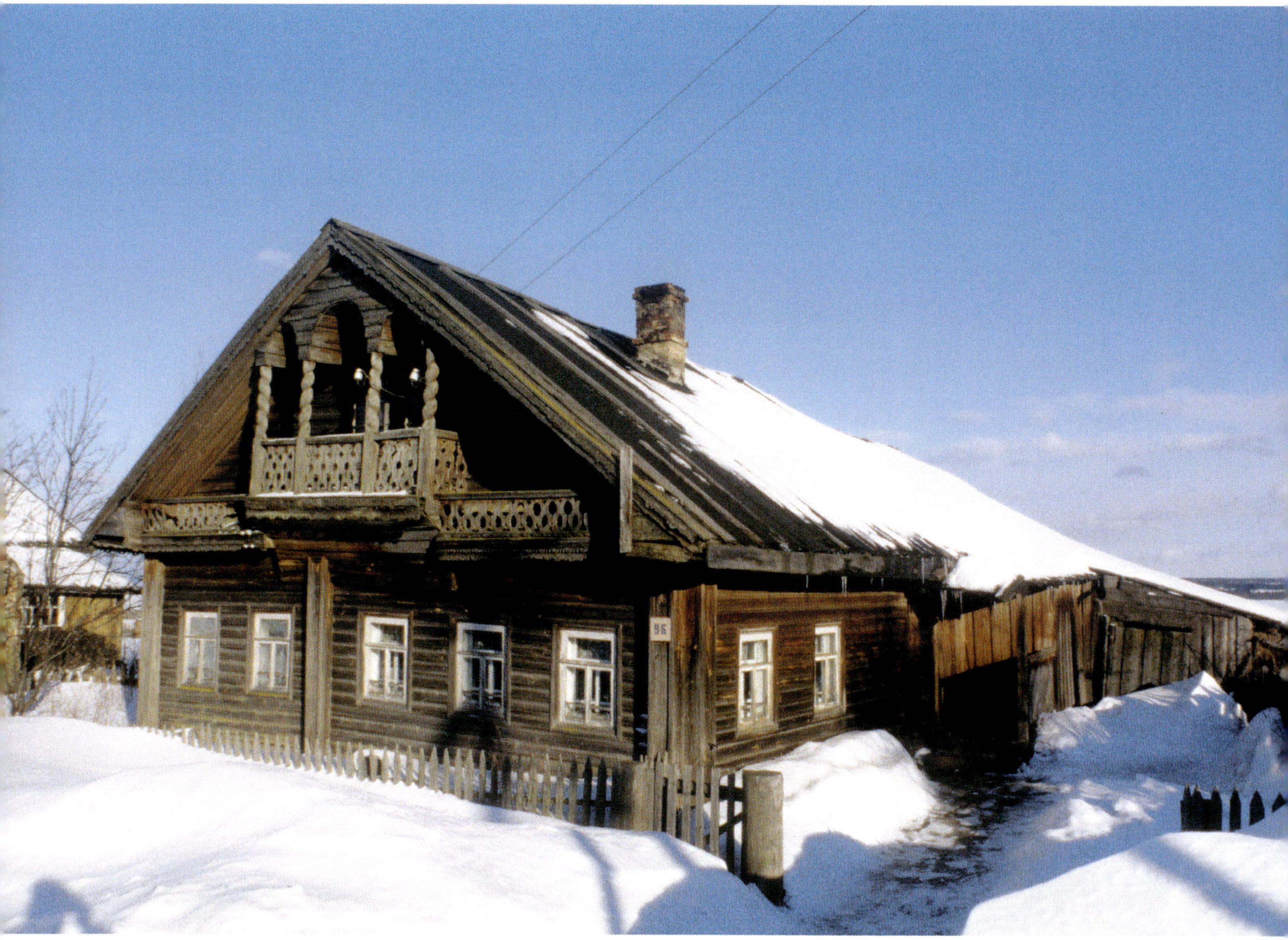

MOROZOVITSA (Pukhovo village). Nineteenth-century wooden house. Photograph: March 7, 1998.

FIVE *Along the Northern Dvina and Beyond to the Arctic Circle*

SOLVYCHEGODSK: SALT ON THE VYCHEGDA RIVER

Of the many treasures of the Russian North, few seem as improbable as the town of Solvychegodsk (population ca. four thousand), located on the north bank of the Vychegda River, a tributary of the Northern Dvina that stretches some eleven hundred kilometers northeast toward the Ural Mountains and Siberia. Despite its sleepy appearance, Solvychegodsk contains two of the most elaborate examples of religious architecture and applied arts in the North.

The first Russian settlements in the area probably arose in the fourteenth century with the support of Novgorod, whose explorers would have recognized the value of a site near the crossing of two major river routes: north to the White Sea and east to the Urals. As Moscow expanded during the sixteenth century, the northern river network became a crucial transportation artery for trade. Wealthy entrepreneurs such as the Stroganovs, who arrived in the middle of the sixteenth century, received privileges from the Muscovite state to establish and maintain settlements in the area.

The main source of their wealth was salt, which in the medieval era was one of the most valuable of commodities. Solvychegodsk means "salt on the Vychegda," and the area is replete with salt springs, as well as a small brackish river, the Usol, and a salt lake, the Solonikha. The Stroganovs created a salt monopoly in the sixteenth century that brought them enormous wealth, and Solvychegodsk became the center of a private empire.

The patriarch of the dynasty, Anika (Ioannikii) Stroganov (1497–1570), began the lavish Stroganov patronage of the arts. His wealth was incalculable, from salt refining, trade, and the exploration of Siberia. Ivan the Terrible allowed Stroganov to maintain an army of his own and to exploit the wealth of vast areas of the Urals and Siberia, in return for which the domains of the tsar were greatly expanded at relatively small expense.

Anika Stroganov's primary contribution to Russian architecture is the Annunciation Cathedral, begun in 1560 and apparently concluded in the early 1570s, although it was not formally consecrated until 1584. Its design is idiosyncratic, with only two interior piers, yet it has the five cupolas usual for major sixteenth-century churches. The structure originally culminated in arched gables, whose outlines are still visible beneath a four-sloped, eighteenth-century roof. The original bell tower at the northwest corner was replaced in 1819–26 by an oversize neoclassical bell tower.

The interior walls of the Annunciation Cathedral were painted with frescoes in the summer of 1600, as noted in an inscription at the base of the walls. They were subsequently overpainted in the eighteenth and nineteenth centuries, particularly after a fire damaged the interior in 1819. A restoration effort since the 1970s has uncovered original frescoes on the west wall. The centerpiece of the Annunciation Cathedral was an elaborate five-tiered iconostasis, originally installed by the end of the 1570s. Its present form dates from the 1690s, although the Royal Gates leading to the altar were donated by the Stroganovs at the beginning of the seventeenth century.

The florid style of the Stroganov school of religious art culminates in Solvychegodsk with the late seventeenth-century church at the Monastery of the Presentation of the Virgin. Its patron, Grigory Stroganov, acquired a dominant position in the Stroganov mercantile empire and would soon figure prominently in the political and cultural changes effected by Peter the Great. In 1688 he commissioned a new cathedral to replace one of wood in the monastery (founded in 1565) that formed part of the family compound at Solvychegodsk. Although the church was not consecrated until 1712, some of the lower parts of the structure were already functioning by 1691, and the basic construction was completed by 1693.

The Presentation Cathedral is distinctive for many reasons, not the least of which is the carved limestone decoration on the brick facades, which are also decorated with polychrome tiles. During the eighteenth century the gallery—originally an open terrace—was enclosed in a brick arcade with an intricate limestone cornice (now partially obscured).

The soaring interior of the Presentation Cathedral is created by a vaulting system of paired arches that support the large structure and its five cupolas. The absence of free-standing piers creates an effect of bright spaciousness, intensified by the lack of frescoes. All attention is focused on the elaborately carved seven-tiered iconostasis, created by Grigory Ivanov in 1693. The icons within the Presentation Cathedral were painted on canvas (instead of treated boards) in a western style by a Stroganov painter, Stepan Narykov. During the winter, worship services are held only in the warmer south gallery. Rarely has a small parish received such lavish premises.

As new trading routes led to a decline in its significance in the eighteenth and nineteenth centuries, the town became a small resort, known for its mineral waters and springs. At the beginning of the nineteenth century, there was still sufficient commercial activity for the Pankov merchant family to build a grand neoclassical mansion.

Solvychegodsk was subsequently used by the tsarist government as a place of exile. The local Political Exile House Museum includes a log cabin where Iosif Dzhugashvili (later Stalin) spent one of his many northern exiles. The Soviet period would inflict much damage on the cultural heritage of Solvychegodsk. Of the town's twelve brick churches at the beginning of the twentieth century, eight were destroyed and two others left in ruined state. But the jewels in the crown, the two Stroganov "cathedrals," still stand in their monumental glory.

VERKHNIAIA UFTIUGA: ALONG THE UFTIUGA RIVER TO THE FORESTS OF SOLVYCHEGODSK

The high artistic culture of the magnificent Stroganov churches provides a telling contrast with the more traditional design in neighboring villages. Among the region's notable historic villages is Verkhniaia (Upper) Uftiuga, located on a dirt road along the small, winding Uftiuga River some forty-five kilometers inland from the Dvina. The village contains one of the defining wooden monuments of the North, the Church of St. Dmitry (Demetrius of Thessaloniki), erected in 1784 and carefully restored in the late 1980s.

The most striking feature of the St. Dmitry Church is its "tent" tower, which comprises over half the forty-meter height of the church. The eight-sided tower rises above a low octagonal log base, which in turn rests on the large cuboid basic structure. The tower culminates in a cupola covered by wooden shingles. On the east side is an extension for the apse (with the main altar), which is crowned with a small gable and cupola. The church is constructed of stout pine logs, tightly fitted and notched at the ends. Just beneath the base of the "tent" tower, the logs are extended in length to support a flare (poval). This extension bolsters the tower and also creates a roof overhang (politsa) that protects the lower walls from excessive moisture runoff. The flare design is both functional and graceful.

The powerful vertical presence of the Church of St. Dmitry is further emphasized by the lack of the usual extension for a vestibule on the west side of the church. In this case the west facade is fronted by a simple raised gallery from which a covered stairway descends to the ground level. This elevated approach lifts the main entrance above the snow drifts that accumulate during the long winters. In every season the soaring form of the Church of St. Dmitry served as a beacon throughout the area.

To the south of the Uftiuga, back-country roads (often little more than sandy tracks) wind through the pine forests in the direction of Solvychegodsk. This region between the Uftiuga and Vychegda Rivers has a number of traditional wooden houses. Many of them have been abandoned, yet they still give a sense of the folk traditions characteristic of the North. These large structures usually have two levels that encompass living quarters in the front and a barn for storage and livestock in the back. All components are under a long extended roof. Log houses traditionally have decorative window surrounds (*nalichniki*) as well as end boards (*pricheliny*) along the front edges of the roof. A distinctive feature of houses in this area is the slightly curved form of their roof. This bowed form was considered to facilitate the shedding of snow, although roofs in most areas of the North have a simple pitch. Whatever the origins, this unusual design creates an appealing aesthetic accent.

The path to Solvychegodsk goes through the once-flourishing village of Tsivozero. Its brick Church of Saints Peter and Paul, completed in the 1860s, was closed and despoiled in the Soviet area. Cleaned by local residents, the exterior of the church is appealing even with the ruined bell tower.

Tsivozero's most remarkable monument is the darkened form of a log bell tower. This intriguing structure was built in 1658 to accompany a church dedicated to Saints Florus and Laurus. Although the church was frequently rebuilt and has long since disappeared, the intricate design of the bell tower provides a rare example of ancient traditions in log construction and decoration. And it is still on its original site.

Other villages in the area have small wooden chapels as well as an occasional brick church (usually abandoned).

FROM KRASNOBORSK AND CHEREVKOVA: THE UPPER REACHES OF THE NORTHERN DVINA

During the nineteenth century, the Northern Dvina continued to play an essential role in connecting towns along its route, including tributaries such as the Sukhona and Vaga. By the beginning of the twentieth century, the region's modest prosperity was reflected in merchant houses built in quiet towns along the river. Among these towns were Cherevkova, Krasnoborsk, and Permogorye, on the left bank of the river in its upper reaches.

Today Cherevkova still has imposing examples of such wooden houses, elaborately decorated with carved facades. The skill of their anonymous carpenters is a marvel, and the houses are especially poetic in the summer, when the fading light of long days seems to bring the ghosts of the past back to life. Unfortunately, meager local resources make it unlikely that the houses will be restored.

APPROACHES TO ARKHANGELSK: HISTORIC SETTLEMENTS ON THE DVINA RIVER

In 1584 growing trade with western Europe led Ivan IV (the Terrible) to establish a settlement near the mouth of the Northern Dvina. Known as Arkhangelsk, after the nearby Monastery of the Archangel Michael, the new outpost would soon become one of Russia's most important ports. Yet there were far older places in the area.

The most important of these was Kholmogory, located near the left bank of the Dvina about eighty kilometers south of contemporary Arkhangelsk. As early as 1138 a document from Novgorod referred to the settlement of Ivani Pogost on the site. The first mention of the name "Kolmogory" occurred in a 1335 document from the court of Moscow's grand prince Ivan Kalita, who also served as prince of Novgorod from 1328 to 1337.

Although Novgorod built a wooden fort at the turn of the fifteenth century to protect the strategic location, by the end of the century the entire territory had entered Moscow's domains. During the sixteenth century, Kolmogory (called "Kholmogory" by the end of the seventeenth century) was fated to play an important role in the opening of Russia to the West.

In 1553 King Edward VI granted a royal charter to the Company of Merchant Adventurers to New Lands, founded no later than 1552 to explore the area beyond the North Cape and investigate the possibility of a northeast passage to China. In May 1553 three ships under the command of Sir Hugh Willoughby departed London, but two of the vessels were lost with all hands on the coast of Russian Lapland (now the Murmansk area) after discovering the inhospitable terrain of Novaia Zemlia. However, Richard Chancellor (?–1556), captain of the ship *Edward Bonaventure*, succeeded in making landfall in August 1553 not far from the St. Nicholas-Korelsky Monastery (now in the city of Severodvinsk on the south shore of the Dvina Bay near Arkhangelsk). Local inhabitants directed him to the mouth of the Dvina River, and from there to the settlement of Kholmogory.

In the meantime local authorities, having granted Chancellor full hospitality, sent riders with the news to Tsar Ivan IV (the Terrible) in Moscow. The tsar brought Chancellor to that city (where he stayed until February 1554), showed him every courtesy, and granted trading privileges to the English that would last until 1698. Kholmogory thus played a critical role in one of the first Western visits to Muscovy, a momentous event that was vividly described in Chancellor's account of the journey. Henceforth, Moscow found its place on the map of European consciousness.

Kholmogory is also known as the birthplace of the renowned Russian scientist and author Mikhail Lomonosov (1711–65). And in the mid-eighteenth century, it served as a place of exile during Romanov family court intrigues. Today, Kholmogory is officially designated a village, with some four thousand inhabitants. Its historic architecture centers on an ensemble that originated in 1685, when Archbishop Afanasy initiated the construction of the Cathedral of the Transfiguration, completed in 1691. At that time the Bishopric (eparchy) of Kholmogory and Vaga stretched over an enormous territory, and the Transfiguration Cathedral became the largest brick structure north of Kargopol. The cathedral ensemble contained a monumental free-standing bell tower (1681–83), as well as the chambers of the archbishop's court, whose windows were crowned with fanciful ornaments (*koruny*). The young Tsar Peter I visited the site in 1693 and commissioned an elaborate icon screen.

Additions to the ensemble include the small Church of the Twelve Apostles (ca. 1760) and the Church of the Pentecost (1865). In 1798 the buildings were converted for use by the Convent of the Dormition, which had occupied several different sites over the centuries. The Dormition Convent was closed in 1920, and during the Soviet period the ensemble fell into extreme disrepair. Restoration of the Transfiguration Cathedral began in 2010 in connection with the tercentenary of Lomonosov's birth, but funds are limited and a proper renovation will require many years.

Near Kholmogory is the village of Matigory, known for its Church of the Resurrection, picturesquely located on a bluff near the small Kurapolka River. Originally built by Fedor Stafurov in 1686–94, the church had additions in the eighteenth century, including a bell tower. The church interior is graced by a majestic icon screen that miraculously survived during the twentieth century.

Complementing the historic monuments at Kholmogory and Matigory is the venerable Trinity–St. Antony Siisky Monastery, located near the west bank of the Dvina about 160 kilometers south of Arkhangelsk. It was founded in 1520 by the monk Antony (1477–1566) on an island in Mikhailovskoe Lake, from which flows the small Siya River. The monastery gained favor in the Muscovite court and subsequently became one of the most important spiritual and cultural centers in the Russian North. Among its treasures was a large manuscript collection.

A sign of the monastery's importance was the construction of the brick Trinity Cathedral in 1589–1606. Despite unusually primitive conditions, the cathedral was competently built and became one of the first large masonry structures in the distant North. In the mid-seventeenth century, the cathedral was complemented by the building of a large bell tower with its Chapel of the Three Prelates. During the same period the monastery gained other brick structures, including the Refectory Church of the Annunciation (1643) with its large dining hall. In 1679–86 the Church of St. Sergius of Radonezh was erected at the main entrance gate.

Like the Kholmogory ensemble, the Trinity–St. Antony Siisky Monastery was closed in 1920. During the late Soviet period the monastery served as a summer resort and its buildings were poorly maintained. In 1992 the monastery island was returned to the church, and the gradual process of restoration began. Today the monastery again serves as a flourishing center for the Russian Orthodox Church.

IZHMA: BEYOND ARKHANGELSK

One of the few remaining historic villages in the Arkhangelsk area is the village of Izhma, situated on the small Izhma River some twenty-five kilometers northeast of the city. The proximity to Arkhangelsk has enabled Izhma to maintain a viable existence. Its log houses are generally well kept; and although there is limited farming, many of the some two hundred inhabitants work in Arkhangelsk. Indeed, Izhma is readily accessible through a road that passes by the city's main airport, Talagi. Despite the urban presence, a visit to Izhma conveys a sense of moving back in time. This impression is due above all to the distinctive form of the log Church of the Transfiguration, crowned with a high four-sloped roof and five wooden cupolas.

Although the origins of the village are obscure, pioneers from Novgorod were in the region as early as the twelfth century. The location was advantageous. The Izhma River—only fifty-five kilometers long—empties into the Kuznechikha River near its merger with the Northern Dvina estuary. Thus the settlement was protected from flooding and still had ready access to the White Sea.

There is evidence of a parish at Izhma village in the fifteenth century. By the early seventeenth century, there are references to a log Transfiguration Church, which was subsequently replaced. Documents date the present Transfiguration Church to 1679. The original form built in 1679 differed from the appearance of the church today. Soon after its construction, chapels were attached on the north and south sides of the main square structure. These chapels contained secondary altars dedicated to the most revered northern saints: Zosima and Savvaty (the founders of Solovetsky Monastery) and Antony Siisky, who founded the Trinity Monastery near Kholmogory.

Apparently, each of these three components was crowned with a tower, similar to the design of the wooden Dormition Cathedral in the Karelian town of Kem. The Orthodox hierarchy frowned upon such towers as deviations from canonical church design, and in 1717 the regional bishop had them replaced with the pitched roof and cupolas visible today. The chapels were later dismantled.

Despite its losses the Transfiguration Church possesses a massive, archaic strength. Some critics would dismiss such architecture as primitive. But in this severe climate the form of the Transfiguration Church proclaims the virtue of survival in the northern forests. Indeed, its stout proportions and diminutive windows suggest the blockhouse of a log fort.

In the late seventeenth century, the Transfiguration Church was complemented by a smaller church used for worship in the winter. Because it was heated, the church repeatedly burned. Its present version was built in 1887 and dedicated to the Resurrection of Christ. The simple elongated form is now empty, lacking its cupola and open to the elements. During the nineteenth century, a wooden bell tower stood between the two churches, but it has since disappeared.

The two abandoned churches are surrounded by wooden houses that are well defended against the severe climate. The houses are one story, usually with another half story containing a summer room at the top. The logs are tightly fitted to minimize heat loss during the long winters. The windows, with their painted frames, are double glazed and carefully insulated. Here, as elsewhere, the traditional wooden houses are being refurbished or replaced by more contemporary designs. But there are exceptional villages, in more remote locations.

BACK TO THE ARCTIC CIRCLE: KIMZHA AND THE MEZEN RIVER

The village of Kimzha, in Arkhangelsk Province, is one of the most significant surviving traditional settlements in the Russian North. It is situated close to the Arctic Circle near the point where the small Kimzha River flows into the Mezen, one of many waterways that drain northern Russia. Slightly farther to the north, the mouth of the Mezen River is flanked by two towns, Kamenka and Mezen, both with a population of about five thousand. Mezen is the regional administrative center; Kamenka has the region's largest employer, a lumber factory. The population of Kimzha varies between winter and summer: a couple of hundred in the winter, with a hundred or so more at various times in the summer, when relatives return to visit parents and grandparents.

For much of the year, Kimzha lies buried under severe winter conditions, stiff wind, and treacherous snowdrifts. Formerly, there was limited scheduled transportation by water from Arkhangelsk, but that long ago ceased to exist. A year-round transportation option is by small plane from the Arkhangelsk's Vaskovo airport to Mezen, and from there by car (and boat) to Kimzha. During the winter there is a temporary road, or zimnik, but this is an exhausting, nerve-wracking route, whose usefulness has been curtailed in recent years by the earlier spring thaws. An all-year dirt road is nearing completion and will in theory open the way to Arkhangelsk.

In the meantime Kimzha continues in its traditional ways. The place has a certain magic perhaps best represented by the aquamarine shimmer of the aurora borealis that can be seen from here. And the village itself makes an extraordinary impression, with its massive log houses built in the late nineteenth and early twentieth centuries. Although some houses have been abandoned or shuttered for the winter, and others have been modified with plank siding, this is not an open-air museum with a few reconstructed log buildings. Kimzha is a living environment.

Some residents are employed by the village administration, others live on the remnants of agriculture, and others have connections with the lumber plant in Kamenka. Although the former dairy kolkhoz, surrounded by rusting machinery, has withered, a large part of the dairy herd is now individually owned. The villagers are also sustained by the forest (berries, mushrooms) and waterways (fishing). Locals are adept at growing and preserving much of their own food. Nonetheless, modern life requires certain amenities that are difficult to provide in this environment. With so many complications, the preservation of Kimzha—the buildings and the community—seems remarkable. While many former residents of the village have left for work elsewhere, this emigration has helped Kimzha retain its age-old dimensions. And the arduous journey required to reach the village has also protected the integrity of its environment.

Yet these factors alone cannot explain the survival of Kimzha, when hundreds of other villages throughout the North have vanished. Its primary landmark is a church, dedicated in 1763 to the Hodegetria Icon of Mary. Perhaps the physical existence of the church has played a major role in the village's endurance. With its tall vertical form — over twenty-seven meters high — the Hodegetria Church defines Kimzha from every perspective. The Russian North was rich in examples of log churches such as the famous Transfiguration Church on Kizhi Island, with its twenty-two domes. But the Kimzha church is the sole surviving example of its type (high central tower and cupola closely flanked by four small cupolas) that was created by a group of carpenters active only in this part of the North, near the Pinega River.

Begun in the early eighteenth century and consecrated in 1763, the Kimzha church has survived decades of neglect and the threat of accidental fire. In the 1870s its stout logs were covered with plank siding, painted white with blue and green trim. At the same time a bell tower was erected over the west porch. (An earlier bell tower stood separate from the church on the bank of the Kimzha River.) Soviet restoration practice frowned on such nineteenth-century cladding, and in the 1980s some of the planks were removed. Lack of funds halted the restoration, and the church remained as a textbook display, half with plank siding and half without.

A dedicated church committee succeeded in 1999 in having the padlock removed from the church, which was then reconsecrated. For a few years thereafter the church was open for worship, but preservation efforts have forced parishioners to move to a small house for services. Two years ago the church structure was disassembled for a thorough restoration, but work has since been halted. If current problems are resolved, there will be hope for the preservation of this masterpiece.

Despite its difficulties, Kimzha has found a delicate balance between past and present. A slowly increasing number of artists and specialists in the history of the North visit the village. Tour companies talk of the possibility of building a small hotel. The opening of the new road might bring new resources, but also new problems. Without a source of local pride and spiritual values, conservation will be questionable. It comes back to the church that stood at the center of the village. Russia can ill afford to lose such treasures.

SOLVYCHEGODSK. Cathedral of the Annunciation, northeast view. Cathedral was begun in 1560, completed in the early 1570s, but consecrated — like the Vologda St. Sophia Cathedral — only in 1584 (apparently due to Ivan the Terrible's anger at the church hierarchy). Photograph: June 26, 2000.

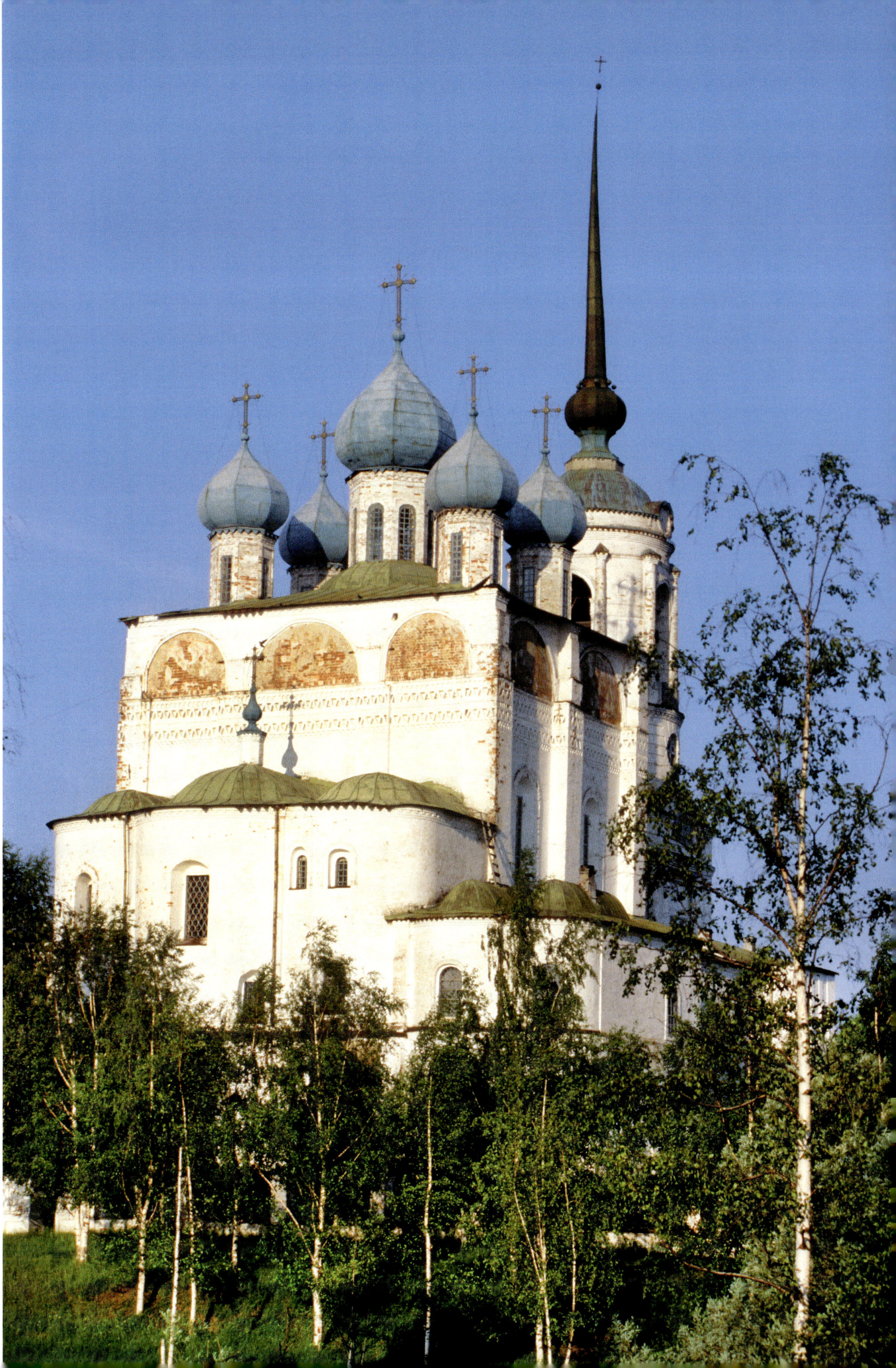

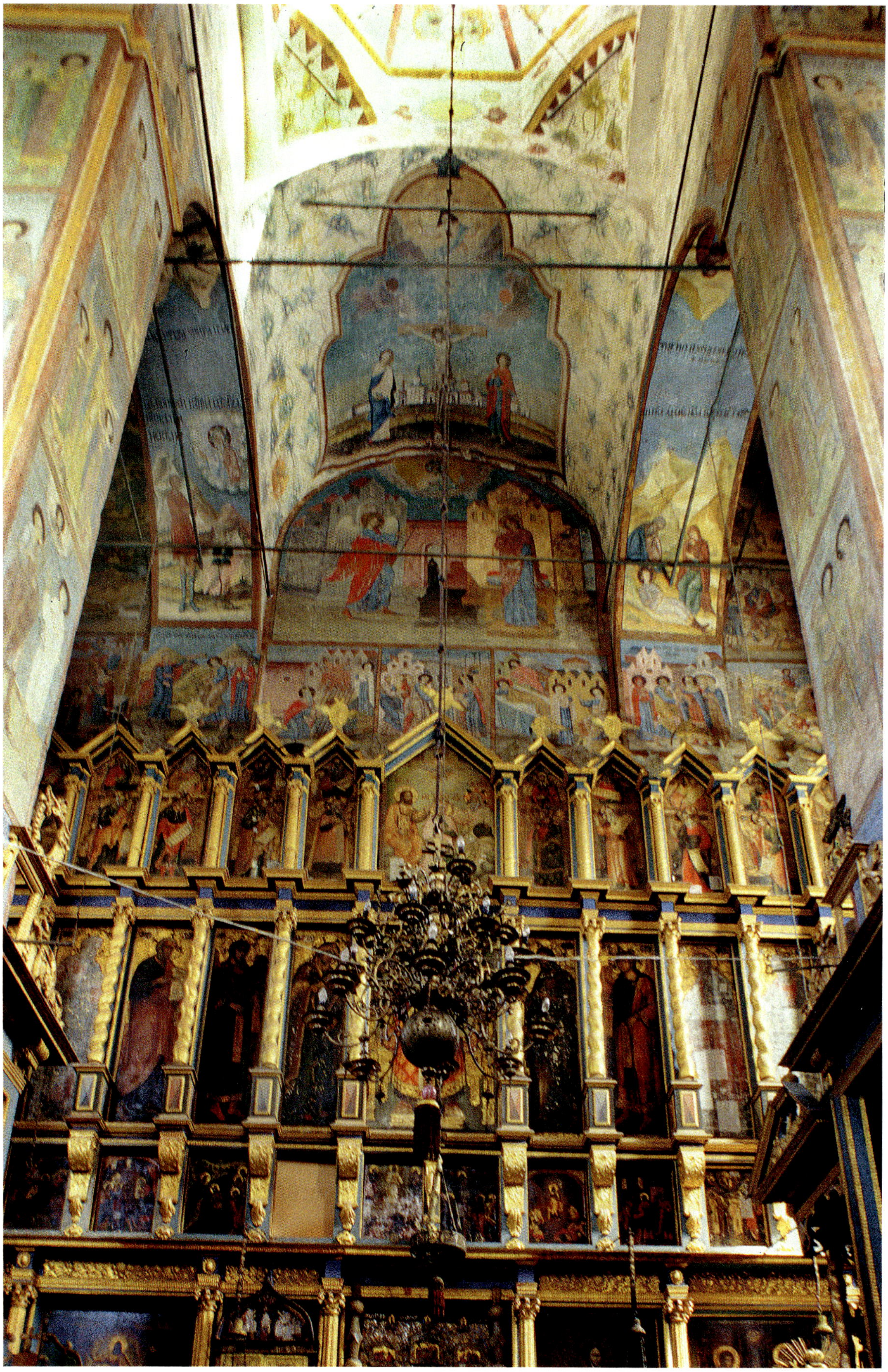

SOLVYCHEGODSK. Cathedral of the Annunciation, interior, view east toward iconostasis.
Frescoes originally painted in 1600. Photograph: June 26, 1999.

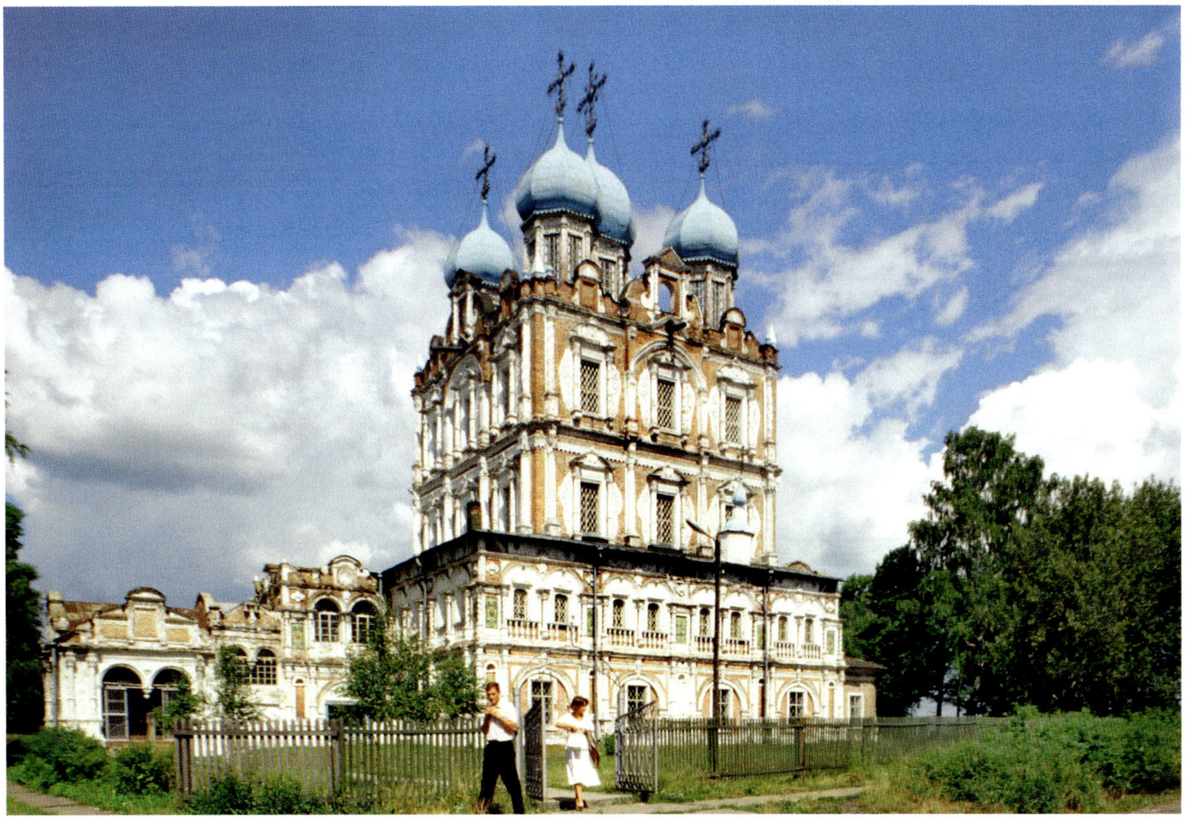

SOLVYCHEGODSK. Cathedral of the Presentation, southwest view. Built between 1689 and 1693, consecrated in 1712. Photograph: July 17, 1999.

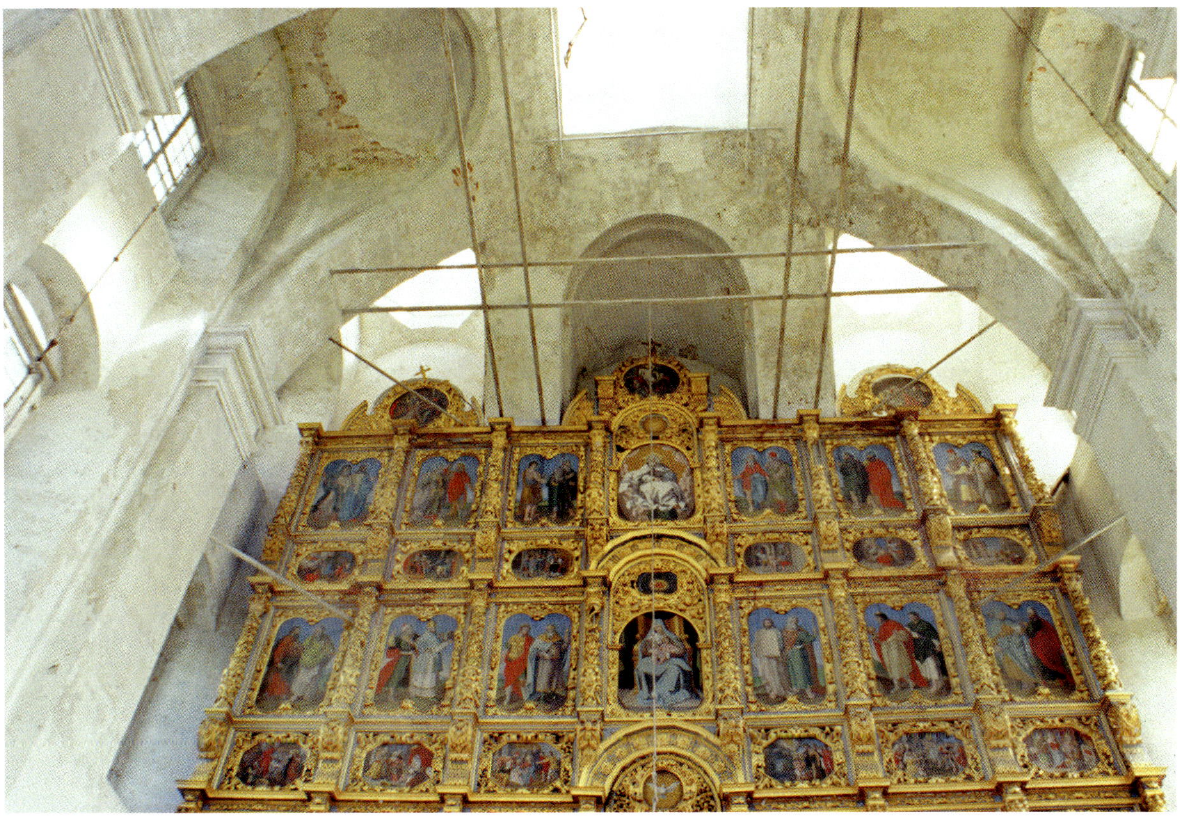

SOLVYCHEGODSK. Cathedral of the Presentation, interior, view east toward vaulting and upper part of magnificent icon screen, created by Moscow master craftsmen in 1693. One of the definitive examples of "Stroganov baroque." Photograph: June 26, 1999.

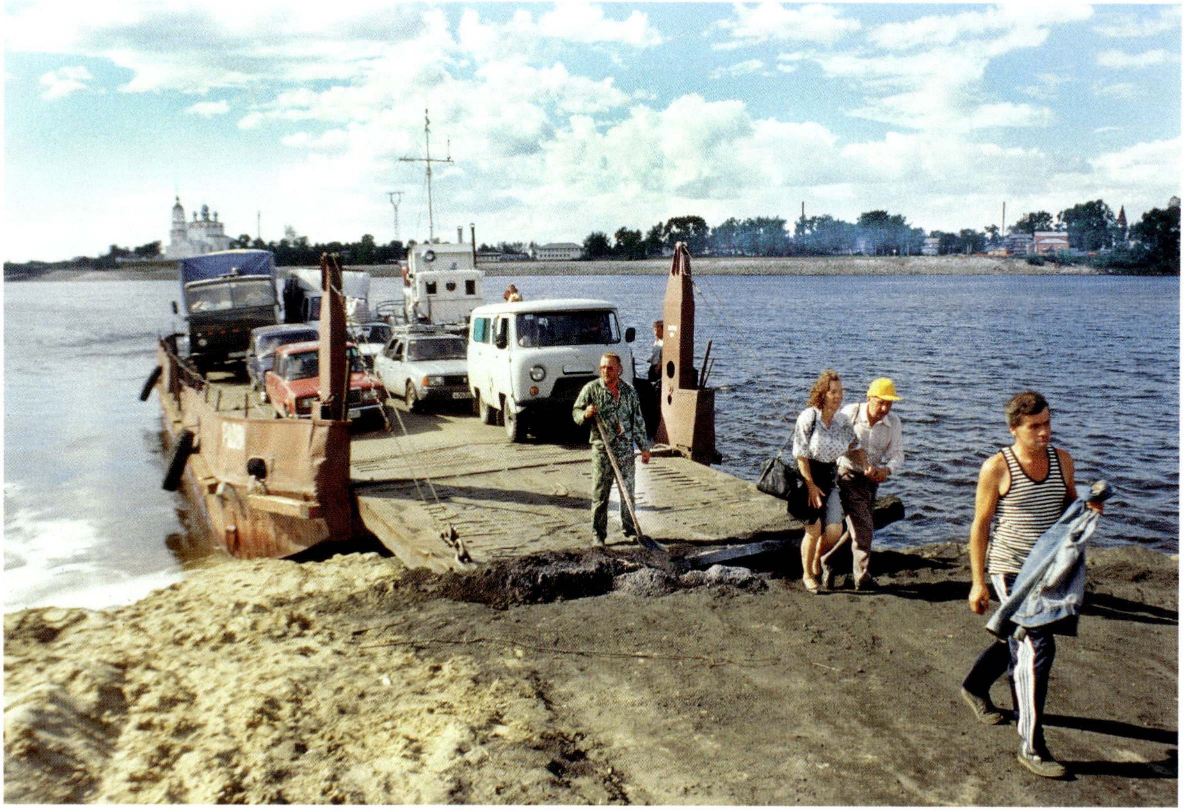

SOLVYCHEGODSK. Vychegda River ferry, south bank. Background: Annunciation Cathedral. Photograph: July 17, 1999.

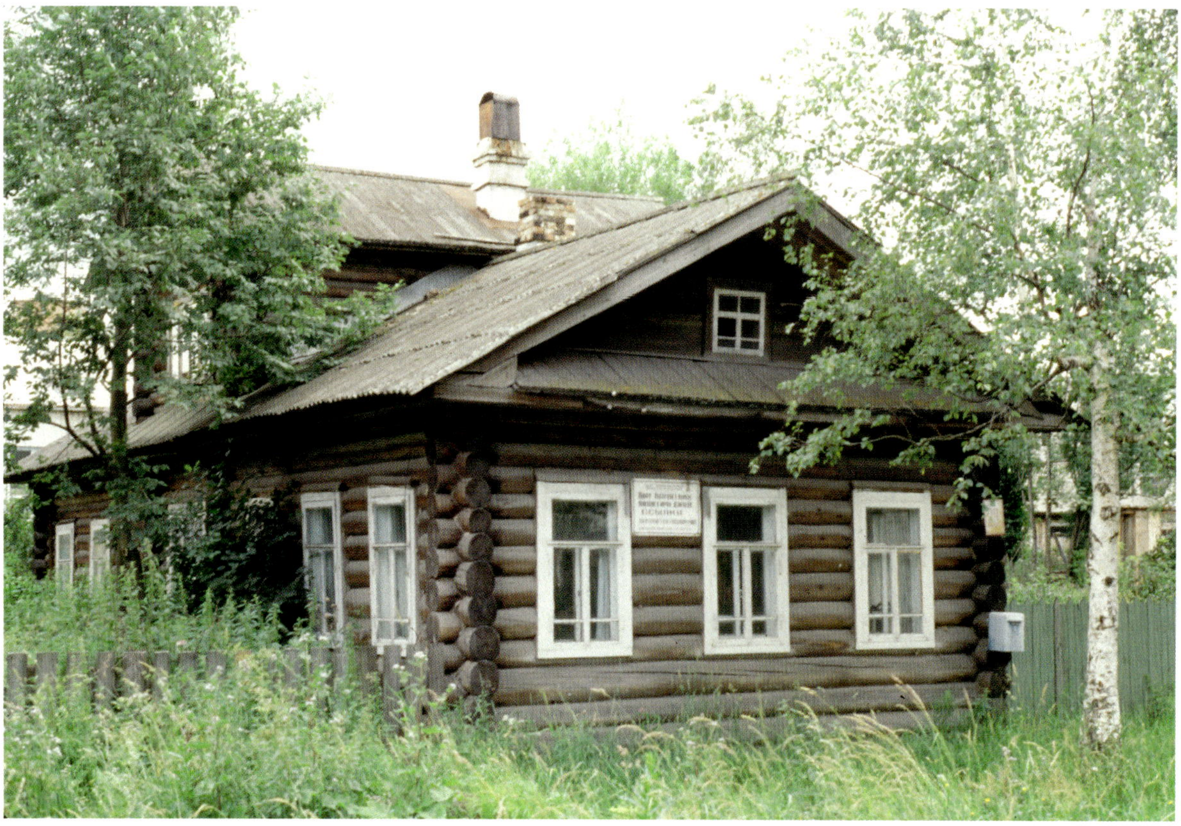

SOLVYCHEGODSK. Political Exile House Museum. Log house where Iosif Dzhugashvili (Stalin) lived in exile from late 1910 until July 1911. Photograph: July 28, 1996.

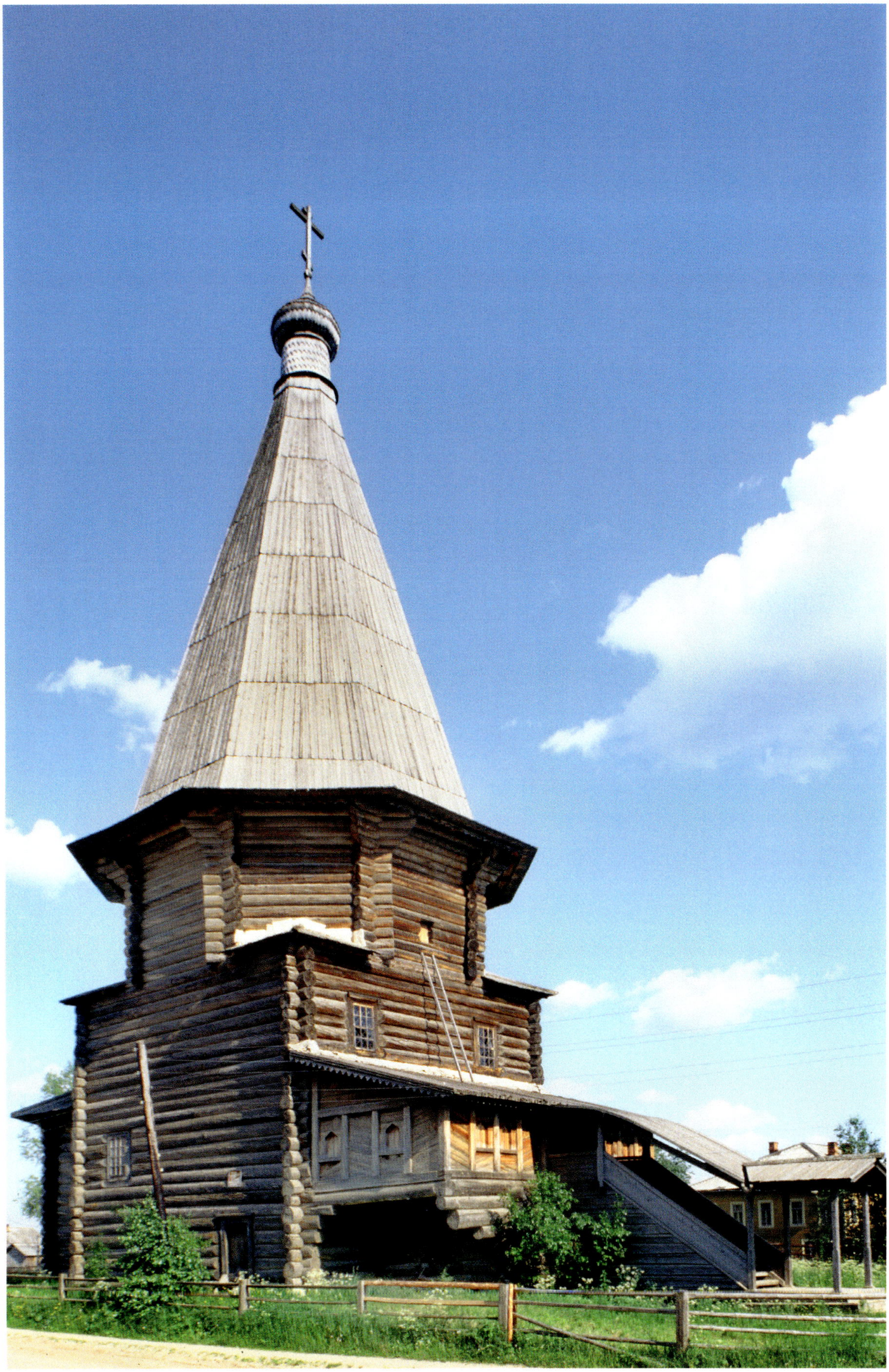

VERKHNIAIA UFTIUGA. Church of St. Dmitry Solunskii (Demetrius of Thessaloniki), northwest view. Built in 1784. Photograph: June 25, 2000.

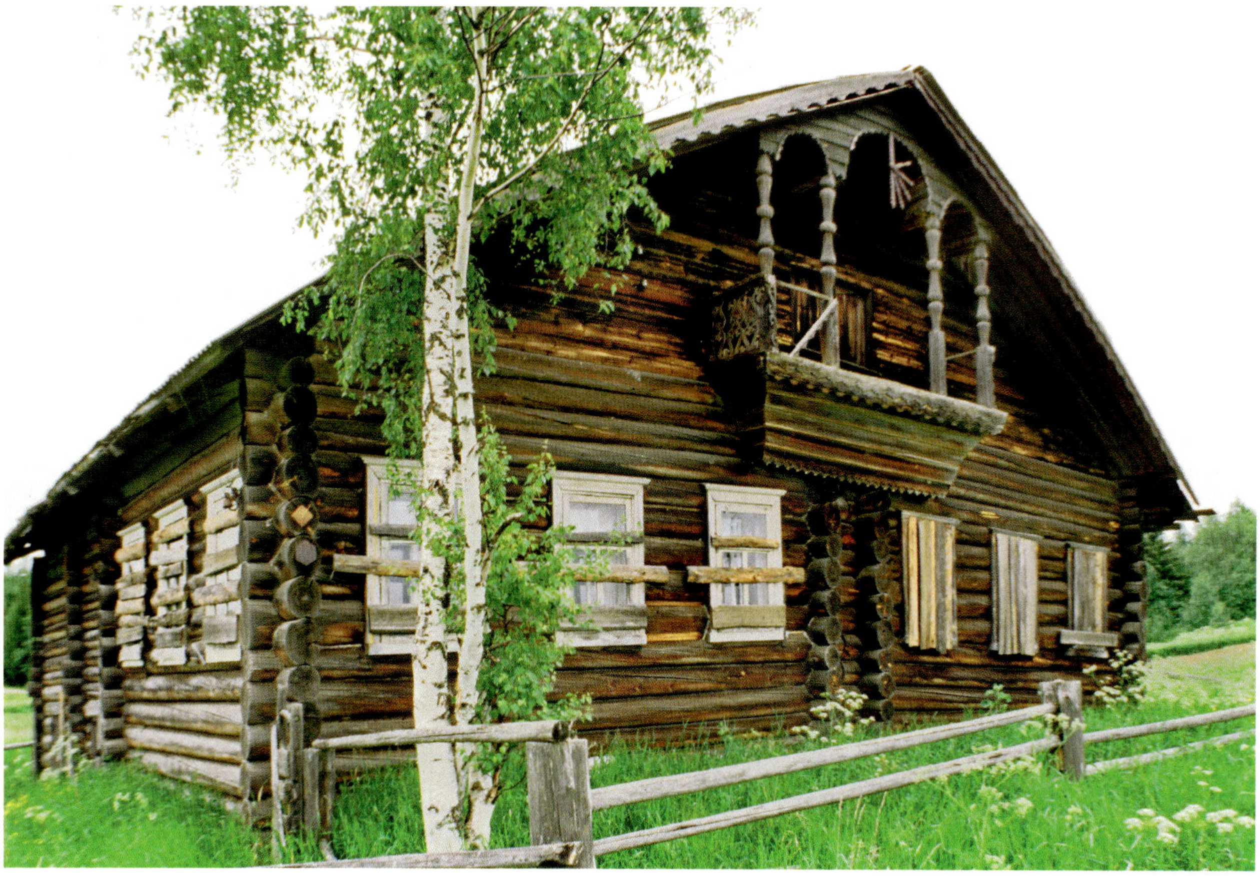

ZABOLOTYE (Terekhino). Log house with balcony and bowed roof. Photograph: June 21, 2000.

TSIVOZERO. Wooden bell tower of Church of Saints Florus and Laurus. Built in 1658. Photograph: June 25, 2000.

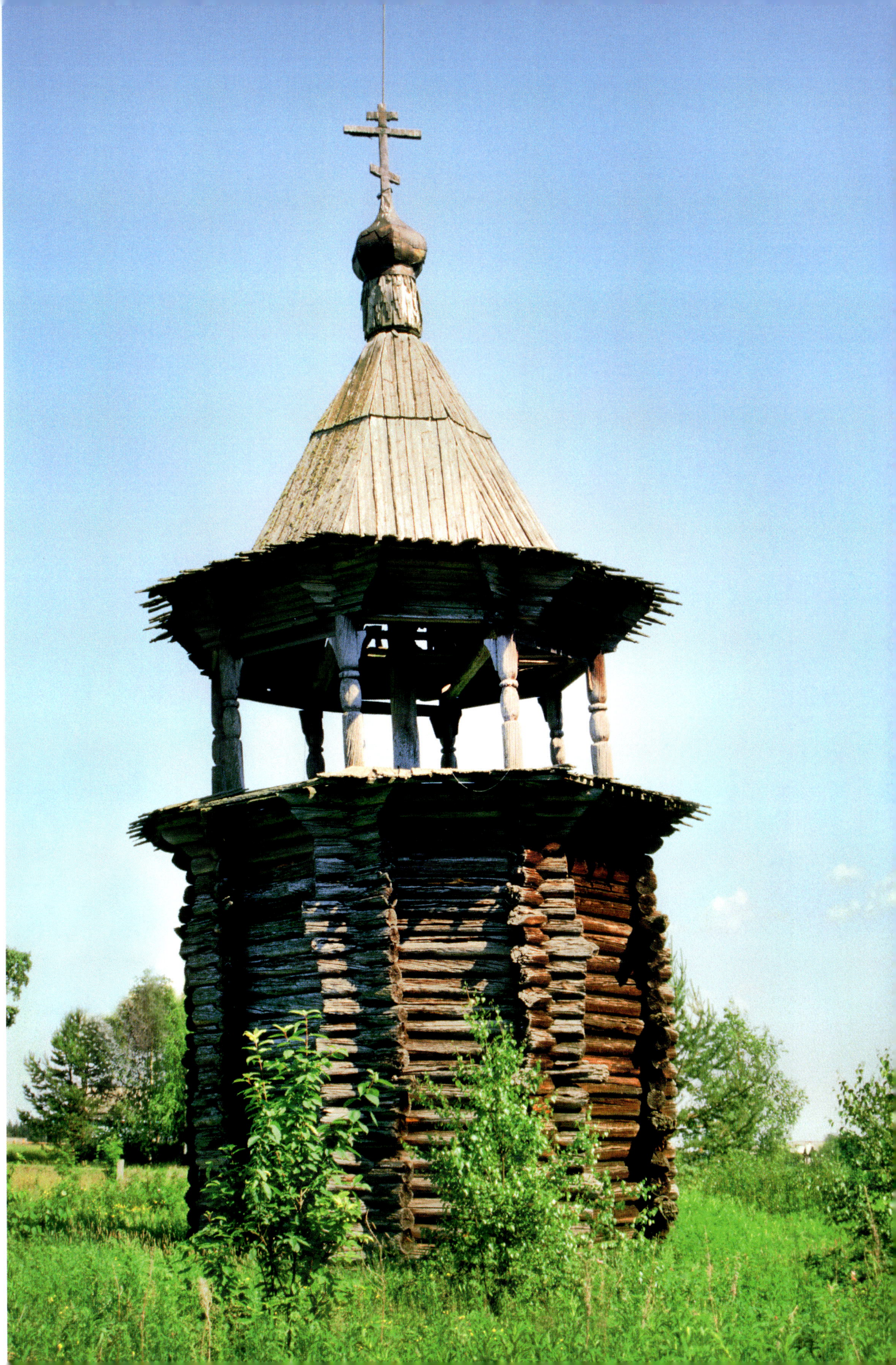

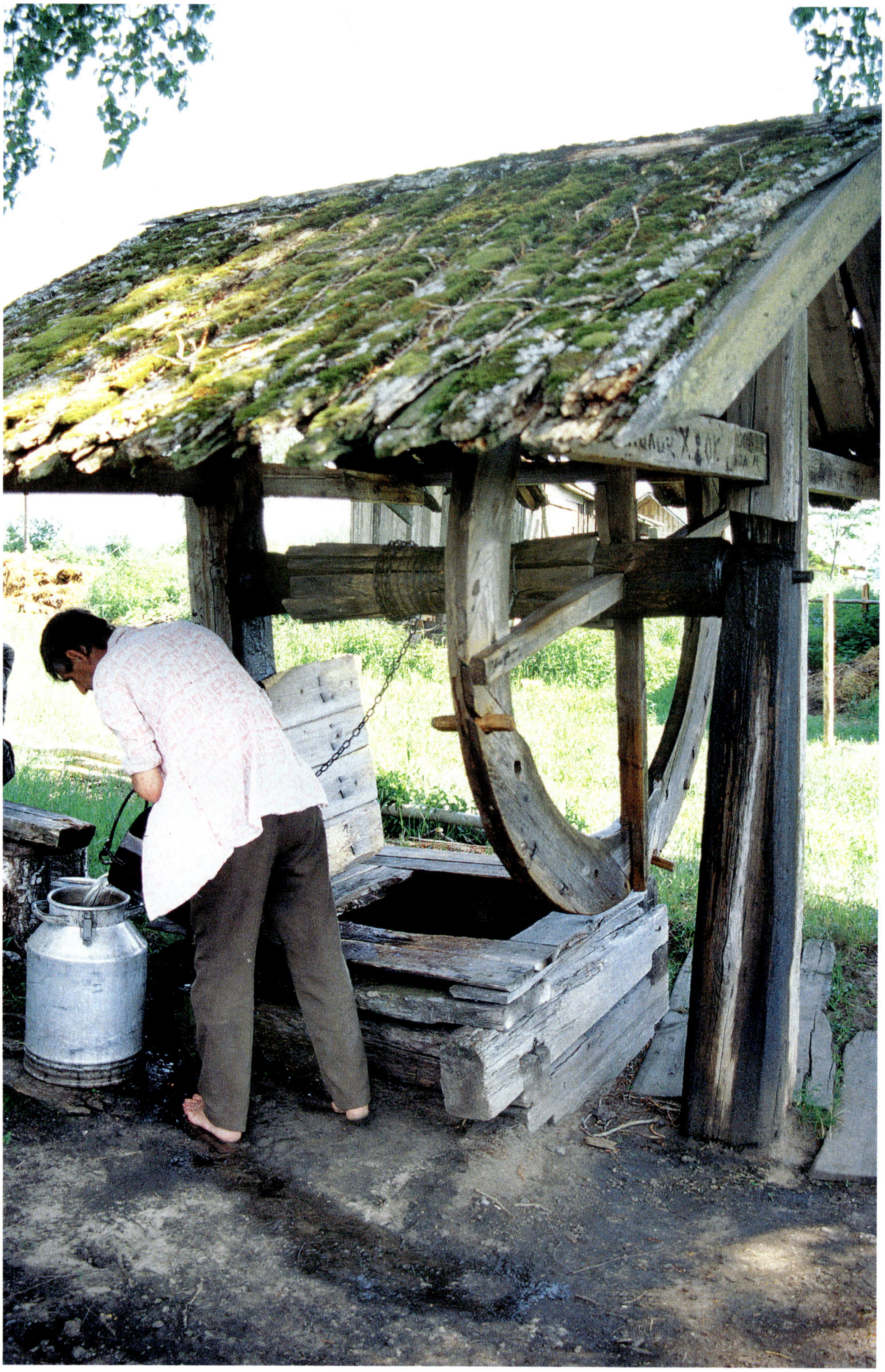

TSIVOZERO. Village well with wooden roof. Photograph: June 25, 2000.

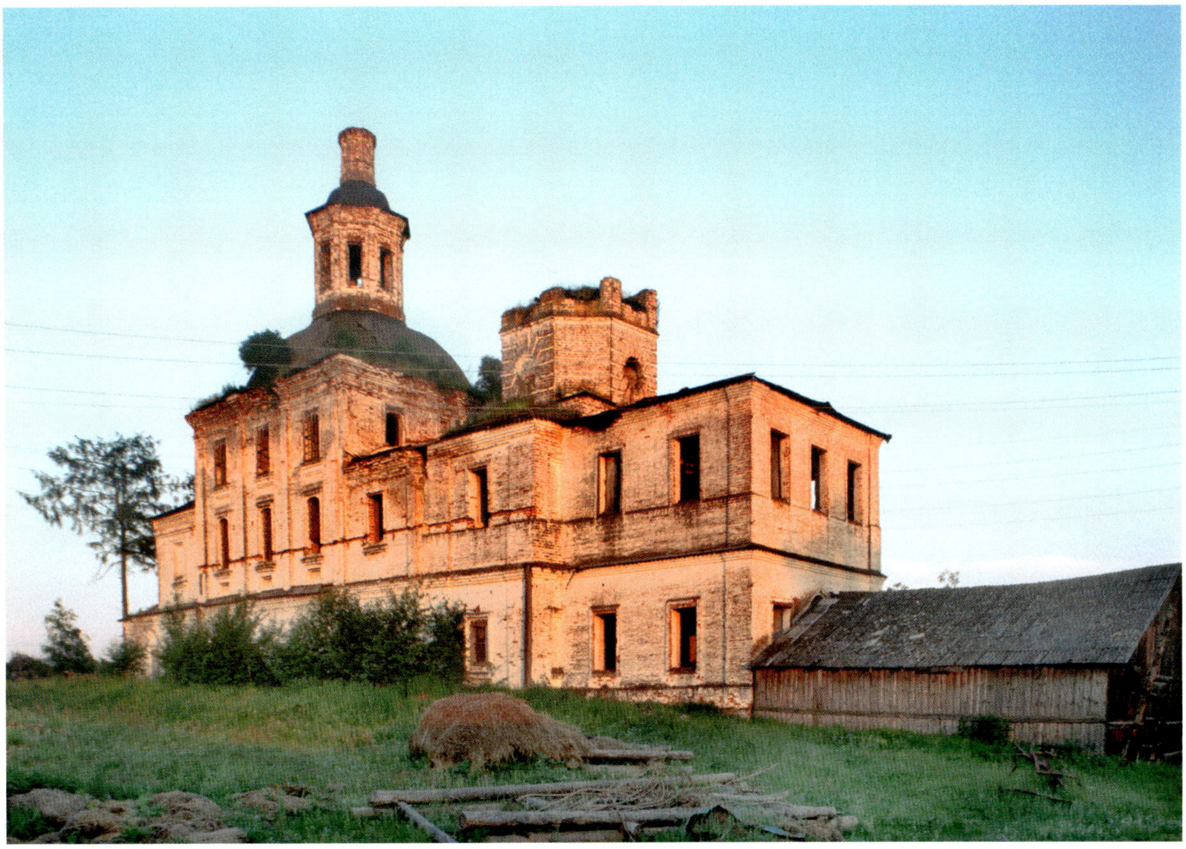

PESCHANITSA (Grigorovo). Church of the Trinity, northwest view at sunset. Built in 1789; upper part of the church collapsed around 2010. Photograph: June 25, 2000.

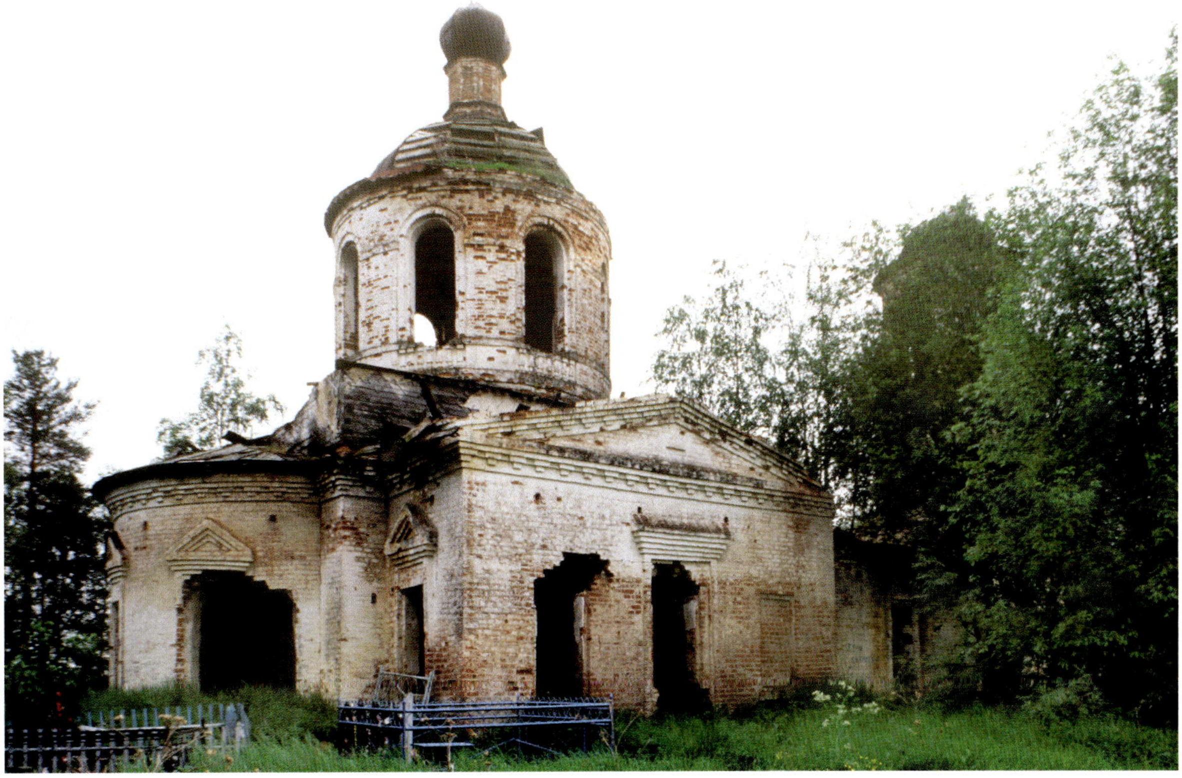

EVDA. Ruins of Church of the Ascension, north view. Built in 1835. Photograph: June 21, 2000.

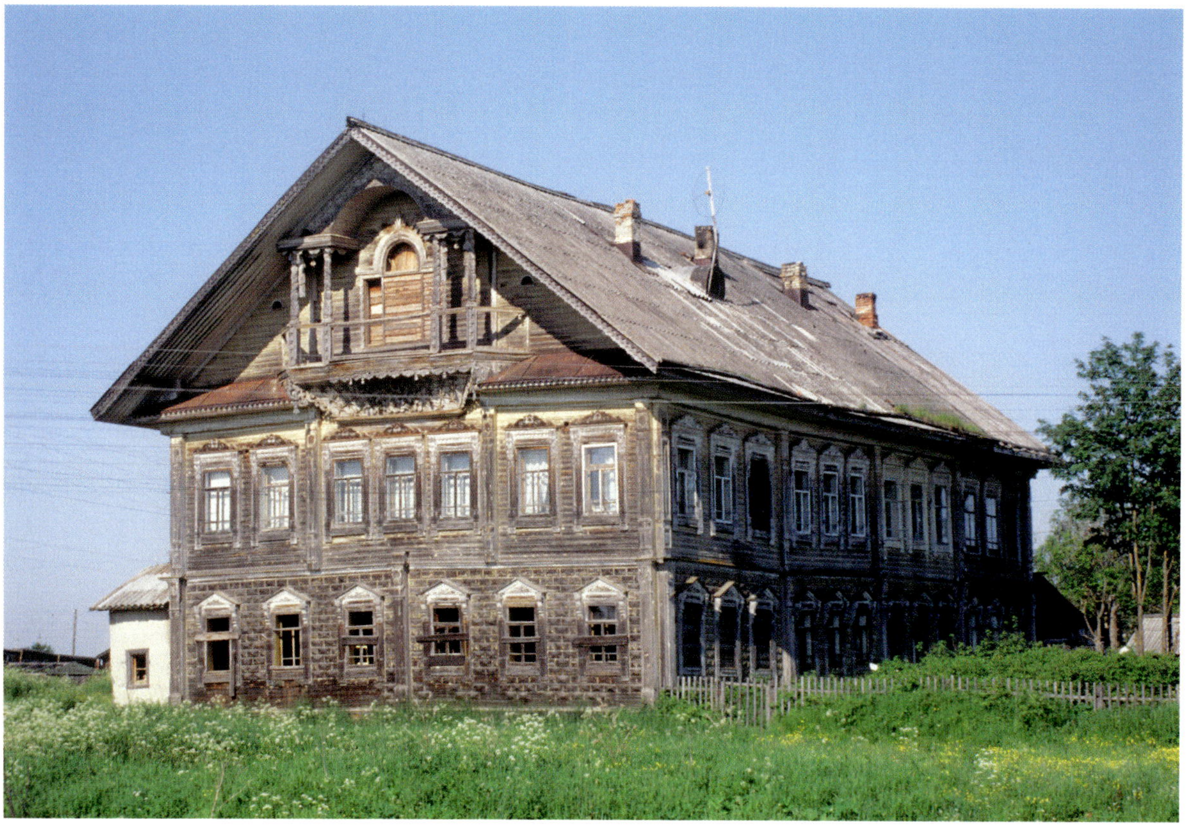

OVSINNIKOVSKAIA (Cherevkovo). M. S. Gusev house. Built in the late nineteenth century. Photograph: June 24, 2000.

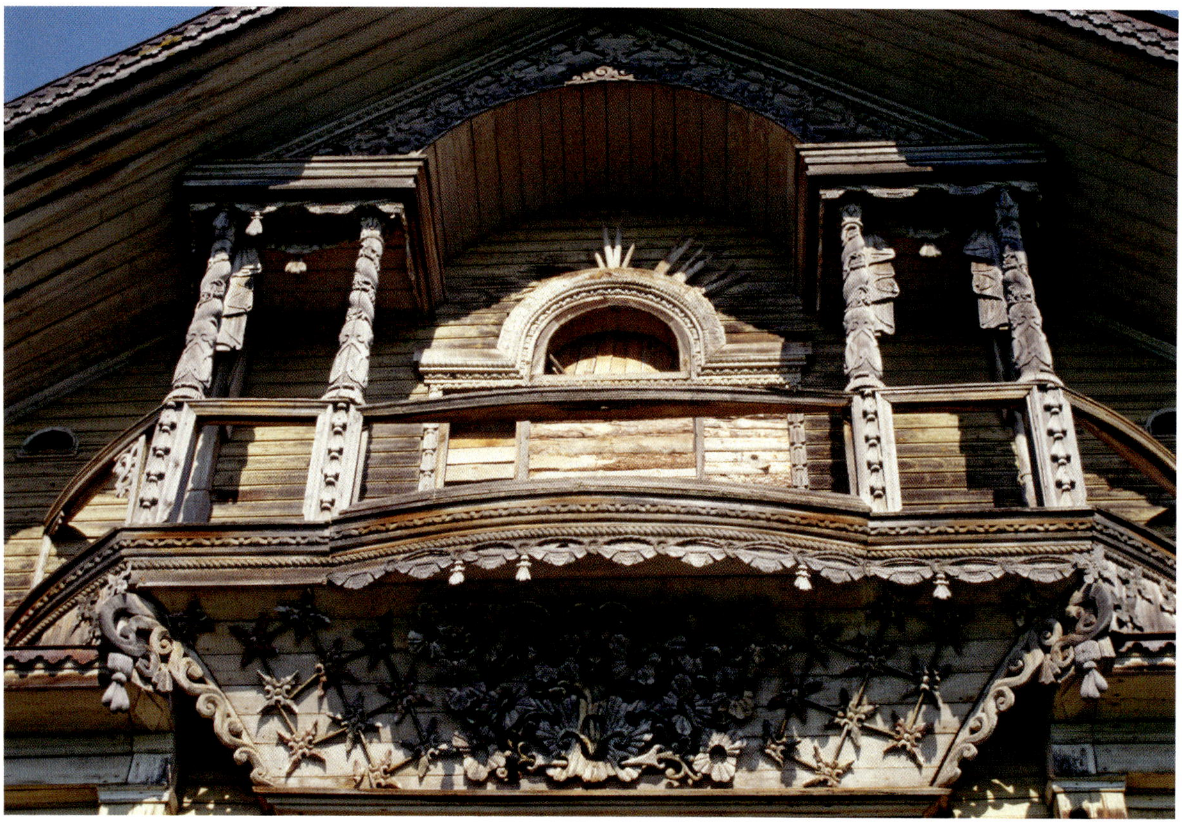

OVSINNIKOVSKAIA (Cherevkovo). M. S. Gusev house, balcony. Photograph: June 24, 2000.

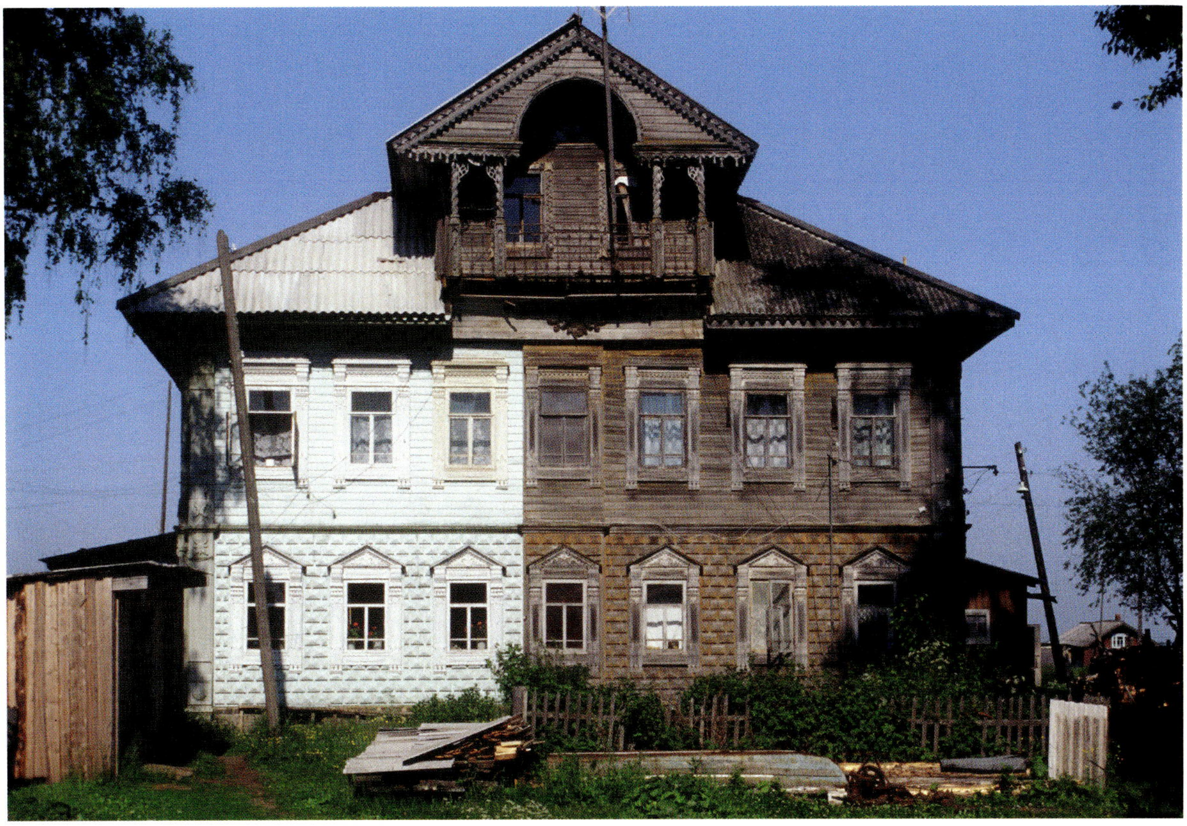

OVSINNIKOVSKAIA (Cherevkovo). I. S. Gusev house. Photograph: June 24, 2000.

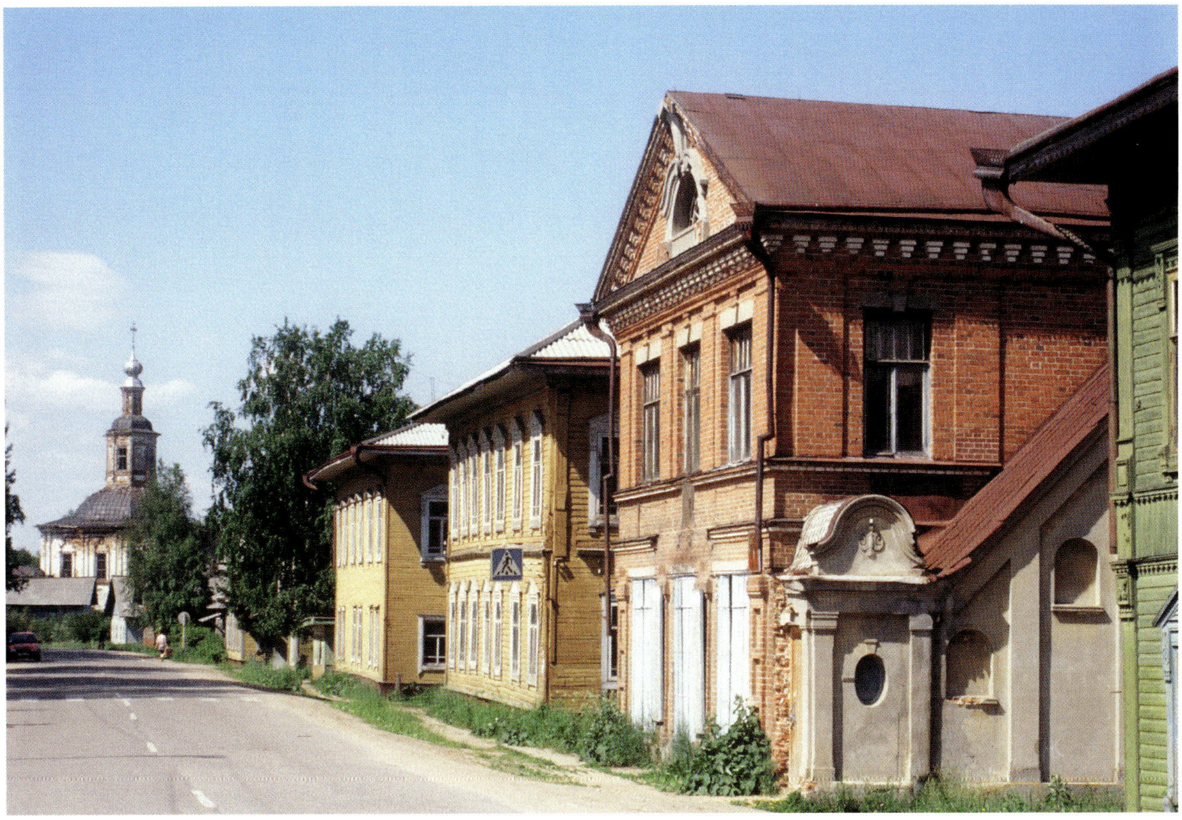

CHEREVKOVO. Houses, First of May Street. Left: Church of the Trinity, southeast view. Photograph: June 24, 2000.

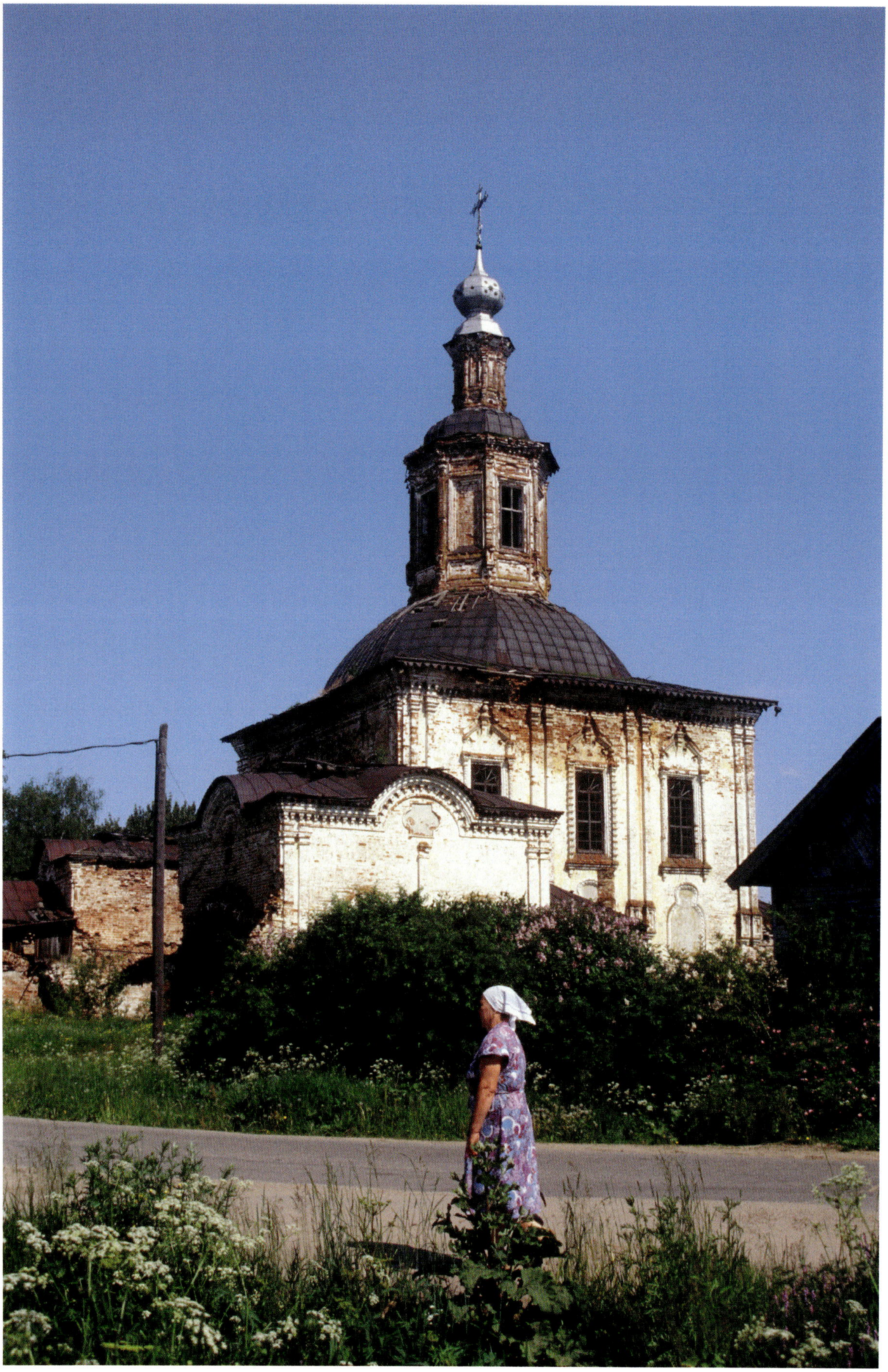

CHEREVKOVO. Church of the Trinity, south view. Built between 1727 and 1731. Photograph: June 24, 2000.

PERMOGORYE. Wooden Church of St. George, northwest view. Built in 1665. Photograph: June 22, 2000.

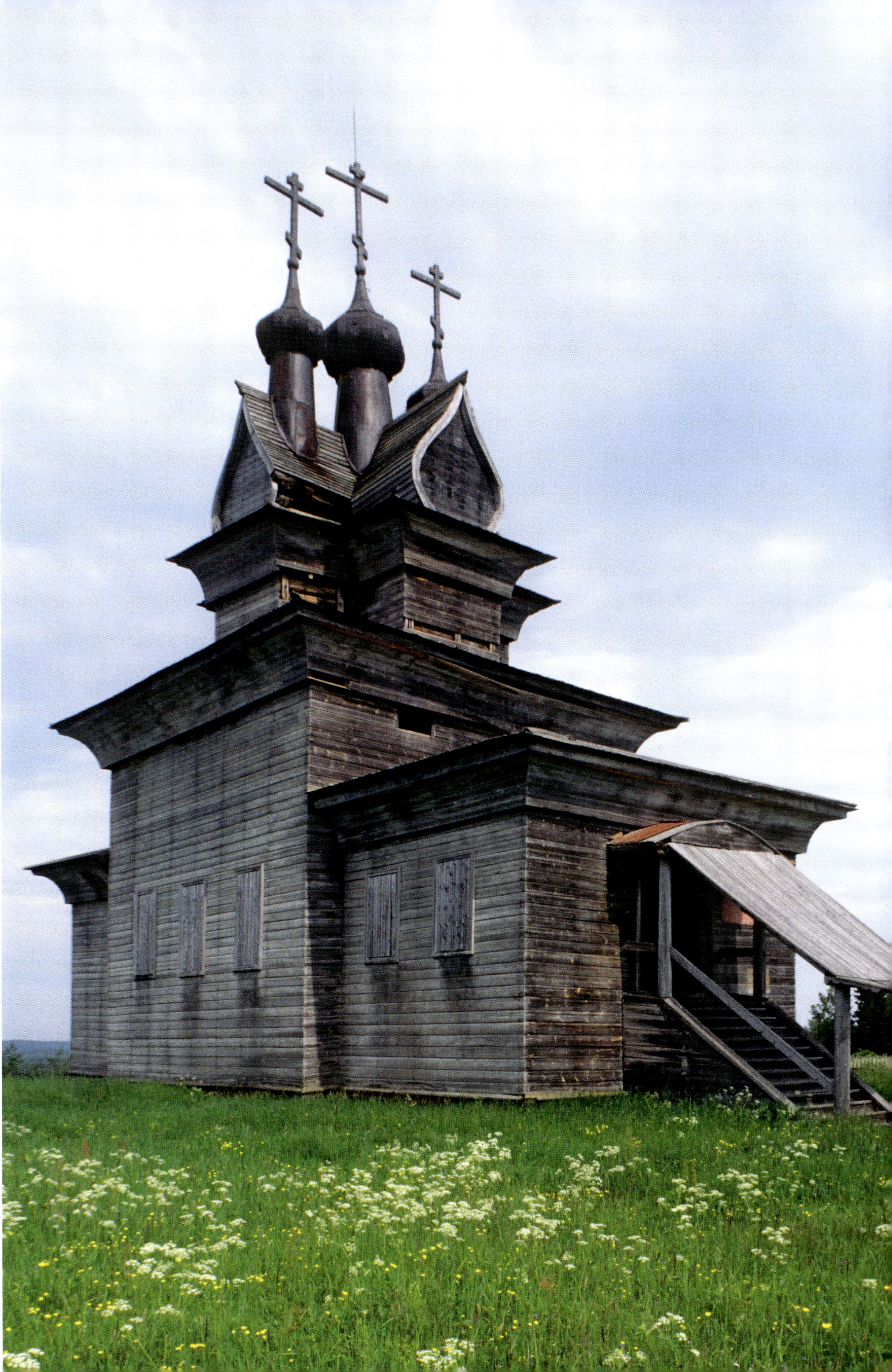

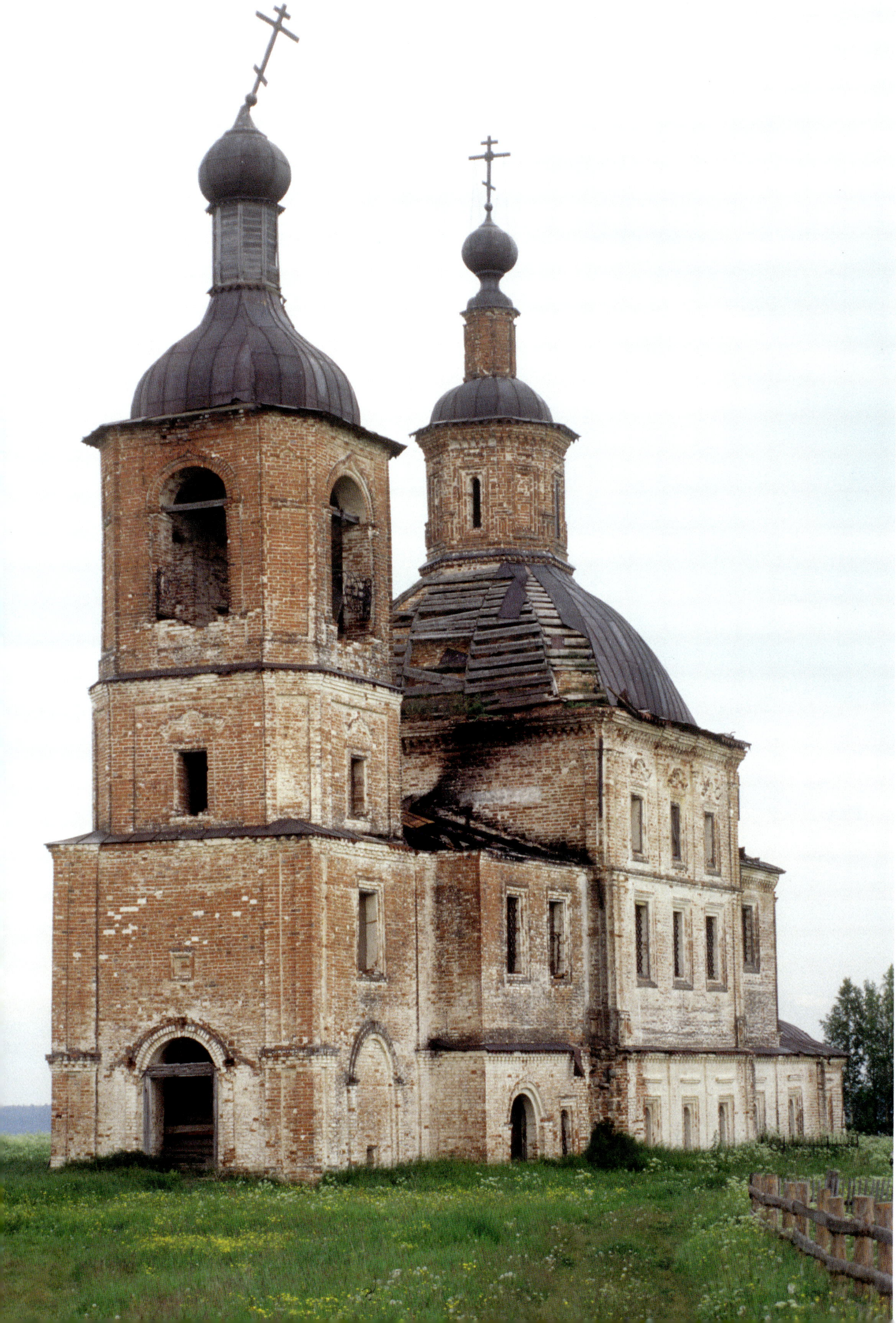

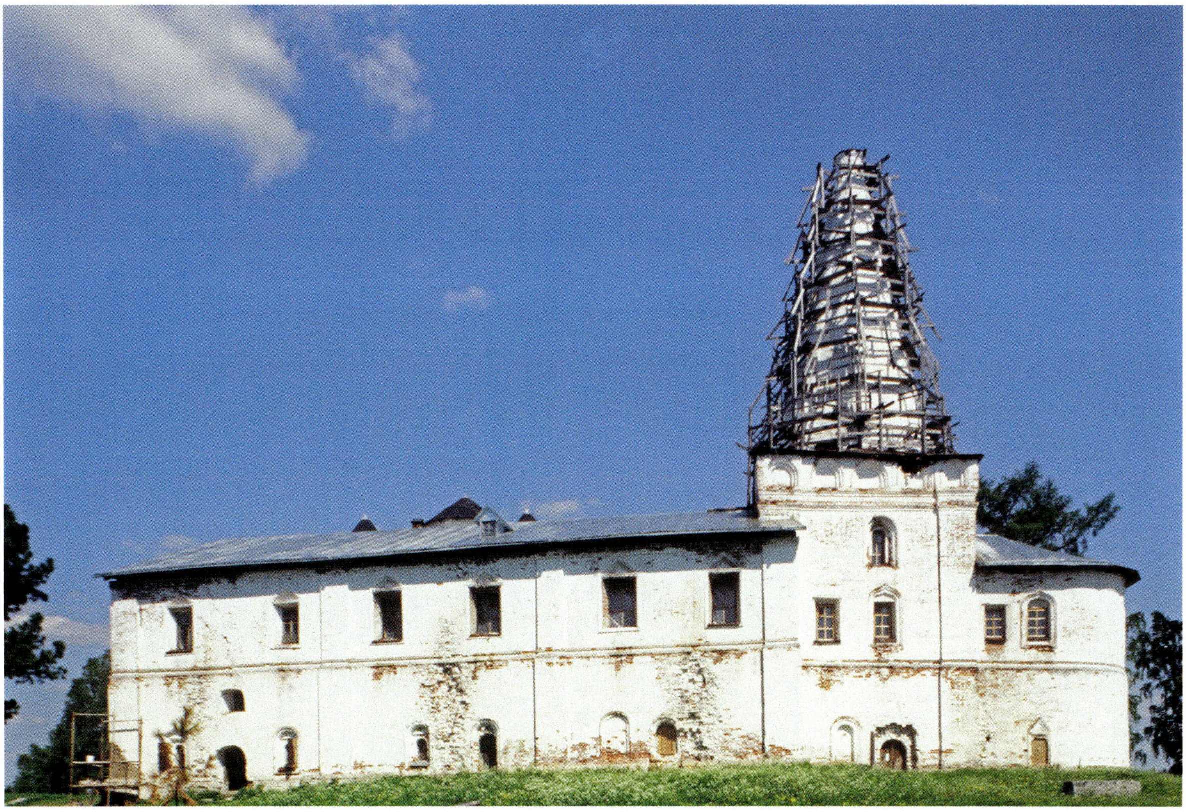

MONASTYR. Church of the Annunciation, with refectory, Trinity–St. Antony Siisky Monastery, south view. Built in 1643. Photograph: June 23, 1999.

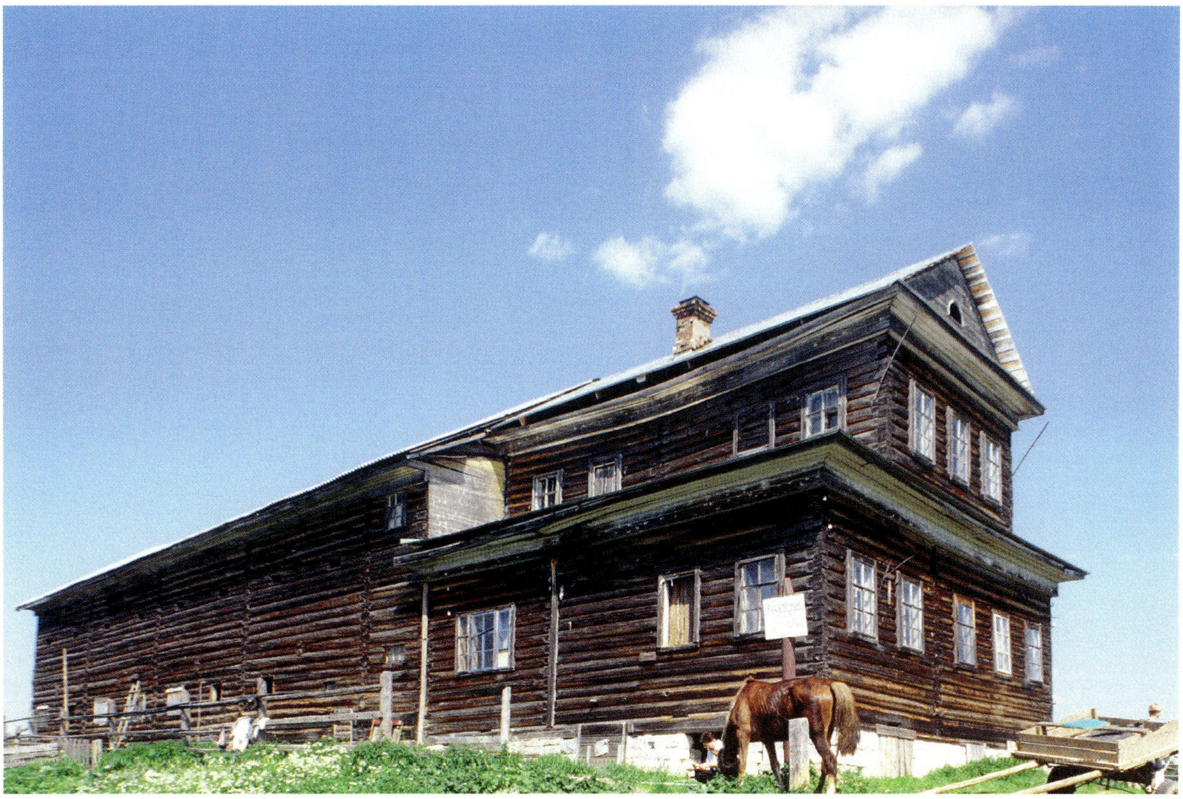

MONASTYR. Log house with attached barn. Photograph: June 23, 1999.

PERMOGORYE. Church of the Resurrection, southwest view. Built between 1748 and 1762. Background: Dvina River. Photograph: June 22, 2000.

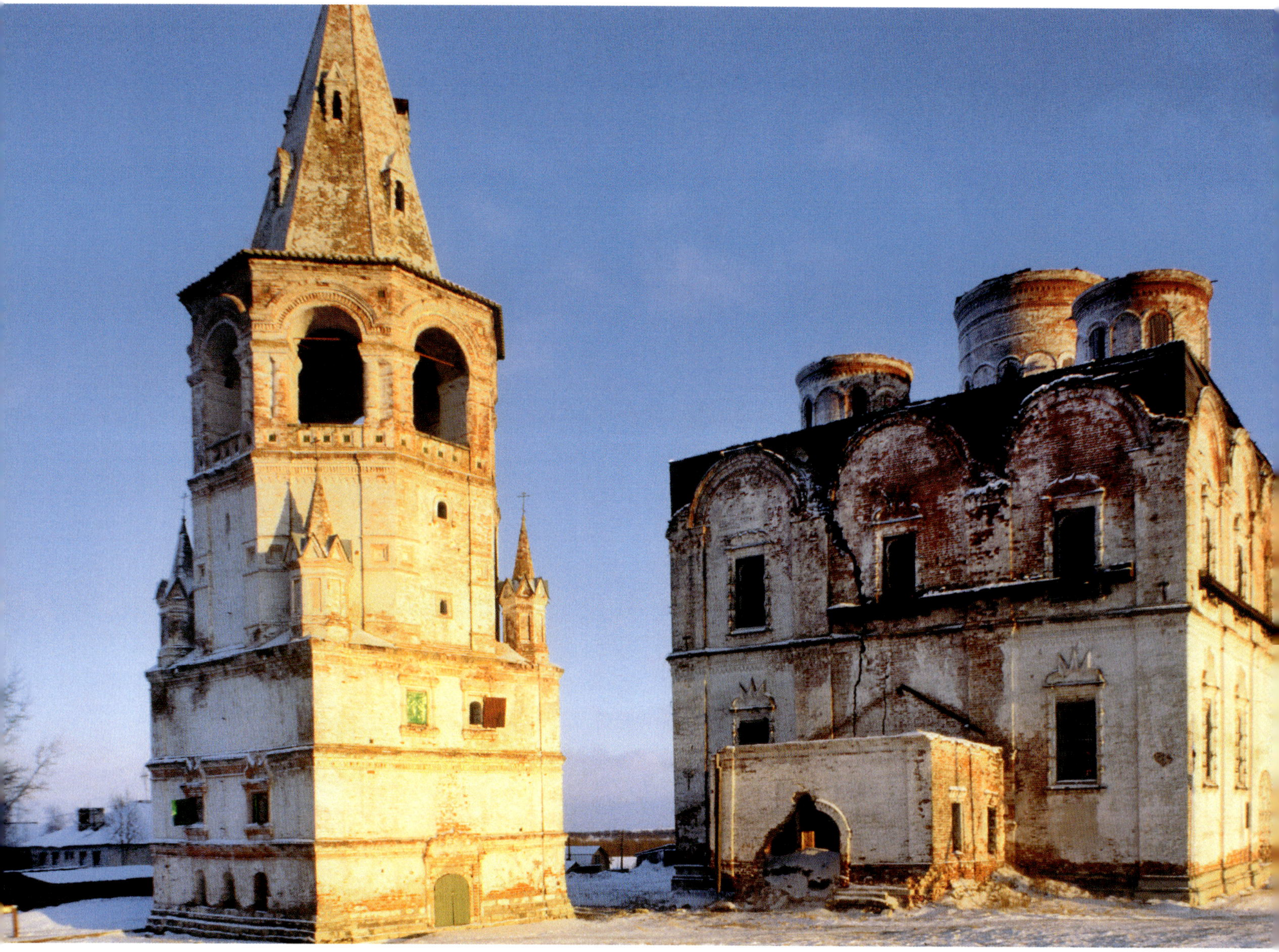

KHOLMOGORY. Bell tower and Cathedral of the Transfiguration. Built between 1685 and 1691. Southwest view. Photograph: November 23, 1999.

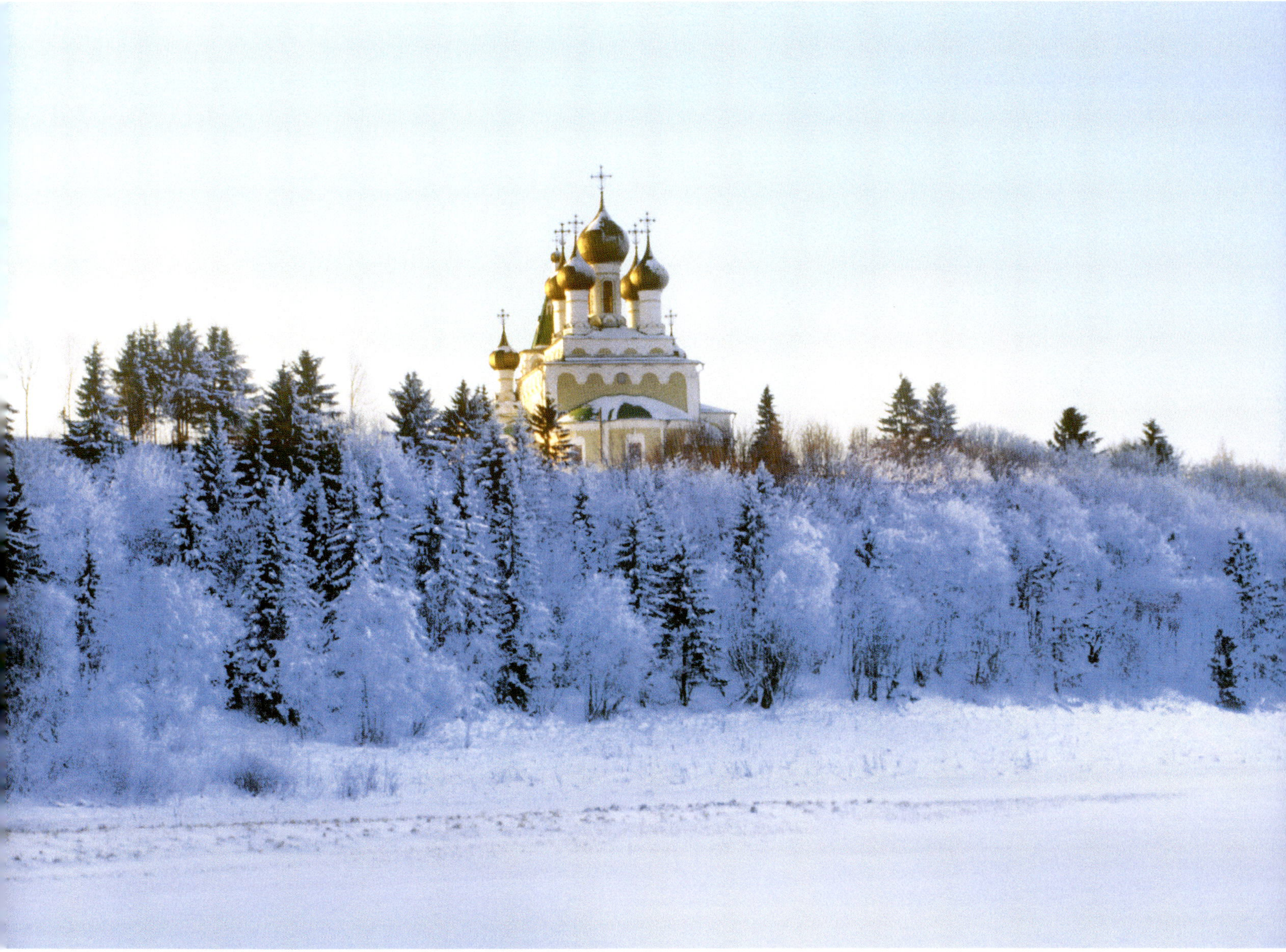

MATIGORY. Church of the Resurrection. Built in stages: 1686–94; 1708; bell tower modified in 1765. East view over pines and firs. Photograph: November 23, 1999.

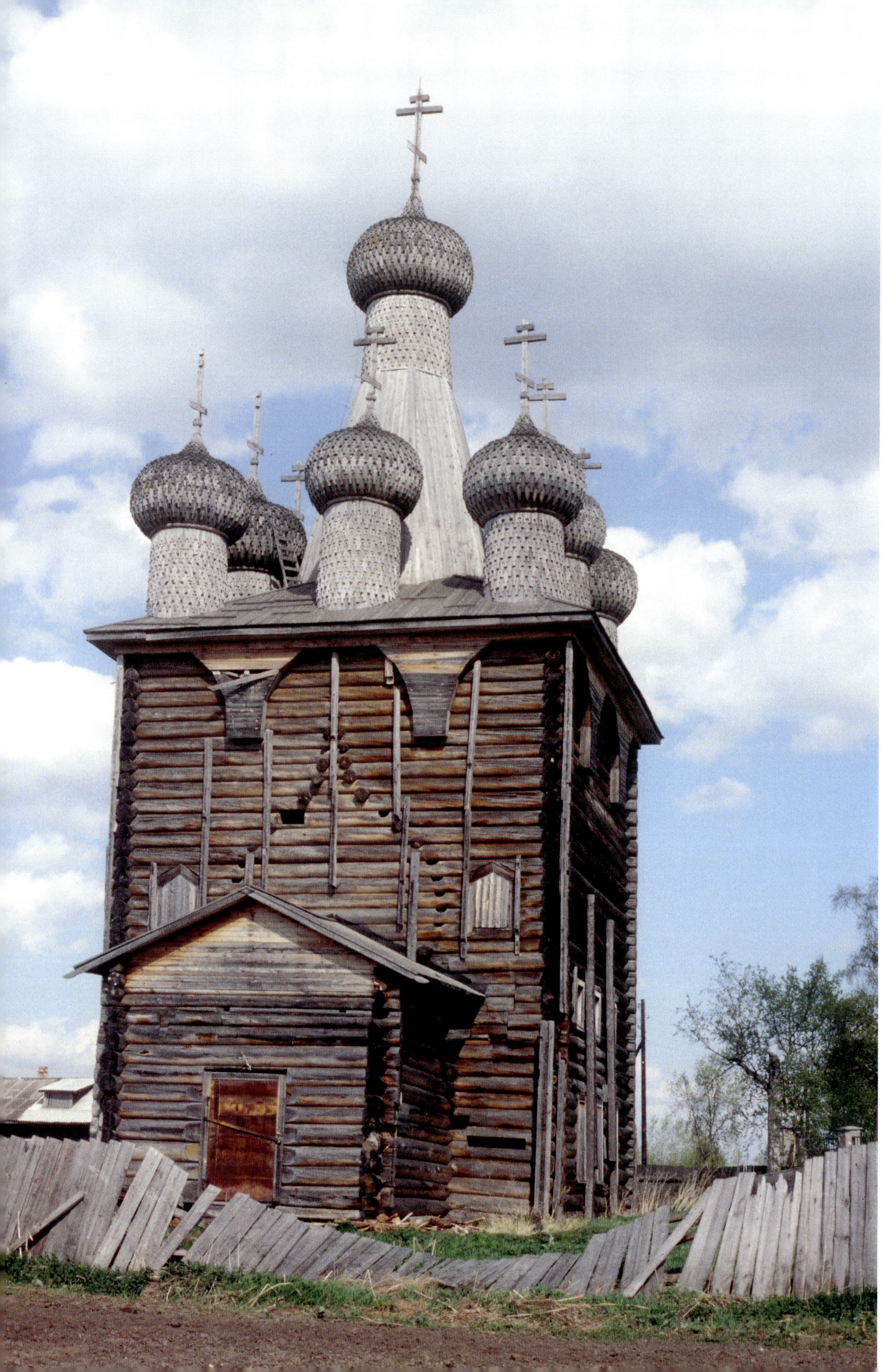

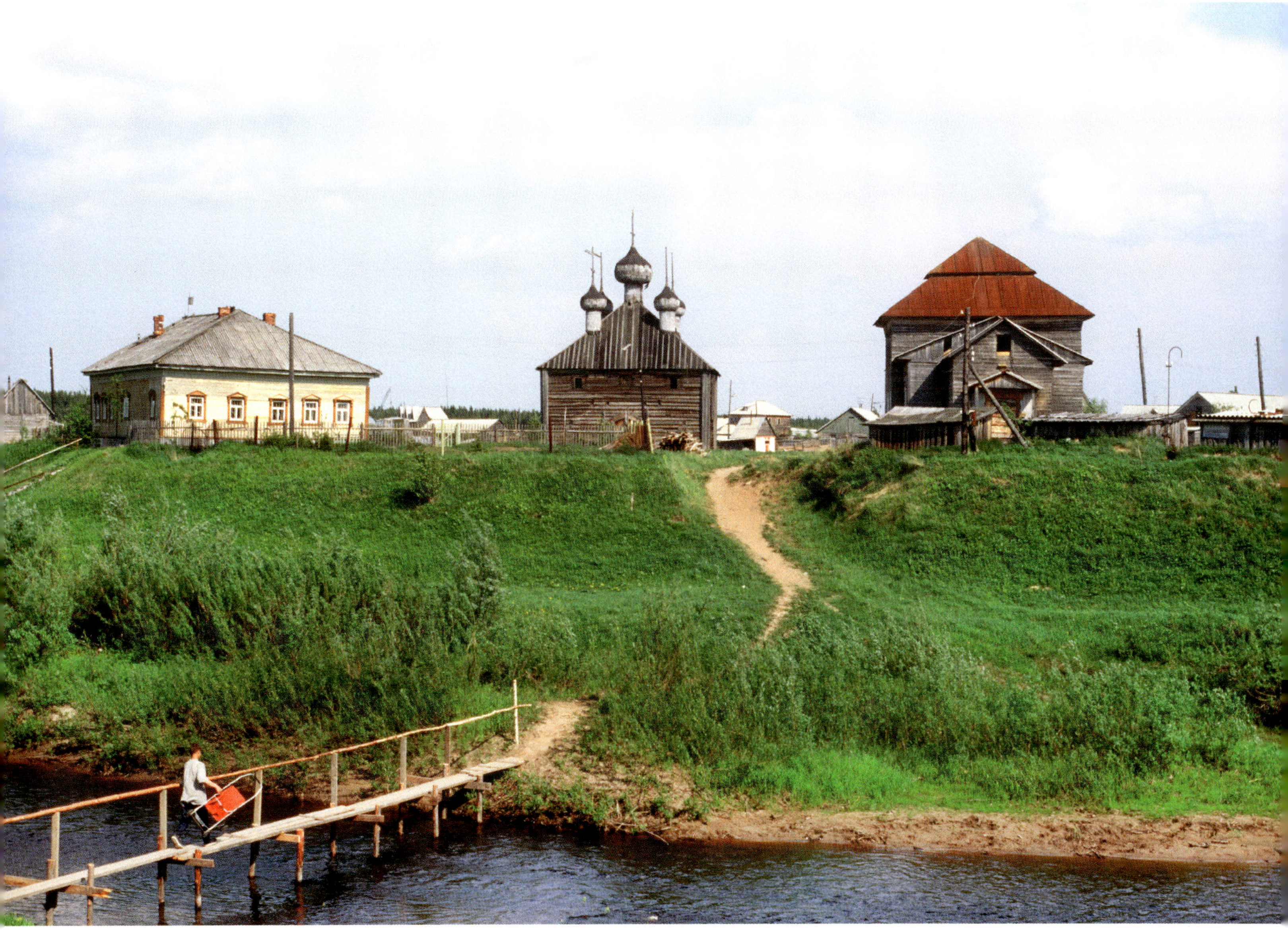

IZHMA. View across Izhma River, Church of the Transfiguration (center) and Church of the Resurrection (1881–87; right), west view. Photograph: June 21, 1999.

ZAOSTROVYE. Wooden Church of the Purification (also known as Intercession). Built between 1683 and 1688. West view. Photograph: June 10, 1998.

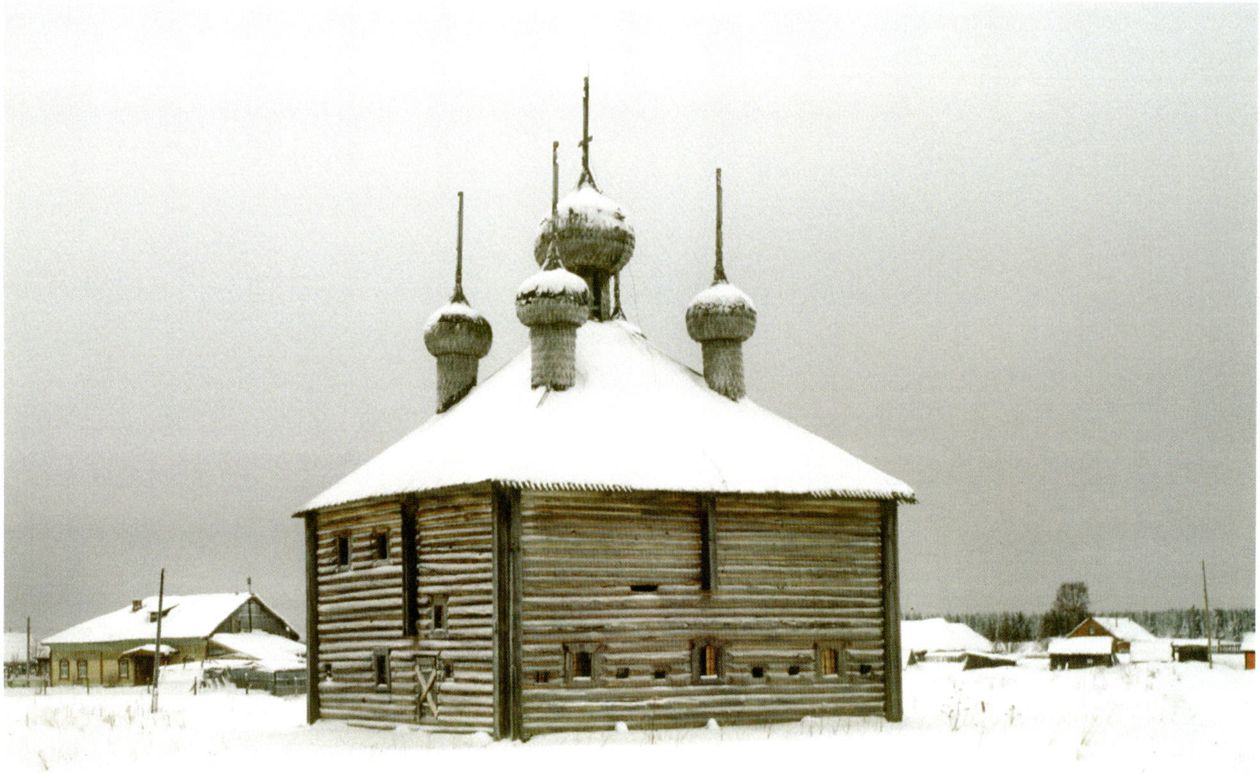

IZHMA. Wooden Church of the Transfiguration, southeast view. Built in the seventeenth century, the church was modified in the eighteenth century and relocated farther from the Izhma River in 1911. Photograph: January 3, 1999.

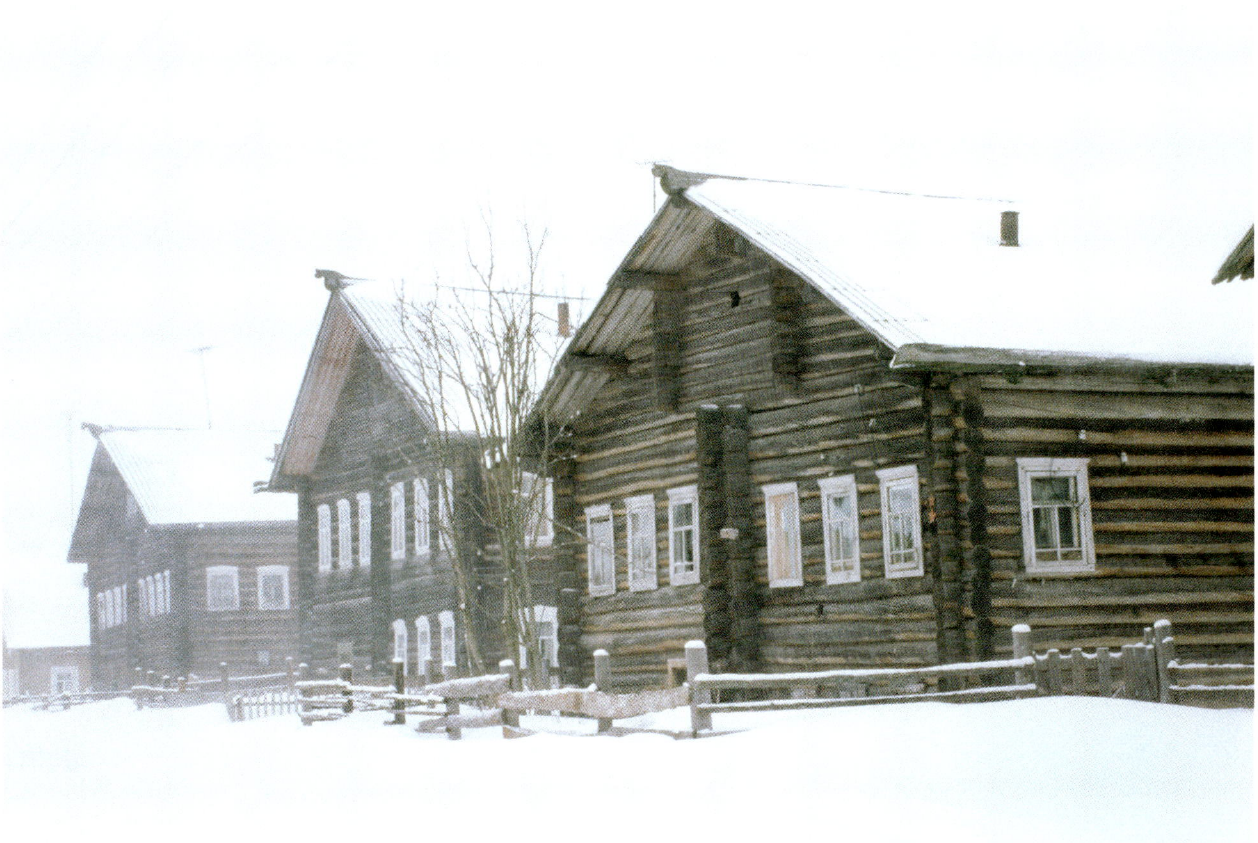

KIMZHA. Log houses in snowstorm. Photograph: March 7, 2000.

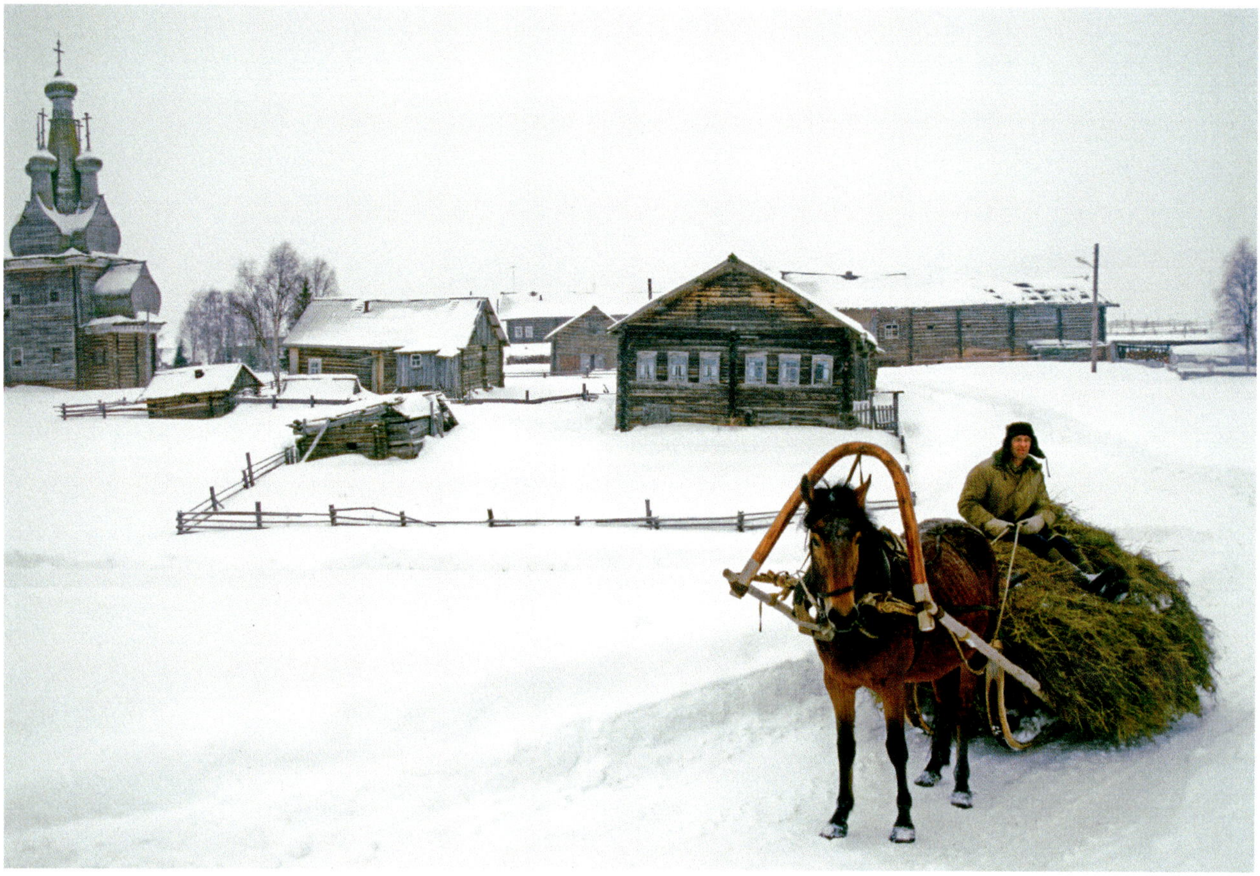

KIMZHA. Horse pulling sled with hay. Background: Church of the Hodegetria Icon of the Virgin, south view, with log houses and stables. Photograph: March 7, 2000.

KIMZHA. Church of the Hodegetria Icon of the Virgin, east view. Begun in 1700, the church was built slowly and not consecrated until 1763. The bell tower was added in the nineteenth century. Photograph: August 1, 2000.

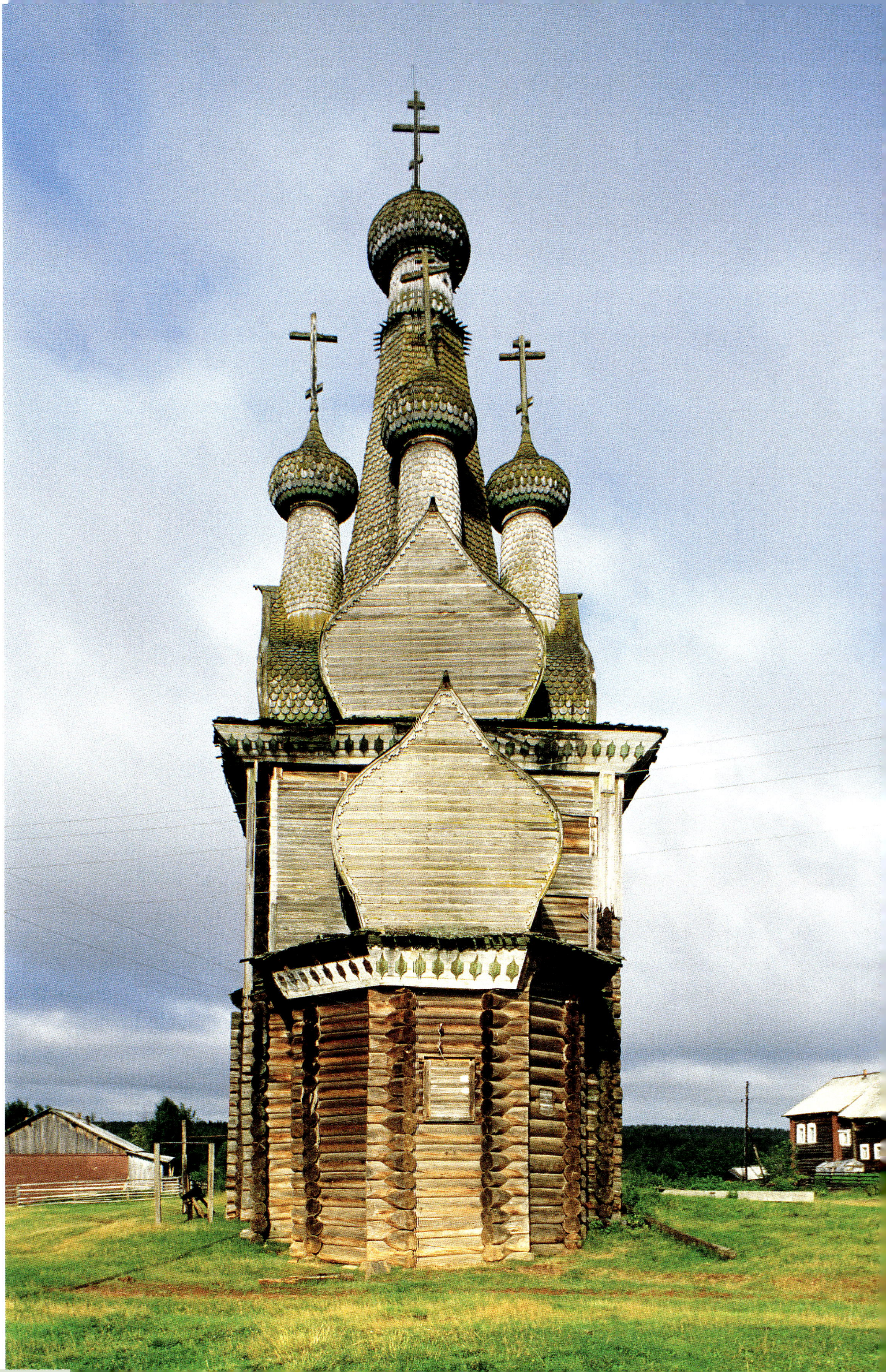

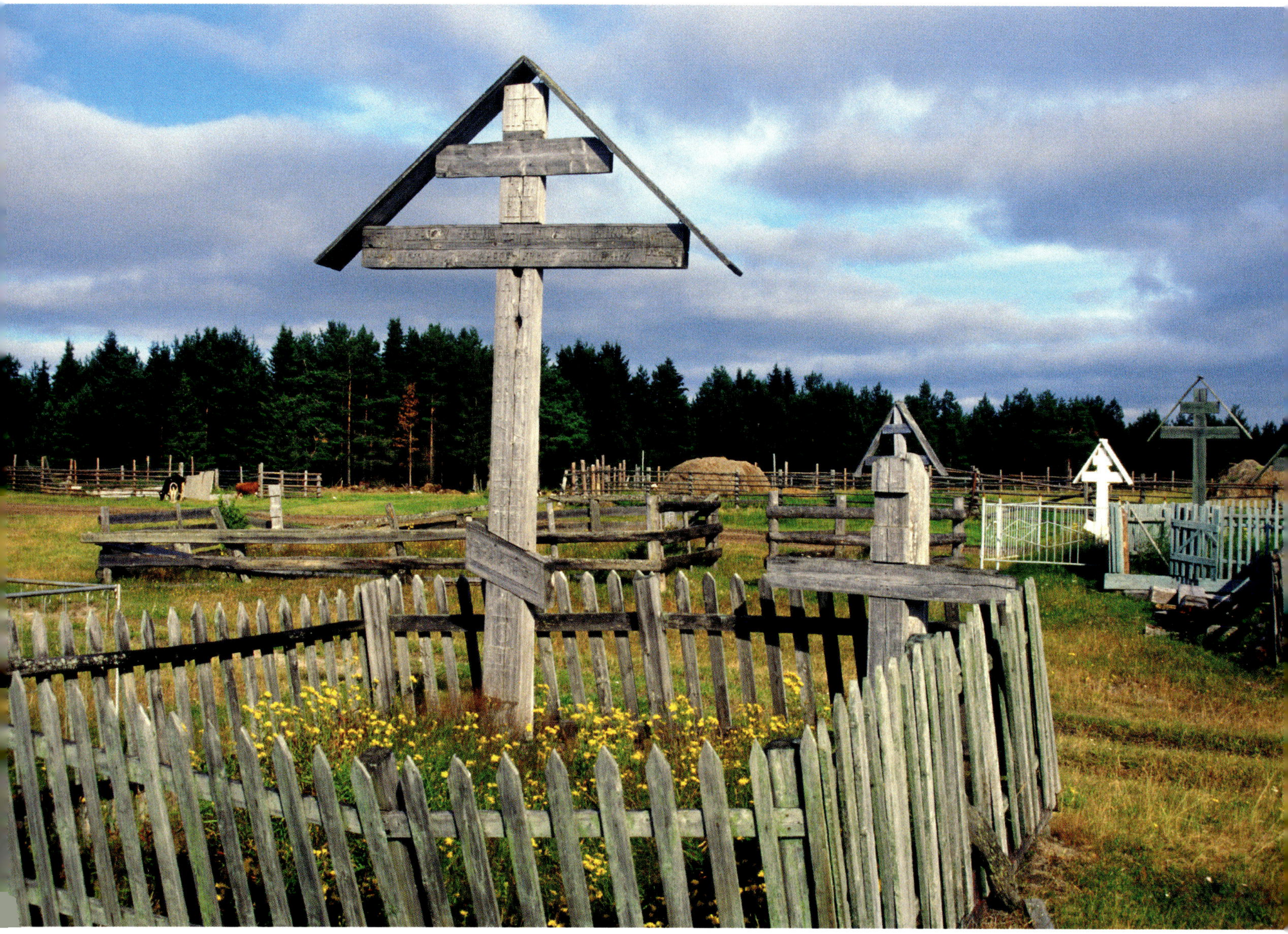

KIMZHA. Cemetery with hooded crosses. Photograph: August 2, 2000.

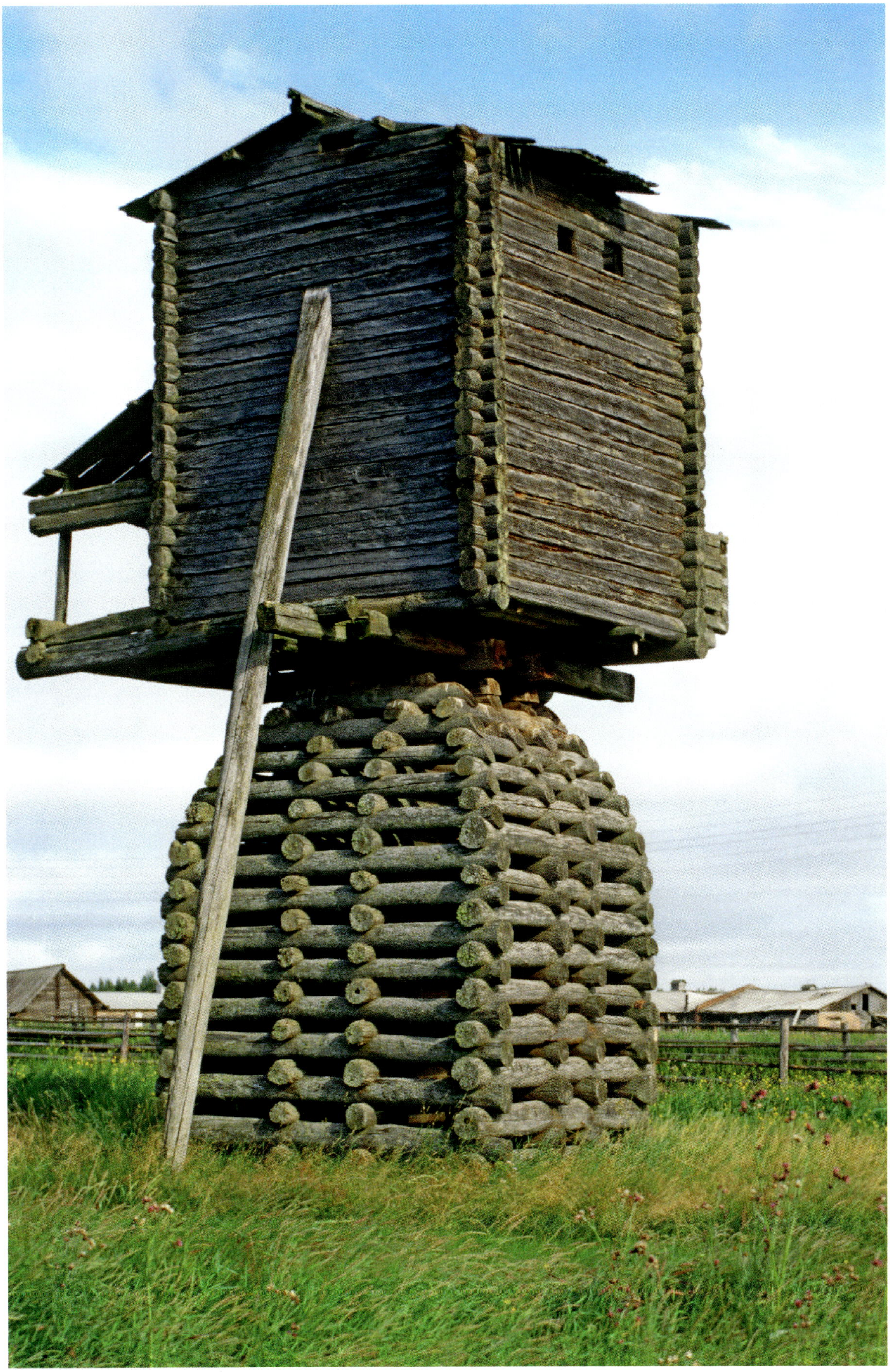

KIMZHA. Log windmill. Photograph: August 2, 2000.

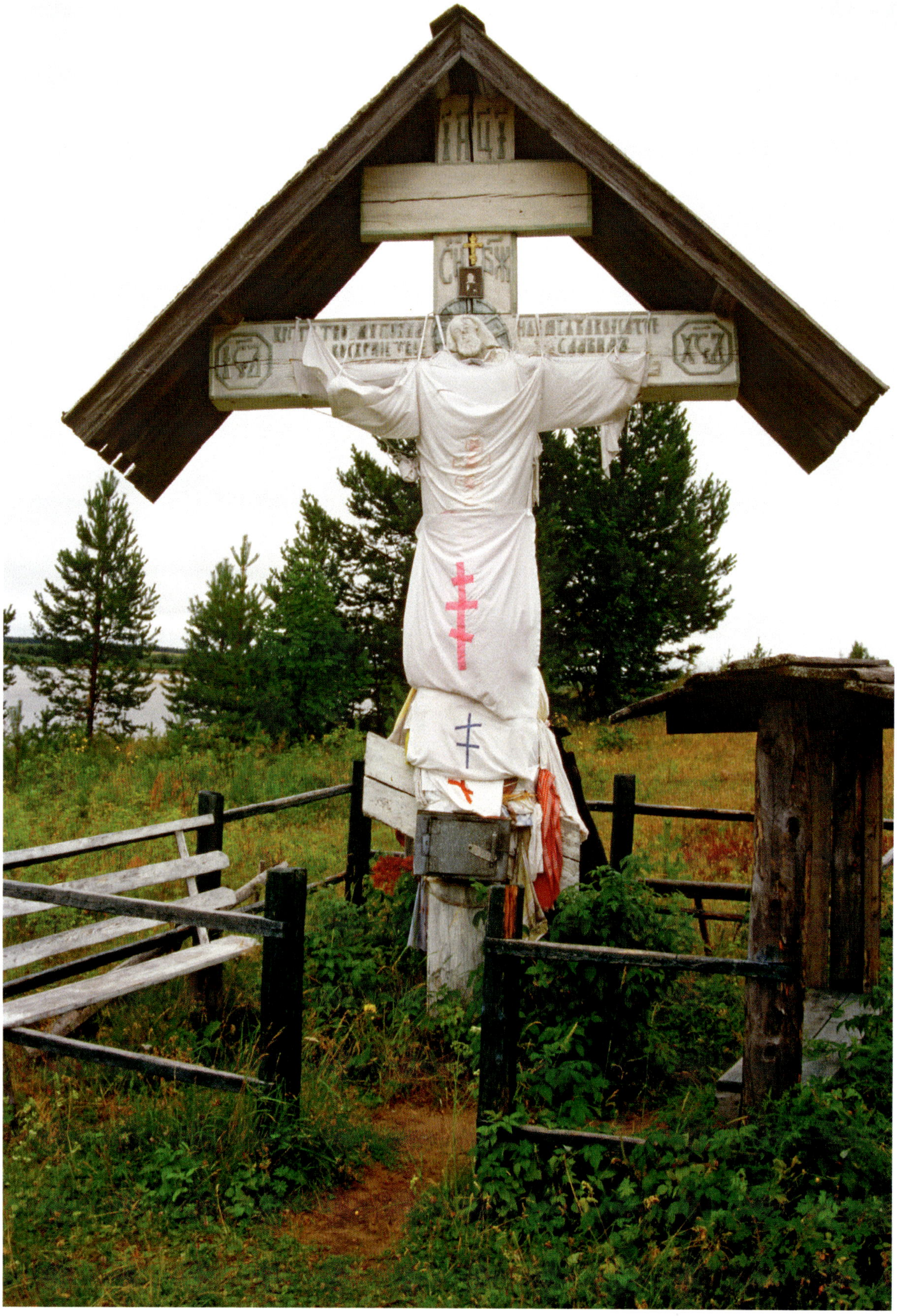

KIMZHA. Votive cross on Mezen River. Photograph: August 3, 2000.

Postscript

What Will Remain of the Heritage of the Russian North?

The preceding pages have provided a view of the traditional, historic architecture of the Russian North. The photographs followed a trajectory from the village of Varzuga—on the Kola Peninsula in the far northwestern part of Russia—to the village of Kimzha, located on the opposite side of the White Sea. Both situated near the Arctic Circle, these two villages represent the extremes within which the journey unfolds.

In their historic amplitude a number of the points on this journey could themselves be the subjects of separate books. Indeed, I have published a number of such books in Russia. But I have long thought of gathering the northern material in a single volume for a Western audience. Thanks to the generosity of Richard and Betty Hedreen, this is now possible.

I began photographing in Russia during the summer of 1970, but my initial forays into the North began only in 1988. (Until the perestroika era, most of the North was off-limits to Westerners—and some of it still is.) Throughout this period I have worked with a variety of Nikon cameras and lenses, as well as a Bronica ETR medium-format camera. Several years ago I made the switch from film to digital cameras, but most of the photographs in the book were taken on film. Over the years, the distances traveled, the climate, and the intensive pace of work have taken their toll on the equipment, but the work has continued to this day.

The larger question is how much of the legacy that I have photographed will

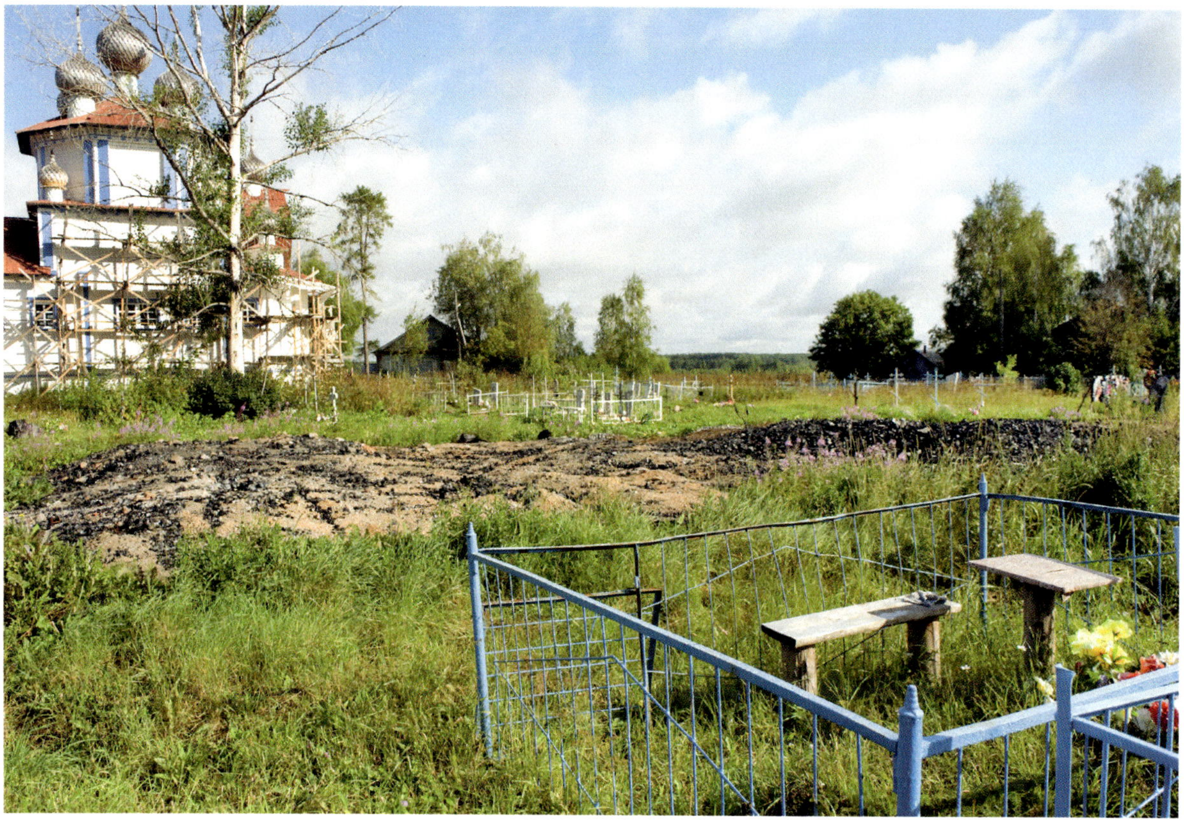

remain by the middle of this century. The record is not reassuring. The remarkable Dormition Church at Varzuga has been "restored" with new painted plank siding that obscures the log structural details that I photographed in July 2001 (see chapter 1). And a few years after I photographed the wooden Church of the Hodegetria Icon at the village of Kimzha, the structure was dismantled for a restoration that became an object of prolonged dispute.

View of the burned ground and charred remains of the monumental wooden Church of the Intercession at Liadiny village (see chapter 3). The structure and a nearby log bell tower were consumed by flames on May 5, 2013. The author photographed the interior and exterior of the church, including its extensive wall paintings, on repeated visits in 1998. Surrounding the site are burial plots of the village cemetery. In the background is the surviving Church of the Epiphany, with recently painted plank siding. Photograph: August 14, 2014.

Villages such as Kimzha and Varzuga are living environments that tenuously exist in a changing world with modern expectations. They are not museum displays. Outdoor museums play a legitimate role in preserving public memory of the cultural legacy of the Russian North, but traditional wooden architecture has greater meaning in its original site. That is why I decided in this book to exclude wooden structures reassembled in museum settings.

And if those once viable sites are no longer sustainable? In August 2014 I returned to the small village of Liadiny, over fifteen years after my trips there and in the Kargopol region during 1998 and 1999. As noted in chapter 3, the wooden tower Church of the Intercession was leveled by fire on May 5, 2013. Now I could see and touch the charred pine remnants of the once magnificent structure that stood on the site. Chapter 3 has a selection from the some two hundred photographs that I took of the exterior and interior in the winter and summer of 1998.

Now, nothing remained of the Intercession Church or its adjacent bell tower. The surviving structure in this ensemble, the wooden Church of the Epiphany, now has brightly painted white plank siding with blue trim — the result of a prolonged, and controversial, restoration. (There is no parish in the tiny village, which led some to question why a historic monument had been painted like a new parish church.)

During a conference in August at the excellent Kargopol Museum I heard that substantial funds had been approved to rebuilt the Intercession Church, but this will result only in a reproduction of the structure without the extraordinary eighteenth-century paintings and other artwork that graced the interior. In the meanwhile there are authentic log churches in the area that are not being restored for lack of funding. The Kargopol Museum, under the leadership of Lidia Sevastianova, has been a major force in sustaining regional culture in this part of the north, but the museum does not have final authority over funding decisions. With such limited resources, what is the appropriate basis for these decisions? The creation of tourist sites? The preservation of national heritage monuments? Or some vaguely defined mixture of both?

Northern communities, and those who advise them, continue to search for a balance between heritage and a level of development necessary for a living community, to support families within the community. Ideas of self-reliance might seem attractive, yet contemporary social mobility is a powerful force. Who remains behind in these enclaves of tradition? The photographer is an outsider, there briefly, recording what the camera can capture. Careful research and years of experience enhance the meaning of the image, but the image itself is often the final message from a past that recedes and vanishes.

MOSCOW, SEPTEMBER 22, 2014